ECONOCIDE

Econocide

British Slavery in the Era of Abolition

Seymour Drescher

University of Pittsburgh Press

Published by the University of Pittsburgh Press, Pittsburgh, Pa. 15260

Library of Congress Cataloging in Publication Data

Drescher, Seymour.
  Econocide.

  Bibliography: p. 261
  Includes index.
    1. Slavery in Great Britain—Anti-slavery movements.
2. Slavery in the British West Indies. 3. Slave-trade—
Great Britain. 4. Slave-trade—West Indies, British.
I. Title.
HT1093.D7   301.44′93′0941   76-50887
ISBN 0-8229-3344-6

For
Michael, Jonathan, and Karen

Contents

Tables

Figures

Acknowledgments

A scholar's chief pleasure is to be able to follow where the spirit leads. This study was originally focused on another place and another aspect of history. Perhaps it was inevitable that sooner or later my interest in the demise of French colonial slavery should lead me across the Channel. It was surely less likely that I should end up hypnotically compiling tables and figures on pounds of muscovado sugar, cotton wool, and sterling. Lengthy cruises in such unfamiliar waters have put me so deeply in debt that I must acknowledge at the outset what I can never hope to repay in full.

A Senior Fellowship award from the National Endowment for the Humanities enabled me to spend a year of research in Great Britain in 1973–1974. Subsequent grants by the American Philosophical Society, and by the Center for International Studies of my university allowed for some crucial follow-up research at Liverpool, Manchester, and Paris. The efforts of librarians and archivists spread over three countries helped me to put these travel opportunities to good use: the staffs of the municipal libraries of Liverpool, Manchester, Sheffield, Birmingham, and York; the university libraries of Duke, Durham, Edinburgh, Cambridge, Oxford, and London; of the Historical Manuscripts Commission, Friends House Library, the British Museum, Lambeth Palace Library, the Institute of Historical Research, the House of Lords Record Office, and the Public Record Office in London; and of the Scottish Record Office in Edinburgh, and of the Archives Nationales in Paris. The staff of Hillman Library in Pittsburgh were unmatched for enduring and courteous service. A special note of gratitude is due the hardworking secretaries of the Department of History at the University of Pittsburgh, and those of Sociology and in the dean's office who came to the rescue at a critical juncture. I am equally fortunate to have had Catherine Marshall, a former colleague, as my editor.

Of unique value to me were occasions when I could test out fledgling ideas on friends and colleagues. George Shepperson, Christopher Fyfe, and Hugh Kearney cannily provided me with an excellent resuscitation of trial by ordeal at a seminar in Edinburgh. E. P. Thompson's seminar at Pitt later continued the tradition. Paul Hair's organization of a conference on the African slave trade at Liverpool in the spring of 1974 assembled an invaluable critical mass of expertise. I was fortunate in having had access to informed opinions or unpublished manuscripts from Roger Buckley, David Brion Davis, Ralph Davis, Barry Drake, John McCusker, Duncan Rice, Frank Sanderson, Michael Sanderson, Howard Temperley, and James Walvin.

My initial overview of the subject appeared as "Le 'Déclin' du système esclavagiste britannique et l'abolition de la traite" in the *Annales: ESC* of 1976. A number of friends and scholars also gave of their time and insight as the manuscript passed through its subsequent metamorphoses. At Pittsburgh, Richard Hunt, Michel Roublev, Richard Vann, Julius Rubin, and Neal Galpern read extensive portions of the manuscript. Of more remote readers Philip Curtin, E. Phillip LeVeen, and Howard Temperley provided me with valuable suggestions. Duncan Rice offered a lengthy and suggestive commentary at a late stage in the writing. Finally, Stanley Engerman, who read the study at its earliest and latest stages has been an indefatigable and consistently helpful critic.

In the recounting of my variegated debts there is one friend whom I would have had to mention under every rubric. When I first arrived in England, Roger Anstey literally laid before me the feast of his unfinished manuscript, his years of research, his scholarly experience and contacts. We spent hours, sometimes days together in interchange over the course of three years. His home more than once afforded me a cherished family away from family in the delightful Kentish countryside. Roger has read every draft of this study, and whatever divergences of interpretation are apparent in our works, the impact of his findings will be evident throughout.

If a scholar is sometimes free to wander up and down creation in pursuit of elusive data and empathic spirits, his family perforce is not. Mine has had to make peace with a world of rapid movement and temporary abandonments. They have always reacted with resiliency. To my children I return this small slice of myself in token of their patience. To my wife, my partner, no further words are needed after all these good years. None would suffice.

ECONOCIDE

1
The Decline Theory of Abolition

The Emergence of the Decline Theory

For one hundred and fifty years a sense of the extraordinary has pervaded interpretations of the abolition of British slavery. To its supporters abolition represented an almost miraculous example of the triumph of the spiritual over the material, and of "humanitarian" over "interest" politics. The fact that the West Indies were the main theater for the contest encouraged this conception. Just as North American colonization displayed certain characteristics of European politics, released from the encumbrances of tradition, the Caribbean colonies were in their own way caricatures of the European capitalist ethic. In these colonies almost no thought had been devoted to the idea of establishing a community founded on reciprocal relations. The plantations were set up as pure agricultural factories, and the forces of the world market had been allowed to determine the nature of social relations to a degree unknown in Europe. Labor approached the status of a pure commodity more completely than anywhere else in the world ruled by Europe. The colonies' very reason for being was to serve the material needs of the inaptly named mother country. That this vast enterprise, which loomed ever larger in the political economy of the eighteenth-century Atlantic world, should crumble so rapidly before the onslaught of those who insisted on their economic disinterestedness, struck many contemporaries as incredible.

The historiographic tradition has been deeply affected by this dramatic reversal of fortune. The quality of mysterious triumph provided assurance for those who shared the abolitionists' vision of providential progress. It was cause for celebration in periods of imperial optimism and a refuge from disheartening events in periods of social violence and disintegration.

3

A cynical historian was ultimately led to remark of this tradition that one might almost believe that the British had founded slavery merely for the purpose of abolishing it.[1] For those who were as offended by the aroma of self-righteousness in abolitionism as by the stench of slavery in the colonies, or who were simply uncomfortable so far outside the world of *realpolitik,* there were two alternative explanations at hand. One was that the abolitionist movement was merely a humanitarian cloak covering economic interests of diabolically Machiavellian cleverness. Some grand strategy, such as the destruction of rival systems, must have lain behind the willingness of the nation of shopkeepers to close down a shop. This theme was a favorite among opponents of humanitarian abolition everywhere in Europe, from the earliest period of antislavery agitation. It also left its mark on histories of British slavery.[2]

The second alternative, and the most popular, was to emphasize the long-run economic weakness of slavery. In this schema, whatever temporary economic loss was entailed by the dismantling of such a system was a necessary and perceived prerequisite of long-term recovery and growth. This free labor theory was also as old as the debates over the abolition of the slave trade. It was given its conceptual framework by Adam Smith, its empirical plausibility by Alexander von Humboldt.[3] Smith provided the rationale for the basic long-run superiority of wage over slave labor. Von Humboldt, writing at the height of the controversy over the international slave trade, believed that he had located the heirs of the slave empires in the "free labor" cane fields of Mexico and India and in the beet fields of Europe. By the time of emancipation, the British West Indies could be dismissed as an aging hothouse growth of a bygone era. First metaphorically, and then causally, their decline came to be seen as a cause of British abolition and a paradigm of abolition elsewhere. This historiographic tradition was strengthened by the relative decline of all the older Caribbean slave colonies during the nineteenth century.

The concept of "failure" now clings as closely to the history of the West Indies as success does to the history of abolitionism.[4] In 1928 Lowell Ragatz published his carefully researched *The Fall of the Planter Class in the British West Indies*, detailing the decay of the British West Indian system and dating it from the end of the Seven Years' War. His work, in turn, became the basis for Eric Williams's wholesale devaluation of the significance of noneconomic forces in his *Capitalism and Slavery.*[5] Williams's analysis offered, in neo-Marxian terms, an explanatory model that served three scholarly functions. It was the first general explanation of the rise and fall of European colonial slavery with recourse to only one major variable. Its focus on long-term economic development afforded the possibility of moving beyond the narrative of abolition in single cases to a general causal explanation of the destruction of slave systems throughout the world during the nineteenth century. The thesis was both simple and theoretically testable: economic interest giveth, economic interest taketh away. Finally, it helped to redirect attention to the economic and temporal contexts of the various European abolitions.

By identifying economic agencies of social change at every juncture in the process, Williams also dispensed with the equivocal, and therefore untestable, historiographic recipe of one part Wilberforce, one part Adam Smith. Wherever the humanitarian school had seen a crusade of saints against ruthless degradation, Williams saw the invisible hand of capitalism. Wherever they had observed the storming of a mighty complex of entrenched interests by a gallant band of disinterested humanitarians, Williams found powerful economic interests sweeping aside a sclerotic colonial system. The "disinterested" forces of abolition were shown to be the ideological cover for another, more powerful force. It had simply not been properly identified and measured. Against the economic network that supported the slave system, Britain's domestic industrial revolution produced a new, hostile set of economic interests. They determined the fate of the failing slave systems in a direct and economically logical way. Once the balance sheet was properly drawn, slavery was shown to have lost its economic underpinnings before any successful assault was launched against it. One of the charms of this hypothesis was its aesthetic simplicity: a see-saw of rising industrial metropolis and falling agricultural colony.

Williams's picture of the British colonies is in turn linked to a much broader theory of economic development and political economy which explains the abolition of slavery as a profit-maximizing or loss-minimizing operation by specific economic groups in a given society.[6] If the demise of at least one major part of Western slavery can be described in such a way, the British system, as the first to be dismantled, seems to be the best candidate. Its slaveholders are characterized as the most capitalist of all colonials. Its imperial metropolis was obviously the most capitalist and industrial of all European societies by 1800. In concentrating on the British case one is dealing with the market model of abolition on its own grounds and on its home grounds.

Williams's sweeping thesis, that slavery was a phase of commercial capitalism which aroused opposition only when it had ceased to perform its function, was repeatedly attacked for its analysis of the motives of various political figures.[7] Other minor flaws in his account have since been subject to continuous scrutiny by more precise and more thorough scholarship. On one central point, however, Williams changed even the perspective of those who rejected this rigorous historical materialism in principle and his treatment of the abolitionists in particular. G. R. Mellor, who vigorously defended the abolitionists from Williams's charges of hypocrisy, took it for granted that the "power of the West India interest was weakened by the growth of industrial capitalism." He only differed in asserting that "the idealism of the humanitarians, however, was the determining factor."[8] He offers no suggestion as to how one could go about testing either statement. David Brion Davis summed up this view in his masterly overview of the origins of abolitionism in *The Problem of Slavery in Western Culture.* He noted that it was difficult to get around the fact "that colonial slavery was of greater importance to the British economy in 1750 than in 1789" or that "no country thought of abolishing the slave trade until its economic value had considerably declined."[9]

Davis's sequel to his first work, *The Problem of Slavery in an Age of Revolution,* judiciously qualified these earlier statements by taking note of short-term changes affecting the British slave system, such as the St. Domingue revolution and the Napoleonic wars. But in this case qualification is verification. These events are still characterized as parentheses in the long-term process: British abolition occurred in the context of the secular economic decline of its slave system after 1770, caused by such factors as soil depletion, competition, and monopolistic privilege, on the one hand, and the emergence of laissez-faire industrial capitalism on the other.[10] In a far more subtle and convincing fashion than Williams, Davis depicts the task of the abolitionists as a series of symbolic acts which expressed the social hegemony of the British ruling class and morally legitimized its rule. Although it is not absolutely necessary to all elements of his interpretation, there is an aesthetic economy in the principle that the emptier the solemnly broken vessel, the more obvious is the ritualistic content of the act itself.

Even Roger Anstey, the most recent and thoroughgoing critic of Williams's view of abolition, was originally more royalist than the king on the decline of slavery. Anstey rejected Williams's analysis as a reading of later metropolitan economic development backward into the world of 1800. While rejecting the Williams "rising capitalist" interpretation, however, he accelerated the Ragatz-Williams "falling planter" interpretation. For Anstey, the West India interest was a "shadow of its former self," an "old incubus" by 1790. It was almost pitiful in its decrepitude, merely surviving on the reputation of its former glory. The delay in the abolitionist victory was fundamentally a sociopsychological problem, that of overcoming a crippling national self-deception about the importance of the slave system. In this schema, if Williams erred, it was in giving too much substance to a specter. The paradigm of destruction is Jericho—one final blast of the trumpet shattered slavery's brittle, fragile, outermost wall.[11] Duncan Rice, another historian of abolition not at all partial to Williams's deterministic explanation, refers to the "Williams thesis" of decline as the new orthodoxy and finds it "difficult to see how the thesis that economic change made abolition *possible* in 1807 and 1833 *can* be challenged, in view of the obvious growing weakness of the West India planters by the end of the eighteenth century."[12] In his *Rise and Fall of Black Slavery,* Rice is reluctant to accept the decline thesis as applicable to some cases, but accepts it fully for the case of British slavery.

The decline thesis also impinges on more general interpretations of slavery. One may be led to look for a natural history of the institution in a sequence of youth, maturity, and senility. The fact that Britain was the leading economic entity and a model for social change during the century of abolitions is also significant. The planetary network of capitalist slavery seems to unravel beginning with the threadbare British Caribbean. Initial abolitionist successes against the economic "sick man" of plantation America by the dynamo of Europe provided invaluable momentum for victories over admittedly vigorous economies.

In the decades following the publication of *Capitalism and Slavery,* most scholars have therefore been inclined to look for a correlation between the declining importance of the colonial area to the political economy of Europe and the relative ease with which British slavery was transformed by an emergent capitalist society. The argument has been constantly, if cautiously, reaffirmed, accepted as part of the "core" of substantive conclusions about the abolition of slavery and the slave trade in the Caribbean. The decline theory attained the status of a simple empirical statement largely because behind Williams stands the factually more formidable study of Ragatz.[13]

The empirical validation of the "decline" of British slavery is thus the first subject to be faced. We will present an overview of the economic development of the British West Indies in relation to the metropolis prior to abolition. The impact of the Caribbean revolution of the 1790s and of British imperial expansion in the same decade also need to be explored. But the description of economic developments in the West Indies is not an end in itself. Our main focus is on the implications of those developments for British abolition of the slave trade. We will consider how well the process of abolition fits into the context of economic change, in the Caribbean and the metropolis, prior to the rise of abolitionism and during the two momentous decades before its triumph in 1807. Since the problem must be approached at various levels, we must treat short-term conjunctures separately from secular trends.

Finally, our analysis should lay the groundwork for a fresh investigation of political abolition. The study of the political process in relation to economic change was given an enormous thrust forward by *Capitalism and Slavery*. That study incorporates not only the Ragatzian concept of the declining West Indies, but an overarching concept of a shifting balance of interests in both metropolitan Britain and the empire. From a suggestion of C. L. R. James in *The Black Jacobins,* Williams developed the theme that British abolitionism was demonstrably linked to the rise of the industrial bourgeoisie of Britain, and especially of the cotton industry. Also, giving a unique twist to a fundamental historiographic concept of Reginald Coupland and the imperial school, Williams tied Britain's shift to abolition with the loss of America and with Adam Smith's attack on the protectionist ideology of the "old" empire. Williams concludes that slavery was destroyed by, or because of, the impact of certain interest groups emerging under the banner of laissez-faire, in other words, by a particular form of capitalistic political economy. This assumption has appeared in whole or in part in subsequent histories.[14] In this study we will test the validity of this frame of reference.

It is necessary to enter a preliminary *caveat.* We will not be testing just one theory of political economy as applied to the abolition of the slave trade. Williams, and those who follow him this far along his analytical path, explicitly identifies abolition as a political process linked to the emergence of a laissez-faire ideology. We hope to show that the decline theory really presumes the action of two coequal and, in part, quite contradictory theories of political economy. One is laissez-faire capitalism; the other is mercantilist capitalism. They are used by Williams as a general might use regular and guerrilla armies to explain one or another phase of the process as the terrain demands. A situation that would explode the theory in laissez-faire terms is explained only in mercantilist terms, and vice versa. Since the terrain, Parliament, remained the same, one is at a loss to know what one set of economic premises was doing in men's minds while its alter-ideology was in the field. This switching of premises to meet every turn in the situation makes the decline theory more difficult to test. We will isolate the premises appropriate to each explanation and ask whether each, taken separately, helps to account for abolition. We further propose to see whether using both together vitiates the usefulness of such explanations as applied to particular sequences of political action, and of abolition in general. We hope to suggest that a more coherent explanation of British abolition may be achieved by looking for an alternative hypothesis.

The Problem of Measuring Slavery

Economic decline meant much the same thing to contemporaries of abolition as it has to historians of abolition. It implied a measurable deterioration in the significance or performance of some enterprise or economic network. A decline in the value of British slavery would therefore mean a perceptible downturn relative to its past, to the metropolis, to other imperial units, or to other slave systems. Moreover, in eighteenth-century Britain, the political value of a colony was largely a function of its perceived commercial value. This was especially true of the slave colonies. They had little attraction as havens for the British laboring poor, or even as dumping grounds for convicts. As for any intrinsic moral value, the slave islands did not figure among the preferred locations for utopian settlements or visions. The worth of the slave colonies was therefore quantifiable in pounds and products.

The most common indicators of economic value in the eighteenth century were figures on production, population, capital, and trade. By the 1780s political economists could plot the course of British commercial development as graphically as their counterparts in physics or engineering could plot the trajectory of a missile. William Playfair, in his *Commercial and Political Atlas,* congratulated his society for its newly acquired ability to trace the course of its growth. "Had our ancestors," mused Playfair, "represented the gradual increase of their commerce and expenditure . . . what a real acquisition would it not have been to our stock of knowledge?"[15] Colored graphs of a century of trade conveyed the impression of progress to even the economically illiterate. His figures were "nothing more than those piles of guineas represented on paper." The acquisitive society could see its collective progress in a series of line drawings. Publicists could also entertain contemporaries with quantitative tales of progress and decline by tabular representations and maps of values, volumes, and weights.

Ample materials were also at hand for measuring the significance of individual sectors of the empire through the flow of trade. Thomas Irving, the British inspector-general, stood guard over the customs records, not only vouching for their accuracy, but providing a continuous flow of data to Parliament and to the public. As keeper of the holy numbers he was endowed with an aura of authority. At one point special arrangements were made by Parliament so that he could testify in the evidentiary hearings on the slave colonies.[16] Irving's ordinal cornucopia was supplemented by major fact-finding bodies for every economic activity as the need for specific information was felt.

In parliamentary debates, in political economy, and in public parlance, rise and decline thus had the same fundamental meaning. The same information was manipulated in the same ways. Growth and expansion implied improvement, and contraction, decline. In arguing against regulation of the cotton industry in 1803, for example, two parliamentary speakers cited prodigious growth as sufficient evidence of improvement and of the need for caution in laying on regulatory hands.[17] Contemporaries could also calculate economic importance as a fraction of some larger economic endeavor in regional, national, or international terms. An increasing fraction indicated progress; a decreasing one, decline. By the end of the eighteenth century these calculations, and their graphic representation, had become the common cultural symbols by which a society knew itself and could gauge the significance of its constituent parts. Historians have also used the same "political arithmetic" to calculate values, rates, percentages, trends, and comparisons.

While measures of production and exchange served the purposes of general national policy, other information on slavery became accessible only when the system came under challenge. The mortality rates of slaves and sailors in the African slave trade and the islands were collected by agitators or in official response to agitation.[18] This problem-related data did not usually flow in as regularly as the trade figures, but it offered the possibility of observing slavery in a broader context. Such an opportunity came with the Privy Council's report on the British slave trade in 1788, and with subsequent parliamentary reports. These accounts formed the basis of most arguments used in both polemical and analytical discussions of the British slave system.

The debate over abolition also led to questions about the position of the British slave trade vis-à-vis related systems and to discussions of the impact that British abolition would have on the competitive situation of British slavery. Yet once one probed beyond the British system the reliability and availability of the data fell precipitously. Polemicists often rushed in where officials feared to tread. Even the Privy Council report shows that the information gathered on French slavery, the significant referent for the British system, was random and impressionistic.[19] The report's figures on the French colonial population were ten to fifteen years old, so that comparisons were being made between French estimates for random years in the mid- and late-1770s and British estimates for 1788. This comparison, widely disseminated by the press, left an initial impression that the French and British systems were about equal in size, although the French system was in fact the larger. Foreign production estimates were sometimes as rough as those of population. For example, at various times during the two decades of debate on abolition, estimates of the average annual value of sugar production on St. Domingue ranged from well under equality with the British colonies, to twice the British figures. The French figures were likely to be compiled with care only where real economic commitments were at stake.[20] For other French islands, the estimates were usually based only on a fixed proportion of St. Domingue's figures. While the outbreak of revolution and war made the task of assessing French colonial slavery more difficult in one respect,[21] British occupation of every island sometime during the 1790s provided the government with firsthand information.

Impressionistic as they were, the early figures on French slavery were more readily accessible to the British than those on other systems. It is not clear that any concerted effort was made to gather and publicize information on minor European colonies in 1788. As in the French case, British conquest of all the Dutch and Danish colonies provided firsthand information at a later time. In general, the picture of slavery outside the Anglo-French empires was so diffuse at the beginning of the abolitionist campaign in 1788 that the reading public was informed that the Spanish Empire was the largest employer of slave labor in the Americas. As late as 1807, James Stephen, the most assiduous fact finder among the abolitionists, had difficulty in obtaining up-to-date information on Cuban production and trade.[22] Only for certain products was it possible to measure the total output of all European slave colonies with something approaching precision. The African slave trade yielded more figures but hardly absolute certainty. The Privy Council itself was content to reply on the testimony of a single British merchant for its estimate of the British share of the trade. However, while the total estimated human cost to Africa since the beginning of the trade ranged erratically from nine to fifty million and beyond, the *annual* toll in 1788 was realistically put at eighty to one hundred thousand.[23]

Considering the point of departure, knowledge of the slave system in imperial and international context was remarkably accurate. The range of error tended to narrow after 1788. Grosser misconceptions were eliminated by the governmental reports. Within a year or two most aspects of British slavery that were readily quantifiable had been diffused to the public through the newspapers, printed propaganda, and public meetings. For those who made the effort, most of the information subsequently used in the decline theory was available in print. By 1807 parliamentary committees could estimate the commodities flowing from the European slave economies with justifiable assurance. The statistics of British slavery and the slave trade were carefully measured elements in one of the most thoroughly discussed questions in British parliamentary history.

The Destruction Process

While the initial part of our analysis will deal primarily with developments in slavery rather than with abolition, it is important that the reader have some idea of the political chronology of British abolition. Prior to 1787 the only major step limiting the expansion of British slavery had been to place some legal restrictions on the intrusion of the institution into Great Britain itself. The juridical contests sponsored by Granville Sharp appeared to have assured the civil rights of thousands of slaves or ex-slaves resident in Britain, whatever the uncertainty of their rights if they returned to the islands.[24]

With the 1780s came the first attempt at collective association for the legal abolition of imperial slavery and the slave trade. Under the initial impetus of the Quakers in America and England, a national committee to abolish the slave trade was founded in London by 1787. It formed the center of an active provincial network which soon extended into Scotland. The following five years, 1788–1792, are usually bracketed as the period of mass abolitionist agitation, led by Thomas Clarkson and coordinated with parliamentary initiatives by William Wilberforce and William Pitt. This period witnessed two sharp bursts of nationwide agitation. The legislative accomplishments of these years were the Dolben act of 1788, which regulated the slave trade, and the House of Commons bill in 1792, requiring the abolition of the entire trade by 1796. There were also other, unsuccessful initiatives in this period: an abortive attempt at coordinated international abolition in 1787–1788, the defeat of the first bill for general abolition in 1791, and the sidetracking of the 1792 bill in the Lords. The next four years, from 1793 to 1796, were marked by a series of severe setbacks. All attempts to implement abolition, whether partial or total, failed. One bill, designed to abolish only the foreign slave trade, survived the Commons in the spring of 1794, only to be brushed aside by the Lords. Extraparliamentary abolitionist activity almost vanished. Meanwhile, Martinique, Tobago, and St. Lucia were added to Britain's slave system, and St. Domingue was partially occupied.

The next seven years, 1797–1803, are often combined with the previous four, because again all attempts at general abolition failed. The London committee ceased to meet altogether. No abolition bills were introduced from 1800 to 1804. Even a bill in 1799 to exempt the environs of Sierra Leone, a free-soil colony in Africa, from the slave trade was narrowly defeated in the Lords. New West Indian colonies, Trinidad and Guiana, were seized by Britain. The British government began large-scale purchases of African slaves to fill out its West India regiments. From another point of view, however, this period was far less barren than 1793–1796. In 1797 a resolution was passed affirming the British desire to see amelioratory legislation initiated in the West Indies with a view toward abolition. In 1799, the slave transportation act, hitherto renewed annually, was made permanent and far more stringent. Steps were also taken by the British government to prevent the opening of Trinidad to unrestricted development by slave labor. Thus at the moment when general abolition was still unobtainable, important strategic gains were made in both principle and practice. By 1803, the abolitionist forces had been more successful than in 1793–1796.

A fifth period may be said to run from mid-1804 to the triumph of total abolition in 1807. It was characterized by major abolitionist successes in the House of Commons in 1804, 1806, and 1807, and only one narrow defeat, in 1805. In the more hostile upper house there was one technical setback in 1804, and then the three substantial victories of 1806–1807. Even 1805 was marked by a decisive extraparliamentary abolitionist victory. Despite the continued governmental policy of Caribbean expansion, the slave trade to the conquered colonies was sharply reduced by executive order, and the rationale was prepared for abolition of the foreign trade in 1806. The London abolition committee was also revived in 1804 and the propaganda campaign renewed in 1805. Public opinion was again mobilized, although within narrower, self-imposed limits than in 1788 or 1792.

From 1808 to 1815 there was a final period of abolitionist activity directed against the African slave trade. On the parliamentary level it was marked by quiet, continuous elite initiatives for tightening imperial enforcement and international extension. The period was climaxed by another extensive popular and parliamentary campaign in 1814. That year also marked the beginning of a vigorous new abolitionist foreign policy by the British government. After 1820, British abolitionism began to transform itself into a general emancipation movement and to move back toward the broad aims which its leaders had apparently abandoned for tactical reasons in 1787.

The temporal boundaries of political abolition in Britain are quite clear. In 1785 not one major figure in either house of Parliament conceived it to be a practical option, whatever their individual moral reservations about the slave trade.[25] In 1814 not one figure in either house dared to suggest that its restoration was either politically possible or morally defensible. We must analyze the extent to which the economic development of British slavery provoked or encouraged abolition by British capitalism.

2

The 1770s as the Pivot of British Slavery

The decline thesis, however elaborate, comes to this: In the first half of the eighteenth century the slave economies were far more important to the mother country than afterward. Small islands in the Caribbean could rival continents in significance because of their relatively rapid rates of development. Their specialized production was of undisputed value in the imperial system, and their profits may have helped to fuel the capital needs of the industrial revolution.[1] Somewhere after the middle of the century, the slave economies began to lose their developmental lead and were unable to maintain their former position either as customers or as tropical producers. As they became encumbrances to emergent British capitalism, the door was opened for the destruction of their inefficient, anachronistic economy. Their decline was only accelerated by the abolitionist campaigns and legislation from 1788 to 1807.[2]

The argument that abolition was a result of either the relative or absolute decline of the slave economy may be further broken down into two general statements: British slavery diminished as a factor in the imperial political economy before and during abolition; at the same time, it succumbed to competition with similar economic systems in the international market. In both cases the assumption is that the West Indian colonies were less valuable and less vigorous in the last third of the eighteenth century than before. Although there is no general agreement on when the secular decline in proportionate value begins, the American Revolution is most often depicted as the decisive event in the cycle.[3] Some turning point is of course significant for any causal argument, since the decline must be shown to have preceded the major political initiatives in the dismantling process.

The Value of the West Indies

No area of the empire, either before or after the American Revolution, was more totally identified with slavery than the British Caribbean colonies. The principal standard for measuring the value of the slave colonies to Britain is the position of the British West Indies in British overseas trade accounts.[4] Williams presents statistics to show a general rise in the value of the colonies, both as exporters and importers, in the first three-quarters of the eighteenth century. He thus demonstrates that the slave colonies were expanding, both absolutely and relatively, in the period prior to 1773. He then presents much more scattered evidence to illustrate the decline of their value in the period immediately prior to emancipation. They were in decline, at least relatively, at the beginning of the 1830s.[5] But what of the period between about 1770 and 1820, well after abolition, and just before the British Parliament resolved to bring the slave system to an end as soon as it was deemed practicable? This was the critical political period of great mass campaigns against the slave trade and of the effective closing off of African labor to the British colonies. To establish firmly the Ragatz-Williams thesis, it would also be necessary to demonstrate the relative decline of the slave economies in this interval.

Neither imports from nor exports to the British West Indies declined at the end of the eighteenth century. On the contrary, both categories increased sharply in value toward 1800 and reached levels well above *any* putative "golden age" before the American Revolution (see figures 1 and 2). They therefore point to precisely the opposite conclusion from that indicated by Williams. Even more impressive are the figures of British West Indian trade as a percentage of total British overseas trade. Table 1 shows that, if we use Williams's terminal data year (1773) as our pivotal year between 1723 and 1822, the British West Indian trade accounted for a higher proportion of total British trade after 1773 than it did before. Figures 3 and 4 and table 1 show this to be equally the case when imports and exports are measured separately. Therefore, Williams's own principal measure of significance shows that the British West Indies were absolutely and relatively far more valuable to Britain during the period of intense debate on the imperial slave trade (1788–1807) and on the world slave trade (1814–1820) than during the period when there had been no organized British pressure against the trade (1720–1775). Using tables 2, 3, and 4 one can also compare the British West Indian slave colonies with

FIGURE 1: AVERAGE ANNUAL VALUE OF EXPORTS AND REEXPORTS FROM ENGLAND AND WALES TO THE BRITISH WEST INDIES

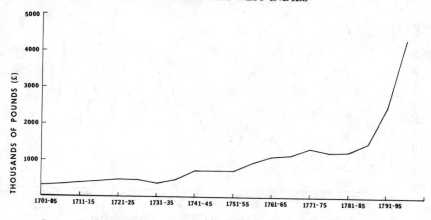

Source: E. Schumpeter, *British Overseas Trade,* p. 17.

FIGURE 2: AVERAGE ANNUAL VALUE OF IMPORTS INTO ENGLAND AND WALES FROM THE BRITISH WEST INDIES

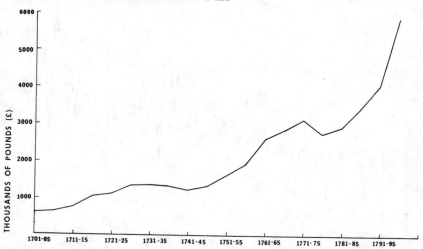

Source: E. Schumpeter, *British Overseas Trade,* p. 18.

Britain's other major overseas trading areas. They show that of all the non-European areas, British or foreign, the British West Indies were generally the most important sector to Britain for the entire century between 1722 and 1822. Furthermore, they were actually pulling away from their closest competitors during the period 1793–1797 to 1808–1812.

FIGURE 3: BRITISH WEST INDIAN IMPORTS, 1722–1822

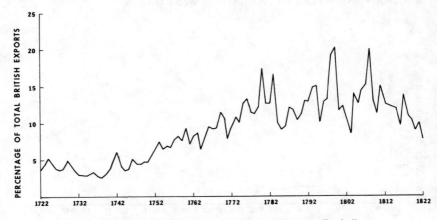

Source: Mitchell and Deane, *Abstract,* pp. 309–11, "Overseas Trade."

FIGURE 4: BRITISH WEST INDIAN EXPORTS, 1722–1822

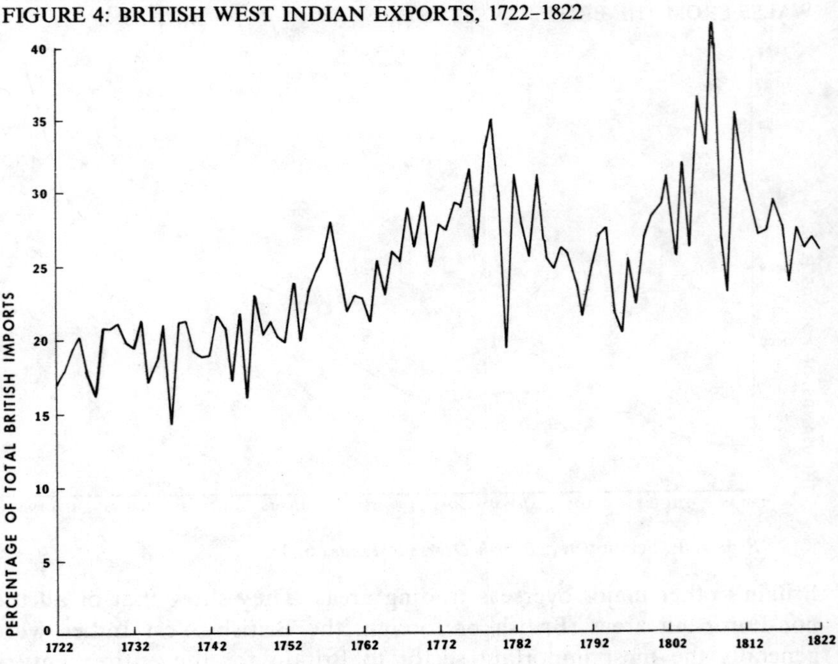

Source: Mitchell and Deane, *Abstract,* pp. 309–11, "Overseas Trade."

An observer, looking back in 1822, would still have felt the force of this comparison. As late as 1821, the West Indies accounted for more of British overseas trade in both imports and exports than they had fifty years before. More important, he would also have obtained a similar statistical result whether he matched the previous ten years, or twenty-five, or the whole fifty years with corresponding periods before 1770 (see table 1). His picture would have looked like that in figure 5. Moreover, taking the West Indian total after 1814 is a conservative estimate of British slavery's "value." It was no longer the measure of the whole colonial slave system. A percentage of Britain's Afro-Asian trade (Mauritius and the Cape Colony) had to be added to the account of slavery. The most that can be

TABLE 1: BRITISH WEST INDIAN SHARE OF TOTAL BRITISH TRADE, 1713–1832 (by value)

	Imports	Exports	Total
1713–1717 EW	17.9%	5.0%	10.7%
1718–1722 EW	16.7	3.9	9.9
1723–1727 EW	18.3	4.4	10.9
1728–1732 EW	20.4	3.9	11.7
1733–1737 EW	18.6	3.0	10.1
1738–1742 EW	19.9	4.1	11.6
1743–1747 EW	19.4	4.3	10.3
1748–1752 EW	20.9	5.3	11.5
1753–1757 EW	23.5	7.1	14.0
1758–1762 EW	23.7	8.2	14.3
1763–1767 GB	24.0	8.4	15.3
1768–1772 GB	27.2	9.7	17.7
1773–1777 GB	28.7	11.6	19.7
1778–1782 GB	29.3	13.4	21.0
1783–1787 GB	26.8	11.3	19.1
1788–1792 GB	24.3	12.0	17.8
1793–1797 GB	24.3	13.2	18.0
1798–1802 GB	27.6	14.3	20.2
1803–1807 GB	30.5	13.1	20.8
1808–1812 GB	30.3	14.0	20.9
1813–1817 GB	27.6	11.9	17.6
1818–1822 GB	25.8	9.7	15.9
1818–1822 UK	25.7	9.9	16.1
1823–1827 UK	21.1	8.6	13.8
1828–1832 UK	20.1	7.0	12.3

Source: Mitchell and Deane, *Abstract*, pp. 309–11, "Overseas Trade."

Note: Prior to 1755 all figures are for England and Wales only. Between 1755 and 1758, imports are to Great Britain and exports are from England and Wales. From 1759 to 1822 all figures are for Great Britain. Thereafter they are for the United Kingdom.

said of the West Indian devaluation is that it became visible only a decade or two after 1806–1807. Decline followed abolition.

These trade figures were the staple of parliamentary measures of significance in the debates on the slave trade. They do not, of course, measure the precise value of the British West Indies as a consumer of British exports. Some of the goods sent to the British West Indies were re-exported to foreign colonies, as were a proportion of the African slaves. The export totals assigned to the foreign West Indies further understate

FIGURE 5: BRITISH WEST INDIAN TRADE,
1722–1822

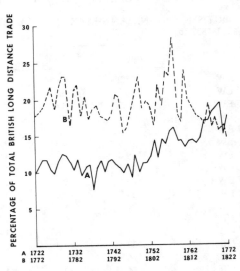

Source: Mitchell and Deane, Abstract,
pp. 309–11, "Overseas Trade."

the importance of that area in the long period of war prior to abolition. Part of the British trade to the United States was really a war detour to the enemies' colonies under the cover of a neutral flag. In 1807, over one-fifth of British exports to the United States went on as U.S. reexports to the hostile West Indies.[6] On the export side, British reexports to Europe, which included a high percentage of colonial goods, were not credited to the account of tropical slavery in the ordinary trade figures. The figures also exaggerate the "decline" of the British West Indies as a customer after 1815, because a direct trade with newly independent Latin American colonies began to replace the British reexport trade in the Caribbean area.

TABLE 2: NON-EUROPEAN SHARES OF TOTAL BRITISH TRADE, 1713–1822 (by value)

	British West Indies	North America	Latin America	Asia	Africa
1713–1717 EW	10.7%	6.5%	1.8%	6.3%	0.9%
1718–1722 EW	9.9	7.2	1.7	8.3	1.2
1723–1727 EW	10.9	7.8	2.4	6.6	1.7
1728–1732 EW	11.7	7.8	2.2	7.2	1.8
1733–1737 EW	10.1	8.7	1.3	7.9	1.4
1738–1742 EW	11.1	10.3	2.1	8.6	1.4
1743–1747 EW	10.3	9.4	2.1	9.2	1.1
1748–1752 EW	11.5	11.5	0.6	9.2	1.3
1753–1757 EW	14.0	12.8	0.0	10.2	1.3
1758–1762 EW	14.3	14.9	2.6	9.3	1.5
1763–1767 GB	15.3	14.6	1.1	10.6	2.3
1768–1772 GB	17.7	16.6	0.4	12.1	3.0
1773–1777 GB	19.7	12.1	0.3	9.8	2.8
1778–1782 GB	21.0	7.9	0.7	12.6	1.5
1783–1787 GB	19.1	14.3	0.4	15.1	3.0
1788–1792 GB	17.8	15.9	0.9	15.4	2.9
1793–1797 GB	18.0	17.5	2.4	16.6	1.7
1798–1802 GB	20.2	17.3	4.1	13.7	2.3
1803–1807 GB	29.8	19.1	2.9	12.7	2.1
1808–1812 GB	20.9	13.8	14.4	9.6	1.1
1813–1817 GB	17.6	14.4	9.1	12.1	0.9
1818–1822 GB	15.9	15.1	8.7	13.2	1.0

Source: Mitchell and Deane, *Abstract*, pp. 309–11, "Overseas Trade."
Note: Prior to 1755 all figures are for England and Wales only. Between 1755 and 1758, imports are to Great Britain and exports are from England and Wales. From 1759 to 1822 all figures are for Great Britain.

It might be argued that for the period 1793–1814 secular trends were distorted by the fortunes of war, and that calculations for the long term should exclude these years. Certain considerations weigh against such a procedure. First, the very opposite strategy, which emphasizes the economic results of the American war years, lies at the heart of the decline thesis. If we discount the upward march of slave production and trade after 1792 as distorted by war, we must also discount the short march downward between 1775 and 1783. Only the expansive peacetime decade of 1783–1792 would be left between 1775 and 1815. A final consideration is crucial. The abolitionists' triumph came amid war and after fifteen years of almost continuous war. They did not, as some of their opponents urged, shelve the question for the duration. We must therefore weigh the economic retrospect and prospect during these fourteen years of war (and one of peace). This was all that was available to the decision makers, and

TABLE 3: NON-EUROPEAN SHARES OF BRITISH IMPORTS, 1713–1822 (by value)

	British West Indies	North America	Latin America	Asia	Africa
1713–1717 EW	17.9%	7.2%	0.7%	12.9%	0.4%
1718–1722 EW	16.7	8.6	0.5	16.1	0.4
1723–1727 EW	18.3	8.4	1.0	12.4	0.7
1728–1732 EW	20.4	9.0	1.0	13.3	0.6
1733–1737 EW	18.6	10.2	0.3	14.1	0.8
1738–1742 EW	19.9	11.4	0.2	15.2	0.7
1743–1747 EW	19.4	11.0	1.0	14.0	0.3
1748–1752 EW	20.9	12.0	0.4	15.3	0.6
1753–1757 EW	23.5	11.7	0.3	14.2	0.4
1758–1762 EW	23.7	10.6	4.6	12.1	0.4
1763–1767 GB	24.0	11.6	2.4	14.5	0.5
1768–1772 GB	27.2	11.4	0.7	16.7	0.7
1773–1777 GB	28.7	9.8	0.5	13.7	0.6
1778–1782 GB	29.3	2.1	0.5	14.6	0.5
1783–1787 GB	26.8	6.8	0.6	20.4	0.7
1788–1792 GB	24.3	8.2	1.6	20.1	0.5
1793–1797 GB	24.3	8.2	3.3	23.7	0.5
1798–1802 GB	27.6	9.4	6.4	21.6	0.5
1803–1807 GB	30.5	9.8	3.3	20.3	0.5
1808–1812 GB	30.3	9.8	15.8	16.1	0.7
1813–1817 GB	27.6	8.2	11.3	25.7	1.0
1818–1822 GB	25.8	13.8	7.3	22.8	0.8

Source: Mitchell and Deane, *Abstract*, pp. 309–11, "Overseas Trade."
Note: Prior to 1755 all figures are for England and Wales only. Between 1755 and 1758, imports are to Great Britain and exports are from England and Wales. From 1759 to 1822 all figures are for Great Britain.

the annual enumeration of official overseas trade flows remained the unrivaled primary source of commercial comparison.

If one turns from trade figures to the relative value of slave property between 1775 and 1815, decline is not more perceptible. The British West Indies were valued by the British West Indian planters at £50–60 million in 1775 and at £70 million in 1789.[7] After 1789 the trend was not reversed. The old value of the colonies alone was being set at over £80 million by the late 1790s, with £20–30 million added for the conquered colonies. By 1807 the West Indians claimed a value of £85–100 million for the British slave colonies (including Trinidad). There was naturally a great deal of dispute over these assignments, which were often declared to be overstated to twice their value. But the distortion would appear to have been consistent: in 1775 the West Indian planters assessed their own value at £60 million, while Southey estimated it at £30 million; Edwards claimed a valuation of

TABLE 4: NON-EUROPEAN SHARES OF BRITISH EXPORTS, 1713–1822 (by value)

	British West Indies	North America	Latin America	Asia	Africa
1713–1717 EW	5.0%	5.9%	2.7%	1.1%	1.3%
1718–1722 EW	3.9	5.9	2.8	1.5	1.8
1723–1727 EW	4.4	7.2	3.6	1.4	2.6
1728–1732 EW	3.9	6.7	3.2	1.7	2.8
1733–1737 EW	3.0	7.5	2.1	2.6	1.6
1738–1742 EW	4.1	9.4	3.6	3.5	2.0
1743–1747 EW	4.3	8.4	3.4	6.0	1.6
1748–1752 EW	5.3	12.2	1.0	5.2	1.9
1753–1757 EW	7.1	13.6	0.0	7.3	2.0
1758–1762 EW	8.2	17.5	1.3	7.5	2.2
1763–1767 GB	8.4	17.1	1.0	7.6	3.7
1768–1772 GB	9.7	20.9	1.0	8.1	4.9
1773–1777 GB	11.6	14.1	0.1	6.3	4.8
1778–1782 GB	13.4	13.3	0.9	10.7	2.5
1783–1787 GB	11.3	22.0	0.2	9.7	5.3
1788–1792 GB	12.0	22.7	0.3	11.3	4.9
1793–1797 GB	13.2	24.7	1.7	11.1	2.7
1798–1802 GB	14.3	23.6	2.2	7.5	3.8
1803–1807 GB	13.1	26.6	2.6	6.6	3.4
1808–1812 GB	14.0	16.8	13.4	4.8	1.4
1813–1817 GB	11.9	17.9	7.9	4.3	0.8
1818–1822 GB	9.7	15.6	9.6	7.1	1.2

Source: Mitchell and Deane, *Abstract*, pp. 309–11, "Overseas Trade."
Note: Prior to 1755 all figures are for England and Wales only. Between 1755 and 1758, imports are to Great Britain and exports are from England and Wales. From 1759 to 1822 all figures are for Great Britain.

£70 million in 1790, when the Privy Council report had estimated it at about £36 million. In Parliament, in 1807, George Hibbert put the capital worth of the "old" West Indies at slightly under £100 million, as did a witness testifying for the colonies. If we also discount this figure by 50 percent, the low valuation would be £50 million. The value of the "old" colonies alone would therefore have increased by 20 percent between 1775 and 1790, and by almost 40 percent in the following seventeen years. Using P. Colquhoun's figures in his *British Empire*, the 1790 colonies alone were worth £100 million before the end of the Napoleonic Wars.[8] If one adds to them the value of the slave colonies conquered by 1806, and ratified in 1814, the total figure was £145 million. Whether one uses the inflated figures of the West Indians or the deflated figures of their opponents, the property value of the slave colonies would appear to have doubled between 1789 and 1814. Excluding India, most of whose capital did not belong to British subjects, Colquhoun assigned to the slave colonies 5 percent of the total annual income of the British Empire in 1814 (see table 5).

These contemporary assessments took no account of inflationary factors. Between 1760 and 1790 this would have been almost negligible to the most discerning eye. During the period as a whole, and even for the inflationary war decades, the rate of increase of the West Indian property assessment outran the general rate of price increases in Britain.[9] This may explain why, whatever other objections might have been raised to West Indian claims, inflationary distortion was not included among them. All the valuations, whether self-interested or otherwise, were in fact nothing more than a combination of demographic estimates and current prices for slaves. Global estimates of the value of land, stock, machinery, and

TABLE 5: ESTIMATED VALUE OF THE ANNUAL PRODUCTION OF THE BRITISH EMPIRE, 1812

Area	Value (in thousands)	Percent
Britain and Ireland	£430,520	91.6
North American dependencies	13,220	2.8
European dependencies	1,820	0.4
Free settlements in Afro-Asia (excluding India)	290	0.1
Total nonslave	445,850	94.9
British West Indies (including those retained in 1814)	22,500	4.8
Slave settlements in Afro-Asia (excluding Ceylon)	1,490	0.3
Total slave	23,990	5.1
Grand total	469,840	100.0

Source: Colquhoun, A Treatise on the British Empire, table 3, pp. 97–98.

buildings were simply computed as a constant multiple of the total value of slaves. The usual procedure was to double that total to encompass all other items in the account. This is probably the reason why maximum and minimum value estimates differed by a factor of two. In any event, slave labor was, in a very literal sense, the unique measure of the value of the West Indies.

In terms of both capital value and of overseas trade, the slave system was expanding, not declining, at the turn of the nineteenth century. The secular decline of the slave colonies within the imperial political economy prior to abolitionist successes seems to be a statistical illusion created by ignoring the period 1783–1815.

The Slave Trade

In focusing first on the Caribbean component of the system we have not overlooked the fact that abolition began not with the slaves already in the West Indies, but with the transatlantic slave trade. We have followed the historical tradition in its emphasis on the colonial nexus, rather than the African trade, as the crucial variable. This is quite logical if abolition derived its strength from the decline of the slave system as a whole. Nevertheless, the slave trade was the first target of the abolitionists. From a tactical point of view the priority was quite appropriate. The capital in the slave trade was but a fraction of that in the American sector. Even more significantly, the African trade did not sustain large colonial settlements of British subjects with special claims on imperial good faith. Petitions of distress from the native African slave traders would certainly have been given short shrift in London. They would more likely have provided additional ammunition to those abolitionist wits who busily composed mock petitions from the chain manufacturers of Birmingham and from the sharks in African waters, bewailing the deprivations they faced under abolition.

The political reasons for the abolitionist strategy against the slave system are clear. But perhaps it was also the economically logical place to begin the work of destruction. Insofar as the slave trade was an end in itself, was its end likewise a decay in itself? The evidence indicates that the British African slave trade also reached its apogee at the end of the eighteenth century. During this century, when extra-European trade was a growing component of British trade,[10] the West Indies and Africa were among its most dynamic areas. Table 6 shows the value of British exports to Africa from 1749–1755 to 1817–1823. As in the West Indian case, British trade with Africa was not diminishing after 1783 either in relation to the period before 1775 or compared with the rest of the empire. Africa never loomed as large in trade as many other areas of the non-European world, but to the extent that it played a role in the overseas network, it was more important during the abolitionist attack after 1787 than in any previous period. Moreover, in terms of absolute value, the African trade was measurably greater for any period after the American Revolution than for any period before it. Twice as much money was invested in the slave trade during

1791–1807, at the height of the abolitionist agitation, as in the agitation-free decades 1761–1780.[11] In this it also parallels the West Indian trade down to 1807. If we turn from value to volume, the results are identical. Tables 7 and 8 show that the British trade reached its apogee in the last two decades of its existence.

TABLE 6: BRITISH EXPORTS TO AFRICA, 1749–1822

	War	Peace	Index
1749–1755		x	100
1756–1762	x		112
1763–1774		x	285
1775–1783	x		180
1784–1792		x	379
1793–1797	x		287
1798–1802	x		589
1803–1807	x		488
1808–1812	x		232
1813–1817		x	199
1817–1822		x	265

Source: Mitchell and Deane, *Abstract*, pp. 310–11.
Note: The time sequences are keyed to the outbreak of war and the restoration of peace until 1792, when five-year averages are used, breaking at 1807. If one clustered any sequence of periods prior to 1792 and compared them with the period 1792–1807, the result still indicates rising trade in 1792–1807 compared with earlier periods. The drop in exports to the slave-trade coast after 1803–1807 is actually larger than shown on the table. By 1810 exports to the Cape Colony, conquered in 1806, accounted for almost half of total British exports to Africa.

Although at this point we are concerned with long-run trends, a word is in order on the comparability of the decades after 1781–1790 with the preceding ones. In briefly interpreting his figures, Philip Curtin argues that the British slave trade "really" peaked in the 1780s and 1790s. This would already be uncomfortably late for the Ragatz-Williams thesis. Curtin maintains, however, that the continued high rate of exports from 1801 to 1807 was "accountable to the planters' expectation that the trade would soon be cut off by Parliamentary action." This last period would therefore constitute "only a short-term peak. The sustained peak of the English trade had already passed."[12]

Curtin's distinction between sustained and short-term peaks in the period 1780–1807 may be arbitrary. Annual figures within this period show a sharp rise in the trade occurring in 1789–1792, when the first campaign for abolition was coming to a head. This may have triggered a speculative increase of exports. Certainly, when the abolition bill passed the Commons by a substantial majority in 1792, there was an immediate rush to fit out every available ship.[13] The sharp subsequent falls and rises in volume seem to have depended largely on wartime and market conditions down to 1798–1799, when the slave trade reached its absolute peak. In that year, however, a new version of the slave transportation act was passed. It not only lowered the number of slaves that could be carried per ton of shipping, but set new standards for overhead space so high that it drove a substantial number of smaller ships out of the trade. The volume of trade in 1801–1804 was 30 percent less than in 1798–1800.[14]

TABLE 7: AVERAGE ANNUAL SLAVE EXPORTS BY BRITAIN, FRANCE, AND PORTUGAL, 1701–1807

	Total Annual Average	British Annual Average	British Share
1701–1710	31,000	12,000	39%
1711–1720	33,200	14,100	42
1721–1730	38,100	14,200	37
1731–1740	49,800	20,700	42
1741–1750	54,400	25,500	46
1751–1760	48,500	23,100	48
1761–1770	60,700	30,600	50
1771–1780	56,800	25,400	45
1781–1790	84,000	36,000	43
1791–1800	75,300	44,800	59
1801–1805	61,800	37,500	61
1801–1807	59,300	35,000	59

Sources: Curtin, *Atlantic Slave Trade*, pp. 150, 211, for all three nations for the period 1701–1761; Anstey, "Volume and Profitability," pp. 5–9 for the British trade, 1761–1780; Anstey, "The Slave Trade of Continental Powers," MS, for the Portuguese and French trades, 1761–1807; and, for the British trade, 1781–1807, Appendix II of this study.

The years 1801–1807 certainly do not form a block as far as pressures for stocking are concerned. The political stimulus to speculation was absent for most of the period. After 1799 no further attempt was made to introduce an abolition bill until late in the session of 1804, and there was really no probability of an end to the trade for another two years. June 1806 to May 1807 is clearly the maximum period in which there were incentives to speculative buying. But by then the trade

TABLE 8: ESTIMATES OF THE VOLUME OF THE BRITISH SLAVE TRADE, 1777–1807

	Tonnage (in thousands)[a]		Estimates of the Number of Slaves Loaded in Africa (in thousands)					
	1	2	Curtin	Inikori	Anstey	Drescher[b]	Drescher[c]	Drescher[d]
1777–1788	161.4	165.0	339.2	462.7	304.6	332.2	322.0	339.1
1781–1790	187.5	191.1	325.5	–	323.4	360.0	348.5	367.6
1791–1800	312.7	320.0	325.5	486.4	419.6	447.5	433.3	462.7
1801–1805	191.4	201.0	190.0	–	176.2	187.3	182.5	207.2
1801–1807	250.3	264.0	266.0	393.7	226.6	245.0	238.3	272.6
1781–1805	691.6	712.2	840.0	–	919.2	994.8	964.3	1,036.5
1789–1807	612.5	633.8	656.7	955.8	712.4	766.8	743.5	810.8
1781–1807	750.4	775.1	917.0	–	969.6	1,052.4	1,020.1	1,102.9
1777–1807	773.9	798.8	995.4	1,481.5	1,016.9	1,099.3	1,065.5	1,150.0

Sources: See Appendix II.
a. Column 1 represents British tonnage clearing for Africa from British ports. Column 2 includes foreign tonnage.
b. Slaves loaded on British carriers assuming 5% nonslaving tonnage (preferred series).
c. Slaves loaded on British carriers assuming 8% nonslaving tonnage.
d. Slaves loaded on British and foreign carriers from British ports assuming a 5% nonslaving tonnage.

was already crippled. Although the planters of the old islands could engage in heavy buying through 1807, those in the conquered possessions found themselves almost entirely cut off from direct African exports; the British trade to the unconquered foreign areas was abolished in 1806. And finally, to dampen any last minute slave rush, special legislation was passed in 1806 to prevent the use of any shipping for the trade which had not been previously registered for it. Thus, unlike 1792, stocking was largely nullified by 1806–1807. The total volume of the trade for 1806–1807 was down by almost one-quarter from the 1801–1805 average, and the volume for 1807 alone was lower still (see figure 6).

FIGURE 6: THE BRITISH SLAVE TRADE, 1780–1810

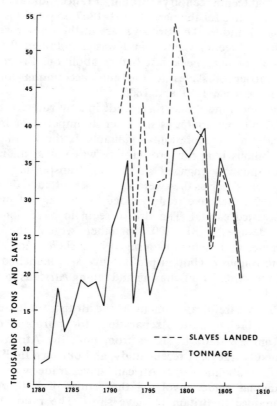

Source: Anstey, "Volume and Profitability," tables 1, 2, 3.

It would appear that the slave trade was artificially suppressed, not stimulated, after 1799. The unrestrained market was no longer the arbiter of the trade. From this point of view the figures for 1800–1807, and especially those for 1806–1807, are not totally comparable with the eighteenth-century totals. Another consideration permits us to view the British figures as a considerable underestimation. After 1796, and especially after 1802, both domestic carrying restrictions and war conditions made it increasingly attractive for British slave-trade capital to work under neutral colors. The British had developed a vigorous informal slave-trading empire alongside their visible one by 1806.[15]

The British slave traders were, even officially, faring quite well during the period 1750–1807. Both Curtin's figures for the Big Three exporters of the early eighteenth century (Britain, France, and Portugal) and Anstey's global figures for the period 1761–1807 help tell the same basic story (see tables 7 and 9). The British share of the trade rose sharply at the end of the eighteenth century and was maintained through 1805, reaching a peak or near peak just before abolition. Britain remained the premier carrier of slaves to the end, accounting for over half the world total between 1791 and 1806.

The profitability of the British slave trade in long-run terms, a measure less accessible to contemporaries in either its imperial or international context, provides a corroboration as valuable as the volume and share indicators. Fabulous long-run profitability was not at all necessary to keep British capitalists engaged in buying, transporting, and selling human beings for as long as they were legally permitted to do so. Over the period 1761–1807, the slave trade yielded an average of just under 10 percent on invested capital. The British seem to have done especially well in the decades 1781–1800. In other words, the abolitionist movement, rather than being encouraged by a slave trade already bled white by a precipitous decline in profitability, was launched at the very moment when rewards for purchasing and selling Africans were sustained at a high level.

Anstey offers a careful assessment of the British trade and a cogent survey of the foreign trades, separating, for purposes of analysis, the profits from the trade in slaves from both the African and West Indian commodity trades. A recent study, and our own findings, suggest that just before abolition the African slave trade was again very much a triangular trade, involving the return of both African and Caribbean produce to Britain in slave ships. The ratio of goods per ton carried by the direct West Indian trade to Liverpool in 1805 was only one-sixth higher than that carried by the African ships on their

TABLE 9: NATIONAL SHARES OF THE SLAVE EXPORTERS, 1761–1805

	British[a]	Portuguese	French	American	Danish/ Dutch	Total Number of Slaves Exported (in thousands)	Annual Average of Slaves Exported (in thousands)
1761–1790	40%	25%	23%	4%	7%	2,277.9	75.9
1791–1805	52	30	5	11	2	1,220.6	81.4
1761–1770	43	24	17	6	11	730.4	73.0
1771–1780	39	31	16	5	8	661.3	66.1
1781–1790	41	22	32	2	3	886.2	88.6
1791–1800	53	29	7	9	2	851.5	85.2
1801–1805	51	31	1	16	1	369.1	73.8

Sources: See Appendix II.
a. Includes only ships sailing under the British flag.

home voyage. The proportion of consigned cargo (which would be carried only as freight on commission) was also only one-sixth less in the triangular than in the shuttle trade.[16] From the perspective of investing capitalists the profits of the two commodity trades would naturally be added to proceeds from the sale of slaves. The separation of slave from "commodity" sales is only an heuristic strategy which isolates one trade from the compound profits of continuous voyages.

Triangularity was characteristic not only of the period just before abolition. Until the shortages caused by the French Caribbean uprisings, it was customary "to return five-eighths of the net proceeds in the vessel, or to freight her home full; cash and produce were then plenty, and proportioned to the trade . . . ; both produce and bullion were shipped in British bottoms, and to British ports only, and more than proportioned to the demand."[17] Only in times of scarcity, like the nineties, did large numbers of Liverpool slave ships return in ballast or light freight.

International comparisons indicate that the British slave trade might have sustained a far lower rate of return without causing its practitioners to abandon the field. Anstey calculates an average profitability of about 10 percent for the British slave trade for the period 1761–1807. The Dutch Middleburg Company, with an annual rate of return of 1.43 percent per year between 1761 and 1800, doggedly persisted in the trade. In the last thirty years of that period it showed no average profit whatever. In fact, in each succeeding decade of that period, it showed a progressively increasing average loss. Similarly, in the French seaport cities, the slave traders of Bordeaux, Nantes, and La Rochelle averaged no better than 6 percent, and as little as 1 percent.[18]

If one thus incorporates slave-trade profitability into the story of abolition, economic ironies are more abundant than iron laws. Slavery was first attacked where and when it was leading the international pack. Launching an attack at that point of the system was like attempting to restrict the flow of labor into Manchester as the first step in the dismantling of the British textile industry. Yet it is hardly necessary to compare the slave trade to Britain's premier growth industry in the period after 1780. It would be fairer to compare it to average expectations from, and the performance of, other British overseas trades in the eighteenth century. It seems that general expectations in other areas of the globe were extraordinarily low, even for relatively risky overseas investments. The British Levant traders, for example, would probably have been quite content to turn a profit of 10 percent per year for half a century.[19]

The Continental Colonies

The third component of the British slave system in the eighteenth century poses a preliminary problem of another order. The North American slave colonies were politically severed from the empire after 1775.[20] The long-run impact of their absence from the imperial slave ledger cannot be assessed without some reference to their political context, which was now different from that of their erstwhile tropical counterparts. The historical tradition requires such a compound assessment. The departure of the continental colonies is cited by Williams and others as both a political and economic blow to the sugar colonies, weakening slavery's ability to resist assaults after 1783. While we cannot measure the impact of independence, our purpose will be amply served if we can show that the American separation did not alter the balance of economic forces against British slavery and, above all, against the British slave trade.

The loss of the American colonies clearly entailed a severe short-run diminution of the imperial slave labor force (see table 10). The trade of the new slave states henceforth appeared in the foreign trade column. However, the empire lost a number of colonies dependent on free labor at the same time. A far larger number of her former subjects were free rather than slave laborers. The change in their political status is of less moment, however, than the general thrust of American policy even prior to 1775. Therefore, before discussing the implications of Anglo-American slavery in economic terms, we must consider a striking feature of British imperial policy during the eighteenth century.

In contrast to the rest of the colonial world, the slave trade was a live political issue in North America long before it emerged anywhere else. Abolitionism had a political base of its own in North America, which was able to effect abolition in perfect temporal parallel with the British system in 1807. Before 1776, the Americans were far more active against the trade, if only for political reasons, than were their metropolitan counterparts. It was the agent of the American colonies who taunted the English for freeing Negro slaves in England while producing new ones on the African coast. Virginia unsuccessfully petitioned for prohibition, as had South Carolina in 1760. The first petitions against the slave trade were collected in Philadelphia in 1772. Initiatives by Pennsylvania, Georgia, and Jamaica to tax the slave trade were disallowed by the British. In Massachusetts, only a governor's rejection prevented an abolition bill from becoming law. The Americans were also willing to use a boycott of African slaves as an economic weapon in the imperial struggle. It was the metropolis which uniformly opposed restrictions or abolitions and wished to maximize slave imports.[21] The British apparently had the greater stake in the African trade.

The postwar attitudes of the American slave states are too variegated to permit general conclusions about the long-run implications of pre-Revolutionary moves against the slave trade. But the pattern of the northern and middle states after independence seems to indicate a continuity of sentiment against the slave trade, especially into their own territories. They also maintained their resistance to its continuation in

TABLE 10: FRENCH AND BRITISH SLAVE POPULATIONS,
1710–1814 (in thousands)

	In the Caribbean		Total	
	French	British	French	British[a]
1710	88	148	90	197
1730	169	219	169	310
1750	265	295	270	531
1770	379	428	445	880
1790	675	480	735	480
1805	175[b]	585[c]	290[b]	605[d]
1814	178	755	230	870

Sources: For the Caribbean 1710–1770: McCusker, "The Rum Trade," I, 602–712. For the American continental colonies: Southerland, "Colonial Statistics," in United States Department of Commerce, Bureau of the Census, Historical Statistics of the United States, Colonial Times to 1957 (Washington, D.C., 1960), p. 756. For other areas, 1750–1814, and for the Caribbean 1790–1814: Moreau de Jonnes, Recherches statistiques sur l'esclavage colonial et sur les moyens de le supprimer (Paris, 1842), chapters on French and British colonies. Approximate deduction for free nonwhites is made from McCusker's tables for individual islands in using his summary table on p. 712.

a. Excludes slaves in India but includes those in Ceylon.
b. Excludes Haiti, St. Lucia, Tobago.
c. Excludes St. Lucia, Tobago, Demerara, and Berbice. If all were included, the figure would be 715; if only St. Lucia and Tobago were included, 620.
d. Including St. Lucia, Tobago, Demerara, and Berbice, 735; including only St. Lucia and Tobago, 640.

the larger unit of which they were a part. Finally, on the question of the trade, many of the large slave states threw their weight toward abolition in the political councils of the federal government. One must either include all political elements in the equation or abandon the thesis that America, by remaining within the imperium after 1775, would have caused a net diminution in the growth of abolitionism or an alteration of its first target.

On the economic side, the rhythm of American slavery after 1775 seems to run along lines approximating those of the rest of the British Empire.

The war years were clearly times of stress. Recovery returned about the mid-1780s, and the demand for slaves rose fairly steadily from then until abolition. Nor did the purchase of Africans by Americans stop after 1783. On the contrary, despite abolitions or suspensions in every state but Georgia by 1787, trends were as strongly positive thereafter as those indicated in the British African trade figures.

Recent estimates indicate that slave imports into the United States between 1790 and 1807, far from declining, "were higher in this period than in any previous twenty-year period." As many Africans entered the country between 1780 and 1810 as during "the previous hundred and sixty years of United States involvement in the slave trade." [22] Even more significant in its implications for British abolition, the trade to America was still very much a British trade. British ships continued to furnish the lion's share of Africans, half the total slave imports to South Carolina just prior to American abolition. [23] British merchants to the Carolinas were among the petitioners against abolition in 1806. The North American slave-trading interest continued to be represented in Parliament along with the African and Caribbean interests. They clung together and were hung together.

Moreover, the British slave trade to America was immune from certain abolitionist arguments. The first, directed against the British African slave trade, was that British slave exports to foreign colonies intensified sugar competition. The second charge, directed against the British colonial trades, was that African-born slaves increased the risks of colonial revolution. The first charge was always irrelevant to America, which was viewed principally as a source of tobacco before 1790 and a major cotton producer after 1800. The second charge was equally irrelevant to America after 1783. The British could henceforth write off both the social risks and the social costs involved in selling fresh slaves in the United States. Finally, none of the wartime strategic, social, or economic arguments applied by the British abolitionists against the foreign West Indian trade were transferable to the United States. Yet the abolition of the British foreign trade was applied equally to America in 1806.

America's political posture, not her economic potential, appeared to be most significant in the final moments of the British parliamentary debates on abolition. It was not America's enormous ability to absorb Africans, but her ability to do without them which counted most in 1807, as it had in 1770. Continental and insular slavery diverged in that important respect throughout the eighteenth century. Continental slavery had long since reached the point of self-sustained growth. Despite America's increasing volume of imported slaves, Africans accounted for only half as much of the growth of America's black population as did natural increase.[24] Their contribution, while considerable in certain areas, was not overwhelming. By contrast, the British, and all other European-controlled systems, were unable to maintain their slave population levels, much less grow, without annual imports from Africa. It would seem that the loss of the continental colonies in 1783 deprived Britain of just that portion of its empire which was always most easily severed from the African connection. In terms of getting rid of its ties to the slave trade, the British held on to the wrong end of their empire. Had Britain in fact defeated the contintental colonies, the demographic pattern of British slavery would thereafter have been far more vulnerable to the attacks of British abolitionists.

Abolition in 1807 was a more crucial turning point for British than for American slavery. After 1790 British slavery expanded almost as rapidly as American slavery, without natural increase. From 1790 to 1815 the American slave population increased by 90 percent, while the British slave population increased by 80 percent. From 1790 to 1805 the American increase was 49 percent while the British was between 26 and 53 percent. Between 1805 and 1814, when the American increase was 28 percent, the British slave population increased by a maximum of 44 and a minimum of 18 percent, depending on the perceived permanence of various British conquests (see table 10).[25] The geographical indeterminacy of the British system from 1792 to 1814 will be discussed below. The significant point is that over the whole period, the relative expansion of the two systems was parallel. Each increased, through a combination of acquisition, natural reproduction, and imports, to nearly twice its 1790 figure. The difference between them was in the weight of each ingredient in the combination.

The comparison between the American and British experiences with slavery after the revolution reveals striking continuity and parallelism in economic development as well as political process down to the abolition of the slave trade. The loss of America did not, at the very least, doom the British slave system to stagnation. By concentrating on the slave system losses of 1783, the decline school fails to note the corresponding losses in the free and saturated slave zones. But the more important question remains as to why the war losses of 1775–1783 constitute a turning point, and not the war gains of 1792–1814. By such an assertion, one arbitrarily assigns a second order of causal potency to the results of British expansion at the very moment when English naval and mercantile supremacy were producing the Pax Britannica of the nineteenth century. The decline thesis might have been applied just as well to American as to British slavery by 1830, if the former had been denied access to labor from the old states or territory in the West.

The continued positive role of American slavery in the British economic system to 1807 poses another, more general problem, which we deliberately avoided in the organization of this chapter. In dealing only with the three imperial components of eighteenth-century British slavery, we followed the traditional historiographic dichotomy between the British and foreign slave systems. The assumption of *Capitalism and Slavery* is that foreign slave systems were competitors and rivals. Their economic development would logically have a negative impact on British slavery. This is also presumed to have been the perspective of British statesmen and is the source of what we will refer to as "beggar-my-rival" political economy. The American case offers a forewarning that this mercantilist assumption of the relationship between the British Empire and foreign slavery is problematic. It remains to be seen to what extent the assumption accorded with British interests in the development of the Caribbean in the era of abolition.

3

The Protected Economy Before the French Slave Revolution

British abolitionist agitation and colonial developments reached a critical moment in the years from 1788 to 1792. Abolition became a national issue in 1788, and the Commons first voted to eliminate the slave trade in 1792. At the same time the French began to experience serious metropolitan conflict, together with social disorders in the colonies which culminated in the explosion on St. Domingue in the summer of 1791. In this chapter we will attempt to show how the British slave economy appeared to contemporaries on the eve of the milestone vote in the Commons and the momentous uprising in the Caribbean. There is one serious problem involved in treating the period 1788–1792 as a single terminal unit. The great slave revolt on St. Domingue created a situation so favorable to British tropical producers that we would be bending the argument in our favor to use 1792 alone as our retrospective year. Although contemporaries could not eliminate the immediate implications from their thoughts, we will reserve consideration of this climactic year for separate analysis. The development of the colonies, as they appeared about 1790, is our immediate concern.

The analysis can focus on three questions. First, was there a secular change in the performance of the British slave colonies about 1790 which warranted a more pessimistic assessment of their future than might have been the case a generation before? Second, was there a similar trend or shift in the balance of power between British slavery and the "free" labor zones such as to produce a weakening of, or a gloomy outlook for, slavery as a constituent element of the empire? The same question can then be asked about the British slave system in relation to rival systems in tropical America or elsewhere. Later we must ask whether the slave trade itself was, like the sorcerer's apprentice, producing consequences which threatened British slavery.

At the outset we can rule out certain theoretical economic arguments against colonies in general which were circulating among some economists by 1790. In the first place, Britain and its leaders were as yet far from embracing the ideology of anticolonialism. It was simply too broad a blade to use selectively against slavery. All British dependencies in Asia, Africa, America, and the Pacific would have felt its edge. No parliamentary abolitionists wished to disband the empire. The normal administrative costs of running the British slave colonies were recognized to be lower than those of Britain's nonslave colonies, including those just being founded in the 1780s and 1790s, using convict labor or freedmen. Even abolitionists recognized that the slave colonies made direct contributions to both colonial and imperial revenue which were not matched by their temperate zone counterparts.[1] It is on the weaknesses peculiar to the British West Indian economy that the decline theory rests its case.

The British Caribbean in 1790

Ragatz and Williams believe that British slavery was rapidly deteriorating until reprieved, albeit momentarily, by the French colonial cataclysm. The general list of charges against the system include absentee ownership, chronic indebtedness, the flight of whites from the islands, and the exhaustion of the soil by monoculture. All of these disabilities are compared with the robust French system, which was also the yardstick used by contemporaries down to 1791.[2]

The weaknesses, however, if they were such, were not unique to the British system, or even to slave systems. They were certainly not unique to the generation just prior to 1790. Absenteeism had been a characteristic of Caribbean agriculture for generations, and, while it might have induced hostility among those who had to witness the absentees' conspicuous consumption in Britain, it is unclear that it made the slave system either less or more efficient in 1790 than before.[3] Regional depopulation was more characteristic of eighteenth-century Britain than of her slave colonies. In Britain, however, selective depopulation was often described as the natural consequence of general prosperity, representing the optimal geographical division of labor.[4] Nor were absentee English, Scottish, or Irish landlords, resident in London, likely to regard themselves as convincing evidence of a pathological economy.

Similarly, while the West Indians themselves complained bitterly about the extent of their indebtedness to the metropolis, and the ease with which their lands passed into the hands of outsiders, this was not news to Britain. Prior to the American Revolution, the Commons was already informed that seven-eighths of the planters were deeply in debt to Great Britain and that credit for improvements was often difficult to obtain. Since this, as well as most other distress signals, came from planters who were crying poor from the beginning to the end of slavery, we must take with a grain of salt their claim that they were always on the verge of total ruin. Indebtedness was no recent discovery or rediscovery of the late 1780s. An agent for the sugar planters, describing their "miserable consumptive life . . . filled with great Debts, perplexing Accompts, protested Bills of Exchange at Tenn per cent. loss," was referring to the Barbados of 1700, not of 1800.[5] Nor is it clear why the increasing share of West Indian capital actually located and spent in England via absentee ownership and absentee consumption should have decreased the stake of British capitalism in the system.

The British slave colonies were certainly not demographically stagnant during the half-century before American independence. If the island colonies as a whole grew at a more moderate rate than those of the mainland, their showing still represented a population explosion by any European standards. The growth rate of the British Caribbean was far greater than that of the home islands. The complaint about the flight of whites from the West Indies, especially to North America, was also a hoary observation whether made in 1787 or 1783. In one sense it was more easily made in 1774 than in 1787. The American Revolution sent numbers of mainland loyalists to the islands, with consequences which will be discussed later. From the long-run perspective, in 1780 the white population in the British West Indies stood in about the same proportion to the black population as it had in 1740. In absolute terms, Jamaica's white population actually increased steadily during the eighteenth century. The relative diminution of the white population was a phenomenon of the late seventeenth century. Finally, soil exhaustion, while considered a serious problem, had been observed at least a century before the Seven Years' War.[6] The crucial question was always whether there were new lands within the system which were available for maintaining and expanding production, and whether old soils could be refurbished.

If we turn to the inevitable contrast with the French colonies, we find that they were subject to the same range of charges: absenteeism, indebtedness, lopsided demographic ratios, and soil exhaustion. France's premier colony of St. Domingue had immense absentee holdings, yet it was by no means thought to be less efficient than the more "resident" French islands of Martinique and Guadeloupe. Comparative absenteeism was never a critical variable in the discussions of intra- or intercolonial productivity, and its impact is difficult to assess.[7] British capitalists thought they were complimenting the French islands in conceding that the risk of bad debts was not much worse there than in their own islands.[8] Nor was French colonial agriculture, even on fabulous St. Domingue, immune from soil exhaustion. The British were also at the forefront of technological innovation in the sugar islands. They were apparently the pioneers in the introduction of the plow into the cane fields, and the intricate and costly new machinery brought into the sugar mills of St. Domingue after 1780 were dubbed "à l'anglaise."[9] The two systems were almost identical in demographic structure and had been so from the early decades of the century.[10] The British, when they started seriously counting at the end of the 1780s, were able to observe that the French racial ratios were no more advantageous than their own. The fate of the French islands after 1789 confirmed that observation in blood.

It is not the century-old demographic or physical features of the plantation system in which the decline thesis has the greatest stake. Since it is a theory of change it properly focuses attention on deterioration as a result of the struggle over American independence. Both war and weather, runs the story, combined to pile difficulties upon the slave colonies. The dearth of American provisions drove the islands to, and over, the brink of famine. The subsequent peace, which blocked U.S. shipping from the old provisions trade, kept prices high. The result, it is assumed, was to render the metropolis more critical of this mendicant remnant of the empire, and to set it dreaming of other empires in India and America.[11]

On top of man-made disasters came those of nature. Jamaica had six hurricanes in the first seven years of the 1780s. The plagues of the British West Indies vie with those of Egypt in many of the chronicles of abolition. What is overlooked in this "war and weather" assessment of the West Indies after 1775 is that the rivals of Britain were equally subject to them. The French West Indies suffered even more severely from the war. Metropolitan prices rose as French supplies became irregular. The islands were glutted with sugar, despite the fact that droughts, tempests, and provisions shortages kept down staple production. During 1779–1780 many planters in St. Domingue were not able to ship off "a single ounce for France. . . . It was such a Drug on that Island, as to be offered to sale at 10S per cwt . . . the planters having no prospect of shipping it, were willing to accept any price, rather than lose the whole of so perishable a commodity."[12]

Nor did nature deal kindly with the French islands. Just before the beginning of the great agitation against the British trade, the French East and West Indian islands were both devastated by hurricanes with enormous losses to French traders.[13] Finally, if the weather conspired to retard production by hurricanes before 1787, it ceased to do so thereafter.

Neither the global statistics of demographic ratios nor the eruptions of disaster and conflict are at the core of the evidence presented for decline. This is located in the specific record of Caribbean economic development. The central argument is that after 1783, the British slave economy was already tottering from structural weakness.[14] The colonies were simply failing to fulfill the very function for which they had been founded. One argument for economic decline rests on the supposition of a progressively deteriorating position of the planters as capitalist entrepreneurs. A second declares that the competitive and productive position of the British colonies deteriorated progressively after 1775. The first argument is supported by the assertion that the West Indian planters underwent a profit squeeze of increasing intensity after 1770-1775.[15] The total number of executions against property in Jamaica is one of the principal indicators used to prove the fragility of the West Indian system during the decade before the votes on abolition. The Jamaicans themselves used the data to prove that the war had caused them enormous distress, making them all the more deserving of sympathy. The decline school converts the distress to a trend. Between 1772 and 1791, notes Ragatz, "the amazing number of 80,021 executions, totalling £22,563,786 had been lodged in the office of the provost marshal of Jamaica."[16] A closer look at these statistics, divided into their annual components, affords a different perspective. The value of executions rose from a low of £0.56 million in 1772 to a high of £2.45 million in 1777 and, after again falling, reached a second peak of £2.1 million in 1785. Every subsequent year saw a decrease in the figure. By 1791 the sum had fallen to the level of 1772. The annual average for the period 1789-1791 was in fact slightly less than for 1773-1775. The number of executions per year reveals a similar pattern, except that the average number for 1789-1791 (2,875) was even further below its counterpart for 1773-1775 (3,626). Whatever the very real blows the island had suffered during the war and hurricane years, the Jamaican documents showed that the outlook was again brightening. The citation of bankruptcies and turnovers as a simple index of decline can be quite misleading as an indicator of economic decadence. Using such criteria one might have cited the following as evidence of the decline of the British cotton industry in 1815:

"there is but one out of five [Manchester cotton mills] remaining in the hands of the original proprietors; the others have changed hands once or oftener out of the sixty-two factories . . . generally from the ruin of the proprietors."[17]

We have an alternative way of gauging the relative position of the planters in 1788–1791, at least of those who survived the winnowing of the war decade. The Ragatz-Williams account includes a West Indian profit squeeze among the symptoms of decline. References to profit usually refer to the figure of 4 percent cited by Fuller, the agent for Jamaica in 1789.[18] This is usually accepted as an extremely unremunerative rate, because the planters often claimed that 10 percent was a fair rate for the risks and dangers of working in an alien land and climate. As indicated in chapter 2, real expectations in overseas ventures were probably lower than these "fair profit" claims by interested parties would imply. But more important, there has been no attempt by the decline school to estimate even roughly the change in the rate of profit over the period 1775–1792, which should certainly have some bearing on the argument. Williams presents one bit of data to show a falling profit rate between 1771–1781 and 1788. Unfortunately he compares two different things, the actual 9.5 percent profits of one family, the Longs, in 1771–1781, with Fuller's 4 percent estimate for all of Jamaica in 1788.[19] Even if both figures are accurate, the difference in what is being measured in the two cases vitiates the comparison.

We have some direct evidence, published during the period under discussion, on profits in Jamaica before and after the American Revolution. Even more important, from the evidentiary point of view, the information comes from the same source as the data on executions for debt cited by Ragatz.[20] From the accounts presented by Mr. Taylor, a large Jamaican planter, we can calculate his costs in two periods, before and after the war-weather interregnum in Jamaica. The base period used by the Jamaicans, 1772–1775, is, incidentally, from the "golden age"; the second period, 1788–1791, is from the spring tide of abolitionist activity. Taylor's accounts reveal that in *1790* he was paying 71 percent more per slave than in *1773*.* His hired labor costs rose 67 percent. The cost of provisions rose too, although the protein of the masters (salted Irish beef up 22 percent and pork up 10 percent) increased much more slowly in price

---

*To eliminate the repetition of cumbersome dates, a given period will sometimes be referred to by a single, central, italicized year. In this case *1773* = 1771–1775, and *1790* = 1788–1791.

than herring, the protein of the slaves (up 66 percent). American lumber rose 37 percent, only a little more than a third. Since the cost of slaves occupied a far greater proportion of the budget than lumber, the rising cost of African labor was of far more concern in *1790* than the relatively moderate rise of wood.[21] From this perspective, abolition was far more serious to the planters' prospects than the mercantilist consequences of American independence in *1790*.

The Ragatz-Williams account is justified in highlighting the increased costs to the planter. But what of sales, prices, and profits? Mr. Taylor's accounts showed that from *1773* to *1790* his volume of sales rose 48 percent, from 51,634 cwt. to 76,365 cwt. More significantly, the price paid for his sugar increased 69 percent. Finally, where it really counted, the average "balance at the disposal of the sugar planters, after all deductions" was 75.5 percent greater in *1790* than in *1773*.[22] Mr. Taylor had apparently more than kept pace with his rising costs of production. While the figures may not be representative for other, smaller producers, it should be noted that this was evidence presented in a document which consciously wished to paint an overall picture of planter distress. Recognizing that they had returned to prosperity by *1790*, the planters were anxious to remind the mother country of the preceding trauma. Ragatz's conclusion, that the decade 1783–1793 brought no relief to the planter, is simply not demonstrated by the data. The very opposite is the case.

In a twentieth-century analysis Michael Craton and James Walvin find that on Worthy Park plantation in Jamaica, the average income for 1776–1796 (twelve years of war and nine of peace) was equal to, or slightly above, that of the period immediately before the American war, and possibly double that of the period before 1750.[23] They further estimate that between 1775 and 1800 the average profit of the estate was between 15 and 20 percent of the assessed value. The planters were not "saved," even momentarily, by the collapse of St. Domingue. Recovery had returned before then.

The Imperial Factor

Since the fate of the colonies ultimately lay in metropolitan hands, their value was judged less by how well they did for themselves than by how well they were doing for the empire. As the last decade of the eighteenth century opened, the slave colonies were doing what they had always done, raising staples, principally sugar, with by-products of rum and molasses, along with lesser crops of cotton and coffee. They were still purchasing slaves from Africa and still purchasing provisions and finished goods, now transported almost exclusively in British ships. They were still insuring with, borrowing from, and defaulting to, metropolitan capitalists. The more successful planters were still sending their families to England and joining them as absentees. How then did the years of turmoil and tempest after 1775 alter the imperial equation or British perception? Did the political economists or capitalists have cause to grow restive and look beyond slavery to new pastures?

Wartime losses alone, of course, could not have made either political economists or politicians of Britain see strange new handwriting on the West Indian wall. The domestic economy itself suffered from the war, so that no relative decline whatever was apparent. If one looks more closely at the figures in table 1, another striking observation may be made. The West Indian share in British imports actually reached its eighteenth-century peak, just over 29 percent, in 1778–1782. While it fell back in the decade 1783–1792 to just over one-quarter of total imports, throughout the period it stayed at a level above any five-year period before 1768. Their share of British imports for the whole period 1778–1792 was actually slightly greater than in the halcyon years 1763–1777, and far better than any previous comparable period. The export figures made a still more impressive picture. Before the American revolutionary war, the West Indies had never accounted for as much as 10 percent of the value of British exports. After that period they never took as little as 10 percent of that trade.

Jamaica also carefully reminded the metropolis that between *1773* and *1790* its consumption of herring had more than doubled and consumption of British coal had more than tripled. Such information was not likely to produce restive murmurs among their suppliers. Demonstrating the ability to recover lost ground, the West Indies stood above their prewar production peaks even by 1785–1788, despite the residue of hurricanes and earthquakes. Their recovery lagged about two years behind the metropolis, whose revival occurred almost immediately after 1783. This may have been due as much to metropolitan mercantilism as to any situation in the islands. The British decision to favor British suppliers of provisions by excluding American ships from the direct West Indian trade created a severe, but temporary, transportation problem. British vessels had filled the supply gap by the mid-eighties, and the problem of peacetime provisions then quickly dropped from the West Indian grievance list.[24]

By and large, down to 1791, British slavery was deemed capable of more than adequately filling its old niche in the imperial system.[25] However, it is neither in the British islands, nor in the imperial nexus, that the decline school ultimately rests its case. The whole planet is called into the argument. And there we must now follow, judiciously applying the statistics of cane to the core of the decline theory.

French Sugar: "The Most Amazing Phenomenon"

The ultimate weapon of the decline thesis lies in its portrait of a shifting economic balance of power. This consists in pointing to both the positive lure of alternative nonslave markets and the rising competition of the powerful French slave system in 1790. We begin with the French threat. It is always less vaguely defined than the positive alternatives and is supposedly backed by empirical evidence. It was also the system against which British contemporaries measured their own. The French system was, as Williams notes, "an object of particular inquiry with the Privy Council Committee of 1788."[26]

The theoretical underpinning is presented as clearly and as precisely as any element of the story of decline. Slavery historically declined in both profitability and productivity as sugar monoculture wreaked its inevitable havoc on the fertility of the soil. Leadership in sugar culture, the principal indicator of economic development, passed from one virgin colony to the next, in a centuries-long relay race. Soil exhaustion and declines in productivity were the consequences of this crop and labor system. With the technology available in 1783, developed colonies could neither grow their sugar as cheaply nor expand their production as rapidly as could the frontier regions. In accord with this model, the British West Indian sugar colonies are described as bowing before the French juggernaut. So runs the argument.

The principal period of differentiation between the two systems is also precisely defined. "Between 1783 and 1789 the progress of the French sugar islands, of Saint Domingue especially, was the most amazing phenomenon in colonial development."[27] The symmetry of rising French and setting English satellites parallels that of rising British capitalism and falling British slavery. The chief indicators of growth were the trade figures, but, like both contemporaries and subsequent historians, we are faced with problems in assessing the French data. A certain percentage, usually exaggerated, was always added to the islands' export figures to account for smuggling. For our purpose, however, which is to measure change over time, the exact percentage of smuggling is irrelevant, so long as it either remained constant, or fell, over the century.[28] For purposes of estimation we need only assume that the ratio of smuggled to unsmuggled goods was roughly constant. Our manipulations of the data are dealt with in Appendix II.

What then of the putative "take-off" of French sugar before 1789? Is it reflected in the figures? The story seems to be somewhat more pedestrian. As indicated in table 11, in *1770* the Caribbean colonies of Britain and France together accounted for just under 75 percent of the sugar reaching the North Atlantic market. About twenty years later their combined share had expanded to 80 percent. Of the Anglo-French exports, the French colonies accounted for 53.2 percent in *1770* and 54.1 percent in *1787* for a net gain of less than one percentage point over the intervening generation. The difference, in terms of an average annual gain of the French colonies over their British rivals, was simply invisible to contemporaries. And none calculated any.

If, however, we are talking of economic change, irrespective of political alterations, even this small spread is a statistical illusion. Risking the hazards of misplaced precision, the bulk of the French gain over Britain was produced not by Saint Domingue, the old jewel of the French empire, but by the more modest little island of Tobago. Its mere acquisition by France in 1783 accounted for more of the increase in France's share of the sugar market between *1770* and *1787* than all of her remaining West Indian colonies. To be precise, in *1770* the French could claim 53.24 percent of Anglo-American exports. In *1787* she had moved up to 54.14 percent for a net gain of nine-tenths of one percent. If we drop the Tobago account from the French sugar total, without adding it to the British, the *1787* French colonial share of Anglo-French sugar falls to 53.87 percent. Finally, if the British had retained Tobago in 1783, even allowing for Tobago's stagnation under French control, the French figure for *1787* would fall to 53.56 percent. That is, other things being equal, in the generation between *1770* and *1787* the French, without benefit of Tobago, would have increased their share of Anglo-French production by a little more than three-tenths of one percent. Had the Privy Council bothered itself with such absurd four-digit precision, only a pun lover could have described the Anglo-French "gap" as a yawning one. The obvious point is that between *1770* and *1787* the stability between the Big Two is far more striking than the change.

One can also look at the broader international situation. The French colonies increased their share of the North Atlantic market from 39.6 percent in *1770* to 43.3 percent in *1787*, a relative gain of 3.7 percentage points. In the same period, the British boosted their share

TABLE 11: COLONIAL SOURCES OF NORTH ATLANTIC SUGAR IMPORTS, 1770–1787

Colony	Years used in Averaging for *1787*	*1770*	*1787*	*1787* Average Muscovado Equivalent (in tons)
St. Domingue	1786–1789	28.8%	29.8%	86,300
Martinique	1786–1788	5.0	6.5	18,790
Guadeloupe	1790	4.0	5.8	16,910
St. Lucia	1780	1.8	0.6	1,850
Tobago	1789	—	0.5	1,350
French total		39.6	43.3	125,200
Jamaica		16.4	17.0	49,130
Anguilla		—	0.0	90
Antigua		3.3	4.3	12,450
Barbadoes		4.3	2.9	8,510
Dominica	1785–1788	0.5	1.2	3,410
Grenada		3.5	4.0	11,550
Nevis-Montserrat		1.9	1.5	4,310
St. Kitts		3.7	3.4	9,780
St. Vincent		0.6	1.3	3,660
Tortola		—	1.1	3,150
British total		34.8	36.7	106,040
Surinam	1784, 1787, 1790, 1792	4.2	3.3	9,640
Demerara, etc.	1784, 1787, 1790		0.9	2,530
St. Eustasius	1781	3.5	0.1	300
Java	1786–1790	0.1	0.1	390
Dutch total		7.6	4.5	12,860
Cuba (Spanish)	1786–1790	3.9	6.3	18,250
Brazil (Portuguese)	1788	10.8	6.6	19,150
West Indies (Danish)	1785, 1793, 1796	3.2	2.7	7,800
Grand total				289,300

Sources: See Appendix II.
Note: 1770 designates the average for 1768–1772; *1787* designates the average for the years indicated in the second column.

from 34.8 to 36.7 percent for a corresponding gain of 1.9. However, if we retain Tobago in the British column, the French gain would have been 3.2 points and the British 2.3 from *1770* to *1787*. War therefore accounted for at least half the small differential between the relative French and British market shares between *1770* and *1787*. A thin margin, it would seem, on which to build a thesis of dramatic decline. In terms of the French sugar rivalry, the British West Indies were not perceptibly weaker in *1787* than before the American War of Independence.

A different question may now be interposed. The French colonies did not forge ahead during *1775–1787*, the "Williams" period. But perhaps they did so between 1763 and *1787*, which would at least fit the Ragatz account. If the French colonies were the principal sugar exporters of the world even before the American Revolution, is that position to be attributed to the Seven Years' War or to the peace which returned Guadeloupe to the French? We now push the sugar census back two generations. Based on contemporary estimates made in the early 1740s, and allowing for appropriate muscovado–clayed sugar ratios, our survey shows that the French system already accounted for 42.2 percent of the North Atlantic market, a figure only 1.1 points less than its share in *1787*.[29] Its position was actually slightly better in the forties than in *1770*. More significantly, by 1745 French slavery was already the premier sugar producer of the world. Even if no allowance is made for clayed sugar conversion to muscovado (following most eighteenth-century calculators), the French share stood at 38.5 percent in 1745, at the top of the heap. The British share of 28 percent (26.1 percent, if no clayed conversion is made) in ca. 1745, indicates that Britain's share in *1787* still represented a marked improvement over its mid-century position. Might one now argue for a disproportionate surge in British efficiency between 1740 and *1787*, and conjure up a hitherto unperceived French decline? The explanation is perhaps far simpler. Just as war accounted for much of the French gain in *1770–1787*, it accounted for the British surge in 1745–*1770*. The Seven Years' War brought four new colonies into the English fold, enabling the British system to improve on its standing between 1745 and *1770* and to almost match the French pace during the decades between the peace of 1763 and the outbreak of the French Revolution.

All told, the British benefited more by the Caribbean warfare between 1750 and 1790 than did the French. By *1787*, the colonies acquired by France (St. Lucia and Tobago) added only 2.5 percent to French colonial sugar exports. The British acquisition of the ceded islands of Grenada, Dominica, and St. Vincent increased the British total by more than 20 percent. According to such comparative imperial criteria, Postlethwayt, in the eighteenth century, was on firmer ground in asserting that the Seven Years' War reversed a deteriorating British colonial position, than was Ragatz in the twentieth, marking 1763 as the beginning of the downturn.

We are left with one general conclusion. Between the Big Two the relationship was one of stability, not change. The most striking demonstration of this relationship, virtually ossified for generations before *1787*, is obtained by focusing on St. Domingue.This star of French expansion in the decline thesis may be compared with its exact British counterpart from 1745 to *1787*. It is asserted that the sugar production of St. Domingue at the outbreak of the French Revolution equaled that of the entire British colonial system: "St. Domingo was then [1783] producing substantially two-thirds of the French-grown tropical produce, and nearly as much sugar as all of the British Caribbean colonies combined!"[30] What is more significant, in temporal perspective, is that after two full generations St. Domingue still exported almost exactly the same proportion of sugar as those same British colonies against which it had been matched forty-odd years before. According to my estimate, if we combine the production of St. Domingue around 1745 with the then British West Indian colonies (Jamaica, the Virgin Islands, Antigua, St. Kitts, Nevis, Montserrat, and Barbados), St. Domingue exported between 48.0 and 50.6 percent of the grand total. In *1770* St. Domingue, in relation to the same colonies, exported 48.7 percent of the total. In *1787* St. Domingue's proportion stood at 49.7 percent of the same colonial total. The rate of fluctuation throughout the entire period from 1740 to *1787* did not amount to more than 2 percent.[31]

If anything more were needed to indicate the astonishing lack of change in St. Domingue's sugar position before 1789, one might add that between 1783–1785 and 1787–1789 its sugar exports increased by less than 1 percent. Jamaica's increase for the same period was almost 7 percent. If we compare only the years 1783–1784 and 1788–1789 we find that St. Domingue sugar exports rose just under 10 percent while Jamaica's rose 25 percent.[32] In short, between 1783 and 1789, Jamaican sugar exports were increasing faster than St. Domingue's. It was between 1720 and 1740, not 1770 and 1790, that St. Domingue overtook Jamaica in sugar, reached her pinnacle, and held firm. While St. Domingue was increasing its share of the Atlantic sugar trade from 29 to 30 percent during the period *1770–1787*, Jamaica and the ceded islands were able to raise their own joint share from 21 to 23 percent.

A look at the sugar world of *1770–1787* beyond the Anglo-French rivalry, which has riveted the attention of both contemporaries and posterity, indicates that there were indeed symptoms of relative stagnation and dynamism in sugar production. Those terms are more applicable to the Dutch, Portuguese, and Spanish systems in *1787* than either the British or French colonies (see table 11). While a Spanish renaissance was beginning to be apparent, her colonial exports had not yet emerged from the pygmy class. The giants of *1787* were those of 1740. For British slavery alone, the continuity was still greater. In 1700 her share of total colonial sugar was almost exactly what it was to be ninety years later.[33] If 1790 denotes anything, it marks the unforeseeable end of an era of surprising structural stability. Caribbean slavery was on the eve of the most dramatic moment in its history, but the chief beneficiary of that change was to be the British slave system.

In terms of volume, the evidence does not lend itself to a decline thesis. Nevertheless, there is a second argument to be seriously considered. It derives from the comparison of relative costs of sugar production and profits in the two colonial systems in 1788. The Privy Council report, as Williams points out, devoted an entire section to "the advantages which the French West India Islands are supposed at present to enjoy over the British Islands."[34] The British planters themselves agreed with the assumption embodied in the title. They assigned various reasons, including soil fertility and water available for irrigation. Relying on private estimates, and based chiefly on a comparison between St. Domingue and Jamaica, the consensus also seems to have been that profits in the French colony averaged from 8 to 12 percent or higher, compared with 4 percent in the major British colony. While there may have been some offsetting British gains in the costs of slaves, technology, shipping charges, and the purchase of certain supplies, two facts were unquestioned. First, French sugar undersold most British sugar on the Continent. Second, French sugar was overwhelmingly the product consumed by noncolonial European societies in *1787*.[35]

How does all this concur with the decline thesis in 1788–1791? Whatever the reasons, the French were obviously number one. Yet there is nothing here to support the decline thesis. The British position on the Continent in 1790 was one of inferiority. But, as with the rate of growth, France's great leap forward in the international market came not in the 1770s or 1780s but in the 1720s and 1730s. With the aid of import and export figures dating from the early eighteenth century it is, and was, possible to pinpoint the moment of defeat with precision. Between 1724 and 1728 almost 22 percent of British sugar had been reexported. In 1729–1733 the proportion fell to 17 percent. In 1734–1738 it dropped to 10 percent, although Britain's own sugar supply dropped off by one-sixth in the same period. The reexport rate never recovered its mid-twenties level except in war years. French Continental supremacy had been consolidated and recognized well over fifty years before the first abolitionist petition presented to Parliament.[36] To explain the initial triumph of abolition in 1788–1792 in terms of a loss of the foreign market would require a rather flexible theory of delayed action.

The British position in this area actually improved after 1775. In 1791 Mr. Irving provided the relevant figures to the House of Commons Slave Trade Committee. They showed that in 1772–1775, the British reexported only 2.2 percent of their colonial sugar imports. In 1787–1790 they reexported twice as much by weight as well as by share.[37] And during the American war years the rise was even greater. This is another indicator that on the whole, even in this worst of colonial wars for the British, the French sugar producers suffered more than their British counterparts. While the British exporters had certainly not undermined the French Continental hegemony between 1775 and 1790, they were edging upward.

The economic development of a system whose competitive international position had remained basically unchanged between 1740 and 1790 was not likely to cause a sudden upsurge of antagonism. The revolt of America did not "leave the British sugar planters face to face with their French rivals."[38] The British colonies had been out of the race except in wartime for two full generations before 1783. The British had long since recognized that unpleasant economic fact without abolitionist consequences. The planters had turned to the metropolitan market after 1730, and on that market alone British slavery survived. It simply continued to grow on the increasing wealth and population of Great Britain, as sugar became an item of mass consumption. By 1750 "the poorest English farm labourer's wife took sugar in her tea."[39] By 1790 sugar was considered a necessary, if not deserved, luxury of even the very poor. The "ideal typical" poor family was alloted 6 percent of its budget for sugar. During the winter of 1792, when sugar prices had reached new peacetime peaks, a number of parishes hit upon a "sugar test" as a measure of eligibility, denying relief to anyone who was still consuming sugar or tea. Sugar was a substantial item in the budget of the Liverpool infirmary at the turn of the century, and, in the hungry winter of 1800, when substitutes for corn were desperately needed, Manchester's relief recipes called for brown sugar and treacle.[40]

By the time of the French Revolution the British colonies were doing a shade better than in *1770* in their share of world production, in their reexport turnover, and perhaps in their profit margins.[41] They did not seriously challenge their French rivals in foreign markets, but nestled comfortably in the arms of their own. Political economists might tally the cost of monopoly to the British consumer, but the league of interests bound together by the system in manufacturing, shipping, commerce, and planting maintained its unity. The expansion of the French sugar system was neither a novelty nor a direct threat to the British system. The long reign of King Sugar remained placid and serene.

Metropolitan commercial and political magnates were not aware of any broadening sugar gap between the British and French sugar systems on the eve of the St. Domingue revolution. Nor did they perceive any decline in the British system. The East India company, surveying its chances of penetrating the sugar market in 1792, concluded that "notwithstanding the loss of the Foreign Markets, the [British] Islands have been in a state of progressive improvement. It must, however, be remarked that there is the strongest reason to believe the French islands have been equally successful, and that this has not proceeded from either nation having made inroads upon the Commerce of the other, but from the increased demand for West India commodities, as well in Great Britain, as in every part of Europe."[42]

The rest of the "sugar rivals" of *1790*, conjured up by the decline theory, can be dismissed fairly rapidly. In his discussion of the growth of world sugar production after 1783, Williams lists, in addition to the French islands, Brazil, Cuba, and India.[43] Brazil, says Williams, was, along with the French islands, the British sugar system's chief competitor, Cuba being hampered by Spanish mercantile exclusiveness. A glance at table 11, however, shows that Brazil's share of the world market had actually fallen between *1770* and *1787* from 10.8 to 6.6 percent. That fall was the sharpest decline of any major producer. Brazil had been reduced to the status of a minor producer, and the Privy Council in 1788 manifested no concern for its progress. Cuba was, in fact, the only obviously progressive sugar producer of the minor entrants, and its size gave no cause for alarm. Only the French slave system received serious attention from the British.

One final, and rather curious candidate is included in the list of sugar rivals of 1787. That is British India. India is really Williams's nominee despite Ragatz, who notes that no sugar had been commercially imported from the Far East for more than a century and a half when a committee of the East India Company first recommended an agricultural experiment in 1789. The directors of the company were themselves skeptical of the outcome of the experiment before 1791. Only after the St. Domingue revolt did Indian sugar begin to be thought of as a serious contender. It played no role whatsoever in the gestation of abolition in the 1780s; its rivalry before 1791 is purely a product of the imagination. Williams pushes this speculation of the 1790s back to 1783 only by three unconnected statements linking the British prime minister to a Machiavellian scheme against all branches of Caribbean slavery.[44] Under scrutiny the West Indian rivals' list of 1783–1791 shrivels to the already considered French connection. Insulated from its rival, British slave-grown sugar stood unthreatened by the world beyond the empire.

4

The Unprotected Economy Before the French Slave Revolution

Slave Cotton and "Laissez-faire" Abolitionism

The decline theory does not rest on sugar alone. Innovations outside the old sugar systems were supposedly decisive factors in the decline of British slavery. A new imperial political economy of laissez-faire and a new tropical product, cotton, rendered the slave system a fetter on the British imperial economy and caused it to be broken. An empire revolving around sugar, monopoly, and stagnation was incompatible with an open market empire.[1] Because of this, a system which enjoyed the approval of every economic interest in the middle of the eighteenth century had its position "eroded" dramatically until every interest was indifferent or hostile to its existence.[2]

Here the theme of rising capitalism enters, a component of the decline thesis that is Williams's special contribution. The broad outlines of the theory have been widely echoed. Britain at the end of the eighteenth century was undergoing an industrial revolution, and, as Eric Hobsbawm aptly writes, "whoever says Industrial Revolution says cotton."[3] With British productive capacity increasing enormously, further demands were put on British slavery. But according to Williams the system was caught in its own rut. "The British West Indian planter, faithful to his first love, sugar, could not keep pace with Manchester's requirements. The sugar islands provided seven-tenths of British cotton imports in 1786–1790, one-fiftieth in 1826–1830."[4] The steam engine pushed Manchester from alliance, to indifference, to "downright hostility." The Lancastrian Gulliver, tied down by the Lilliputian colonials, tore Britain loose from its mercantilist moorings and destroyed the slave system. Williams's classic linkage of cotton and laissez-faire

55

to British abolition is not without either plausibility or later supporters. It deserves extended appraisal.

Throughout most of the eighteenth century cotton was not an exclusively slave-grown product, much less a monopoly of the British slave system. The story of its spread was, however, like that of sugar, one of migration from the old world to the new. In the case of cotton the shift began only about a generation before the emergence of abolitionism. Especially after the expiration of Arkwright's patents, in 1785, cotton production increased, prices rose, and new tropical sources of supply were immediately needed.[5] By 1787 the British cotton industry already depended on the production of the foreign West Indies and Brazil, as well as upon Turkey and, to a small extent, India (see table 12). Because the Levant could not increase its cotton shipments rapidly enough, the decade following 1783 was the "West Indian age" of the British raw cotton trade.[6]

Cotton, even when grown in British islands, was in the unprotected zone of the imperial economy. The inauguration of the Caribbean free port system in 1766, confirmed and extended in 1787 and 1792, allowed foreign slave cotton to enter the imperial economy on the same terms as British.[7] Both figures were fused in British resource estimates (see table 13). The Caribbean free ports were a carefully controlled breach in the mercantilist network. They also provided a funnel through which British manufactures and African slaves could penetrate the protected markets of other mercantilist empires. They were thus an admirable prototype of free trade imperialism, in which the complementary trades of the foreign systems could be regularized and encouraged to Britain's advantage. The reciprocity of the cotton and slave trades appears vividly in one year for which the record of the British West Indian trade is particularly full. In 1791 the reexport of "Negroes" to the foreign West Indies was officially valued at £633,300. The corresponding figure for imports of cotton from foreign colonies into the British West Indies was £700,000. The free port trade was regarded in the British colonies as a singular triumph over the protectionism of baffled rivals. At home, in the succinct words of Mr. Irving, the system helped the empire to enjoy the trade of foreign colonies without "the expense of protecting or defending them."[8]

However, the British were far from ignoring their own colonies as a cotton source in 1787; they accounted for almost a third of British requirements when the abolitionists opened their campaign.[9] The period after the American war was marked by particularly vigorous

TABLE 12: SOURCES OF BRITISH COTTON IMPORTS, 1786–1787
(in thousands of lbs.)

	1786	1787	1786–1787
British West Indies	5,800	6,600	5,050
French West Indies	5,500	6,000	3,375
Spanish West Indies			1,339
Dutch West Indies	1,600	1,700	1,500
Total West Indies	12,900	14,300	11,264
Portuguese Brazil	2,000	2,500	2,500
East India	—	100	90
Smyrna or Turkey	5,000	5,700	6,000
Total imports	19,900	22,600	19,854

Sources: For 1786, Baines, *History of Cotton Manufacture*, p. 304. For 1787, Edwards, *History of the British West Indies*, 322–23. For 1786–1787, BT 6/140 (1788), fol. 56.

TABLE 13: BRITISH IMPORTS OF WEST INDIAN COTTON, 1761–1805

	Cotton (thousands of lbs.)	Percent Change
1761–65	3,338	—
1771–75	2,587	– 22
1781–85	6,131	+137
1791–95	11,603	+ 89
1801–05	16,007	+ 38

Source: PP 1808 (IV), Report from the Committee on the Commercial State of the West Indian Colonies, July 24, 1807, p. 78.

governmental attempts to extend cotton culture in the British islands. The best seeds were sent to them from South America, Asia, and Africa. In resettling some of the American loyalist refugees, a new and promising cotton frontier was opened up in the Bahamas. Special sanction was given to open up waste lands of Jamaica and the ceded islands. The cotton manufacturers of Manchester were more than disinterested onlookers. In 1787, a circular was dispatched to the governors of the West Indian islands in direct response to a representation of a delegation of the cotton manufacturers which asked the government to promote cotton culture in the British West Indies, "in order that we may have from our own islands the raw material in such perfection as we are under the necessity of drawing from other powers." The government recommended the cultivation of that staple "in the most forcible terms," and asked the governors to "afford any assistance in your power" to planters so inclined. In September 1786, Governor Orde of Dominica proclaimed free grants of thirty to sixty acres for any planter who moved into cotton, along with ten to thirty acres for provision grounds. The metropolis objected only to his "provision" grants and wanted largess to be reserved to cotton acreage. At the very moment that the first abolition committee was forming, Parliament was informed by none other than Lord Hawkesbury that Britain could anticipate self-sufficiency in cotton culture from the growth of the British slave islands.[10]

As with sugar, if one compared British cotton imports from the West Indies between the American and French revolutions, there is clear evidence of both vigor and continuity. In 1781–1785, as in 1771–1775, over half of Britain's raw cotton came from the West Indies. Their share was still a respectable 42 percent in 1788–1791. By weight, average West Indian cotton exports more than doubled between 1771–1775 and 1781–1785, and almost doubled again during the first abolitionist offensives, averaging just under 12 million pounds a year in 1788–1791.[11]

By the beginning of the nineties, however, it was clear that the expansion of British cotton was not catching up with British requirements. As sugar prices rose in response to increasing French colonial turmoil, there was no possibility of closing the gap from British culture alone. Especially after 1785, the cotton growth of one foreign area after another began to be drawn into the British network. The cotton crops of the French, Portuguese, and Dutch colonies found an outlet in the British market. The Spanish, encouraged by growing British demand, were also actively in the British cotton market by 1788 (see table 12). At the very moment that the abolitionists launched their first campaign, Spanish commissioners arrived in London offering the whole colonial cotton crop reaching Spain in exchange for British manufactures.[12] A large portion of the Latin American crop that did not find its way to Britain through the free ports was thus reexported from the Continent, after complying with foreign mercantilist requirements. In 1789, of 32 million pounds of cotton coming into Britain, over 10 million came through European ports from the Americas. In 1790 an anonymous memorandum on the cotton supply, written for the government, noted that the expansion of southern European colonial cotton was entirely benign: "The Spaniards and the Portuguese had never had any cotton manufactories. The French have hardly any.

They have lost them partly by the powerful operation of the Commercial Treaty, partly by their present troubles."[13]

By the late 1780s there was even some discussion of Africa as a potential source of cotton, although the difficulties were already suggested by the failure of the first Sierra Leone settlement in 1787–1788, and an earlier Dutch failure.[14] Although Africa could grow cotton rated as equal to the best in the Americas and superior to the British West Indian or Carolina varieties, its potential as a major commercial producer was still highly problematic. But as far as the cotton manufacturers were concerned, there was no more conflict between importing cotton from both Africa and the West Indies than from Brazil and the West Indies. Their major concern, in the midst of an unprecedented boom, was to increase the supply of their raw material.[15]

This concern did not at all imply, or lead to, a clash between an insatiable British industry requiring open imports and a closed colonial monopoly. By 1788 cotton planters had been an integral part of the free market sector for a full generation. They neither received nor asked for prohibitive protective tariffs. From their situation there could be no logical connection between a generalized antimercantilism and antislavery. But there is a more fundamental reason why the emergent capitalists of the cotton industry did not launch an attack on slavery under the laissez-faire banner. They themselves had not emerged from their protectionist swaddling clothes.[16] Their mercantilist reflexes could be observed in their anxiety over the possibility of an Anglo-Irish customs union in 1785.[17] Their official spokesman on that occasion was none other than Thomas Walker, soon to be the principal leader of Manchester abolitionism.

Cotton's continuing dependency on protectionism was equally evident at the precise moment that abolitionism got under way in the industrial towns of England and Scotland. In February 1788 a general meeting of the cotton spinners and manufacturers of Glasgow protested the influx of East Indian white cotton and muslin goods into Britain. Supported by other manufacturers in Paisley and Manchester, this group explicitly aligned itself with West Indian, and indeed, all slave production. They attributed their own "unexampled increase" in muslin production to the expansion of cotton production in Barbados, Surinam, and Brazil. To dramatize the impact of their own potential losses they registered the total value of West Indian trade on their side of the economic equation. It was the *East* Indian competitor which had to be curbed. Thus cotton manufacturers, in the *annus mirabilis* 1788, were requesting protection from colonial cottons. Despite the mercantilist compromise quota worked out in the summer of 1788, the cotton spinners and muslin manufacturers of Britain continued to petition against East Indian cotton goods down through 1792.[18]

Neither the vigor of cotton growth in the Americas nor the expansion of its manufacture in Britain prejudiced the British slave system during the postwar decade. If the British planters could not themselves fill the gap opened up by the mechanical explosion of the industrial revolution, that was certainly no reason to eliminate the growth capacity of any other tropical system. Williams's central conclusion, that the new age of cotton produced hostility to slavery and the slave trade on the part of the antimercantilist forces of cotton capitalism, rests on empirically unsupported assumptions. In 1790, if industrialization meant cotton, cotton meant slavery. It also meant the slave trade.

There is a radical defect in the entire chain of reasoning connecting the rise of British abolitionism to a shift in political economy after the American Revolution. The rising cotton industry was not alone in its conservative and pragmatic commercial policy in the 1780s. Neither Pitt and his cabinet, nor Fox and his opposition, nor Parliament, nor the Committee of Trade, clamored for the abandonment of the protectionist framework. In 1790 British policy was, as it had been before the American Revolution, to move selectively toward the liberalization of trade, while legislatively reaffirming its commitment to imperial protectionism. The move toward reciprocal lower tariffs in the Anglo-French treaty of 1787 must be set off against Parliament's rejection of trade reciprocity with Ireland two years before.[19] The renewal of the Caribbean free port system in 1787 was preceded by the exclusion of American carriers from the British West Indies and by the reaffirmation of the Navigation Acts in 1786. Its sponsor, Jenkinson (later an antiabolitionist), could claim that it was the only major commercial act in fifty years to pass without objection. Continuity was the keynote of the imperial economy after 1783.[20] Accounts of abolitionism that have interwoven its emergence with that of laissez-faire have unconsciously manufactured an eighteenth-century tapestry of imperial history with nineteenth-century threads. As with the decline of the West Indies, the elementary chronology is flawed. The illusion of economic retrogression in the British West Indies is thus balanced by the symmetrical illusion of emergent laissez-faire.

Slave Trading and "Mercantilist" Abolitionism

Williams finally asserts that slavery was first attacked at its "weakest and most indefensible spot."[21] As a description of the British slave trade in 1790 this would be false. After a sharp dip during the previous decade the trade was flourishing by the late 1780s. Tonnage increased by over a quarter from 1771–1780 to 1781–1790. The trade surpassed its prewar profit levels in the 1780s and was recognized to be in satisfactory condition by its practitioners.[22] In fact, the African link in the trade was probably the most competitive sector of British economic activity within the slave system. Slaves were a preferred item of the reexport trade under the free port system.

By contrast, the slave trade of other European powers operated under monopoly charters or subsidies, apparently without overwhelming success. In Dutch Guiana, the cotton producers complained to the government of severe labor shortages. The Danish African factories were unable to meet the demand of even their own small system. The Spanish Empire began to open its colonies to British carriers in earnest after 1783: Cuba, Puerto Rico, San Domingo, Caracas, and Buenos Aires. In 1790 the prospects for British traders were as bright as the profits.[23]

The decline theory does not assert that the slave trade lacked vigor in 1783–1791. Instead, it reverses the prevailing metaphors of decrepitude applied to the rest of the system. The dynamism of the slave trade is supposed to have been killing the British slave system in 1788. The same cluster of forces which were attacking slavery in its weakness were supposedly moved to abolish the slave trade because it was a principal source of the weakening process. We have referred to this before as the "beggar-my-rival" theory. In *Capitalism and Slavery,* Williams outlines a vast scheme whereby Pitt offered to strangle the British slave colonies if only the French would consent to do the same with theirs; British India was to emerge as the beneficiary of the suicide pact.[24]

We are not concerned with the plausibility of Williams's account of Pitt's motives. His underlying premises, however, have gained acceptance as an explanation for the victory of abolition and require serious consideration. In contrast to his laissez-faire argument regarding cotton, Williams's argument about the role of the slave trade is based on a mercantilist explanation of British political behavior. It is, nevertheless, founded on respectable capitalist premises of impeccable pedigree. We must be ready to acknowledge that each model may explain a different aspect of the decline thesis. Theoretically, if the slave trade were helping to destroy British slavery, a political force might have been unleashed, regardless of Pitt, aimed at destroying the destroyer of British imperial interests. The first question to be posed, however, is whether the slave trade was in fact undermining British slavery by building up its rivals before or after the American War of Independence.

Around 1790, the British African trade contributed more than one half of each year's human harvest to the development of foreign colonies. This was not an innovation of the 1780s. Well before the Seven Years' War over half the slaves shipped by Britain went to foreign colonies. As far back as the beginning of the eighteenth century Britain had fought to gain control of the *asiento*, the exclusive right to carry slaves to the Spanish colonies. If there was a time when the British foreign slave trade had decisively helped to build rivals against the British colonies, it was during the development of the French sugar islands after 1715.

The pattern of the foreign slave trade after 1783 represented no major change. It represented no major threat either. The Spanish trade was largely a revival of old patterns, exchanging bullion and livestock for slaves and British manufactures. No major conflict of interest existed with any major imperial interest group. In fact, the Spanish trade helped to sustain a merchant as well as a planter class in Jamaica and elsewhere.[25] Even where the Spaniards began to enlarge their sugar as well as their cotton production after 1783, direct conflict of interest was still negligible. Spanish sugar competed in the Continental, but not in the British imperial market.

The British slave trade to the French colonies was likewise neither a novelty before 1783 nor a threat thereafter.[26] The astonishing development of St. Domingue after 1783 was no illusion. Its annual imports of slaves suddenly doubled after the peace of 1783, partially supplied by British carriers. The increase had a major impact on the island, but not where Williams and others saw it. It came where the British welcomed it. From 1783–1785 to 1787–1789 St. Domingue's sugar export increased less than 1 percent. In the same short interval her cotton exports increased 31 percent. The new infusion of slave labor after 1783 was being harnessed to the British economic mechanism. A steady stream of foreign cotton flowed to Britain to feed its industrial revolution. After 1787 the foreign cotton imports increased, because of the combined impact of the Anglo-French commercial treaty of 1787 and the increasing disruption of economic life in France during the Revolution. All this was fully apparent to contemporaries.[27] It is no accident that a member of the Committee of Trade, Lord Hawkesbury, drew Parliament's attention to cotton and insisted that the link be investigated by the Lords when they began to hear evidence on the slave trade.[28]

The reexport slave trade was regarded as good for the British West Indies too, since it was a form of insurance against temporary shortages in the British islands—the equivalent of a reserve army of slave labor in a trade subject to shortages. It kept both the slave supply and the currency supply stable. All the free port colonies therefore opposed the abolitionist movement. Jamaica fought with the greatest determination, but even Barbados, which was relatively full, which was a substantial cotton exporter, and which stood to benefit relatively by a rise in slave prices if the overseas supply disappeared, did not accept the "beggar-my-rival" opportunity offered by British abolition in 1790.

The postwar revival of the British foreign slave trade after 1783, and especially after the free port act of 1787, had the effect of broadening the British slave system. Offers came from French capitalists for joint ventures in the trade to the French colonies, and British slave traders helped to build up British capital investments in them. The British traders thus became capitalists and absentee owners of foreign as well as of British plantations. In all these respects the end of the eighties marked a new burst of internationalization in a trade and a system which had always revealed this dimension. By the early 1790s the merchants of Liverpool and London had become so deeply involved in the French islands that when the British military attempted to enforce mildly confiscatory policies in the conquered islands in 1794, they deluged the government with protests and forced a Parliamentary intervention.[29]

If the British traders had been more reluctant to respond to foreign demand in 1787–1791, the possibilities for expansion were so bright that every major power encouraged it where it existed and launched it where it was absent. The British merchants complained bitterly that theirs was the only trade that had to function without bounties or monopolies, and according to regulations for slaves and seamen which hindered no other entrepreneurs.[30] The French and Portuguese stayed vigorously in the trade, and the Americans and Spanish began to move back into an activity from which they had almost withdrawn. Even the Dutch and Danes tried to reorganize their trades at the end of the eighties. The Danish decision for gradual abolition in 1792 seems to have been contingent upon the presumed imminence of British abolition. The Dutch apparently took a more businesslike approach to the question. When the British vote for abolition was announced in 1792, the Dutch ambassador in London was reported to have immediately dispatched a special messenger to the Netherlands, so that the Dutch could make maximum use of the opportunity.[31]

Prospects in 1790

On the eve of the Caribbean revolution the metropolis had little reason to regret its economic relationship to the West Indies. The imports of sugar and cotton from slave labor and the exports of slaves and manufactures to all the slave islands were apparently still of benefit to both ends of the Atlantic economy. The prospects were no less bright. The British islands had not nearly fulfilled their potential. The existence of a tropical frontier is the final important consideration in evaluating the decline thesis as of 1788–1792. Taken as a whole, the slave colonies had exhausted neither their soil nor their potential. Some, such as Barbados and the Leeward Islands, were considered to be at or past their optimum development. But this was only one segment of the islands. In the 1780s the influx of loyalists and the opening of the Bahamas to cotton production added a new dimension to the picture. A report on those islands in 1790 indicated that the black population had doubled since 1785 and the white population had tripled. Acreage under cultivation rose from 2,500 in 1785 to an estimated 18,000 in 1790, with 20,000 acres more under location by grants. The unsettled lands in the ceded islands, especially in St. Vincent and Dominica, were also considered ripe for further development following American independence.[32] But the largest frontier was still where it had been throughout the eighteenth century, in Jamaica. In the 1770s Long estimated Jamaica's still undeveloped acreage at over 1.9 million acres, excluding provision grounds. The Jamaicans themselves claimed that at least half the commercially arable land on the island was patented and still undeveloped in 1789.

Jamaica's chief economic problem continued to be a shortage of labor. Her planters contended that the West Indies were not Europe, where a labor shortage would produce a rise in wages and an immediate response from the surrounding densely populated regions.[33] It is no accident that Dundas, the principal metropolitan spokesman against immediate abolition in 1792, emphasized the imperial network of British investments in undeveloped or incompletely developed lands as a major argument against hasty abolition. The abolitionists reacted with the assertion that full development meant indefinite postponement of abolition and un-counted thousands of new slave imports to the British islands.[34] The image of decrepitude or saturation of the old slave system was one shared neither by abolitionists nor their antagonists in 1790. On the contrary, as the old regime in the islands drew to an end, the debate over abolition was essentially a debate over whether the slave system should be allowed to fulfill its maximum economic potential.[35]

5

The Growth of Slavery
in the Era of British Supremacy

The year ending in June of 1792 marked a new period for the abolitionist cause in Britain and for slavery in the Caribbean. At the far end of this period (1805–1807), a sequence of orders and acts finally prohibited the transportation of African slave labor by British subjects.

A preliminary ambiguity must be noted before we attempt to estimate economic trends during this dramatic era. Before 1792, annual averages could be based on comparable peacetime periods. In 1787–1791, 1772–1775 was usually regarded as the historical base period. After 1791 these constellations of economic analysis simply disappeared. Between 1791 and 1800, the Caribbean enjoyed only two years when a major revolt or civil war was not in progress in one area or another. Such areas did not have to be in continuous turmoil to upset long-run estimates. A few months of guerrilla warfare might require years of recuperation and fresh imports of slaves, as was the case in St. Vincent and Grenada. War and blockades compounded the uncertainties of revolution. With the exception of the short-lived Peace of Amiens (1802), Britain and France were locked in permanent and deadly combat. There was not a single calendar year of peace between 1793 and 1815. One had to use an average of "abnormal" years to gauge trends, or to treat 1802 or 1803 as representative of the normal peacetime situation, or simply to revert to the last prewar years and assume that all figures thereafter were abnormal.[1] Methods of computation in 1806 or 1807, however, continued to follow patterns laid down before. Parliamentary accounts favored five-year averaging for calculating long-term trends. Polemicists on both sides of the question were fully aware of the need for averaging to make a convincing point and to allow for fluctuations due to disease and weather as well as war. James Stephen, perhaps the most authoritative abolitionist propagandist after 1800, measured the dynamics of the slave trade between 1792 and 1807 in terms of averages for 1788–1794 and 1795–1804. On the opposing side, Sir William Young's *West India Common-Place Book* argued that natural hazards alone required that no less than four-year averages should be used to measure the dynamics of cotton production.[2] Estimates for the European end of the Atlantic world also became less manageable. The Continental market for British colonial produce might shift with every major change in the fortunes of war. Especially after 1804, calculations about European demand were even more precarious than those about Caribbean supply.

The facts of permanent war and revolution posed one additional difficulty, which had existed only in embryo in the decades between 1763 and 1792. Before 1792, it was quite clear to everyone what areas actually constituted the various colonial empires, with the exception of Tobago. Even the Seven Years' War did not appreciably alter the intercolonial balance of territory, production, or population. After 1792 the situation was completely reversed. The boundaries of all Caribbean systems lost their eighteenth-century outlines. Between 1793 and 1807 there was not a single year in which the British slave empire incorporated the same areas as in 1763–1792.[3] In 1793–1794 it appeared that the entire French system was falling to the British. For the next two years it was unclear whether most of the British system might not itself fall prey to French Revolutionary warfare. From 1797 to 1802 the expanded British slave empire included among other colonies, Trinidad from the Spanish, Guiana from the Dutch, and Martinique from the French empires. By the treaty of Amiens, both the British and French slave empires were extended beyond their 1792 boundaries at the cost of the Spanish, Dutch, and Portuguese colonies. With the resumption of hostilities in 1803 the British system again began to expand. Demerara, Tobago, and St. Lucia were reconquered at the outset. This time the process of expansion continued unbroken through, and beyond, 1807.

For the moment we only note that for the British Empire the overall political and military trend was one of growth. After 1792 the British colonial slave empire never returned to its original boundaries. For most of the period the expansion was quite substantial. In three periods, 1793–1794, 1797–1802, 1803–1807, British conquest moved toward a hegemony of colonial power.[4]

Bearing in mind this penumbra of spatial boundaries, trends for 1792–1806 must be treated with caution. However, although there might never have been a worse time for policy makers to hazard decisions based on estimates about the future of British slavery, these were the years in which the critical decision was made. We must therefore attempt to deal with the trends of 1792–1806 insofar as they indicated the course of development of slavery and its future within the empire. We shall necessarily have some recourse to a method of maximal and minimal estimates. Minimum figures for the slave empire include all slave areas, populations, and products recognized *de jure* as belonging to the British crown. Maximal figures include all areas under *de facto* British control at a given time.

The Trade Network

The imperial stake in slavery between 1792 and 1806 can easily be summarized, following the method described in chapter 2. The status of the British West Indies as a partner in the empire improved between 1791 and 1807 (see table 1). In regard to imports, exports, and total trade, their share of metropolitan trade increased. Their import share rose from 1793–1797 to 1798–1802 and again in 1803–1807. The gain of more than 6 percentage points between 1793–1797 and 1803–1807 was a greater increase than for any similar amount of time in the eighteenth century. North America was runner-up to the West Indies in this trade sector, gaining less than 2 percent between 1793–1797 and 1803–1807 (see table 4). Asia's share moved steadily downward. The heralded "take-off" of Britain's eastern empire after 1783 was obviously still experiencing severe difficulties early in flight.

As a customer for British exports, the West Indies also showed no signs of flagging. From 1793–1797 to 1803–1807 its share remained at a level equal to, or above, the best quinquennium before 1792, reaching 14 percent in 1798–1802 (see table 4). North America was a more dynamic export customer, but part of its share in 1803–1807 represented exports destined for the foreign West Indies, themselves growing customers of Britain. The Asian showing under exports was even more dismal than for imports. In 1788–1792 Asia (including India) had received from the metropolis almost as much as the British slave system. In 1803–1807 Asia accounted for only half as much. The trend was continuously downward in each successive quinquennium. If British capitalism were looking for mercantilist fetters to break, India was the more visible target by 1803–1807. The case for the "rising East" as the imperial trade replacement for British slavery might be regarded as closed.

The overseas trade patterns of outlying metropolitan ports support the results indicated by the general flow of trade. Scotland shared England's involvement in the British slave system. At the turn of the nineteenth century, for example, Jamaica was listed as Glasgow's largest single trading partner. In terms of the previous decade, Glasgow's trade by 1801 grew most quickly with Jamaica, the Carolinas, Portugal, and New York. Of these only the last was not linked directly with slave production and the slave trade.[5] Glasgow merchants figured among the petitioners against abolition in 1806–1807. The overall pattern of British trade during the years prior to the abolition of the slave trade would appear to be one of continuity and intensification of bonds with both the British and foreign slave systems.

British slavery was also doing quite well as a customer of the two premier metropolitan growth industries usually cited as its opponents. For Williams the cotton manufacturers and the iron masters occupy the front ranks of slavery's enemies after 1788. Table 14 shows the state of British exports to the West Indies in 1805–1806 by industries. At that time the West Indies were Britain's major trade customer for British brass and copper (37 percent), for iron and steel (37 percent), as well as for fish, hats, leather goods, and linens. Even the exporters of earthenware and glass (21 percent), and of cottons (18 percent), had to regard them as very substantial customers. The West Indies ranked as the third best customer of cotton goods. And if one combines the Afro–West Indian system for slavery's contribution to British trade, 40 percent of exported iron products and 23 percent of exported cotton products went to that system. Neither her prime growth industries nor her traditional trades provided any evidence of slavery's dispensability, let alone a cause for hostility.

While we have not emphasized the weight of short-run economic factors, it would be well to take note of them as they appeared in the statistics of trade on the eve of abolition. A special relationship between slavery and the empire was rapidly evolving in 1806–1807 as the debate on abolition reached its denouement. If reliability is a factor in economic planning, the value of the stable West Indian market rose even more than the trade figures indicate. After 1805, the Continental market became a speculation, with the bravest rushing their merchandise from area tó area as opportunities arose, risking total loss or defaults in payment.[6] By the end of 1806, large amounts of British goods had been seized by the French in Continental ports. Relations with America, Britain's largest single trading partner besides the West Indies, were becoming strained. Britain was beginning to launch a counterblockade involving severe restrictions on neutral carriers from enemy ports and colonies. It was obvious "to spinners and brokers, quite early in 1807, that relations with America were fast deteriorating."[7] Psychologically, then, the overseas

TABLE 14: WEST INDIAN SHARE OF SELECTED BRITISH EXPORTS, 1770–1806

Percentage by Weight

	Brass	Wrought Copper	Iron	Iron Nails	Earthen-ware	Silk	Printed Cotton & Linen	Beaver Hats	Flannel
1770	15	45	33	–	25	10	12	30	4
1775	16	53	41	50	30	14	29	38	10
1780	11	10	26	79	18	8	19	24	10
1785	10	16	22	25	1	5	15	14	3
1790	12	–	27	19	16	4	–	21	15
1795	15	18	26	24	13	6	25	27	19
1800	9	24	21	30	17	6	16	19	12

Percentage by Value

	Brass Copper	Iron Steel	Earthenware Glass	Silk	Printed Cotton	Linen	Fish	Haber-dashery	Hats	Leather
1805–06	37	37	21	5	18	60	39	34	50	52

Sources: For 1770–1800, Schumpeter, *British Overseas Trade Statistics,* pp. 62–69; for 1805–1806, PP 1812 (X), 79 ff., and PP 1813–1814 (XII), 225.

slave systems still open to British ships or goods were never more important than after Jena.

British possessions were also far more securely bound to the metropolis in 1806–1807 than were those of any other power. The possessions of France, the Netherlands, Spain, and Denmark could come under blockade or change hands overnight. The British tropical empire alone did not depend on an increasingly tenuous American connection for economic survival. Nor was it threatened by internal social disorder and metropolitan military collapse. This was the perspective of William Windham, the secretary of war and the colonies, in arguing against abolition in 1807. Why, he asked, should Britain risk "such a resource as the West India Islands? Did they not see empire after empire tumbling like so many nine pins all around them?"[8]

For a combatant whose economic prospects in the winter of 1807 seemed to depend on how many doors it could keep open outside Europe, tropical slavery was a very reassuring element in the world scene. From 1805 to 1806, the value of Britain's trade with both northern and southern Europe had decreased. Asian trade had fallen off even more sharply, down over a quarter from the previous year. All areas which were not identified in some way with slave production were moving downward. The very opposite was the case with areas dependent to one degree or another on slavery. Improvement varied almost in proportion to involvement in the slave trade. Trade with the United States, the area least dependent on the slave trade, was up almost one-fifth from 1805 to 1806. Trade with the British West Indies rose over 28 percent. Trade with Africa went up over 40 percent (although the preabolition rush may have been a factor) and that with the foreign West Indies and Latin America leaped by over 185 percent. For any member of Parliament who sought guidance in very short-term trends, the trade pendulum was swinging sharply slaveward.[9]

Moreover, 1806 was a record year for metropolitan trade with the British West Indies, reaching £13.5 million sterling by official valuation, and topping the previous peak year, 1801, by 6 percent. The area's 28 percent increase over 1805 represented the largest absolute increase in value of any of Britain's trading partners. The British West Indies now constituted the empire's largest single trading entity, unless the entire total for northern Europe is calculated as a single unit. Its absolute value was five-sixths as large as all of northern Europe in 1806. Measured against the two other major areas of expansion, the increase in British Afro–West Indian trade for 1806 was just short of the total increased value of British trade with the United States and all of Latin America combined.

This is why contemporaries failed to see any declining significance of slavery on the eve of total abolition.

The Slave Trade—Arrested Growth

One British-based trade calls for separate scrutiny after 1792. In general, the story of the slave trade is analogous to that of British trade to the West Indies. For the period as a whole neither the merchants nor the empire had any cause whatever for concern about decline. From 1791 to 1805 British ships landed an average of 52 percent more slaves each year in the New World than they had in the previous decade and a half. The value of British exports to Africa rose by 88 percent; the tonnage increased by 126 percent (see table 15). Taking only the final decade of this period yields the same result. The trade stood at the summit in value, in volume, and in weight. Even in the last quinquennium, when the absolute peak was passed, more slaves were being loaded on British ships in Africa than in the corresponding period before the American Revolution. With half of this trade moving under the British flag, and more invested under other flags, British capital was playing an enormous role in the slave trade on the very eve of abolition.

Yet, for all its general similarity, the slave trade, as shown by the figures for 1800–1807, was not commensurable with the West Indian trade. The ebbs and flows of the slave trade during the 1790s, although affected by conflict as well as by the market, were still only minimally restricted by legislation. From 1793 to 1796 British conquest in the West Indies alternated with French and slave revolutionary victories. The African trade was also disrupted by a French raiding expedition which raked the coast. From 1797 to 1802 the combination of British naval supremacy and conquests allowed the remaining Caribbean colonies to recoup their losses and to deal with the backlog of demand for slaves in the West Indies and for colonial produce in Europe. British slave loadings in 1798–1799 reached an average of 56,000. Then, at the pinnacle, the law intervened.

The slave transportation act of 1799 was far more stringent than the original Dolben act, setting new standards for space between decks that drove certain ships out of the trade. The impact of the 1799 legislation is clear not only from table 15 but from figure 6. In 1801–1805 the ratio of slaves per ton of British shipping fell by over one-third from the 1796–1800 figure. Other colonial systems, restored by the Peace of Amiens, turned down British ships because of their high costs and offered special inducements for British capital to move slaves from Africa under foreign flags. The British legal system then explicitly sanctioned such peacetime

TABLE 15: THE BRITISH SLAVE TRADE, 1791–1805

| | Average Annual Value | | | Average Annual Tonnage | | | Average Annual Number of Slaves Landed | | |
| | In Thousands | | | In Thousands | | | In Thousands | | |
	Base Period	Prior Equivalent	Percent Change	Base Period	Prior Equivalent	Percent Change	Base Period	Prior Equivalent	Percent Change
1791–1805	£ 971.3	£ 515.6	+88.4	31.9	14.1	+126.2	40.3	26.5	+52.1
1796–1805	1078.1	773.9	+39.3	36.3	24.5	+ 48.2	40.5	40.0	+ 1.3
1796–1800	1102.6	757.6	+45.5	32.6	26.8	+ 21.6	45.0	39.9	+12.8
1801–1805	1053.6	1102.6	− 4.4	36.4	32.6	+ 11.7	36.0	45.0	− 20.0

Sources: For cols. 1-3, Mitchell and Deane, *Abstract*, pp. 310–11; cols. 4–6, PRO Customs 17/4–27; cols. 7–9, ibid., and "Volume and Profitability," tables 1–3 for mortality rates.

Note: "Prior Equivalent" means that every period listed in cols. 1, 4, and 7 is compared with an identical time span just preceding it. Thus the value for the fifteen years 1791–1805 in col. 1, is matched by the value for the corresponding period 1776–1790 in col. 2, etc. This is done for four paired time periods before 1805 to minimize the possibility of distortion on the basis of one arbitrarily chosen cluster of years during the period of abolitionist agitation.

transfers of capital.[10] The difference between the regulated and unregulated trades could be substantial. James Stephen cited the instance of a ship sailing under Dutch colors which had been taken as a prize. It carried 413 slaves; under British regulation its weight and its crew-slave ratio would have permitted a maximum of 260. It is no wonder that the relative profitability of British-regulated ships fell sharply after the legislation of 1799.[11] British ships were allowed half as many slaves per ton as they had averaged before 1788, and their profit rate under the British flag was cut by more than half. Unregulated American ships now entered the slave trade in increasing numbers. The British slave interest claimed that the American fleet was almost three-quarters as large as the British by 1806.[12] Had the Peace of Amiens endured, British-owned ships, if not British capital, might have lost the whole foreign slave trade on the basis of slave costs per ton alone. The volume reduction for the year 1803 (see Appendix II) gives some indication of the potential peacetime loss.[13]

Nevertheless, there are indications that even though the 1799 act depressed exports on registered British ships, the trade showed signs of both vigor and stability until the implementation of the order-in-council of August 1805 and the acts of 1806. During the Peace of Amiens, British slave-trade capital supplied restored Dutch Guiana on British ships under the Dutch flag. The nominal drop in the British slave trade in 1803 represented only a transfer of national flags and some trade goods. On top of this, "a large proportion, perhaps all the American Slave Ships that are now fitted out in our Ports, are owned by British Subjects."[14] Therefore the British figures given by Curtin and Anstey for the slave trade just prior to abolition understate the role of British capital. It is possible that this British "foreign ship" trade extended even beyond the American connection. The British began seizing Danish ships in 1807. The Admiralty prize records show a Danish ship seized on the Brazil run, some of whose capital led back to London via Lisbon.[15] If it were possible to trace all the subterranean passages taken by British investment during the war, the British neutral slave trade may represent a substantial trade in its own right. James Stephen estimated that this legal but concealed British trade raised the actual figure for British-financed shipments of Africans by over 40 percent in the years just prior to 1807.[16] If his estimate were even double the actual figure for those years, it would still more than compensate for the nominal drop of 20 percent in British-carried slaves between 1796–1800 and 1801–1805. The British slave trade had not declined after 1796–1800. It had probably been redistributed under more flags. When Britain moved first to destroy its "foreign" slave trade, it moved against the most profitable per capita branch of the trade.

When Parliament passed the foreign abolition act in May 1806 prices of slaves were at an all-time peak. Prices had moved steadily upward, through peace and war, from the opening of the Spanish colonies in 1789. Contrary to all abolitionist hopes, the supply of slaves had risen along with their price. While profits of the regulated trade certainly fell after 1799, profits on the unregulated British foreign trade, disguised under the American flag, were far higher. "Unhappily," wrote James Stephen of one British-African trade group just after the foreign abolition of 1806, "the supply [of slaves] has increased so much that in this and all other branches of the trade their success must have far exceeded their estimate; and after losing their foreign customers they will have a larger market than they could reasonably have expected when they laid out their money to found it."[17]

British tonnage alone remained just under the turn-of-the-century peak. Nor did this tonnage simply represent a sunken investment in specialized ships with nowhere else to go. The slave-trade fleet continued to be among the technological pioneers of the British merchant fleet. The use of copper-bottomed merchant ships, which began in the last quarter of the eighteenth century, "was first taken up on any scale in the slave trade where vessels sheathed with copper were widespread by the late 1780s. By the early nineteenth century sheathing was almost universal in the slave trade." Most significant, the slave fleet was a relatively young one in 1807, half of its ships being less than ten years old at the time of their last slaving voyage.[18]

This final burst of youth was not a deviation within the larger slave system. It corresponded to a similar trend in the whole shipping network serving slavery. In 1784 there were seven ships in that trade over twenty years old to every six ships under three years old. By 1794 the proportions were only three in the over-twenty category to every nine less than three years old. In 1804 the ratio of the over-twenties to the under-threes was three to twenty-six. It is quite clear that all slave-related shipping was continually being rejuvenated.[19]

The demonstrated versatility of the slave ships after 1807 shows that their owners stuck with the trade even when alternatives were available. By the end of 1808, one year after the trade had formally ceased, over 64 percent of the slave-trade vessels had been successfully redeployed. A year later the figure stood at 77 percent, and the following year at 80 percent. Moreover, this transition was not achieved in an optimum conversion situation. Both the American and European trades were in a period of enormous distress.[20] There was ample unemployed tonnage on hand in Liverpool, even without abolition. The flow of relocation also casts light on the vitality of slavery at the moment of abolition. None of the slave vessels went into the trade with northern Europe, and very few with North America. The overwhelming proportion of the slave ships went to the newer slave economies of Britain and Latin America.

Barry F. Drake's study of Liverpool shipping lists in 1805 provides further evidence that alternatives were available to the slave traders. The triangular trade, contrary to historiographic tradition, was very much alive. There was a significant carrying trade in West Indian produce from the chief slave-importing colonies in slave ships on the final leg of their voyages. The trade ships were kept on the African run, not because they were overspecialized sunken capital, but because they brought equal or superior returns to the entrepreneurs. With abolition, many of the ships simply shifted to the shuttle trade with tropical America. If the slave traders exaggerated the threat to their invested capital in ships by abolition, they did not exaggerate the market incentives to remain in the slave trade.[21]

In terms of international areas for redeployment, it should be borne in mind that Liverpool merchants were in a worse position in 1806–1807 than they had been in 1792. The slave trade was part of Britain's secure zone in 1806. The French, and their Spanish and Dutch allies, had either lost their most effective footholds on the African coast, or traded at British sufferance. Gorée had been recaptured from the French in 1804 and the Cape of Good Hope from the Dutch in 1806. French Senegal had only minor nuisance value and was routinely swept into the British net after abolition. There were no major enemy ports available for privateering, as in Europe, the Caribbean, and the Indian Ocean. Slave ships did not even travel in convoy, as they did to other areas. More slavers were lost in the West Indies than near Africa. British inventories were more secure on the coast of "uncivilized" Africa than in European ports, where they were liable to suffer disastrous seizure by the new warrior-chieftain, Bonaparte. Compared with the captious winds which were assailing British merchants almost everywhere else, Africa was a quiet haven.

Four points of major significance emerge from the story of the slave trade between 1792 and 1806. First, in terms of the usual standards, the British trade was bigger and better over the period as a whole than it had ever been. Second, the "national" downturn (relative only to 1796–1800) came when a major legislative blow successfully decreased the competitive position of British slave ships. Third, the British African traders had a wider choice of secure alternative markets to choose from in 1791–1792 than in 1806–1807. Finally, any account that emphasizes the very short-run correlation of abolition and the economics of slavery must deal squarely with the fact that the restrictive legislation of 1799 was introduced, and passed, at the absolute peak of the British African slave trade by volume and by profitability.

Staple Production During The Caribbean Revolutions

The great slave uprising on St. Domingue in 1791 marked the end of an era in Caribbean history. An enormous gap in production for the European market opened up. Almost immediately, the destruction was reckoned as equivalent to half that island's productive capacity, or almost the entire annual production of runner-up Jamaica.[22] By April 1796, General Forbes, the British commander on St. Domingue, confirmed the trend. Of the 400,000 slaves in 1790, no more than 60,000 were still working on plantations. Sugar culture had been reduced by a minimum of 80 percent, cotton by over 90 percent, and coffee by about 40 percent. In 1797 the British estimated the value of St. Domingue's exports to be down fully 75 to 85 percent. Under Toussaint L'Ouverture's new regime, sugar exports temporarily stabilized at under one-quarter of their prewar level.[23] They again sank rapidly after Bonaparte's abortive reconquest of the island in 1802–1803. St. Domingue's steep fall was paralleled by production losses in other French possessions: St. Lucia, Guadeloupe, and Cayenne. Only Tobago and Martinique, which fell early and easily to the British, maintained their prewar levels.

For almost an entire decade, from 1791 to 1799, the market was overwhelmingly favorable to the producers (see figure 7). The result was the greatest redistribution of slave-produced staples in well over half a century, and probably the most rapid shift in the entire history of the Caribbean. The results are apparent if we look at the shifting locus of the principal Caribbean cash crop. Tables 16 and 17 illustrate the impact of revolution and war on colonial shares of sugar exports from *1787* to 1805–1806. These figures show the sources of North Atlantic sugar imports, with allowance for clayed conversion of muscovado (see Appendix II). While some contemporary documents included such a conversion in their estimates of sugar production, most did not. Without such an allowance, the British share of the market would appear even higher than in tables 16 and 17. The tables therefore represent the *lowest* plausible share of British colonial sugar exports that contemporaries could have calculated.[24] At the outbreak of the French Revolution, France's Caribbean colonies exported over 43 percent of the sugar shipped to the North Atlantic market. By 1805–1806 that share had dropped to 10 percent.

FIGURE 7: AVERAGE LONDON PRICES OF BRITISH WEST
INDIAN MUSCOVADO SUGAR, 1793–1812

Source: Ragatz, *The Fall of the Planter Class,* p. 340.

During the same period British-controlled sugar moved from less than
37 percent to over 57 percent of the total market. This is a minimal figure,
including only exports from those colonies which were *de jure* British
dominions by 1806 (i.e., the colonies of 1792, plus Trinidad). With the
addition of the Dutch colonies conquered between 1803 and 1805, the
British share rises to 59 percent of the total. Looking at the end of the
period does not distort the general situation over the intervening years.
Britain's possession of Martinique, Tobago, Trinidad, Surinam, and
Demerara gave her control of over two-thirds of the European colonial
sugar supplies (69 percent) in the three years before 1802. The cross
section of the sugar market in 1805–1806 probably represents an understatement of the general British position from 1794 to 1806.[25]

TABLE 16: SOURCES OF NORTH ATLANTIC SUGAR
IMPORTS, *1787–1806*

| Controlling | | 1805–1806 | |
Power	*1787*	Maximum[a]	Minimum[b]
Britain	36.7%	58.4%	57.3%
France	43.3	10.2	10.2
Portugal	6.6	15.0	15.0
Spain	6.3	12.2	12.2
Holland	4.5	0.9	2.1
Denmark/Sweden	2.7	2.5	2.5
United States	–	0.7	0.7

Sources: American State Papers 14, imports for 1805–1806;
PP 1808 (IV), Reports from the Committees on the Distillation of Sugar and Molasses (1807–1808), 304, Account of . . .
Sugar Imported into Great Britain from all Parts, 1798–1806.
Note: For method of estimate, see Appendix II.
a. Represents *de facto* control in mid-1806.
b. Represents *de jure* control in mid-1806.

TABLE 17: SHARES OF SUGAR EXPORTS TO THE NORTH
ATLANTIC, 1805–1806

	Tons	Percent of Total
Swedish West Indies	1,810	0.6
Danish West Indies	5,880	1.9
British West Indies	170,440	55.0
French West Indies	30,240	9.8
Dutch West Indies	3,470	1.1
Spanish West Indies and America	36,790	11.9
Total West Indies	248,630	80.2
Louisiana	2,170	0.7
Portuguese Brazil	46,600	15.0
Total Americas	297,400	95.9
British East India		
To Britain	3,100	1.0
To the United States	4,030	1.3
Total British East India	7,130	2.3
French East Indies	1,360	0.4
Spanish Philippines and Africa	1,030	0.3
Dutch East India	2,850	0.9
Cape of Good Hope	190	0.1
China	50	—
Grand total	310,010	

Sources: Same as table 16.
Note: For method of estimate see Appendix II.

One of the major assumptions of the decline thesis is the inelasticity of British colonial production after 1763–1775. But this characterization is even more obviously unfounded for the period 1791–1805 than for the period which immediately preceded it. The "old" empire, above all Jamaica, responded vigorously to the unprecedented opportunity to fill the St. Domingue vacuum. Jamaica increased its sugar exports by 50 percent between 1788–1792 and 1801–1805 (henceforth, *1803*). Between the prewar peak of 1791 and 1805–1806, the increase was over 60 percent (see table 18). In other words, Jamaica, whose pre-1790 exports amounted to less than 60 percent of St. Domingue's, was by 1805–1806 exporting more sugar to Europe than had St. Domingue at the outbreak of the French Revolution. Jamaica had literally replaced St. Domingue. The other colonial system exhibiting similar dynamism was the Spanish. The years

TABLE 18: JAMAICAN SLAVE POPULATION, COFFEE
AND SUGAR EXPORTS, 1783–1814

	Slaves	Coffee (in thousands of lbs.)	Sugar (tons)
1783	—	—	47,972
1784	—	—	46,428
1785	—	—	54,800
1786	—	—	40,481
1787	—	—	41,235
1788	226,000	1,035	58,700
1789	—	1,493	59,400
1790	—	1,784	55,600
1791	250,000	2,300	60,000
1792	—	—	54,644
1793	—	3,984	51,600
1794	—	4,912	64,200
1795	—	6,319	62,800
1796	—	7,204	64,000
1797	300,000	7,869	51,600
1798	—	7,894	63,400
1799	—	11,745	73,200
1800	300,000	11,116	70,100
1801	307,940	13,401	90,200
1802	307,199	17,962	92,300
1803	308,668	15,866	76,200
1804	308,542	22,064	74,900
1805	308,775	24,137	99,600
1806	312,341	29,298	97,100
1807	319,351	26,761	89,800
1808	323,827	29,528	77,800
1809	323,704	25,587	76,000
1810	313,683	25,885	73,700
1811	326,830	17,460	87,900
1812	319,912	18,482	62,100
1813	317,424	24,624	66,500
1814	315,383	34,046	72,417

Sources: For col. 1, Bean, "The British Trans-Atlantic Slave Trade," p. 229. For 2 and 3, Deerr, *History of Sugar,* I, 198; PP 1789 (XXVI), vol. 646a, part IV; PP 1840 (VIII), Appendix 32.

from 1791 to 1804 were boom times for Cuba, Mexico, and Louisiana as rival producers. Yet, vigorous as they were, Mexico and Cuba together exported only half as much as Jamaica in 1805–1806.[26] Between Jamaica and the new runner-up in the Caribbean, Cuba, the tonnage spread was even wider in 1805–1806 than it had been between St. Domingue and Jamaica in *1787*. Once again Jamaica was the queen of the Antilles. In the great sugar race, the prize returned to the island that had lost it three-quarters of a century before. It was a feat never to be repeated in the history of sugar.

The British slave economy improved in more than its relative productive position. After having been virtually confined to the empire for over half a century, British sugar again flowed abundantly to the European continent. Table 19 indicates how the reexport trend appeared to Parliament at the moment of abolition. At the end of the Seven Years' War, British reexports of sugar, swollen by captured French islands, represented almost 25 percent of imports into Britain. The reexport figure dropped to under 5 percent in the golden years before 1775. Only in 1791–1795 did the British sugar industry regain the high reexport ratio of the early sixties. The years just prior to abolition witnessed the climax of the upward trend. In *1803*, one-third of all imported British-controlled West Indian sugar was sent on to the Continent. One must go back a full century, to 1707–1714, to find a comparable import-export ratio.[27] Including even 1806, the average reexport figure for 1801–1806 stands at over 31 percent.

TABLE 19: BRITISH SUGAR IMPORTS, 1761–1806

Period	Average Annual Import (in thousands)	Reexported Excluding Ireland (in thousands)	Percent Reexported
From the British West Indies			
1761-65	1,485 cwt.	354 cwt.	23.8%
1771-75	1,835	83	4.5
1781-85	1,580	158	10.0
1791-95	2,021	496	24.5
1801-05 (*1803*)	3,333	1,111	33.3
1801-06	3,577	1,273	31.2
1801	3,729	863	23.1
1802	4,120	1,747	42.4
1803	2,925	1,377	47.0
1804	2,969	762	25.7
1805	2,922	808	27.6
1806	3,673	791	21.5
Worldwide			
1801-05 (*1803*)	3,577	1,273	35.5
1801-06	3,617	1,204	33.3

Source: PP 1808 (IV), Report from the Committee on the Commercial State of the West Indies.

The years before abolition were, of course, primarily war years. Traditionally, because of Britain's general naval supremacy, her sugar reexport ratio was always more favorable in wartime. However, if we take only the two most peaceful years of the period 1801–1806, the usual "rule of war" is reversed. Britain's peacetime reexport figure, in 1802–1803 ran to more than 45 percent of imports compared with 31 percent for 1801–1806. Britain, at the beginning of the nineteenth century, had reached a level of reexportation never even approached during the entire eighteenth century. For members of Parliament calculating normal year potentials, this was significant.[28] Expansion was the only term that could be applied to the reexport trade whether in the perspective of a decade or a century.

The sharp increase in the volume of sugar production and the enormous expansion of the reexport market between 1791 and 1806 meant that the good old days of imperial market protection were over. Sugar's exit from pure mercantilism was ended not by metropolitan legislation but by colonial growth. By responding to the Continental opening, the British sugar islands also increased their vulnerability to fortune as well as their chance to make new fortunes. They were more exposed to a Continental environment of unprecedented volatility. This also altered the rules of competition in a manner quite beyond the control of either the British planters or the British Parliament. The market was now more subject to foreign pressures. Furthermore, by having to transport all their produce in British ships, they might also find themselves at a competitive disadvantage in selling their products to neutral or enemy consumers. Finally, in wartime, the victories of their enemies might result in a contraction of the neutral outlets on the Continent. All of these conditions obtained with special force at the very end of the period. As a result, prices, which were generally high during the period 1790–1799, reached their preabolition low point in 1802–1803. They then rose again and held firm until the spring of 1806.

We may now take a look at the problem of profitability in this period. No general survey of planter profits was presented to Parliament, either by the planters or others, before 1807. The first parliamentary report containing specific estimates of planter profits after 1792 came in 1807, after the final resolution of the abolition question. It would therefore be plausible to discard the category of profit movements as being outside the public realm in 1806. But we can take up the question *as if* the data were known and widely diffused in 1806.

For the period 1792–1805, as for 1772–1791, the information is scattered and impressionistic. In 1807 the relevant parliamentary committee concluded that colonial profits had averaged 10 percent during the good years of the nineties. Profits were 2 percent or less around 1807. The average annual profit of a very well-run estate was 12 percent from 1795 to 1798, averaged 6 percent from 1801 to 1804, and fell to 3 percent in 1805.[29] It does not appear that the planters had done worse over the fifteen years between 1791 and 1805 than they had in the previous period. If we assume for all the colonies a drop in profitability similar to that of the "well-run" estate, Parliament's overall estimate of 10 percent at the end of the nineties would have dropped to 4 or 5 percent between 1801 and 1804 before dipping to the low point of 1807. In this context, one must recall the Jamaican estimate of 4 percent per year reported to the Privy Council in 1788.

As in 1792, the planter interest presented data of typical estates to illustrate the rates of profit for the period 1801–1806 in order to demonstrate distress. According to one planter, his average rate of profit for 1801–1806 was "a little over 4 percent." However, this estimate was made *after* abolition, and included the year 1806. Therefore, at the beginning of 1806 he must have estimated his profit for 1801–1805 at about 5 percent per year. This brings the estimate very close to the other estate figures cited in evidence which showed a net profit of 12 percent for 1795–1798, 6 percent for 1801–1804, and 3 percent for 1805.[30]

It therefore comes as no surprise that the Jamaican legislature, in a report designed to detail the difficulties of their position to the metropolis, but written before the export crisis of December 1806, produced a schematic account of plantation costs showing that the average Jamaican planter could continue to run his enterprise profitably in normal peacetime conditions. The better planters might count on "ample" returns under similar conditions.[31]

Finally, abolition was a metropolitan and not a Caribbean innovation. The profit squeeze before late 1806 applied almost exclusively to the planter of sugar, and not to the British capitalist network which shipped, insured, refined, and sold the product. Sir William Young's comparative data show that while planters' proceeds per cwt. dropped over 35 percent between 1796–1800 and 1801–1805, the profit share per cwt. tipped absolutely in favor of the grocers, who gleaned 33.8 percent compared with the planters' 31.5 percent.[32] The grocers were more insulated against a fall in prices and could actually increase their profit rate if the reexport market was reasonably open. Thus their returns peaked with the peacetime reexport peak of 1802–1803, when returns to planters reached their lowest level. The shippers, whose rates rose after 1803, the merchants, whose commissions rose, and the provision suppliers, whose prices rose, were likewise unhurt. Insurers had little cause for complaint as they insured shipping, not sugar, coffee, or cotton. Thus slave-grown sugar, which had done well for the entire configuration of extraplanter interests during the 1790s, still afforded very few grounds for complaint from the metropolitan interests during 1792–1805. The planters' difficulties before the end of 1806 were not synonymous with distress for the metropolitan interests.

In 1806, sugar remained the most valuable agricultural staple imported from the slave colonies by the metropolis. Cotton, however, was moving up rapidly. Britain remained its chief importer and continued to demand ever larger amounts. Imports rose to over £20 million at the end of the eighties. After a brief stagnation between 1793 and 1795, the import figure went to over £35 million in 1796–1800. By 1804–1806 it stabilized momentarily at £60 million a year.[33] The revolution in the French colonies was less disruptive to cotton than to sugar consumption because cotton was already more broadly dispersed among producers. The French colonial share of the British market had amounted to less than 20 percent in 1787. The collapse of that system was, however, enough to trigger a sharp rise in prices in 1791 and to hasten the dispersion of cotton production. Within fifteen years the cotton frontiers had moved decisively. Table 20 shows the distribution of Britain's cotton suppliers between 1786 and 1805, based on information made available to the House of Lords during the abolition debates of 1806.[34]

Important changes had occurred since 1790. The foreign and conquered West Indies, after a relative fall during the 1790s, recovered by *1803* to a point where they occupied second place among the suppliers. Brazil moved steadily upward in absolute terms and was Britain's third biggest source of cotton during the period 1796–1805. For the British West Indies, the future was less promising. In 1786–1787 they were Britain's third ranking source of raw cotton behind the foreign West Indies and Asia Minor. For a brief moment during the nineties, between the temporary falling off of the foreign West Indies, and the rise of the United States, they became Britain's chief supplier. By 1801–1805 however, they had clearly been superseded by the United States, the conquered West Indies, and Brazil.

There was no question of a new "Empire of the East" displacing slavery in cotton any more than in sugar. The trend of British East Indian cotton was similar to that of West Indian production. After the supply shortfall created by the collapse of French Caribbean production, East Indian exports to Britain expanded for a brief period. But by *1798* the British slave system was supplying over 22 percent of metropolitan imports, while India was accounting for less than 9 percent. By *1803* Asiatic cot-

TABLE 20: SOURCES OF BRITISH COTTON , 1786-1805 (in thousands)

Area	1786-1787		1789	
	Lbs.	%	Lbs.	%
Eastern				
Noncolonial	–	–	4,541	14.1
Northern Europe				
Mediterranean	6,000	30.2	–	–
Asia/Cape of Good Hope	90	0.5	4,464	13.9
Africa	–	–	–	–
Total Eastern	6,090	30.7	9,005	28.0
Western				
Tropical America				
Caribbean				
Foreign W. Indies	6,214	31.3	–	–
Conquered W. Indies	–	–	–	–
British W. Indies	5,050	25.4	–	–
Southwest Europe				
Portugal (Brazil)	2,500	12.6	–	–
Spain	–	–	–	–
Denmark/Netherlands	–	–	–	–
Total Tropical American	13,764	69.3	22,750	70.6
North America				
British	–	–	–	–
Louisiana	–	–	–	–
U.S.A. (incl. reexports)	–	–	467	1.4
Total N. American	–	–	467	1.4
Total Western	13,764	69.3	23,217	72.0
Prize	–	–	–	–
Grand total		19,854		32,222

Sources: For col. 1, BT 6/140, fol. 56 (1788); for col. 2, Add MSS 38350, fols. 6–18, "Facts Relating to the Growth of Cotton," 1790; for cols. 3–5, HLR MSS, "Account of . . . Cotton Wool imported into Great Britain . . . 1796–1805," May 12, 1806.

ton represented only 5 percent of British imports.

The most dramatic development of all was America's surge to prominence. The United States supplanted both the British and the foreign West Indies as Britain's principal source of cotton after 1800. In *1803* however, the American South did not yet dominate all other British sources to the extent that it was to do in the following generation. From the Lords' figures, Britain was still as dependent on tropical America

1798 (1796–1800)		1803 (1801–1805)		1796–1805	
Lbs.	%	Lbs.	%	Lbs.	%
1,751	4.7	368	0.6	1,959.5	2.2
1,237	3.3	700	1.2	968.5	2.0
3,600	9.7	2,822	4.8	3,211.0	6.7
3	—	3	—	3.0	—
6,591	17.8	3,893	6.6	5,242.0	11.0
1,483	4.0	405	0.7	944.0	2.0
5,871	15.8	9,834	16.9	7,852.5	16.5
8,312	22.5	7,915	13.6	8,113.5	17.0
6,855	18.6	9,098	15.6	7,976.5	16.7
425	1.2	114	0.2	269.5	0.6
190	0.5	80	0.1	135.0	0.3
23,136	62.6	27,496	47.2	25,316.0	53.2
58	0.2	43	0.1	50.0	0.1
10	—	2,895	5.0	1,452.5	3.0
6,883	18.6	23,073	39.6	14,978.0	31.4
6,951	18.8	26,011	44.6	16,480.5	34.6
30,087	81.4	53,507	91.8	41,796.5	87.8
273	0.7	911	1.6	592.0	1.2
36,951		58,311		47,631.0	

Note: This table coalesces the Lords data into three major subdivisions: Eastern or nonslave suppliers include all African, Mediterranean, and Asian suppliers. Northern European areas without slave colonies are also included for two reasons. The original source of their cotton being unknown, we deliberately include them among the nonslave areas to avoid weighting our evidence in favor of slave production. Secondly, the one official comment on these areas claims a probable origin in the East (Add MSS 38350, fols. 6–18, "Facts Relative to the Growth of Cotton, note k). On the other hand the small amount of Dutch, Danish, and French reexports are placed under the Caribbean subsection of the second area, Tropical America. This includes imports from Portugal and Spain as well as the foreign and/or conquered and British West Indies. Finally, Louisiana is included in the North American category, although before 1804 it might have been equally appropriately placed with Honduras and Guiana in the Caribbean littoral. Prize cottons are unlikely to have originated in North America before 1807.

(47 percent) as on North America (45 percent) for its cotton (see table 20). Moreover, American commercial accounts revealed that some "American" cotton was a West Indian reexport. If this cotton is reassigned to its point of origin, the figures indicate that in *1803* the United States alone probably accounted for from 35 to 42 percent of British cotton (see table 21). As with shifting patterns of sugar supply, a good deal depended on political change. Before the United States annexed Louisiana, more cotton was coming from the European Caribbean basin than from the United States. Including Louisiana, well over half of Britain's cotton continued to come from the slave-importing tropics in *1803*, as it had in 1781–1785 and in 1771–1775.[35]

TABLE 21: ALTERNATIVE AGGREGATION OF BRITISH COTTON SOURCES, 1801–1805

Type	Thousands of Lbs.	Percent of Total
United States domestic (1804 boundaries excluding Louisiana)	20,539	35.2 (min.)
United States domestic (1805 boundaries including Louisiana)	24,651	42.3 (max.)
Caribbean (excluding Louisiana)	20,052	34.4 (min.)
Caribbean (including Louisiana)	24,164	41.4 (max.)
Tropical America (excluding Louisiana)	29,150	50.0 (min.)
Tropical America (including Louisiana)	33,262	57.0 (max.)
Dependent on slavery 1805[a]	53,801	92.3

Sources: Table 20; *American State Papers* 14, imports and exports for 1801–1805.

Note: Discrepancies between tables 20 and 21 derive from the breakdown of American cotton sources in the U.S. trade data. Only rows two and four are mutually exclusive.

a. Assumes that no cotton east of the Cape was grown by slaves, and that none was grown by nonslaves west of the Cape.

During the years 1792–1805, Britain's cotton industry became more dependent on slavery and the slave trade than before. In 1786–1787, 30 percent of Britain's cotton had come from areas not identified with slavery. In *1803* less than 8 percent was certifiable as "free." In absolute terms, *all* of the expansion of British cotton imports between 1796 and 1805 came from the network of slave labor systems. Since the Lords' data was collected in connection with the debate on abolition of the trade to the foreign colonies, it is significant that at least three out of the four dynamic cotton frontiers, Brazil, Demerara, and Louisiana, were unquestionably dependent on slave imports for their rapid expansion.[36] Their combined share of the British market was equal to that of the United

States on the eve of abolition. Moreover, in the spring of 1806, no one could guarantee British statesmen that North America would quickly cease to be a *de facto* or even a *de jure* importer of African labor.

The dispersion of sugar and cotton production between 1792 and 1805 was more than matched by another crop. On the eve of the French Revolution, the British slave system made a respectable showing in both sugar and cotton culture. In the growing of coffee, however, there was almost no comparison and certainly no contest. In 1790 it was accepted without discussion that the French colonists had beaten the British out of both the European and North American coffee market.[37] As with sugar, the supremacy of the French islands was well established before the Seven Years' War. In 1767 Jamaica's exports amounted to less than 5 percent of St. Domingue's. The picture was not much better during the seventies when British coffee exports rose only slightly, or during the early eighties when they actually fell below their pre–Revolutionary War figure.[38]

The British government attempted to stimulate production after 1783 by cutting the excise duty on coffee imports by two-thirds, but because of the four- to five-year lag between planting and harvest, colonial export figures were sluggish until the end of the eighties.[39] Meanwhile, French coffee was progressing by leaps and bounds. A large proportion of new slave labor was directed toward coffee production. Between 1767 and 1788 St. Domingue's clayed sugar exports increased less than one-sixth. Coffee exports increased almost six times. St. Domingue officially exported a little over 12 million pounds of coffee in 1767 and was exporting over 72 million by 1788–1789. Before the revolt broke out the crop for 1792 was forecast at 80 million pounds. The reasons behind this enormous increase in production again seem to lie in expanding European consumption: "The excessive price of the Maroc and Eastern coffee probably amounted almost to a prohibition to the middling and lower classes of the people in Europe; . . . the quantity raised in the island of St. Domingo and continuing at the time of the greatest export at a profitable height for the cultivator, . . . it is impossible to account for these facts, but by supposing the consumers to be augmented by new and numerous classes of the people." Coffee, like cotton, moved west in the eighteenth century, became democratized, and built slavery. The chief producer, St. Domingue, directed large numbers of freshly imported Africans into coffee in the 1780s.[40]

Jamaica, whose coffee production in 1768 had amounted to less than 5 percent of St. Domingue's, was, in 1788, exporting well under 2 percent of the French island's official exports, although Jamaican coffee production had more than doubled between 1773–1774 and 1788–1790. The comparison between Jamaica and St. Domingue was an accurate reflection of the relative situation of British and French colonial production as a whole at the end of the old regime. The revival of the 1780s left the British colonies about where they had been before, producing less than 5 percent of the French colonial coffee output.[41]

In this setting, the French West Indian turmoil after 1789 represented an unprecedented opening for a reversal of French dominance. As the St. Domingue crisis deepened and showed every sign of long-term injury to production, planters all over the Caribbean realized their opportunity. In addition to the sudden shortfall in supply, coffee promised to be an ideal crop in a time of severe European social and diplomatic crisis. It demanded less initial capital and a lower scale of operations than sugar. It was technologically simpler to produce. The small entrepreneur was not at so severe a disadvantage in beginning a plantation. It was also a better wartime crop than sugar. It could be stored for long periods of time, awaiting safer shipping lanes or a better price. The new coffee producers also claimed a social advantage over the old sugar system. They were resident proprietors depending on local credit, mostly of middling wealth, and available for militia duty.[42]

The St. Domingue conflict did more for external development than cut short the supply. The explosion scattered a debris of coffee planters throughout the Caribbean area. As the crisis lengthened, the refugee planters began to invest in new plantations. Jamaica and Cuba, as St. Domingue's closest neighbors, were the chief beneficiaries of this dispersion, although its impact reached the shores of North and South America. Jamaica moved most rapidly. Its virgin highlands provided an excellent climate for coffee. Its economic and communications network was better developed than in any other large island in the Caribbean. By the end of 1792, an observer noted that Jamaican production under British fiscal encouragement had already trebled its pre-1783 figure. On the basis of new plantings in 1792 he predicted an extraordinary growth rate.[43] Within a few years Jamaica had again doubled her production.

Although it is difficult to measure relative growth and decline in the fluctuating war years that followed, we have some indications of relative growth. In 1788 Martinique exported more coffee (excluding any smuggling factor) than the whole British colonial system. By 1795 Jamaica's export was triple that of Martinique.[44] St. Domingue's coffee production suffered sharply, but the loss was not nearly so complete as in sugar and cotton. In 1801 St. Domingue's export was still more than half its 1787–1789 average. It was only after the struggle got under way against

Bonaparte that Jamaica closed the gap with the larger island.[45] Jamaica meanwhile held its own against the new challengers. Although the data is scattered, dynamic Cuba, exporting well under 2.5 million pounds of coffee, and Caracas, exporting less than one million, lagged far behind the Jamaican figure of 22 million in 1804.

The performance of the British West Indies as a whole is shown in table 22. British West Indian coffee exports, after more than doubling from 1771–1775 to 1791–1795, almost trebled again between 1791–1795 and 1801–1805. Generations of historians have seen in the soaring of cotton imports after 1770 the statistical symbol of the British industrial revolution. The significance of coffee to the colonial agricultural revolution of the 1790s was equally graphic. In the early 1770s the official value of coffee imports to Britain was well above that of cotton.[46] In 1780 the official value of cotton imports surpassed that of coffee for the first time.

TABLE 22: BRITISH COFFEE IMPORTS FROM THE
BRITISH WEST INDIES, 1761–1806

	Annual Average	Annual Average Reexported (excluding Ireland)
1761–1765	49,309 cwt.	44,514 cwt.
1771–1775	52,015	49,487
1781–1785	26,144	27,597
1791–1795	114,774	104,569
1801–1805	337,381	323,495
1801–1806	363,905	334,106

Source: PP 1808 (IV), 307, Appendix C.

The distance between them widened during the decade that followed. In 1793, however, the trend was suddenly reversed, as shown in figure 8. With the single exception of 1803 the official import value of coffee exceeded that of cotton for every year between 1793 and abolition. Coffee was also a reexport product *par excellence*. This particular British trade more than sextupled in value between 1771–1775 and 1801–1805. By 1801–1805 it was far more valuable in that category than sugar. By the end of the century the value of coffee exported from England officially equalled that of wool, and these two commodities were far and away the most significant items on the trade schedule.

While the British colonies did not single-handedly fill the coffee gap of the 1790s, they were the biggest production gainers by 1800 and continued to hold their position until abolition. Of course, even more than with sugar, the structure of consumption meant that British coffee was developed for, and dependent upon, the international market. It was part of the continental market from the outset, and subject to all its vicissitudes. The coffee revolution proved, as nothing else, that during the final period before abolition the British colonies were capable, not only of rapidly developing existing agricultural systems, but of responding more quickly than any other slave system to the collapse of the French Empire.

Expanded production also meant an enormous increase in the slave labor force between 1792 and 1807. The shifting balance between the British and French systems was especially dramatic. In 1790 British slaves were only two-thirds as numerous as French slaves. By 1805 the British Empire held more than twice as many slaves as its rival, not including unrecognized British conquests (see table 10). More broadly speaking, British slaves constituted between 46 and 58 percent of Europe's Caribbean slaves in 1806.

FIGURE 8: OFFICIAL VALUES OF COTTON AND COFFEE
IMPORTS TO BRITAIN, 1772–1805

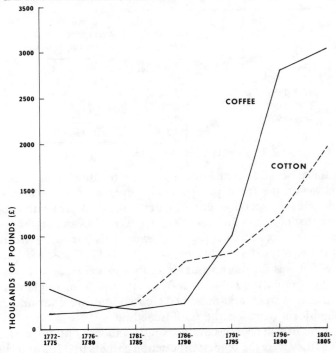

Source: Mitchell and Deane, *Abstract,* pp. 286–89.
Note: Imports are to England, 1772–1791; to Britain, 1792–1805.

The British slave population, both *de facto* and *de jure*, also expanded more quickly than the population of its own industrializing metropolis. Between 1791 and 1806 the population of Great Britain increased by about one-sixth. During the same period the slave population of the British colonies increased by a *minimum* of one-quarter, counting only those colonies recognized by formal treaty. If one adds to them the West Indian colonies conquered by 1805, the increase, consisting principally of able-bodied males, would be reckoned at over half.[47]

The evolution of British slavery between 1792 and 1806 only under-lined the essential continuity of the empire's stake in its own and other slave systems. The West Indies became increasingly dependent on a market of international dimensions, while much of the foreign slave system became British. In terms of control over production and trade, British involvement was continuous and increasing. It increased in terms of British slavery's production, diversification, and value. It increased in terms of metropolitan dependence upon slavery for trade growth and raw materials. Finally, the importance of overseas slave labor to metropolitan survival was never more apparent than in the winter of 1807, when the full dimensions of the Continental blockade were unfolding.

6
The New Frontier and Abolition

The Ever-Receding Threshold of Saturation

British slavery was expanding in 1790. It expanded even more rapidly between 1791 and 1806, despite the dampening effect of political action on the slave-trade component in 1799. But alongside the increase of production, trade, and population there emerged a new frontier which shattered the temporal and spatial assumptions of the debate of the early nineties. The analysis of British economic and political responses to this frontier is crucial for the decline theory or for any other theory of abolition. The decline theory presumes (1) that the British slave system lacked resilience and could not match the growth prospects of the temperate or metropolitan sector of the empire, and (2) that the economic thrust for abolition after 1792 was the result of intensified rivalry between old and new colonies as formerly it had been between British and foreign colonies.[1]

The first supposition hinges on the argument that British slavery was increasingly constricted within its eighteenth-century boundaries, creating a natural barrier to development, while the process of soil exhaustion wrought inevitable decay. This is why Ragatz considers the British retrocession of the French Windward Islands and Cuba in 1763 so momentous a turning point, and why Williams regards the West Indian triumph on that question as a Pyrrhic victory, ultimately fatal to the victors. British slavery, without the French and Spanish colonies, could not keep pace with the other components of the empire for long. The lack of a sufficient frontier is literally a boundary definition of the Ragatz-Williams decline theory.

Contemporary arguments about the proximate future of slavery and the

92

slave trade were also molded by perceptions or assertions about the slave frontier. The slave trade had always been linked to a frontier and to the need for expansion. The end of the slave trade meant the end of expansion.[2] At the beginning of the debate over abolition in 1788, one argument against political abolition had been that the system would reach its natural limit in the not too distant future. With the filling of the British islands, the slave trade would simply wither away. In 1792 Pitt's proabolitionist argument was based on a similar frame of reference which assumed the necessity for only bare maintenance of numbers on existing estates. Any imperial commitment to rapid colonial expansion would be the death knell of this assumption of proximate maturity.

In 1792, however, it was already recognized that to allow Jamaica, with over one million uncultivated acres, to become geographically and demographically saturated would be to acquiesce in indefinite postponement. After 1792, Jamaica showed how unfilled even the "old" colonial vessel had been. Between 1792 and 1806 its slave population rose by a minimum of one-quarter. The Jamaicans, brimming with the vigor of their second childhood in sugar, and their newborn coffee plantations, became more aggressive. Bryan Edwards, with a reputation as a "moderate" West Indian, declared in Parliament that he would indeed accept abolition, "but not until every acre in the islands was cultivated."[3] Jamaica itself had become the dreaded "new" colony denounced by Wilberforce and Pitt in the debates of the nineties.[4]

The British West Indian frontier was alive and thriving in Jamaica before and after 1792. But just as Britain was developing its last "old" frontier at a prodigious pace, she acquired a vast new one. Its precise extent was not clear because of the changing fortunes of war between 1793 and 1807. What is certain is that in 1793–1803 the supposed Caribbean retrenchment that followed the Seven Years' War was clearly revoked. British capital formed the cutting edge of development along the whole slave zone extending from the Carolinas to Buenos Aires. From the 1720s to the 1780s major colonial production of sugar, coffee, and cotton had been largely confined within a rough ellipse enclosing the British and French colonial systems, with Jamaica and St. Domingue at the western end and Barbados and Tobago at the eastern. The colonial revolutions and wars of 1792–1798 caused not only a shift of production within the old Anglo-French area, but a dispersion of production far beyond it.

The Jamaican shipping lists for 1802–1804 show that slaves were being reexported to Trinidad, St. Augustine, Havana, Santiago de Cuba, New Orleans, Charleston, Honduras, and the Spanish Main, as well as to other reexport entrepots at Bermuda and New Providence.[5] Jamaica was thus only one prong of an advancing hemispheric frontier. Other areas vied for British capital. Where successful uprisings and destruction had occurred, the colonies could claim to be underdeveloped areas, requiring extensive new importations of Africans. In the mid-nineties, St. Domingue, Martinique, Grenada, and St. Vincent competed with Jamaica for attention. After 1797 the focus shifted. New areas were rising to prominence, clamoring for the British foreign slave trade.

Within the empire, however, two major new frontiers aroused the greatest interest of the slave traders, and the greatest concern of the abolitionists. By 1799 both groups had already shifted their attention from the smaller islands to Trinidad and Guiana. One can see the transformation at work in the destination of African slaves toward the end of the period. After the Peace of Amiens, an agent for the slave trade in Trinidad, surveying the whole Caribbean, noted that sales to the smaller islands, except St. Vincent, were impossible, that Jamaica and Havana were temporarily overdone, and that the securest markets for slaves were "Surinam, Trinidad, and Demerary." Planters in the last of these places seemed to be getting the best credit terms.[6] Table 23 shows that four-fifths of the slaves retained in British possessions were located in the four frontier areas of St. Vincent, Jamaica, Trinidad, and British Guiana. The latter pair alone accounted for over half the slaves retained for labor under British dominion.

The settlements in Guiana—Demerara, Essequibo, and Berbice—were the most important new slave frontier of the entire period. For the abolitionist fact-gatherer James Stephen, Guiana was the very epitome of British expansionism between 1797 and 1807. If its juridical position was ambiguous, its *de facto* economic and social status as part of British slavery was not. Demerara's potential value for development had been carefully noted by the British government as early as the war with America. With the transfer of Tobago to French sovereignty in 1783, a number of British cotton planters left that island for Guiana. The area began to expand rapidly following the French Revolution. In 1797 the governor of Berbice estimated that since 1789 the slave population of his colony alone had trebled, and Berbice was not the most dynamic area of expansion.[7] By 1794 Demerara and Essequibo probably exported more cotton than any single British colony. All of Demerara's cotton plantations were owned by British subjects, and British capital was so implanted that the government was petitioned two years before the conquest by London proprietors requesting treatment of Guianan cotton as imperial produce. They argued that they had helped to fulfill British imperial policy by expanding cotton production at a critical juncture when demand for cotton far exceeded the capacity of the British colonies. They had been supplied with British capital, British manufactures, and British-shipped African slaves. Finally, Guiana was already looked upon by the slave interest as an area in which profits could balance losses elsewhere. The slave interest, smarting from losses in the French and British revolutionary islands (Grenada, St. Vincent, Guadeloupe, and St. Lucia), saw Guiana as the "only remaining source of remittances."[8]

TABLE 23: AVERAGE ANNUAL IMPORTS OF SLAVES INTO BRITISH-CONTROLLED ISLANDS, APRIL 1803 TO APRIL 1805

Colony	Imports	Reexports	Retained Imports
Tobago	172	—	172
Tortola	438	259	177
Bahamas	2,523	2,230	313
Antigua	436	100	336
Dominica	440	34	516
St. Kitts	971	124	847
Barbados	1,050	28	1,022
Grenada	1,097	2	1,095
St. Vincent	1,540	—	1,540
Trinidad	4,616	33	4,583
Jamaica	7,662	2,402	5,260
Conquered Colonies (chiefly British Guiana)	7,164	—	7,164
Total	28,355	5,212	23,143
Havana			
1803–1804	9,300	—	—
1800–1804	7,650	—	—

Sources: Southey, *Chronological History of the West Indies,* IV, 249–50; Humboldt, *Narrative of Travels,* VII, 146.

After the British conquest in 1797, development accelerated. During the following decade, between £15 and 18 million was tied up in Demerara and Berbice. Slaves, bought on credit, were a major source of investment. Liverpool traders such as Dawson, Bolton, and Tarleton appear in the official correspondence as capitalists deeply involved in the colony. In 1802, Governor Beaujon of Demerara was instructed to pay special attention to the interests of Messrs. Tarleton and Backhouse of Liverpool, who were, "I understand, concerned in property to the amount of 200,000 Sterling in the colony." John Bolton, also of Liverpool, in 1803 had loans out "to the amount of Two Hundred Thousand Pounds" in Demerara.[9] The degree of concern over Demerara was graphically illustrated when war resumed between Britain and France in the spring of 1803. British merchants were desperate to see the colony, which had just reverted to the Dutch, returned to British hands in order to protect not only their investments but their existence. George Baillie, whose house had £100,000 at stake, was terrified that the French would invade before the British navy arrived. If the French descended from St. Domingue, he warned, thirty principal houses in London, Liverpool, and Glasgow, "and many lesser ones, will stop payment." Baillie promised Sullivan backup memorials from Liverpool, London, Bristol, and Glasgow. The government, with such blunt prodding, moved swiftly and successfully. The recapture of Demerara brought a new infusion of capital, Britons, and Africans to the colony. This time they also brought with them the steam engine. Demerara was at the technological as well as agricultural frontier of slavery. Within a few years, steam had superseded wind, water, and cattle mills.[10]

During these early years Demerara was an investor's dream. Fertile, virgin, and almost inexhaustible land lay close at hand. Colquhoun, in his statistical account of the British Empire, did not even attempt to estimate its arable lands as he did with the other tropical colonies. He simply put "*ad infinitum*" in place of a number.[11] Guiana was free of hurricanes. It had plenty of room for provision grounds. Even from the fiscal point of view, the Guiana frontier was a net gain to the empire. As a colonial commissioner wrote in 1804, Demerara plantations grew so rapidly and at so high a rate of profit that "even under a temporary protection, instead of being a dead weight upon our exertions, like so many other colonies, they are able to lessen our general expenses."[12] There can be little doubt that Demerara was the most rapidly developing colony in the slave world between 1796 and 1805. For the abolitionists it was the very embodiment of the situation that they feared most—an expanding colony dependent almost exclusively on the African slave trade. At the beginning of the nineteenth century Demerara demonstrated how quickly capital could be poured into any tropical frontier.[13]

The implications of Demerara's development were not lost on contemporaries. One politician noted just before the Peace of Amiens: "The rapid progress in the improvement of Surinam and Demerary, with their dependencies Essequibo and Berbice, especially since the English were in possession of them, will change the political character of that part of the world." The fertility of its soil, the navigability of its rivers, the regularity of its seasons, were carefully delineated, to show its enormous potential. The fact that "two thirds of the [British] African ships have disposed of their negroes at these settlements in the last two years, and most of the ships are fitting out for the same market," demonstrated that Guiana had already asserted itself as the leading sector of the slave system. For the capitalist there was the further assurance that, in Guiana, a slave would "pay his purchase in twelve months."[14]

We have paid particular attention to the Guiana colony for a number of reasons. First, while illustrating the general trend of the expanding frontier, it was at the head of the pack. Second, it clearly shows the enthusiasm of British participation in the expansion of the slave system between 1792 and 1806. British capitalists liked the protection of the British flag, but they did not absolutely require its presence or guaranteed permanence. Guiana is a prime example of the international dimension of British slavery. The fact that it was not definitively a part of the empire between 1797 and 1806 did not stop British subjects from participating in its expansion. On the contrary, any objections that the planters of the older islands might someday have was, from this point of view, irrelevant to imperial interest. The foreign slave frontier had moved outward from St. Domingue, but the capitalist arguments for expansion, and for British participation in it, remained as compelling as they had been in 1788. Indeed, they had more force after British capital had moved in massively to fill the production vacuum created by the French collapse. Finally, Demerara, between 1797 and 1805, was the one sector of the British-controlled new frontier which was allowed to develop most directly in response to market forces. It is also the frontier most amenable to one explanation of abolition as propounded in the decline theory.

By 1800 the significance of the new frontiers for slavery was abundantly clear to friends and enemies alike. In demographic, as in other terms, the frontiers were now more than adequate for the foreseeable British future in tropical culture. At the outbreak of the French Revolution, the British slave system was relatively densely populated compared with 1806 when almost one-quarter of Britain's slave population was located in the largely underdeveloped new possessions acquired during the French wars. The vistas were expanding even more rapidly than the system. In 1790, there were thirty-seven slaves per square mile in the West Indian colonies. Guiana, in 1803, had less than one slave per square mile. Although overall density statistics are very unreliable indicators of arable acreage, the trend was clear. In relation to its previous potential, the British slave system was opening up after 1792.

It had required a century and a half for the ever-growing slave trade to fill a few tiny islands in the Caribbean and to meet the still relatively modest requirements of eighteenth-century European demand. As the nineteenth century opened, the slave system was expanding in bigger islands, moving to all parts of the Caribbean littoral, and plunging into the great Mississippi valley. Continents were indeed replacing the smaller West Indies, as Williams noted, and machine power was replacing animal power, but it was not at all a question of wage labor replacing slave labor. Despite the twin revolutions in Europe and the Caribbean, slavery was spreading more rapidly in 1800 than ever before. And no one had taken more economic advantage of the general expansion, or of the two revolutions, than British capitalism.

The soothing image projected by Pitt to Parliament in 1792, of a system near saturation, was shattered. Henceforth abolitionists spent less time in publicizing the convergence of birth and death rates in the old islands than in agonizing over the deaths it would now require to develop fully Britain's newborn colonies.[15] Matching the rate of eighteenth-century imports against the boundless spaces opening up to slavery, they foresaw a British slave trade flourishing not for a decade or two longer, but for centuries. Their opponents politely suggested an alternative time span. Because of the high rate of importations at the end of the eighteenth century, the filling process might proceed more rapidly than the abolitionists feared. This was chilling comfort to those whose concern was the total suffering to be inflicted under either projection. It was clear that, given Europe's growing need for sugar, coffee, and cotton, given the African coast with its social machinery in place for delivering up human beings, and given Britain with its capital, its fleets, and its new lands, there existed as devastating an economic combination against abolition at the end of the eighteenth century as at the beginning.

Well might Wilberforce, in 1799, have seriously considered suspending abolitionist initiatives in exchange for only a moratorium on the slave trade. As James Stephen gazed at British slavery a full dozen years after the great victory in the Commons in 1792, he conjured up Leviathan, not Lilliput. "I see my country still given up without remorse to the unbridled career of slave trading speculators. . . . The monster, instead of being cut off, as the first burst of honest indignation promised, has been more fondly nourished than before; and fattened with fuller meals of misery and murder, into far more than his pristine dimensions."[16] Allowing for bitter hyperbole, there was not a trace of contempt or condescension for a dying system in his words.

Demerara and Abolition

The last frontier portion of the decline thesis cannot be considered valid in the last decade before abolition. There remains the other major theme of Williams to be examined, that the slave trade was abolished, not because slavery was insufficient for the needs of the metropolis, but because the new areas were too proficient for the comfort of the older islands. Again, as for the period before 1790, mercantilism is called to the aid of a decline theory supposedly resting solidly on the premises of emergent laissez-faire capitalism.

As in the case of the slave trade before 1790, not failure but success was supposedly the catalyst of annihilation. More particularly, conflict was produced by competitive slave production on the one hand, or competitive capital attraction on the other. Both are varieties of the beggar-my-rival explanation of abolition. In the first instance, the government presumably renounced the advantages of the frontier because it placed the old colonies in jeopardy as sugar producers. In the second instance the government supposedly desired to prevent the use of British capital to build up foreign rivals, or at least rivals which were potentially foreign.[17] Since the battle of each frontier was fought out separately, we must deal with each case as a separate unit. But it must be recognized that it is the cumulative fit of this explanation, as applied to all of them, by which the mercantilist argument must be finally judged.

The most plausible application of the mercantilist argument is to the abolition of the slave trade to Guiana in 1805–1806. As permitted by their articles of capitulation, Demerara and Surinam were allowed to develop without restraint on their imports from Africa in 1803–1805. In reconquering all of Dutch Guiana in 1803–1804, the British were again masters of the largest single slave-importing frontier in the Caribbean. In the year ending October 1805, just before the restrictive order-in-council went into effect, Guiana imported over 12,600 slaves. In the same year Havana's imports were only 5,000. (Her average annual imports for 1802–1805, including even the extraordinary year 1802, were 9,350.)[18] Only Brazil, and perhaps the United States, still exceeded Guiana as an importer of Africans.

The idea of stopping the Demerara slave trade by royal proclamation had been suggested by Pitt before the Peace of Amiens. Wilberforce raised it again after the Lords postponed consideration of general abolition in June 1804. The question really became urgent to the abolitionists after the narrow but unexpected defeat of total abolition in the Commons in March 1805.[19] In August 1805, and after considerable abolitionist pressure on the government, an order-in-council was issued to prevent the importation of slaves for new cultivation as of December 1, 1805. It limited the importation for the upkeep of numbers to a maximum annual quota of 3 percent of the existing slave population. Finally, as of January 1, 1807, no slaves from Africa, even for maintenance, were to be allowed into the colony. The order was issued during a period when the price of sugar was near a five-year peak.

For that part of the decline argument which relies on competition, it is interesting that the preamble, which declared the move to be grounded exclusively on expediency, made no mention of competition as a basis for the order. Demerara's amazing spurt of growth was, of course, used by the abolitionists, who raised the specter of staple competition as an argument against a continuation of the British slave trade. Yet the abolitionists declared themselves bewildered and frustrated at the failure of the older British sugar colonies to rally behind this abolitionist theme.[20] With regard to Demerara, the reason may not have been the perversity or blind prejudice of which the abolitionists accused the West India interest. The growth of the Demerara frontier after 1796, like that of St. Domingue after 1783, was more complementary than antagonistic to the older sugar colonies. Although its sugar production increased between 1796 and 1804, it was as a producer of cotton and, to a lesser degree, of coffee, that Demerara was most valued from the mid-1790s to, and beyond, abolition. In 1803–1804 Demerara's sugar export to Britain was valued, in real prices, at just under £200,000 sterling, compared with £375,000 for coffee and £865,000 for cotton.[21] Even if we include in these totals the large proportion (over 40 percent) of Demerara sugar sent to America, rather than to Britain, the value of that crop was still below that of coffee, and far below cotton. Furthermore, between 1800 and 1804 the production of coffee and sugar had stabilized.

The Demerara proprietors and the British colonial administrators both categorized the colony as primarily a cotton producer.[22] It is thus no accident that when the Jamaicans unleashed a litany of grievances against imperial policy toward the slave colonies in 1804, it was British encouragement of sugar from East India which was attacked as rival-building. Demerara was not even mentioned. As late as 1807, Demerara still exported considerably less than one-tenth as much sugar to Britain as Jamaica did. It ranked below Barbados, Grenada, St. Kitts, St. Vincent, and Tobago, and barely matched Antigua, on the British import list.[23] The assumption that the limitation of the slave trade to Demerara was aided by imperial sugar rivalry is undermined, not supported, by Demerara's staple structure.

The Guiana capitalists in 1805–1806 had their own complaints to voice about unfair slave labor practices and rival-building. They denounced Britain's inconsistency in allowing the British slave trade to continue contributing to the extension of cotton culture in the American South. When the foreign slave trade bill remedied this distinction in May of 1806, the same interest again pointed out that the American-borne slave trade still enabled the United States to expand its own cotton culture, while British production was being curtailed.[24] The main point, however, is that in August 1805, when the British government cut off African imports to the largest cotton colony in its control, it could hardly presume that Parliament would agree the next year to end the contradiction of continuing the British slave trade to North America. In any case, given the demographic situation, Guiana was the greater loser by the two abolitions. The 1805 order-in-council amounted to limiting the growth of a cotton colony which might be lost in the future, in favor of ex-colonies irretrievably lost over two decades before.

The second part of the mercantilist argument is one used by contemporaries. The preamble of the order-in-council explained the action as a prophylactic measure against rival-building. The same motive was announced as the basis for extending the prohibition and for introducing the foreign slave trade bill in 1806.[25] By then, however, the plausibility of the rival-building motive was ceasing to apply to its original object. The British government, by its own decision, undermined its previous position.

The rationale against potential rivals rested on nothing but the likelihood that Demerara would be returned to Dutch sovereignty at the next peace as it had been in 1802. However, although the Fox-Grenville ministry of 1806 was clearly the most proabolitionist since abolition had first been mooted, its peace strategy was quite different from that of 1801–1802. When Fox reopened serious negotiations with Bonaparte in the spring of 1806, the British were determined to hold on to as much of their overseas conquests as possible. Since the emperor had overthrown the balance of power in central Europe and showed no inclination to reduce his influence, British acquisitions were now viewed as a minimal counterpoise to the new Continental system. This time Britain proposed to retain in peace what could not be torn from her by force of arms.[26]

Demerara fitted solidly into these British plans. The mercantile interests involved in Demerara, Essequibo, and Berbice urged the retention of those colonies, even if Surinam had to be given up. Howick, the foreign secretary, also considered Surinam to be a more than sufficient return for a Guiana settlement.[27] In any event, the remainder of Guiana was no longer negotiable. The foreign secretary was unequivocal on the subject. "The quantity of British capital at present embarked in the settlements of Demerara, Essequibo and Berbice presents an almost insurmountable obstacle to their surrender, and to speak quite plainly, the opinion of the leading members of the Cabinet upon this point is so decided, that I have not overstated it in my dispatch when I say that it cannot be abandoned. It was not without some difficulty that I prevailed upon them to allow me to offer Surinam separately, which if our other terms are acceded to, I am not without hope may be accepted."[28] Unlike the British mood in 1801–1802, Demerara had come to be considered a permanent acquisition. This means that restrictions on development were being maintained precisely where the capital-for-rivals idea had lost plausibility. The best way, of course, to insure that British capital did not go into rival-building was to imperialize it politically. Yet despite this decision against retrocession, the previous decision to abolish completely the African slave trade to Demerara by December 1806 was not reversed.

Nor did the government even assume that the surrender of Surinam was to result in a net retrenchment of the British slave system. In exchange for Surinam the British government intended to ask for nothing less than Cuba. Cuba already was not only the largest foreign slave colony in the Caribbean but the largest foreign sugar colony as well. In 1804–1806 it exported roughly forty-four thousand muscovado-equivalent tons of that commodity. This was four times as much as Demerara's total export in 1806. And in the summer of 1806 the price of sugar had dropped considerably below its level at the time of the order-in-council the year before.[29] In surrendering a part of Guiana for the sake of a general peace settlement, then, the British intended that they should be compensated by the acquisition of an island which they regarded as even more valuable, economically and strategically. This largely abolitionist government of 1806 considered it to be their duty to insure the absolute maximum expansion of Britain's tropical empire compatible with a European peace and not to surrender under any condition the conquered portion of the slave frontier already dominated by British capital.

Nor did Britain only talk about getting new slave colonies in 1806. The course of British policy in 1805–1807 was still set for military expansion, even while abolition continued to move forward. In January 1806 the Cape Colony was recaptured. The news reached Britain just before the debates on the foreign slave trade bill. The colony was an importer of slaves, and it was hailed as, among other things, another potential sugar frontier.[30] At the very moment that the government resolved to hold on to gains in Dutch Guiana, it was also helping itself to the mainland of Spanish America. In June 1806 a British expeditionary force captured Buenos Aires, the capital of La Plata. The British government, on receiving word, immediately dispatched reinforcements to hold the colony.[31] La Plata, too, was a slave entrepot, its imports just reaching a peak at the moment of the British invasion. The news of its capture set off a speculative flurry. Ships began fitting out for the slave trade directed to La Plata. Only government intervention prevented another branch of the trade from blossoming.[32]

The case of Demerara reveals some of the analytical difficulties involved in accepting the beggar-my-rival motive as the significant one in explaining British action against its frontier. Nevertheless, it might be maintained that the ambiguity of its political status as a potential rival in August 1805 created an expediency gap which worked. This still leaves open the very important question of why the rival theory was not reversible even a few months later. The situation argues, it would seem, for a more powerful and steady force which froze Demerara once it crossed the threshold to abolition. Setting this reservation aside for the moment, there is another frontier which shows that even the certainty of internationally recognized acquisition did not alter the thrust of political decisions against the new frontiers after 1797, regardless of economic circumstances.

Trinidad and Abolition

Trinidad, like Demerara, had begun to be integrated into the British imperial economy well before its virtually bloodless capture in February 1797. British traders were its principal suppliers of slaves, provisions, and manufactures when the island was opened up for development after 1783. In turn, Trinidad exported cotton to Britain via the free port system. At the moment of conquest Trinidad already possessed almost 160 plantations in sugar, 130 in coffee, 103 in cotton, and 60 in cocoa. However, only 5 percent of its estimated arable land was then developed. The island's immediate potential in lands not yet alienated by the crown was reckoned at almost ten times the existing number of estates.

The sugar land was better situated for commercial transport than that of St. Domingue. Continental draft animals were easily available, which promised to facilitate drainage, a fairly expensive item in Guiana. Even before the peace negotiations required the return of Britain's other slave colony acquisitions, it was regarded as Britain's most valuable conquest. Trinidad was also regarded as a sugar colony *par excellence*. Because of the fertility of the soil, no special inducements or public credit had to be offered as a spur to investment.[33] The Spanish island, conquered in the midst of an enormous boom in tropical products, was in a perfect position to profit by its capitulation in 1797. The British, grown weary of the costly attempts to subdue the French islands, looked to Trinidad as the sugar substitute for St. Domingue. Its lands were known to be comparable in fertility with the best in Jamaica and St. Domingue.[34] Such an island, acquired at an optimum moment, provides a novel test of the decline thesis.

Although it was not fully apparent at the time, the acquisition of Trinidad in 1797 marked a turning point for British slavery and the slave trade. Trinidad was not allowed to follow the traditional line of economic development. Precisely in 1797, at the peak of sugar prices, when no pressure of competition hung over the old colonies, when British revenue was desperately short and capital abundant, when Europe could absorb everything tropical that could be produced, Pitt took the first major step to curb the unlimited expansion of the African slave trade and slavery in the British imperium. He refused to open Trinidad's unsold crown lands for sale and development. "You perhaps may not know," wrote Wilberforce in 1802, "that for several years past Pitt has been assailed by sap and by storm in all directions and from all quarters . . . but he would never give way."[35] The policy was not only adopted but enforced. From the moment the first governor took charge of the island no further grants of land were made.[36] Thus the doubling of the number of slaves in Trinidad between 1797 and 1802 represented an artificially depressed rate of expansion and direct resistance to British capitalist pressure. The last Spanish governor had estimated that Trinidad was capable of absorbing four to five thousand slaves per year. This was before Trinidad was opened to the entry of British capital under British dominion and must be taken as the minimum economic potential for the period immediately following 1797. From the outset the British slave trade to Trinidad proceeded with the demand for slaves already limited by a political decision of the British prime minister. Trinidad, in 1800, was already a chained tiger.

The decline theory offers no explanation for this policy. In view of its dependence on the lack of natural frontiers, the theory overlooks a critical problem. The question is not only how the conflict over abolition affected the Trinidad frontier, but how the Trinidad frontier affected abolition. In *Capitalism and Slavery*, Trinidad plays a curiously mute role. Williams mentions its conquest as a deterrent to abolition in the late 1790s, but then Trinidad drops entirely out of sight in the discussion of the actual fight over abolition before 1807. Of the new frontiers in general, Williams says only that "it was the new colonies, crying out for labor, full of possibilities, that had to be restrained, and they were permanently crippled by abolition."[37] But the decline theory offers no reason why they had to be restrained, and why crippled permanently. In another work Williams, prime minister as well as historian of Trinidad, does briefly touch on the problem. In his *History of the Peoples of Trinidad and Tobago,* Williams abandons his own general model. He hypothesizes that had Trinidad been acquired even a decade before 1797, it would have been regarded as redressing the sugar balance with France. Unfortunately for slavery, concludes Williams, the decision to restrict the slave trade had already been made. But when had it? Who knew it had been made? Neither the British commanders, who conquered French colonies after 1793 and promptly reinstituted both slavery and the slave trade, nor the free blacks, who were often indiscriminately enslaved, whatever their status before the Caribbean uprisings, were privy to any decision to cut off the trade from captured slave islands.[38]

This "just-too-late" hypothesis also conflicts with the history of Trinidad immediately after 1800. By the treaty of Amiens, Trinidad was formally ceded to the British crown. It was publicized to the country as Britain's major gain in the Western Hemisphere. The British government was at that time under a decidedly nonabolitionist cabinet. It explicitly insisted on British retention of Trinidad in order to balance Napoleon's imminent reacquisition of St. Domingue, expanded by Spain's cession of the eastern half of the island to France.[39] Undeveloped Trinidad in 1802 could, of course, redress the balance only insofar as it could match Napoleon's redevelopment of St. Domingue. According to Williams's *History,* this is precisely the motive that would have altered the course of abolition in 1787. The Ragatzian "lost opportunity" of 1763 was now regained by international accord.[40] What the successor of the elder Pitt had surrendered at Paris in 1763, in a moment of total triumph, the successor of the younger Pitt had retrieved in the standoff at Amiens, exactly forty years later. British capital would be free to expand under the protection of permanent British sovereignty, development being the logical future for any acquisition retained for its economic value. This implication was not lost on Wilberforce, who declared in the debate on peace preliminaries in November 1801, that Trinidad would require a million slaves to clear and settle its land. The ministers did not contradict him, and for good reason. The West Indians had exactly the same impression as Wilberforce and considered "the question of the Slave Trade as settled forever by the acquisition of such a tract of land, which it would be madness not to make the most of, and to make the most of which will require an annual importation of Negroes beyond that of all the old islands put together."[41]

The Trinidad frontier was now legally British. Although prices had fallen by 1802, sugar still remained a crop which could be grown very profitably. In the opinion of its governor, sugar could not be "advantageously cultivated or manufactured without slaves." This was also the opinion of James Stephen. The government felt that the normal arrangement would be to open the crown lands to settlement, after which the interests of the persons becoming proprietors, by importations of slaves from Africa, "would operate rapidly and effectively to render them most beneficial to the Planters, and consequently to the Public."[42] There was nothing in the political economy of the situation to hinder such a scheme. Furthermore, for an empire emerging from ten years of conflict, the sale of crown lands was an excellent alternative to further increases in taxes to pay for present expenses and past debts.

Henry Addington, Pitt's successor as prime minister, and a man without excessive abolitionist scruples, intended to do just that. On November 23, 1801, speaking on finances, he announced his intention of selling certain crown properties in the West Indies, including Trinidad, as a means of reducing arrears on the civil list. The ease with which Pitt could earlier have done the same was at no time better illustrated than when Addington was questioned in Parliament regarding the government's intentions in Trinidad. Addington refused even to acknowledge that he was obliged to bring the matter before Parliament as a separate and debatable question.[43]

Plans for the sale of properties in the island were well launched before the transfer of the territory from Spain to Britain was ratified by treaty in March 1802. Here, then, was an island which both businessmen and politicians in Trinidad and Britain regarded as sugar country, capable of rivaling Jamaica in twenty years. It was reputedly able to absorb the total slave trade of Britain for seven years and could help solve Britain's immediate fiscal needs.[44] We cannot enter into the details by which a combination of abolitionists, Pittites, and Canning's opposition friends forced Addington to back down from immediate release of the crown lands. But Parliament only then settled the Trinidad frontier question. It was the good chance that the majority would stand with Pitt, and against the prime minister, which forced the government to retreat twice on the Trinidad issue in the spring of 1802.

Of course neither the frontier nor Trinidad's fertility went away. Nor did the problem of developing Trinidad. Trinidad was suggested as a new laboratory for slave-trade substitutes. Ideas and proposals, with subsidy applications attached, poured into the government. One proposal wished to attract the Scottish and Irish exodus from the United Kingdom and to lure British-born residents back from America. Swiss and Germans, British convicts, and French planters were all recommended. The reservoir of peons from the Spanish American mainland was also considered, especially for clearing land. Veterans from the black slave regiments raised during the previous decade in the West Indies were included on the list. In imagination, at least, the whole planet was scoured to people the island. Finally, a long-delayed and highly confidential plan was set afoot to bring in Chinese labor from the Far East. The end result of all these schemes was that a lone East Indian ship arrived in Trinidad late in 1806 with 192 Chinese settlers on board. The expense and difficulties of the voyage and the subsequent experience with the immigrants were evidence against such plans for some time to come.[45]

The slaves of other islands were also suggested as an alternative to Africans. Proposals were made to encourage the emigration of British planters to Trinidad from islands yielded back to foreign governments. In other parts of the West Indies, where settlers were abandoning their property and emigrating to South Carolina with their slaves, Trinidad was proposed as a lure for redirected slave emigration. But the closing off of the crown lands restricted the inter-island movement of slave labor to Trinidad. Cotton as well as sugar was blocked off.[46] This was important to large numbers of British planters on exhausted lands. Yet a newspaper of Barbados, the most mature slave island in the British West Indies, could only protest at the end of 1805 that eventually Trinidad "must progressively (in spite of the utmost efforts of the envious to prevent it) render it ere many years are past more productive than the whole of the *Caribbean possessions* put together."[47]

This quotation from the oldest of the old slave colonies brings us back to the decline theory's general explanation of frontier restriction, invoked for Trinidad as for Demerara. It might still be maintained that the flow of British capital had to be restricted at least until 1802, because, in case of reversion, the investment would have gone to enrich a foreign rival. Two primary considerations undermine any confidence in applying this explanation to Trinidad in 1797–1802. If fear of plying the enemy with capital had been part of a general policy in 1797 one would have to ask why Demerara, where capital investment could not be so neatly cordoned off by Pitt's simply refusing to act, not only became the premier investment colony at the moment of Trinidad's restriction, but was returned to the Dutch by the treaty of Amiens.[48] The government thus followed precisely the opposite policy and, at the first opportunity, surrendered the colony that had grown fastest with British capital after 1797. The facts of capital flow undermine the idea of any ministerial policy of capital restriction. Even more significant is the British government's intention regarding the permanent possession of Trinidad or its equivalent. As early as the summer of 1797 the British had settled on that island as Britain's compensation in the West Indies for "the augmentation of power accruing to France, from the acquisition of the Spanish part of St. Domingo."[49] Pitt's refusal to throw open the crown lands thus coincided with the decision to retain Trinidad.

One final possible objection remains to the use of the Trinidad case as proof of exclusively abolitionist intentions in the withholding of the crown lands from 1797 to 1802. One could combine the beggar-my-rival theory with the market theory of restriction in the following way. The government, acting on mercantilist premises, held off development because of Trinidad's potential retrocession while the market was buoyant. Just before the rival theory ceased to apply, the price of sugar fell. The old colonies now acted to prevent the development of an *internal* rival. The quotation from the *Barbadoes Mercury* suggests that supporters of the theory have never really investigated the weight of old colony opinions about Trinidad, deriving the entire "old colony opposition" from four or five West Indian spokesmen who were a minority of their own interest. Why the government should have taken a stand on the side of a minority of one imperial interest against metropolitan capitalists, with money in hand, clamoring for the opportunity to develop Trinidad and to provide revenue to the state as well, requires explanation—market, mercantilist, or otherwise. It was, after all, Addington and Hawkesbury, friends of the slave interest, who pressed forward, and friends of abolition, Canning and Pitt, who were decisive in opposing the move. Until research supports the premise that the old West India interest acted decisively, or even cohesively, against Trinidad on the crown lands question, it is totally unjustified for historians to invoke that interest as a force against Trinidad in 1802, much less in 1797.

It must be acknowledged, however, that the case of Trinidad alone can take us no further than demonstrating the implausibility of any mercantilist-cum-market, two-stage explanation, requiring a constant shuttling back and forth between motivations based on two different political economies. Yet the question need not be abandoned at this point. The only critical gap against both theories that the Trinidad question cannot fill with certainty is whether in 1797, rather than in 1802, the government could have resisted the temptation to (1) develop lands in an unequivocally *de jure* British area, (2) with a new frontier, (3) at the peak moment in the slave trade, and (4) at an optimum moment for all sugar producers. There is another island whose story fills in the critical gap.

St. Vincent and Abolition

St. Vincent was unquestionably part of the "old" British slave empire in 1797. It was one of the so-called neutral islands, ceded to Britain by the Peace of Paris in 1763 and reconfirmed as a British possession by the Peace of Versailles in 1783. Its peculiarity, before 1797, lay in its retarded development as a slave colony. This was due to the presence of a powerful community of independent non-Europeans. The "black" Caribs possessed large tracts of territory amounting to one-third of the richest and most cultivated soil on the island. They posed a constant threat to European supremacy. In 1795 the Caribs and some of the French inhabitants on the island responded to revolutionary appeals from Guadeloupe. The island was lost to the British for most of the year. So dangerous was the British situation that the planters allowed troops to be recruited from among their slaves. The war devastated St. Vincent, and British control was not fully restored until the following year. After their defeat, the Caribs were deported from St. Vincent to the island of Roatán in the Gulf of Honduras, leaving the richest land in the island vacant.[50]

A new opportunity was obviously presented for development of the largest sugar frontier remaining in all the British Windward Islands. St. Vincent's case for an intensified slave trade was especially strong in that it could be linked to both the strategic situation in the islands and reconstruction requirements. In 1797, the vacant Carib lands were a potential asylum for still unsubdued groups on St. Vincent and nearby St. Lucia. Even more decisively, the development of the unused lands could easily be joined to a previous commitment. In 1795, with the strenuous support of the representatives of British trade and manufactures, and over the opposition of some of the abolitionists, Parliament had voted a large loan to rescue Grenada and St. Vincent. Pitt himself voted in favor of the loan, making a distinction between restoration and expansion.[51] St. Vincent required capital to renew or replace destroyed plantations, and fresh slaves to replace those who had escaped, died, or served in the military. Moreover, the vacant Carib lands were not actually undeveloped. The Caribs had begun to cultivate sugar and tobacco before the outbreak of hostilities. There were strong technical and fiscal arguments for the immediate development of cleared lands, which would decrease in value with every season "by the growth of woods upon them."[52]

Thus, early in 1797, spokesmen for St. Vincent began to press the government for a speedy opening of the vacant Carib lands. St. Vincent's appeal, made by loyal planters who had fought to keep their island under British control, came at a time when the market for sugar was excellent, and on the heels of a major military success in securing the island. It was addressed to a government that had already invested heavily in rebuilding St. Vincent's shattered economy. Potential objections to the expansion of Trinidad on the grounds that it was a new possession, or not definitively British, did not apply at all to St. Vincent. The two islands were analogous only in their peculiar situation as frontier islands with optimal crown lands. Moreover, while Trinidad had hundreds of thousands of acres available, St. Vincent's Carib lands amounted to only ten thousand acres good for sugar and another fifteen thousand usable for cotton, coffee, and livestock, a relatively modest total of twenty-five thousand arable acres. But because of this single shared characteristic of the frontier, both were treated precisely alike. Pitt, who had approved the reconstruction loan of 1795–1796, refused to allow the lands to be opened for development. In the debate on Wilberforce's annual motion for abolition in 1798, both Undersecretary Canning and Pitt himself made it clear "that no new lands were to be cultivated by negroes from Africa, and the Carib lands of St. Vincent were particularly named." [53]

The ensuing years saw the St. Vincent planters engaged in one stratagem after another to secure the opening of the Carib lands. They initially pointed out the inconsistency of closing the Carib acreage to development while holding open the reexport of African slaves, even in enemy Spanish ships through the free ports. They cited the rush of slaves to Demerara, while not a single acre of Carib land was made available even as provision grounds. [54] In desperation, the planters then offered to import only slaves from unproductive estates in the older plantations or from other islands. Pitt at first professed his interest. [55] He almost assented to a plan for opening the Carib lands on condition that no Africans would be imported but was deterred by the arguments of Stephen and Wilberforce that the mortality of the Creoles in clearing the lands would be prohibitive and that such restrictions were unworkable. Thereafter, Pitt lapsed into stubborn silence while the abolitionists maintained constant vigilance. [56]

During the whole boom period of 1797–1799, not an acre of the vacant land was yielded up by the crown for cultivation. Finally, with the advent of Prime Minister Addington, it appeared that St. Vincent's moment had arrived. Sir William Young, agent for St. Vincent, submitted documents on the case on August 3, 1801, and Addington gave his own views on the subject two days later. On September 26 the new colonial secretary, Lord Hobart, declared himself in favor of immediate settlement. The following day Addington also gave his approval, and by

October 15 the king had done likewise. By November, Young was assured that the approval would leave "in the next packet" sent to the West Indies. Thus, within two weeks of the signing of the preliminaries of peace on October 1, 1801, the colonial secretary, the prime minister, and the king had all assented to the immediate development of the Carib lands. Sir William was even verbally authorized to get in touch with the merchants of the City of London "for publicity and credits." A plan of sale was circulated in the City and in the Leeward Islands. Addington intended to place no restrictions whatever on the importation of African slaves. The Carib lands stood on the brink of a land and slave rush.[57]

Suddenly, the machinery of government stopped. No written authorization was ever sent. A full year later Young could still get no explanation from the prime minister, except that "great difficulties had arisen in respect to that subject, the nature of which he [Addington] declined entering into, and that he could make no other communications at present in respect to such measure."[58] Addington was more convinced than ever of "the richness of the island and its value," but even Young's assurances that its extraordinary fertility would mean that capital would not be drained from the metropolis, that few Africans would be needed, and that the government would gain £200,000 more per year, availed nothing. Young had to depart without permission and without hope. The reversal was due to an abolitionist counterattack. They had succeeded, with Pitt's help, in fusing the question of St. Vincent with that of Trinidad, and both with the question of general abolition.[59]

Far from dampening the abolitionist campaign, the new slaving opportunities, combined with peak imports in British ships in 1797–1799, actually triggered the most determined offensive by the abolitionists since 1792 against further expansion of the slave trade. They rushed from point to point, attempting to build dikes against the rising tide. They failed, in the sense that at the opening of the nineteenth century the British slave trade was still larger than it had been at the opening of the campaign in 1787. But they succeeded in reducing, by regulatory legislation, the number of slaves moving from Africa to the New World in British ships. Equally important, the abolitionists, with or without the West Indians, had also restricted the number of frontiers that could be cleared by African labor under the British flag. They succeeded in doing so when the economic prospects for slave-grown products had never been so bright for so long. Without a single argument from either mercantilist or classical political economy operating steadily in their favor, they had fought the slave system to a standstill in the battle of the frontiers. In the course of doing so they had inadvertently discovered their incremental strategy for the final victory.

The most impressive thing about these three cases is not what they reveal individually about elements of the clash between political and economic forces over the frontier, but what they imply collectively about the whole process of abolition. Whether the frontiers were in cotton or in sugar, whether their status was British or conquered, whether they were large or small, whether supported by old slave capital or new, whether the market was good, indifferent, or bad, their fates were all sealed within a few short years. There were no pardons and no reprieves. In the variegated and mutable economic world of the last decade before abolition, the process of closure was cumulative and durable.

7

Economic Conjuncture and Abolition Bills, 1791–1806

The relation of short-term economic situations to the dynamics of abolition constitute a special category of applied economic determinism in *Capitalism and Slavery*. Williams's specific applications of the theory are by no means as widely accepted as is his secular analysis. Nevertheless, his working assumptions about the relation of political behavior to short-term economic motivation have made sufficient scholarly inroads to warrant separate analysis. Such scrutiny also provides another opportunity to test the validity of the theory at different moments between the beginning of organized abolitionism and its triumph in 1807.

Specific abolitionist political initiatives are portrayed by Williams as rational responses by the metropolis, designed to rectify the maladjustments of a rigid and inefficient mode of production to the requirements of the market.[1] The extreme formulation is provided by Williams in relation to the final abolition bill: "overproduction in 1807 demanded abolition; overproduction in 1833 demanded emancipation."[2] Others, while avoiding such an arresting but inflexible formula, nevertheless argue that the force of market (or mercantilist) premises pointed naturally to abolition, even if they did not "demand" it. The extreme form, and its market-plus or mercantilist-plus versions, require separate consideration.

As in the long-run analysis, Williams explains political behavior in terms of men operating in the framework of two alternative political economies. In the first framework, abolitionist initiatives and victories are logically explicable as laissez-faire reactions to the signals of the market. The abolition act of 1807 was one such response. In the second case, abolitionist victories are supposedly a form of economic warfare against

113

presumed rivals. The order-in-council of 1805 and the abolition of the British foreign slave trade are instances of this mode of response. There is no point in analyzing the context of abolition at every moment between 1787 and 1807. Certain moments are exceptionally good ones for attempting to test the conjuncture of economic and political events. We choose them because they represented high points in the political mobilization against the slave trade and are the principal focus of historical scholarship.

1791-1792

The years 1791-1792 afford an excellent moment to assess the role of the market factor in abolition. In 1791, the House of Commons clearly rejected Wilberforce's first abolition bill. Just one year later, the House reversed itself, deciding that the slave trade ought to be abolished, and chose 1796 as the date of final abolition. The votes of April 1792 were thereafter to be the cornerstone of all abolitionist arguments.[3] We have a stark juxtaposition of consecutive rejection and acceptance. If the economic background of abolition is linked to its political fortunes, one might optimally expect a market situation generally favorable to the slave colonies in 1791, and at least a perceptible deterioration of that situation by the end of 1791 or the beginning of 1792. One would then have a validating empirical congruity between political and economic change.

The first condition of both a favorable staple market and an unfavorable outcome for abolition fits the situation of 1791 perfectly. In 1791 prices were rising. The planters' net proceeds in 1783-1788 were £3.0 million. In 1790 they rose to £4.6 million. In 1791 they reached £5.1 million. It was observed that the West Indian merchants had raised no recent complaints about the sugar market and were satisfied with the prices of the late 1780s, not to mention the sharp rise of 1790 and after.[4] The slave trade itself had likewise grown in each successive year since 1789 and was progressing toward an all-time peak in 1791. The British tropical trade had never been in a more buoyant mood. The British slave system was beginning to feel the effect of French colonial disorder on the market, even before its great denouement in St. Domingue.[5] In these terms 1791 was certainly not a likely year for a positive vote for abolition, and Parliament replied negatively to Wilberforce. On April 19, 1791, the House of Commons, after lengthy debate, rejected the first abolition bill by the decisive margin of 163 to 88, despite the backing of its two principal leaders, Pitt and Fox.

However, even in 1791, when a lively market was reinforced by a peak antiabolition vote in Parliament, when toasts were drunk to the trade in Liverpool, and church bells were rung in Bristol, the British polity did not deliriously abandon itself to the perpetuity of the slave system. Within one month of its defeat of abolition, Parliament voted overwhelmingly to grant a charter for the founding of a free labor colony at Sierra Leone on the African coast. The colony had a double function, recognized by all sides in the debate. It was intended to prohibit the operation or support of the slave trade in the land directly under the colony's jurisdiction, and it was to become an oasis of abolition in the heart of the slave coast.[6]

Even more important, in economic perspective, the new colony was intended to be an experiment against both the slave trade and slavery. It was to prove Adam Smith's principle, that free labor was economically superior to slave labor, on the African coast. A few West Indians and allied imperialists opposed the charter, but other antiabolitionists supported it on precisely those grounds. Alderman Watson of London, who had voted against abolition and did not believe Africa could be profitably cultivated, insisted that if there were men enterprising enough to venture their capital, they should not be denied a fair trial. He declared that he would be happy to admit his error if the venture succeeded.[7] The Sierra Leone bill, supported in these capitalistic terms, attracted overwhelming support, and passed by a vote of 87 to 9. By the following spring, and the second vote on abolition, £200,000 had already been subscribed to the chartered company.

Thus, while caution prevailed against interfering with the slave trade, an overwhelming proportion of the members of Parliament were willing to sanction new economic alternatives, not only to the trade, but to slavery itself, in the spirit of laissez-faire. The metropolis was not committed *a priori* to a single form of tropical labor,[8] nor was it adverse to seeing Africa reduce the West Indian primacy in staples by a victory in the market place. However, neither the imaginative abolitionist "customer counting" of 50 million African consumers nor the promotional claims of tropical exuberance had been accepted without reservation. The Parliament of 1791 seemed both cautious about the present and open about the future. Their action was very much in the traditional mold.

The vote of 1791, however, must be evaluated principally against the vote and events of the following year. After a debate which ran through the night of April 2–3, 1792, the House of Commons reversed itself and resolved, 230 to 85, that the slave trade should be gradually abolished. On April 27, it designated January 1, 1796, as the date of total abolition. If most members were influenced by the prosperous economic picture of 1791 in voting against abolition, how are we to explain the reversal of 1792? A change in the market did occur, but in precisely the opposite direction from that which would be inferred from the political sequence.

The most important Caribbean event between the votes of April 1791 and April 1792 was the massive slave uprising in St. Domingue in the summer of 1791. The details of its progress reached Britain in October. The rest of the French colonial system was seething as well. A drop in production was expected everywhere. Even before the climax of the French troubles, it was obvious that the Continental market was opening up to British sugar. The St. Domingue explosion meant that the British colonies were offered an unparalleled opportunity to regain the ascendency in sugar they had lost over sixty years before. While ships were leaving the St. Domingue ports empty, Jamaica's crop promised to be excellent.[9] Speculation on the market intensified. There were worried suggestions that the price of sugar, which had already been rising steadily for eighteen months before the revolution, should be regulated, as wheat was. Prices rose alarmingly on all tropical produce.[10] By January 1792, cotton prices had doubled and coffee had risen almost 50 percent above the level of the previous spring.

The price rise was an international phenomenon. In January 1792 sugar riots broke out in Paris. Three principal sugar houses were broken into and two more were burned. In the traditional manner, the seized sugar was sold on the spot at the price demanded by the Parisian crowd.[11] If the reaction to the revolt at St. Domingue produced serious turbulence in Paris, anger against the scarcity of sugar took other forms in Britain. Accusations of monopoly profits and hoarding by wholesalers and refiners were made. But the foreign trade reports told the basic tale. British exports of raw and refined sugar rose from 14 percent of imports in 1788 to 23 percent in 1791 and to almost one-third in 1792. Public meetings demanded investigations and a limitation on British sugar reexports.

While even soaring prices could produce no immediate solution to short supply at the end of 1791, the public imagination attempted to fill the gap between supply and demand and to drive down the price. As with more recent shortages, the entire planet was sifted for substitutes. Maple sugar in North America, it was claimed, would soon end the sugar shortage and reduce the need for West Indian slave labor. British patriotism produced other candidates. A sturdy native tree, the birch, was hailed by "some curious persons in the North of England" for its juice, which was "so much more copious and sweet than that of the maple tree in America."[12] "When the object is considered," concluded one provincial proabolitionist newspaper, "he must be entitled to the *birch* who would refuse to adopt it." From the more staid south of England came another strategy. The Kentish Society, meeting early in 1792, resolved to offer a bounty to whoever raised the most bees by the following May.[13]

Less parochial minds roamed beyond the confines of the Anglo-Saxon world. Serious consideration began to be given to encouragement of sugar production in the East. Advertisements for small shipments of "free sugar" from India appeared throughout Britain, although it was recognized that India offered no solution to the immediate problem.[14] The colonization experiments at Sierra Leone and Bulam on the coast of Africa, which were about to be launched, now incorporated plans for immediate sugar production. In 1793 Sierra Leone was scheduled to have 2000 acres in cane. The tropics dependent on slave or convict labor were not disdained. Careful note was taken of the potential of the French slave colonies in the Indian Ocean. There were rumors of planned sugar establishments in the Pacific islands and in Britain's new Australian colony. The geographic, thermal, and imaginative limits were reached in an item published in the *Stanford Mercury* on January 13, 1792. It described a process by which Siberians, on "the frontiers of Irkutz, beyond the lake Baikal," freeze-dried their milk, producing a powdery substance of a saccharine taste, "which may be used instead of sugar."[15]

Never had it been so self-evident that Europe was prepared to absorb everything that the British slave colonies could produce. In the winter and spring of 1792, there were simply no abundant or competitive alternatives to slave-grown sugar. The market for West Indian cotton likewise improved, with prices in early 1792 rising to levels that were higher than at any time since 1786. The link with the slave trade, at a moment when foreign supplies were threatened, was not overlooked by those stressing the imperial interest in cotton expansion.[16]

This optimum moment for new staple expansion was reflected in the slave trade itself. The British slave trade, which had probably hit an all-time peak in 1791, obviously rushed toward a new record during 1792. Almost a fifth more Africans were transported in 1792 than in 1791. Profits from the slave trade were also apparently at an all-time high. One prominent trader wrote that "everything in the shape of a ship that can be come at is fitting out for Africa and I suppose the money made by the voyages just now concluded exceeds anything ever known.[17] The value of West Indian land as well as labor rose. The crops of many of the islands were expected to be good.[18] At the beginning of 1792 only the sugar refiners, who were suffering from a severe shortage of supplies, were really disgruntled. They, of course, had no motive whatsoever to curtail the labor supply to the British West Indies, since their chief concern was to get more sugar, not less, or to block the reexport of raw colonial produce to the Continent. On the other hand, the British planters had leaped in a single year from being beneficiaries of the mercantilist monopoly to being the sector most likely to benefit by free trade. By extension, any arguments against the sugar monopoly reinforced the structural arguments for the continuation of the British slave trade in 1792.

Within a system tied to normal economic incentives, it is difficult to see how 1792, of all years, should have been a good year for parliamentary abolition. The terrain is so unfavorable to a market or even a market-plus explanation that no attempt has ever been made to link the overwhelming vote of April 3, 1792, to laissez-faire interests or ideology. Laissez-faire and abolition were never so far apart. However, one account of 1792, inspired by Williams, shows the difficulties encountered in explaining the vote in mercantilist terms as well. Michael Craton, after briefly referring to the reversal of 1792 in terms of the impact of mass petitions, continues: "It is almost certain, moreover, that a fair number of non-philanthropic MPs were swayed to vote for abolition in the belief that ending the British slave trade would actually damage the French colonies more than the British; for it was commonly held that not only were St. Domingue, Martinique and Guadeloupe expanding rapidly but were also heavily dependent on slaves carried in British ships."[19]

This is an example of the conscientious attempt to preserve a balanced explanation by adhering to the recipe of one part Williams, one part Wilberforce. The assurance of the statement is misleading. William Pitt made the only direct allusion during the debate to French colonial imports. He referred, in the past tense, to "St. Domingo, an island which used to take three-fourths of all the slaves required by the colonies of France."[20] With nearly half of St. Domingue already destroyed by a scorched-earth servile war, and the other islands in the throes of civil conflict, no other tense was appropriate. Craton does refer in passing to the "revolution in France (which seemed likely not only to end the French slave trade but slavery itself)"[21] as a principal ingredient of the movement for abolition. Given this statement, the assumption of a common belief that the British trade principally aided the French colonies is untenable.

Moreover, the "fair number of non-philanthropic MPs" who voted on the basis of that "common" belief is as conjectural as their supposed motive. Since there is no voting list, we cannot know whether there were two or two hundred nonphilanthropists voting for abolition, let alone whether they voted for the particular reason cited in the statement.[22] The speeches themselves provide no evidence whatsoever that the belief exerted a powerful impulse for anyone to vote for abolition nor that it even existed. Not a single member who spoke during the long night of April 2–3, whether for or against abolition, so much as referred to the supposed superior advantage reaped by the French colonies from the British trade.[23]

There is no evidence that any nonabolitionist MPs conceived of the French colonies as areas whose growth was detrimental to the British colonies even *prior* to the St. Domingue revolution. It was not mentioned as an issue in the debate of 1791, when it would have been more plausible to regard the French system as a principal beneficiary of the British trade. In light of our discussion in chapter 4 the absence of the subject is to be expected. The abolitionists, of course, had an argument other than economic rivalry to offer in 1792. The slave trade had not relatively favored the French colonies: every slave carried into the islands was a seed of insurrection.[24] If nonabolitionists had accepted this assessment of the slave trade, they would have voted not for gradual, but for immediate abolition, at least to their own colonies.

The only nonabolitionist allusion to the British foreign trade in 1791–1792 lends further credence to our point. It was made by Henry Dundas three weeks after the debate of April 2–3, where he had played a crucial role in switching the House from immediate to gradual abolition. In a ploy to delay abolition to the British colonies as long as possible, Dundas, on April 27, proposed the immediate abolition of the foreign trade, as part of his "plan" for gradual abolition.[25] Attempting to maximize the sacrifice thereby entailed, he cited the foreign slave-trade statistics— *before* the cataclysm. This particular sacrifice, however, had already occurred as the first fruits of the French slave uprising. Even then Dundas made no reference to the French advantage from its former purchase of British-carried slaves. The fundamental circumstantial fact remains that never before in the eighteenth century did the French colonies seem less likely to be serious rivals to the British, either in the market or the mercantilist sense. Not only laissez-faire, but the whole capitalist lure of windfall profits argued against abolition in 1792.

1797–1802

Other periods prior to the final abolitionist victories in 1806–1807 provide equally fertile grounds for evaluating Williams's basic approach. Although they have received almost no serious attention from historians of abolition, we mention them because the market existed both after 1791–1792 and before 1806–1807 and should therefore be one of the constants in interpretations which rely on *Capitalism and Slavery*.

The period 1798–1799 is an especially interesting moment for testing market or market-plus accounts of abolition. These years marked the absolute pinnacle of the British trade. The British not only accounted for half the total transatlantic slave trade, but had reduced their middle passage mortality rate by half in a single decade. The preabolition peak in the value of British exports to Africa reached a record in 1799 which would stand for another forty years. The price of sugar in Europe also reached extraordinary heights and maintained an unusually steady plateau from late 1795 through the first half of 1799. The price of all tropical products, including coffee and cotton, followed a similar pattern, rising almost uninterruptedly between 1797 and 1799. The boom was based principally on demand from the Continent, virually at peace between 1797 and 1799. Moreover, tropical prices remained high at a moment when the price of metropolitan commodities was moving downward. This further enhanced the inclination to divert domestic capital to slave agriculture. By 1798–1799 the price of corn had fallen 50 percent from 1795–1796, while tropical staples had risen "some a little less, and some a great deal more than 100 percent."[26]

At the same time, the slave colonies were more secure than at any time since the spring of 1794, when the entire French Caribbean had fallen momentarily into British hands. Trinidad, Demerara, Berbice, and Surinam were conquered. The outlook for the British West Indies was one of internal tranquillity, military security, and territorial expansion, all combined with the excellent consumer market in Europe and the abundance of available capital in Britain. It is no wonder that the slave trade climaxed in 1798–1799.

By all the measures of imperial significance the slave economies as a whole stood at all-time peaks in 1798–1799. The value of British colonial coffee exports in 1798–1799 stood at five times the 1792–1793 figure. The value of sugar imports broke all previous records in both 1798 and 1799. The value of cotton imports, after failing to repeat the record level of 1792 throughout the rest of the decade, finally and decisively broke through in 1799. The tale was the same in terms of overall West Indian trade with Britain: British exports to the West Indies represented successive record-breaking years in 1798 and 1799. Not one area whose trade was based to a considerable extent on slavery or the slave trade (Africa, the United States, the British West Indies, Latin America) failed to purchase a record amount of British goods in 1798 or 1799. At the same time, the value of British trade to both southern Europe and Asia in the early nineties stood at figures well below their peaks. Even the northern

European trade was growing less rapidly from 1791–1792 to 1798–1799 than that of the British West Indies. These were surely slavery's most expansive moments in an expansive decade.[27] Yet precisely during these two years the slave trade was attacked on a multitude of fronts. In addition to the usual annual bills for total abolition, a whole series of initiatives was taken, among which we have already discussed the question of Trinidad and St. Vincent, and the slave transportation act of 1799. Quantitatively and otherwise, the achievements and near misses of 1798–1799 constitute the most sustained attack on the slave trade between 1792 and 1804.[28] In terms of either free-market or mercantilist explanations of the process of abolition, these years pose an analytical paradox which has never been discussed with the same attention as the period 1806–1807.

The test can be applied equally well to periods of abolitionist quiescence. There is one period almost identical in market terms to 1807. In 1799–1800 and in 1801–1802 the price of sugar dropped to its lowest point between 1775 and abolition. Coffee and cotton prices followed the same trend, while metropolitan commodities rose. Yet 1800–1802 was as low a point for abolitionist activity as 1805–1807 was high. It is the longest gap in the abolitionist record between 1788 and 1807. The record therefore shows that a June 1806–January 1807 market pattern occurred in 1799–1800 and in 1801–1802 without any parallel abolitionist initiative, let alone triumph.[29]

1806

Given the degree of scholarly attention allotted to the economic nexus of British slavery just prior to abolition, we must focus on that conjuncture with considerable care, dealing first with the mercantilist approach to the bill of 1806 and then with the market approach to total abolition in 1807.

The passage of the foreign abolition bill in 1806 strikes us as the abolitionist initiative most susceptible to explication in terms of economic expediency within the mercantilist framework. Anstey has fully detailed the premises and the initial strategy of the bill's abolitionist sponsors.[30] The government introduced it explicitly as a measure of political economy, based on the need to prevent enemy colonies from taking advantage of the cover of American and European flags. A trade system had evolved to insure a flow of European goods to the French and Spanish colonies, and of their staples to the Continent, despite the fact that the English had swept the Atlantic Ocean of almost all enemy merchant fleets by late 1805.

These colonies, although technically at war, were able to avoid the costs of war insurance and convoys both as producers and consumers. The British colonial trade paradoxically suffered all the inconveniences of war costs, plus the difficulties of having to absorb the risks of forecasting the volatile shifts of Continental ports open to British goods. James Stephen published a book on the subject late in 1805, which was soon the accepted authority on the subject.[31] Carefully calculating the differential advantages, he concluded that both the colonial and metropolitan industries of Britain were paying far more for transportation each way than their rivals were. The West India interest was also able to supply price evidence from the islands to show that while prices for food and provisions at Trinidad were 50 to 250 percent higher than at Martinique, Trinidad's sugar prices were 50 percent lower.[32]

The British slave system was at a significant disadvantage relative to the neutral or enemy colonies. This disadvantage was related not to the comparative productivity or fertility of the British slave islands, but to the comparative handicaps of the British transportation system and marketing facilities.[33] Instead of the metropolis paying the price of "inefficient" colonial production, the colonies were paying the price of high-cost, high-risk, metropolitan transportation. Stephen clearly recognized this when he linked the wounds of the neutral trade to the colonies with damage closer to home: "They [Europeans] supplant even the manufacturers of Manchester, Birmingham and Yorkshire; for the looms and forges of Germany are put into action by the colonial produce of our enemies and are rivaling us [through neutral flags]." American ships were rushing slaves to Cuba. They were glutting La Plata with European imports. The crisis was therefore imperial, not colonial. The progressive evil was to be traced to "this *singular* source," this "present and artificial state of things."[34] Stephen was thus convinced, both before and after abolition, that planters, merchants, and manufacturers were all being hurt.[35] It was simply "enough to raise the charges on [British] commodities so high that all his rivals can undersell him."

The cure was equally clear to Stephen. At the West Indian end, not a single hogshead of "hostile" sugar should pass through to the Continent without having some sort of British toll imposed, equaling the costs of war to the British planters and shippers and canceling the artificial advantage. At the European and African ends of the trade network, Stephen proposed even more drastic measures. Under a British screening system, not a single article (obviously slaves) should be licensed to enter foreign colonies that could serve to extend their existing scale of cultivation. The production of Cuba, like that of Jamaica or Demerara, had doubled and could be doubled again.[36] In this manner Stephen indicated that part of a general action against the neutral trade might include a total blockade of the foreign slave trade. (It is clear, however, that the logic of competition could be used as effectively by antiabolitionists to argue for the postponement of any part of British abolition until the neutral slave trade had also been ended.)

The foreign abolition bill was submitted to Parliament in April–May 1806 under a mercantilist rationale for restraining the growth of rivals. The interpretation of foreign abolition as part of a protectionist strategy in favor of British slavery or imperial economic interests would be quite convincing if the bill had been presented as an element of a grand strategy of foreign colonial semiblockade as outlined by Stephen. Neither the necessary supporting legislation nor even a supporting strategy was suggested in 1806 because the Fox-Grenville government was not yet committed in that direction. It was the following government that fully embraced the economic war plan, in the summer of 1807, and in response to the Continental blockade.

As a measure against rivals, abolition moved in direct contradiction to trade policy toward foreign colonies in 1806. This policy designated the foreign colonies as economic partners, exempted from belligerent status by executive order in 1804 and legislative enactment in 1805. The contradiction between abolition and general trade policy was not lost on those opposing the bill.[37] The best evidence that foreign abolition was not even implicitly part of a mercantilist grand design is Grenville's attitude toward Trinidad within days after the major vote in the Lords. The slave trade to that colony had already been severely curtailed by the freezing of the crown lands. But established planters continued to purchase Africans for estates already in being at the moment of British capture. Grenville proposed an executive order similar to that of August 1805, restricting imports of slaves to Trinidad. Any mercantilist advantage to be derived from the restriction of the slave trade to British colonies was to be immediately foregone by Trinidad. Grenville scrapped the plan only when informed that the trade to any *de jure* British colony was beyond the reach of such administrative action.[38]

The lack of a systematic economic strategy by the government in 1806 is not decisive. It could be very plausibly argued that the majority of those who voted for the bill had a strong implicit commitment to any element of the mercantilist program in time of severe economic warfare. A greater difficulty arises from the immediately subsequent legislative behavior of Parliament. If any significant number of MPs voted for foreign abolition principally to protect the empire's slave colonies rather than for humanitarian reasons, where were they one month after the passage of that bill, when a total abolition resolution was introduced by the same government and carried overwhelmingly? And where was this group when the same government introduced a bill for total abolition, over the protest of the British colonies, only six months later? A close reading of the debates of 1806 reveals that the abolitionists' "mercantilist" strategy became patently and deliberately less necessary before the bill cleared Parliament, and that the abolitionists had gained no more than a superfluous handful of votes by using the mercantilist argument. Our reading of the debates is that Parliament accepted foreign abolition knowing that it was but the second stage (the order-in-council of 1805 being the first) of a rapid elimination of the entire trade. The bill of 1806 called less for a belief in the mercantilist rationale than for a deliberate suspension of disbelief about abolitionist motives by members of Parliament (see Appendix III).

Closely followed, the economic reasons advanced to account for the passage of the act of 1806 disintegrate in the context of general economic policy. We have suggested that MPs deliberately chose not to apply economic reasoning too rigorously to the question. But even this self-contradictory mercantilism cannot be used to account for the elimination of the slave trade to the *de jure* empire, which added up to almost half the total imports in 1806. For the final kill, the forces of the world market are once more summoned to the field by the decline theory.

8
The Market Mechanism
and Abolition

Overproduction

The first steps in the dismantling of the slave trade occurred at the end of the golden decade of the 1790s. But total abolition did not come until seven years after the St. Domingue windfall ended. The economic context of the deathblow therefore calls for careful consideration. Williams attempts to explain the final act of abolition as a response to market conditions. Tempted by the French colonial turmoil after 1791, the British planters overextended themselves in purchasing slaves and in shifting to strains of cane which increased sugar yields per acre. Beginning with 1799, concludes the decline account, overproduction was the constant and increasing bane of the British West Indies. "Overproduction demanded abolition," in the sense that abolition was the "easiest way to limit superfluous production."[1] The decline theory leaves the meaning of overproduction undefined.[2] It is sufficient that it is a term implying to all who use it a specific relationship between changes in supply and in demand.[3] The key to understanding the tropical sugar gluts in Britain between 1799 and 1807, however, is to be found neither in West Indian production nor in European consumption, but in the mechanism of transatlantic shipment and distribution.

The crucial empirical premise of the overproduction thesis is the assertion that production increased faster than demand.[4] To test this premise we can repeat our world sugar census of *1787* in table 11 for the two periods of glut after 1799 to see how the figures accord with the assertion. The first period, 1800–1801, immediately follows the bursting of the sugar bubble in 1799. The second covers the last moment immediately preceding total abolition, 1805–1806. The results are presented

125

in table 24. It would appear that in 1800–1801 total North Atlantic sugar imports had only just recovered their old regime level.[5] By 1805–1806 the figure stood about 9.5 percent higher than in *1787*. The period between *1787* and 1806 was the flattest segment of a supply curve which ascended steadily from the middle of the eighteenth century to the end of the nineteenth.

The most interesting information about the sugar market from *1787* to 1806, however, is not in the aggregate figures for the North Atlantic. There was a dramatic shift in consumption patterns between Britain and the rest of Europe. Between *1787* and 1805–1806 the British increased their consumption of sugar by over one-third. They also increased their share of North Atlantic imports from 27 to 39 percent. During this same period, continental Europe's purchases of sugar dropped by more than one-fifth, while its share of North Atlantic imports decreased from almost two-thirds to just one-half (see table 25). In other words, Britain, with less than one-tenth of the population of the Continent, was consuming four-fifths as much sugar as the mainland in 1805–1806. If one examines the period 1800–1806 more minutely, it is also evident that abolition occurred not at a peak moment of British consumption, but when her imports, both absolutely and relatively, had slipped downward. British sugar imports actually fell by 10 percent between 1799–1802 and 1803–1806.

The volatility of retained imports from year to year was as significant as the average consumption over a series of years. The fact that Britain's per capita sweet tooth could rise or fall by over one-third from one year to the next should make one wary of using any one year's import figures as indicators of the magnitude of British demand. Consumption patterns depended on an equally erratic pattern of war-linked imports and exports. In the partially peaceful biennium of 1802–1803, reexports soared to an unprecedented 45 percent of imports. Thereafter, an increasing percentage of British sugar stayed at home, as the French blockade tightened. Domestic wholesale prices partially, but only partially, reflected the re-export market. The price of sugar, exclusive of duties, reached its lowest quotation in decades between mid-1799 and the end of 1802, rose through 1805, and then moved downward.[6]

How prepared was the metropolitan system to deal with such violent war-related fluctuations? British sugar duties reinforced rather than soft-ened the blows of war and prevented the purchase price paid by domestic consumers from fully reflecting the changing West Indian price. At the outbreak of the war in France in 1793, for example, a British grocer paid an average of 56.2 shillings per cwt. of sugar, plus 15 shillings in

TABLE 24: SUGAR IMPORTS TO THE NORTH ATLANTIC, *1787*–1806 (in tons, muscovado equivalent)

	1787	1800–1801 (War)	1802 (Peace)	1805–1806 (War)
Total North Atlantic	289,300	286,750	307,350	316,920
U.S.A.	–	62,470	46,750	95,120ᵃ
Portugal	–	45,750	45,750	46,600
Britain	–	178,530	214,850	175,200
Total European Continent	186,040	155,910	177,140	158,250
Percent via Britain	2%	38%	53%	29%
European Share of North Atlantic market	64%	54%	58%	50%

Sources: See Appendix II and table 25.
a. Includes estimated Louisiana export.

TABLE 25: BRITISH SUGAR IMPORTS AND REEXPORTS, 1798–1806 (in tons)

	Imported	Reexported	Percent Reexported (excluding Ireland)
1798	134,993	52,349	38.8
1799	169,549	20,368	12.0
1800	158,224	64,939	41.0
1801	198,828	54,008	27.2
1802	214,854	93,194	43.4
1803	159,295	77,082	48.4
1804	162,415	47,060	28.9
1805	158,939	46,832	29.5
1806	190,759	43,932	23.0

Source: PP 1808 (IV), report from the Committee on the Commercial State of the West India Colonies.

duty, for a total price of 71.2 shillings.[7] In January of 1806, he paid 48.5 shillings, plus 27.0 shillings in duty, for a total price of 75.5 shillings. While the delivered price net of duty had dropped almost 14 percent, the price paid by grocers had risen over 23 percent. In 1793 the sugar duty represented less than one-quarter of the price. In 1805 it amounted to more than one-third. A net of duty price fall from 1793 to 1806 was thus converted into a gross price increase.

Lower prices would be expected to have increased sugar demand, not only because of the response within each class, but also because there was a considerable gap between the sugar consumption of different income groups.[8] The doubling of British sugar consumption following the rapid elimination of import duties after 1845 is usually also taken as evidence that there was considerable price elasticity of demand for that product.[9] While suggestive, this phenomenal increase in consumption postdated abolition by almost fifty years. We do have a parallel contemporary example, however, in the case of another tropical staple. Since coffee was far less important than sugar as a source of revenue, it was possible for the government to take greater risks in lowering the coffee duty to increase domestic demand. Coffee followed a pattern similar to that of sugar before 1807. A glut began in 1806 and persisted through 1807–1808. The lowering of the duty on coffee for domestic use in 1808 was a response to this situation. In 1809 British coffee consumption rose 760 percent over the previous year. For the period 1808–1813 it held at 522 percent of the previous five-year average.[10] While this experiment did not indicate exactly how sugar would have responded to an analogous policy, it shows that there was a domestic alternative to the Continental shutdown, and that it was used for a tropical product. In fact, there were more alternatives available to deal with a blockade of sugar than of coffee.

Only by treating the metropolitan market in strict isolation, and by ignoring the existence of war and sugar duties, can one make out a case for periodic, although not systematic, overproduction of sugar between 1799 and 1807. For studying market forces this would be the most artificial of contrivances, ignoring both the implications of the annual trade flows and the perceptions of contemporaries. British sugar production no longer went almost exclusively for domestic consumption. It was linked to a Continental competitive market which absorbed almost half of Britain's imported sugar in the peace interlude of Amiens (1802–1803),[11] and returned to that pattern with the return of peace in 1814. The European market was clearly hungry for West Indian sugar throughout the period 1799–1807. At the close of the French revolutionary wars in 1802, continental European consumption stood at about 163,000 tons (see table 24). This represented a decline of 12 percent, or 23,000 tons from *1787*. Europe's import figure of 158,250 tons in 1805–1806, on the eve of abolition, not only represented a drop of over 21 percent from its level of *1787* but a drop of over 10 percent from its 1802 level.

The low figure for 1805–1806 is all the more impressive if one considers that Europe's population was growing rapidly between *1787* and 1806. In many parts of Europe the increase was greater than 1 percent per year. If we ignore the very exceptional case of the Netherlands, and use the increase in the three other most sluggish societies as a minimal figure for estimating Europe's growth between *1787* and 1806, the result is an increase of about 9 percent.[12] Since continental Europe imported around 186,000 tons of sugar in *1787,* it should have been capable of absorbing almost 203,000 tons per year in 1806, at the same consumption rate per capita. Therefore the 158,250 tons received by Europe in 1805–1806 was about 22.0 percent less sugar per capita than Europe had absorbed with unimpeded distribution in *1787.* If postwar consumption may be taken as another indicator of the magnitude of demand in the early nineteenth century, we need only add that by 1823, after less than a decade of peace, Continental consumption reached 310,000 tons,[13] equal to the entire North Atlantic supply fifteen years before.

On the eve of the penultimate abolitionist thrusts of 1805–1806 in Britain, the French were apparently totally optimistic about the European market for sugar and coffee and the necessity of further expansion through the African slave trade. In 1788, according to their official figures, the kingdom of France imported 106,400 gross tons of sugar (muscovado), 37,900 tons of coffee, and 4,850 tons of cotton from their colonies, in French ships. In 1806 the far larger French Empire imported 29,450 tons of sugar (down 72.3 percent), 8,300 tons of coffee (down 78.1 percent), and 9,400 tons of cotton (up 94 percent), in *all* ships. The bulk of French colonial staples were now imported indirectly via Dutch, American, and Portuguese ports. In the French colonies sugar was still the most alluring crop for those who could afford to make the shift. Martinique's prefect reported that the slave population had risen from 73,400 to 79,800 between 1788 and 1805. The sugar crop had risen by exactly one-third. The coffee harvest, on the other hand, fell by one-fourth. "Sugar stands almost alone in the dictionary of our creoles," concluded the prefect in June 1805. Slave prices had doubled since the Revolution. "It will be necessary," wrote Admiral Villaret, after touring the island, "to give the greatest encouragement to the Negro trade the moment peace returns: the colony could easily absorb twenty thousand Negroes more. There are few inhabitants who are not convinced that, even without new lands, they could use a third more Negroes than they possess."[14]

Another development in the European search for sugar highlights the fact that "overproduction" is an Anglocentric view of the sugar market in 1806. In 1805–1806, Europe's sugar supply depended almost exclusively on slave-importing colonies. The development of European beet sugar was clearly linked to difficulties in obtaining sugar from the West Indies. The first beet sugar factory was commissioned in Germany in 1799, but production was sporadic until after the battle of Jena in 1806. Beet sugar was further encouraged as a consequence of British retaliation to the Continental blockade of British goods beginning in July 1807.

The sugar beet maintained a position on the Continent only just as long as the blockade endured.[15] Maple sugar also began to be listed as a separate export item in the trade reports of the United States in 1805.

European sugar consumption was clearly reduced by the war, while British consumption was artificially increased from the same cause, although British demand was also restrained by high import duties. The impact may be seen by comparing the average price of sugar in Western Europe and in Britain. Until the French conquest of the Netherlands in 1795, the price of sugar and sugar derivatives in Amsterdam was substantially lower than in London. During the war periods 1797–1800 and 1804–1806, the price of sugar in Amsterdam was over 40 percent above the London average. The general result of the French wars was thus to reverse the relative price relationship on both sides of the North Sea. By 1806 the price of Amsterdam sugar was almost three times its 1788 average, while British sugar was up only 10 percent in nominal terms. When British abolition went into effect two years later, sugar in Amsterdam and Paris was selling at twice the London rate. The price differential was to become several times greater before the end of the war.[16]

Overproduction and Abolition in 1807

Having considered the thesis of North Atlantic overproduction for the whole period after 1799, we can now ask the narrower, short-run question. Granting that the slave trade was not abolished because of, or in conjunction with, a system which was overproducing for its normal market, can we still say that the slave trade was abolished between 1805 and 1807 because the abnormal market temporarily required it or made it logical? The short-term question must be approached as it was for 1791–1792. One should bear in mind that this short-run explanation is a radical reversal of the long-run explanation of the operation of capitalist economic forces hostile to slavery. Abolition, in that framework, is presented as a process of discarding a parasitic economic system. In this portion of the theory the process becomes a rational effort, by abolitionists and others, to save that system from its own inability to respond to the market at a critical moment. The permanent enemies of slavery become its temporary saviors.

West Indian sugar prices, after reaching a low of 34 shillings per cwt. in 1802, climbed almost steadily through the end of 1804, and averaged over 50 shillings per cwt. as late as October 1805. Sugar in 1804–1805 was 50 percent higher than in 1802, while average prices for domestic commodities rose less than 5 percent. Coffee, as late as the beginning of 1806 was selling at prices 50 percent higher than their 1802 level. At the end of 1805 both the amount of sugar imported into London and the uncleared sugar were down 5 percent from the previous year-end inventory. At the beginning of 1806 there was still no concern about a glut in the market.[17]

In the spring of 1806 sugar and coffee prices began to sag seriously. The crisis of 1807 was created less on the cane fields of the British West Indies than on the battlefields of Europe. While Trafalgar removed all threats to the sugar supply, Austerlitz, Jena, and Eylau insured an increasingly worsening European market. The English found their outlets drying up. The German market crumbled during 1806. It was no accident that a sharp fall in British sugar prices in 1806 coincided with the war in Germany. Prussian armies closed Hamburg to British shipping in the spring of 1806, a situation which was only worsened by the French takeover of the city following Jena.[18] Toward the end of 1806, Napoleon's Berlin decrees attempted to cut Britain off entirely from the western and central European markets. Sugar backed up in the warehouses and on the docks of London and Liverpool. Reexports to Europe dropped to a seven-year low. The market price of sugar reached its lowest point in over three years. An investigation to consider immediate parliamentary relief was set in motion in December 1806.

We thus have a clear correlation between the final vote on abolition and a declining British market price for sugar. Before any conclusions about overproduction are drawn even from this vote, we must note three things. First, the crisis at the beginning of 1807 had been briefer in duration than two similar dips, in 1799–1800 and 1801–1802. Parliament still believed it was dealing with a short-term wartime contingency. The official parliamentary investigation committee declared, just as the final abolition debate opened in the Commons, that "there seems no ground whatever to believe that this increased quantity of sugar in hand is owing to any cause except the diminution of the demand for raw and refined sugars . . . for Foreign Markets."[19] The committee characterized the problem as a short-term one, beyond any immediate power of imperial remedy. Even at the twelfth hour for abolition, and at the worst moment in three years for the West Indian trade, no thought of curtailing supply entered into the deliberations of the committee. Not only did the Parliamentary report on West Indian commerce ignore the slave trade as an element in the problem; all those afterward did so as well.

Nor was there any reason for singling out tropical staples as oversupplied in January 1807. Napoleon's blockade and his confiscation decrees of October and November 1806 had resulted in an almost complete halt in all British exports to the Continent.[20] The most decisive evidence that overproduction was not considered to be a problem faced by the colonies comes from the record of Parliament's proceedings. At the moment the abolition debate was approaching its climax, the problem of imperial trade was the subject of extensive discussions.[21] They concerned the appropriate response to the Continental blockade, to the neutral carrying trade, and to the continuing flow of exports from enemy colonies to Europe. British colonial production was of course one of the major elements in the discussion. Not a single speaker even referred to the cause of the crisis as lying at the supply end of the network. With Parliament moving from imperial political economy on one day to abolition the next, such an aversion from a topic which looms so large in subsequent historical interpretation is curious. To account for such an oversight we must conclude that either contemporaries did not see the problem in the light of overproduction at all, or that colonial overproduction was too obvious to need any mention. However, at a moment when many MPs were pointing toward the blockade, American shipping, and the enemy colonies as the principal sources of British colonial difficulties, someone with an interest in deflecting the implicit threat to the American or foreign tropical trades would have insisted strenuously on the obvious alternative. Since there were such interests, and they did not so argue, we are inclined to accept the total absence of the idea of overproduction from the debate as evidence of its absence in perception.

The hard-core abolitionists were not subscribers to a tropical over-production theory. The African Institution, established just as abolition was being implemented, immediately published a study calling for the extension of staple agriculture to every part of that continent. It is equally pertinent to recall that the same ministers who were preparing to submit a final abolition bill to Parliament had just concocted a plan to negotiate for the acquisition of Cuba. This would have poured another 39,000 muscovado-equivalent tons of sugar into British ports.[22] A government which was so eager for the empire to swallow nearly 200,000 more sea-soned slaves at one gulp could hardly have strained, for reasons of over-supply, at the few thousands of Africans imported each year into the *de jure* empire. Nor could overproduction have haunted the imagination of ministers who kept seizing one enemy colony after another while they urged Parliament toward abolition.

British tropical production must also be viewed in the context of the economy of the entire capitalist world at the end of 1806. Bonaparte's decree of blockade and confiscation in November produced a chain reaction of crises. Petitions from the chambers of commerce in port and manufacturing cities of France politely suggested to the emperor that his massive seizures of British imports threatened to destroy their own commercial agents in central Europe. They also warned that the Continental blockade of all "British" exports insured severe reprisals against their only source of transportation for incoming tropical raw materials and outgoing overseas manufactures—the neutral carrying trade.[23]

If the anticipation of British retaliation created fearful foreboding among the French metropolitan capitalists, it brought outright disaster to those in the colonial sector. News of the Berlin decree blighted the prospects of the excellent crop outlook. The staple market vanished. American provisions ships would accept payment only in specie. As hard cash hemorrhaged from the French islands, the planters had to shift land and labor from staples to provisions. British merchants also prudently withheld their tropical produce. The Continent began to starve for tropical raw materials, while the French islands choked with them. Rational calculations of supply and demand became hazardous.

Even the usually obsequious reports of the French administrators traced the crisis of their colonies directly to the flamboyant pronouncement of the Continental blockade in Berlin: "European events, the uncertainties facing the neutrals, their fear of most probable and violent British reprisals against all French overseas possessions, due to the Imperial decree of last November 23, have suspended, and threaten to completely deflect their [neutral] ventures from these islands."[24] Amid such paralysis the French were no more prone to view the sugar, coffee, and cotton now stranded in their colonial ports as "overproduced" than were the British to so regard the staples accumulating in the warehouses of London and Liverpool. For the Continental merchant or consumer, it hardly made any difference whether commodities were bottled up on the island of Martinque or the island of Britain. In the Caribbean, of course, the British planters had one edge over their French neighbors. They still had access to the most important single sector of their market.

However one characterizes the relation of economic to abolitionist pressures in 1807, one must explain the different political responses on opposite sides of the channel. Both the British and French colonies were confronted by a sharp contraction of their market. French colonial produce was, if anything, less vendible. Yet the British permanently prohibited their planters from importing African slaves. The French did not even temporarily suspend that right. British abolition was noted in the official *Moniteur universel,* without further comment or consequence, and attacked elsewhere as simply another strategem by *perfide albion* to lure the French colonial system to its destruction.

In the light of such divergent responses to analogous situations, abolition cannot be identified as an obvious or common sense response to the conjuncture of 1806–1807. Neither was there any obsessional concern in Europe with colonial glut, such that one could cite abolition as a psychological response to a mistakenly perceived situation of "overproduction." This term is one which obscures, rather than illuminates the politico-economic nexus of 1807. It suggests that the glut of 1807 represented the cumulative result of the association between tropical supply and North Atlantic demand, when it actually represented a violent dissociation between the two.

There remains a final alternative to be considered. After rejecting the overproduction thesis for total abolition in 1807, one historian suggests that it might conceivably be more relevant to the foreign abolition. In this coda of the thesis, overproduction constitutes one of the two powerful policy arguments in favor of the act of 1806.[25] The concept, in its strict sense, seems to us to have no firmer foundation in the logic or the rhetoric of the foreign than of the general act. With regard to the market, sugar prices were higher, and the sugar supply lower, at the beginning of 1806, than they were a year later. Both the verbal and statistical evidence presented to Parliament indicates that there was no perception of general glut at the beginning of 1806. In terms of constricting the supply of labor, the foreign act of 1806 was a certified underachiever, guaranteed to have less effect on foreign colonies than an act directed toward the British colonies. It could not effectively remove the neutral slave trade to the foreign West Indies or to Brazil. It was, on the contrary, bound to stimulate that trade. The member for Liverpool claimed that Charleston alone had thirty-seven vessels in the slave trade and that the number could be increased rapidly.[26]

James Stephen quietly conceded this point beforehand when arguing against another assertion, that foreign abolition would materially injure the free port trade: "the Spanish colonies were supplied, as they have been during the last and present War, with Slaves brought directly from Africa, in Neutral Bottoms," at no risk of seizure by English or Spanish cruisers. To that extent, the act could not possibly fulfill the mercantilist and monopolist ends elsewhere adduced in its behalf by the government. In anticipation of just such a stimulus to the neutral trade, a second bill was rushed through Parliament almost immediately after the passage of the foreign act. It specifically prohibited the fitting out of any slave ship, whether British or neutral, which had not previously been in the African trade. The bill was declared to be the more urgent in that "foreign ships will crowd their unfortunate victims to the utmost, in order to profit by the high prices which the prohibition of the foreign slave trade in British ships will inevitably produce in the West India islands during the approaching season."[27] Finally, if general overproduction was to be one of the two powerful arguments for foreign abolition, along with rival-building, it is curious that the government did not argue the point, either as a motive for introducing the bill or for passing it. Stephen, their expert, spoke of gluts in the domestic market. But the possible saturation of the Continental market was referred to only in the future conditional, and it could not be suggested that the British domestic supply of tropical commodities from its own colonies could be effectively reduced by the foreign act. Only insofar as the abolitionists might have succeeded in obfuscating the distinction between the domestic and foreign markets could glut have played any role in the passage of the act.[28] From the text of the debates it is clear that overproduction was as peripheral to the arguments of the spring of 1806 as to those of the following winter.

In the final analysis, it is up to historians who wish to insert the concept of overproduction into the decision for abolition to present evidence for its existence and to explain how it played its assigned role in the world of 1807. The thesis may be simply an uninvestigated variant of the general assumption that slave systems were structurally incapable of responding to the messages of the market.

Beyond all the statistics of supply and prices, or of demand and distribution, and beyond the thrust of the circumstantial evidence, there is a more fundamental structural reason why contemporaries did not consider abolition as a device for short-run production control in 1807, or at any other time. Everyone acquainted with slave production was aware of the phenomenon called "seasoning." Freshly imported slaves required two to three planting seasons to become fully productive members of the work force. The abolition bill presented in 1807 allowed ships to land slaves in the West Indies until March 1808. This meant that the slave system would not fully feel the impact of lost labor recuitment until at least three years after the approval of the measure. Coffee, with its even longer waiting period between planting and harvest, plus its more sustained storage life, was even less responsive to a cutback via abolition. In presenting abolition as a solution to oversupply in January 1807, its supporters would have had to declare that, in order to solve a problem which had lasted for six months and might disappear in six more, they were offering a solution designed to take full effect in no less than thirty-six months. It is no wonder that there were neither serious sellers nor buyers for such a solution in 1807.[29]

Most serious historians of abolition have been far less attracted to

Williams's market interpretation of abolition than to his long-run explanation. If they make a passing reference to overproduction as a general economic precondition of abolition, their detailed causal analyses virtually ignore the concept.[30] In 1807 two other circumstances, more strategic and psychological than economic, had entered into the situation along with the structural force of humanitarianism. The British slave economy was faced with only one major problem in 1788–1792, or again in 1797–1799: the metropolitan threat to their labor supply. Neither the threat nor the need had diminished in 1806–1807. But dangers now assailed British slavery from many sides—from enemy colonies, from neutral carriers, from high duties, and from European restrictions.[31] These tricontinental pressures blurred the earlier clarity of the abolitionist threat. With so many sources of immediate danger, slaves could no longer assert that the African trade was synonymous with survival. The focus had blurred and perhaps with it the metropolitan reflex against abolition which had been so potent in 1791. This does not mean that the metropolis was inclined to throw one more stone on the system in order to drown it more quickly. When the survival of the West Indies was clearly at stake only one year later, the imperial Parliament acted promptly to allow the distillation of sugar over the vigorous opposition of one part of the landed interest.[32] But the slave trade had clearly been relatively devalued as an element of immediate survival.

Parliament did not abolish the slave trade to save slavery from itself, nor because the slave colonies were deemed insignificant to Britain's economy. The decision was made at a recessional point, clearly stemming from the shifting circumstances of war. But it also occurred in a period which had witnessed the opening up of enormous new vistas for long-range expansion. Overproduction, structural weakness, and imperial insignificance played no role in the decision to abolish. Britain's control over much of the African coast and the oceans of the world permitted Parliament to be vaguely assured that others would not immediately benefit by Britain's surrender of the trade. Indeed, in the years following abolition British naval power was to create more problems for the West Indian planters than all the sugar in Cuba and Brazil.

Even the abolitionist premise that the British had a monopoly of the slave trade and that no other carriers were available was disputed in Parliament and disproved by events. At no time between 1787 and 1807 could a British government announce the probability of an imminent end to the Portuguese slave trade, either to Brazil or to other areas. American slavers undercut the very premises of legal intervention against the trade. By 1807 they had taught politicians the grim lesson of a dozen years of unenforced American "foreign" abolition. By 1807 the British government had also given up on Bonaparte, "under the strong influence of Creolian prejudices," as a possible cosponsor of international abolition. Since Bonaparte alone determined European trade policy in 1807, the French, Dutch, and Spanish slave trades were "abolished" only until the next European truce.[33]

Looking at the economic and strategic situation of 1806–1807 we may discover many reasons why abolition won, despite the lack of market or structural imperatives. Ultimately, what must strike the historian most forceably is the parallel with the frontier victories of 1798–1805. However unique were the economic, strategic, or political circumstances that may have allowed abolitionist initiatives to triumph from 1797 to 1807, the gains were never reversed, even when the economic circumstances were completely reversed. Abolition was as much a process of guaranteeing that irreversibility as it was a process of destroying an avenue for emergent capitalism.

The Laws of the Market and the Law of Abolition

If the market mechanism alone did not point to abolition in 1807, it must still be asked whether the ideology of the marketplace told against the slave trade or slavery. In this context, we can reexamine the long-range premise that the assault on the slave trade was an aspect of a general attack of proponents of a laissez-faire, capitalist ideology against mercantilism. If laissez-faire was predicated on the optimal utilization of the entire planet as a single market, there had never been a worse moment to make that a working political premise than in the period after 1805. Blockades, counterblockades, embargoes, reprisals, and confiscations were accelerating at an unprecedented rate. Ironically, insofar as the rules of the open system still prevailed, Africa was its haven and the slave traders were its prophets. The slave-trading interest called upon the British government to repeal the order-in-council of 1805 in the name of free and competitive enterprise, and to stay its hand from abolition in 1806–1807 in the same spirit. The slave dealers of Liverpool denounced all interference with the play of market forces in Africa, the limitation of productive labor in the colonies, and the maximization of capital returns to themselves. The interested gentlemen of Manchester went still further. They insisted that the economic progress of England was dependent on two traditional political principles, the protection of private property and the free flow of capital. This meant "the extension of internal Manufactures and the freedom of exporting those manufactures to every state or power whether neighboring or distant that offered an advantageous Market, without attempting to set any limits to the enterprising genius of the people." On what principles, they asked, was British commerce forbidden with nations at peace with Britain (Africa), while other trades were maintained or opened despite their belligerent status (the Spanish colonies in America)?[34] The Trinidad planters analogized their plight to a hypothetical ban on further agricultural production in Britain. The entire antiabolitionist case was based on the traditional sanction of free enterprise within the limits of the market.

We refer to the economic arguments of the antiabolitionist interests and petitions, not because they were inherently more interesting than countervailing economic arguments of opposing interests, but simply because no such countervailing arguments were laid before Parliament in 1806–1807. As for any putative silent majority of interests against the trade, one can only say that their camouflage was perfect, their sense of victory certain, or their real existence questionable. It might of course be politic for proabolitionist interests to mask their arguments by humanity in 1792 or 1807. But in 1806 the foreign abolition bill was specifically introduced as its predecessors had been in 1793–1794, as a contingent and expedient action, designed to help British economic interests. It is therefore significant that not a single petition was presented stating that a specific economic interest would be hurt by a failure to pass any of these bills. The only abolitionist petition came from Manchester in 1806. It was designed specifically to counteract the "public opinion" weight of the slave traders' petition from that area. It did not present a single economic argument in behalf of abolition. It merely stated that the petitioners were "strongly impressed with a deep sense of the wisdom, sound Policy, and Humanity which dictated" the presentation of the bill.[35]

Even the antimercantilist social overhead arguments against the colonial trade could no longer be raised in the case of the slave trade. There were no large British defense or police forces in Africa to shore up British commerce in 1807. The coastal fort subsidy, amounting to £13,000 per year, had remained unchanged since the mid–eighteenth century. While this might have been a minor debating point in favor of abolition in 1787, it had long since ceased to be even that. The free labor settlement of Sierra Leone was already costing the metropolitan budget far more than all the slave-trade forts combined. Its chief investors, led by abolitionists, had declared the colony to be bankrupt both as a private and as a publicly subsidized venture. When the empire took it over as a crown colony in the very year of abolition, it was not cited as an economic alternative to the West Indies.[36]

At the "demand" end of the Atlantic, even with development restricted in Trinidad, St. Vincent, and Guiana, the labor problem was unresolved. No colony, except perhaps for Barbados, had definitively reached demographic equilibrium by 1806. A labor gap would be created inevitably by the time span needed for the appearance of a positive birth-death ratio. This was why Jamaica reacted to the prospect of abolition in 1792 and in 1807 with a flurry of purchasing before, and a flurry of invective after, the votes on abolition. Even if near equilibrium were present in a colony, the difficulties of labor shortages were not necessarily overcome. In the absence of a free market, the slave trade served as its proxy, when the movement of Creole slaves from one sparsely staffed plantation to another was not feasible.

The logical weakness of reckoning only on demographic averages at the colony level had already been argued, with effect, in 1792.[37] The subject was again presented with particular force by J. P. Barham, a member of Parliament and owner of estates on Jamaica. Before 1807, Barham supported the strategies of suspending the slave trade to all colonies and of abolishing the foreign trade. On his own estates he had long encouraged births as a means of doing away with the necessity of renting or purchasing African and Creole slaves. Barham carefully delineated the difficulty of assuring an adequate labor force on individual estates. He had two estates and had offered each the same encouragements to reproduce for twenty years. One was in a healthy climate, high, dry, and with abundant provisions. The other was in a low and wet area, although the food supply was equally good. Yet the greatest rate of decrease had occurred on the high and dry estate. Barham was inclined to explain the difference by the relative proximity of one plantation to an urban area. But his major point was that one could not simply alter the birthrate by shutting off the transatlantic source of labor.[38]

Whatever the demographic ripeness of any individual economic unit or colony, abolition, as an absolute prohibition, introduced a new inflexibility into the slave market. As the final curtain fell on the parliamentary debates of 1807, the besieged West Indians returned to this fundamental theme. They pointed out that the bill of 1807 contained no replacement clause which would permit importations at least to the amount of the annual deficit, now reckoned by them at 7,000, or a little over 1 percent per year for the *de jure* slave empire of 1807. They cited Malthus on the resiliency of African fertility. They revived alternative suggestions of temporary suspension or progressive taxation as a means of experimentally testing the demographic predictions of the abolitionists. Above all, they deplored the fact that the West Indies would be unable to respond to extraordinary losses of slaves, to external colonial competition, or to renewed European demand. Here they merely reiterated a principle raised at the outset of the abolition debates by Charles James Fox, one of the staunchest and most uncompromising abolitionists in Parliament. In 1791, he clearly noted that once abolition was made a question of supply and demand, rather than of murder and oppression, there would be no foreseeable end to it for "our demand was fluctuating, it sometimes ceased, nay for whole years together, as in the case during the last [American revolutionary] war; sometimes again a demand for slaves was very great and pressing." Stephen reemphasized that point in 1807, insisting on unqualified abolition.[39]

The real debility of the slave trade in 1807 lay far outside the realm of demographic imbalance in the colonies or economic incentives in Africa. Neither the viability nor the function of the slave trade as a source of labor had altered between 1775 and 1805. As long as slavery remained insulated from noncommercial metropolitan forces, its role was accepted as wholly positive. It was the dramatic appearance of a massive pressure group in 1788–1792 which shifted the criteria of valuation. Thereafter, only the conflation of abolition with the larger threat of world revolution temporarily sheltered the slave trade. Even at the moment of supreme anti-Jacobin hysteria in Britain, however, the trade was defended as part of its economic, not its moral order. With the return of internal and external security to Britain the criteria of 1792 slowly reasserted themselves. The hair-splitting utilitarian calculus of demographic and economic stress might presage colonial stagnation but not cataclysmic ruin. That was enough to seal the fate of the slave trade.

Abolition was nothing less than the conversion of a market-oriented sanction into an absolute prohibition. In 1807, as in 1777, the usual way for Parliament to deal with economic enterprises affected by non-economic contingencies was to provide sliding scale relief or limited legislation. In 1808 the use of sugar in British distilleries was allowed in order to increase consumption for a limited period. As one supporter put it: "temporary evils required temporary remedies."[40] The response was thus a continuation of the usual policies followed in assuring some protection to industries affected by nonmarket forces.

The difference between the parliamentary attitude toward the sugar and slave trades in 1807–1808 is particularly interesting. In dealing with the former, Parliament was cautious and calculating. In response to the Continental blockade it attempted to weigh the impact of domestic sugar distillation on the grain market and then to compromise between two articulate and visible economic interests. The result was a controlled expansion of domestic sugar consumption for a limited time, renewed periodically until the Continental blockade was lifted. The slave trade however, was simply converted from a commercial to a criminal activity, without allowance for present variation or for future contingencies. In this sense, Anstey's insistence on the profound difference between the "abolitions" of 1805–1806 and 1807 is crucial. The controversial preamble to the abolition bill of 1807 was deliberately couched in strong humanitarian terms designed to eliminate economic premises and to nullify the market. After 1807, the only way to restore the economic flexibility offered by the slave trade to British slavery was by the tedious public process of parliamentary legislation. In this sense abolition was neither a response to the inexorable decline of old economic interests, acting under old mercantilist values, nor to new economic interests acting to defend new laissez-faire values. Removing the value of the slave trade from the market also meant removing the values of the market from the slave trade.

9

Abolition and the Decline
of British Slavery, 1808–1814

At the heart of the decline theory lies the sense that slavery was unassailable so long as its existence was complementary to Britain's major economic interests and unsalvageable once it ceased to be so.[1] Accordingly, abolition in 1807 is the seal of death, ratifying the inevitable downward path of British slavery. The tendency is for historians to rush on to the next great phase of abolitionism, the campaign for emancipation. It is possible, however, that the immediate postabolition period can shed some final light on the decline theory. Strictly speaking, since restoration of the slave trade was never formally submitted to Parliament, the question of its resurrection is not among the mooted options for Britain's political economy. However, the abolitionists were not so sure of the irrevocability of their victory in 1807. Given the fact that France restored the slave trade not once but twice before 1815, these were years when the abolitionist writ quite obviously did not run far south of the Channel. The slave trade continued to intrude itself into both British colonial and metropolitan politics.

For those who are interested in the economic conditions that underlay or accompanied abolition, there are still some postabolition questions to be raised. Were the economic conditions that followed abolition such as to strengthen the decision of Parliament in 1807? Did abolition lead to the resolution of any of the colonies' economic problems in 1807? Our own analysis has placed much of the economic history of the West Indies from 1792 to 1807 in the shadow of Mars. Our final period of discussion logically carries us down through 1814, when peacetime British policy toward abolition was formulated in terms which were to hold good until the end of the transoceanic slave trade fifty years later. The year 1814 is one of the crucial moments in the political history of British abolition. It is also one of the critical moments in the economic history of British slavery.

Decline in Disguise, 1808–1814

The slave system lost none of its outward luster for the metropolis in the period between abolition and the disintegration of the Napoleonic empire. The British West Indian share of metropolitan overseas trade maintained its upward momentum (see table 1). Never in the eighteenth century had West Indian trade achieved such a sustained and high plateau. No five-year period before 1772-1777 showed the British West Indies which were affected by abolition in 1807. British imports from East India, the area totally unconnected with the African labor supply, fell by it was possible for the slave interest to claim that it had literally accounted for over one-fifth of Britain's overseas trade for a decade and a half. The slave system maintained the position of prominence which it had gained in the nineties. The only difference between the periods before and after abolition was that the West Indies became an even better customer for British exports, while the position of North America and Africa declined. The only other area that increased in importance in 1808-1812 was Latin America, to which, of course, the slave trade continued. The British West Indies were also one of Britain's most reliable and stable trading partners during the Continental blockade (see tables 26 and 27). There was only one geographical exception to the general upward surge. Considering only the trade figures, anyone who regarded the slave trade as a lever for lowering the sugar supply might have concluded that it was the East Indies which were affected by abolition in 1807. British imports from East India, the area totally unconnected with the African labor supply, fell by half from 1803-1807 to 1808-1812.

The tale of coffee imports after 1807 was even clearer and more lugubrious, since coffee was almost entirely a reexport commodity at the beginning of the century. It was the postabolition year 1808, when the rate of retained imports jumped over fourteen times its previous average, which marked the real crisis for the coffee trade. To stimulate domestic consumption, drastic cuts in duties were called for in 1808-1809. Yet even the subsequent rise of British consumption could not redress the import-export imbalance.[3]

The increase in retained imports was not due principally to a drop in reexports to Europe because of the Continental system. British reexports of sugar rose after the crisis year 1808 to higher average levels than before 1807. Even during the blockade years, average sugar exports after 1808 always remained above those of 1807, or any cluster of years immediately before (see table 28). Coffee exports, while much more uneven in performance, showed the same characteristics. Except for the sharp fall from 1807 to 1808, average coffee exports after abolition equaled or exceeded pre-1807 totals for all pairings of years between 1803–1807 and 1808–1812. The merchants of Britain therefore showed that they were able to reexport more sugar after 1807 than before, despite the blockade. What they could not do was to keep up with the post-abolition rate of growth in imports.

TABLE 26: ANNUAL RANGE OF VARIATION IN IMPORTS WITH BRITISH TRADING PARTNERS (official values)

	1808	1809	1810	1811	1812	Deviation from Mean Average	Max.	Maximum Change Between Adjacent Years
N. Europe	50	140	177	63	76	56	77	114
S. Europe	67	126	160	54	94	34	60	106
Asia	89	78	109	95	129	15	29	34
Africa	76	98	136	100	91	14	36	38
British North America	106	87	113	103	92	9	13	26
United States	45	119	141	125	70	34	55	74
British West Indies	108	95	101	104	92	5	8	13
Latin America	67	120	164	90	58	34	64	74

Source: Mitchell and Deane, Abstract, p. 311.
Note: 1808–1812 = 100.

The question remains. Why was supply burgeoning after 1807 despite abolition and despite low prices? Did planters irrationally drive their now declining labor force to new heights of productivity in the face of warning signals from the market? Did providence provide year after year of super-abundant harvests as if to demonstrate the redundancy of even the existing labor force? Neither whip nor weather were responsible for the surge of imports into Britain after 1807. The sword, not the hoe, accounted for the paradox of increased supply. While French power was trying with only intermittent success to close Europe to British goods, British power was absorbing the enemy colonial network into its own imperium. The Danish islands fell in 1807. Martinique, French Guiana, Guadeloupe, and St. Martins, the remaining French and Dutch Caribbean possessions, were all under British or allied control by the end of 1810.

The French and Dutch colonies in the East also fell by 1811. Each conquest meant new infusions of tropical products into the metropolitan market. Moreover, where a possession had been long under blockade, its capture would mean that more than one year's harvest suddenly became available. The capture of Guadeloupe in 1810 brought three years' harvests to Britain, accounting for over 40 percent of the total increase of sugar imports between 1809 and 1810.[4] The basic problem was quite clear. Samuel Whitbread, a brewer-abolitionist MP, denounced the policy of expansion in 1808. He was seconded by the West India interest: "By your conquests, almost all the sugar in the world is forced into this market, and, by the conquests of Bonaparte, here it is confined."[5]

TABLE 27: ANNUAL RANGE OF VARIATION IN EXPORTS WITH BRITISH TRADING PARTNERS (official values)

	1808	1809	1810	1811	1812	Deviation from Mean Average	Deviation from Mean Max.	Maximum Change Between Adjacent Years
N. Europe	63	183	150	31	73	53	83	120
S. Europe	62	95	79	119	146	26	46	40
Asia	111	94	98	95	102	5	11	17
Africa	107	142	97	64	89	20	42	45
British North America	70	109	115	119	88	17	30	39
United States	88	115	173	32	92	35	73	141
British West Indies	116	117	94	81	93	13	19	23
Latin America	99	131	122	62	85	18	38	60

Source: Mitchell and Deane, *Abstract,* p. 311.
Note: 1808–1812 = 100.

The real trends in the British slave colonies only became manifest at the end of the conflict. The first comprehensive report on colonial production was compiled for Parliament at the moment of the treaty with France in June 1814.[6] The products measured were sugar, coffee, and cotton, broken down into three categories: British, conquered, and foreign. Information included the years 1805–1807 (*1806*) and 1810–1812 (*1811*). If ever a document on the slave system could be described as handwriting on the wall it was this report. In terms of total trade, the figures in tables 29 and 30 tell much the same tale as those discussed at the beginning of the chapter. The value of the West Indian import trade to Britain had risen almost one-fifth from £8,325,000 in *1806* to £10,189,000

TABLE 28: BRITISH SUGAR IMPORTS BEFORE AND AFTER ABOLITION

Paired Periods	Country of Origin (in thousands)			Total Imports (U.K.)		Retained Imports		Reexports
	British and Conquered Colonies	East India	Foreign Colonies	In Thousands	Percent Change	In Thousands	Percent Change	Percent Change
1807	3,619 cwt.	119 cwt.	33 cwt.	3,801 cwt.	–	2,893 cwt.	–	–
1808	3,687	73	225	3,985	+ 4.8	3,172	+ 9.6	–10.5
1805–07	3,488	93	92	3,683	–	2,906	–	–
1808–10	3,709	49	570	4,338	+17.7	3,137	+11.17	+54.2
1803–07	3,335	101	114	3,555	–	2,695	–	–
1808–12	3,729	48	422	4,205	+18.3	3,276	+21.5	+ 8.0

Source: PP 1847–1848 (LVIII), 528.

Note: For the two lower clusters, the import figures are shown as averages for their respective periods.

in *1811*. British imports of sugar and sugar derivatives had also risen by one-fifth. Coffee imports were up nearly one-third. Cotton imports had stagnated, down 2 percent from *1806* to *1811*. Calculations by weight, rather than by value, showed the same general tendencies.

These figures, however, camouflaged a much more somber trajectory for the *de jure* British component of the West Indian system. In terms of overall imports by value, the British West Indies showed a decline of 4 percent compared with a rise of over 84 percent in the conquered colonial areas. British West Indian sugar exports had declined by 3.5

TABLE 29: OFFICIAL VALUE OF BRITISH IMPORTS FROM THE WEST INDIES, 1805–1807 (*1806*) AND 1810–1812 (*1811*) (in thousands)

Commodity	British West Indies	Conquered West Indies	Foreign West Indies	Total West Indies
Sugar and rum				
1806	£4,328	£ 619	£ 32	£ 4,979
1811	4,344	1,564	61	5,969
Coffee				
1806	1,605	930	141	2,676
1811	1,351	1,606	599	3,556
Cotton				
1806	240	411	27	678
1811	205	442	15	662
Total				
1806	6,172	1,960	193	8,325
1811	5,900	3,613	676	10,189

Source: PP 1813–1814 (XII), 199–200.

TABLE 30: WEIGHT OF BRITISH IMPORTS FROM THE WEST INDIES 1805–1807 (*1806*) AND 1810–1812 (*1811*) (in thousands)

Commodity	British West Indies	Conquered West Indies	Foreign West Indies	Total West Indies
Sugar (cwt.)				
1806	2,936	434	23	3,393
1811	2,834	1,087	45	3,966
Coffee (cwt.)				
1806	239	134	20	393
1811	210	246	88	544
Cotton (cwt.)				
1806	6,602	11,891	803	19,236
1811	5,362	12,180	406	17,947

Source: PP 1813–1814 (XII), 199–200.

percent while British sugar imports from conquered and foreign areas rose almost 150 percent. Even if the entire loss of 100,000 cwt. in British sugar imports from the British West Indies between *1806* and *1811* were ascribable to abolition, the British market was swamped by an increase of 675,000 cwt. in conquered and foreign colonial sugar. This confirmed the utter futility of conceiving of abolition as a crop control mechanism in an expanding empire. While Parliament may have prevented an import of up to 90,000 slaves per year into the *de jure* British colonies by the abolition bill of 1807, by 1814 the British military added four times as many slaves in place to the empire.[7] It was a case of an ounce of prevention balanced against a pound of expansion.

Abolition, while completely failing to resolve the problems created by the Continental blockade, had rigidified British slavery. More important than its inability to maintain production in periods of wartime desolation was the fact that it was losing its resiliency as a normal economic system. Only because of conquests had British-controlled production more than held its own in the period which ended in 1814. In that year, areas under direct British control probably produced over 62 percent of the sugar transported to the American and European market.[8] With the return of some of the conquered colonies, British slave-produced output still amounted to over half of world production. Its situation was serious, but in all respects save one it still had at hand more of the ingredients necessary for maintaining its position than in 1791.

The Crossroads: 1814

For five years after abolition British slavery had to endure the consequences of colonial extension and Continental blockade. Suddenly, in the winter of 1812, the blizzards of Russia revived the tropical economies. The Continental blockade disintegrated in direct response to the defeats of Napoleon. By the fall of 1813, British goods, metropolitan and tropical, were pouring into European ports. Reserves were liquidated. Prices climbed month after month. In the spring of 1814 muscovado sugar was selling at average prices 230 percent above their level on the eve of the French invasion of Russia, and at more than triple their level in the spring of 1802. The record peak prices of the early and late nineties were shattered. The records of the Lord Steward's department of the Royal Household, extending back to 1659, showed that refined sugar was at an all-time peak in 1814. Almost all the world's coffee came flowing into British ports in search of a European market. At the beginning of 1814,

British plantation coffee was selling for two or two and one-half times as much as in the spring of 1812. Cotton shared in the general buoyancy. A pound of Guiana cotton, which had sold at an average of 1.12 shillings at the beginning of the invasion of Russia, also averaged more than twice that price in 1814. Georgia cotton was doing proportionately well.[9]

Riding the roaring boom, and apparently poised at the beginning of an era of unrivaled possibilities, the British slave interest would ordinarily have hailed the present with hosannas and the future with optimism. Yet that interest could see quite clearly that its position was flawed. Without the restoration of the slave trade, production must continue to stagnate until that distant moment when the demographic situation had dramatically altered. At best, this meant a hollow generation of slave labor between the end of the African trade and evolution of a sexually balanced, disease resistant, and normally aging Creole generation. The dearth of labor meant that both the frontier and renewed Continental demand were worthless incentives to expansion. The system could no longer respond.

This was not the worst of the outlook in 1814. The West Indian slave system had been on notice for a generation that it was not beloved by the metropolis. More than ever, its long-term well-being depended on the maintenance of its relative economic importance to the empire. If even twenty years of imperial economic nationalism and Caribbean agricultural triumph over French slavery had failed to persuade the metropolis to favor the growth of slavery, what could the system expect as its significance in that empire diminished year by year, percentile by percentile? Quite clearly, the slave economy was not simply faced with a flawed potential to expand. It must either expand with the metropolis or lose its very *raison d'être,* sketched in the yearly figures of trade statistics and in its traditionally upward curve of progress. There were accusations enough of moral decadence against slavery without the added one of economic decadence.

The situation, until May 1814, contained one ray of hope. If all other colonial powers were frozen at roughly their 1814 positions, the hollow generation might be a universal handicap. If the North Atlantic sugar and coffee supply could not rise dramatically, prices might be sustained at levels which would assure the British planters a comfortable position. The British colonies still produced half of the sugar consumed by the North Atlantic market. Some kind of effective labor adjustments could be maintained either by intracolonial trade or by phasing out cotton plantations for the greater advantages of raising cane.

The British decision to retain Demerara and Mauritius within the empire also meant that British slavery might still be capable of considerable expansion (see figure 9). Demerara was now the second largest sugar producer in the British slave empire. While its demographic position was relatively worse than that of the older islands, it was one of the few British colonies which could hope substantially to increase its preabolition production level. Its fresh soils rendered it competitive with the older colonies. The inclusion of the new expansive colonies, however, also closed the door on a West Indian return to the comfortable imperial ecological niche of 1787. Even if the empire were for the moment inclined to tolerate such agricultural protection, the slave system which supplied so much of Continental consumption in 1813–1814 would find it hard to retreat to the metropolitan market of the old regime.

FIGURE 9: TOTAL SUGAR PRODUCTION, 1790–1835:
JAMAICA, TRINIDAD, BRITISH GUIANA, MAURITIUS

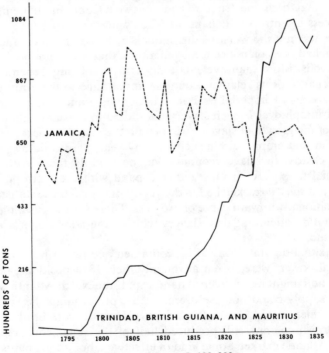

Source: Deerr, *History of Sugar,* I, 198–203.

In 1814 East Indian cane and European beet sugar still had only the same shadowy potential they had in the 1790s. The Eastern peril had too often turned out to be a phantom which disappeared at the first sharp downturn of the market. Much less Eastern sugar was reaching the European market in 1814 than in 1805-1807. One of its two principal carriers, the American merchant fleet, was now the target of the British navy. In the spring of 1814 the sugar beet, too, lay buried in the ruins of the Continental system. The obituary in the *Times* dispatched this budding triumph of "French" chemistry to an island far beyond Elba. "The whole establishment is broken up, and all the implements are to be sold to any Laputan philosopher who chooses to follow the *grande pensée* of the learned Savan Nicholas. There is something exceedingly entertaining in the enumeration of all the articles . . . , the cauldrons, and vats for desecation [*sic*], for evaporation, for steaming, for boiling—in short the whole apparatus of a scheme which was cousin-german to that of extracting sun beams from cucumbers." [10]

The chief cause for concern lay in the more open-ended potential of the tropical producers outside the empire. Many had never stopped importing slaves. The trade to Brazil had continued almost uninterrupted after 1808. The trade to Cuba flickered and flared, but never disappeared. In May 1814 one West Indian spokesman estimated that in the first two years of British abolition, 80,000 Africans per year had been transported to the Spanish and Portuguese colonies. [11] Yet war had also made it impossible to estimate the degree to which the British slave system was threatened by the Iberian systems. The development of the Spanish colonies had been hampered by British withdrawal from the foreign trade in 1806 and by the Anglo-American war of 1812. These successive events may account for the sharp fluctuations in Havana imports between 1807 and 1815. [12]

From 1810 to 1814 there was also an appearance of movement toward the progressive containment of the slave trade, by diplomatic agreement as well as by raw military power. In 1810 the Portuguese were forced to sign a treaty of alliance pledging cooperation in the gradual abolition of the slave trade and agreeing immediately not to operate on any part of the African coast not under Portuguese domination. British support was also responsible for Spanish moves toward abolition during their struggle against Napoleon for independence. Abolitionist motions were discussed by the revolutionary Cortes of Cádiz in 1811 and again in 1813, and it was intended to raise the issue again in the Cortes in 1814. [13] Apart from Peninsular action, the American provinces of La Plata, Venezuela, and Chile had also decreed abolition by 1814. The last northern European entrepot for slaves in the Caribbean, Swedish St. Bartholomew, was closed when Sweden received conquered Guadeloupe as her prize for an alliance with Britain in 1813. The British government, in December 1813, also indicated that pressure would be exerted against the Dutch to include abolition in their treaty of peace. Despite the hostile state of public, or at least elite, opinion in the Netherlands, the Dutch were also in the abolition column by May 1814.[14]

The abolitionists were lulled by the momentum of British diplomacy, while the West Indians basked in the warmth of record prices. Until May 1814 nothing appeared likely to galvanize either interest to a sense of imminent peril. Yet both groups anxiously realized that the decisive weight in the scales of international abolition lay with the one colonial nation whose great power status most clearly matched that of Britain. West Indian and abolitionist voices joined in expressing special anxieties concerning the preliminary discussions of the treaty with France. The government was vague, but reassuring.[15]

On June 6, 1814, Lord Castlereagh formally presented to the Commons a copy of the "Treaty of Peace and Amity signed at Paris on the 30th of May, 1814, between his Britannic Majesty and his most Christian Majesty of France." According to the staid record of the *Parliamentary Debates* it was received with loud cheers. One member, however, remained silent. When Wilberforce rose to speak, it was to announce that Castlereagh had brought back the angel of death under the wings of victory. The minister held in his hand not the instrument of universal relief but "the death-warrant of a multitude of innocent victims, men, women and children," in Africa and the slave colonies.[16] Articles of the treaty restored to French sovereignty all colonies and establishments in French possession as of January 1792 except Tobago, St. Lucia, and Mauritius (Ile de France). French sovereignty over its former colony of St. Domingue was recognized, along with the developed islands of Martinique and Guadeloupe, and the frontier colonies of Bourbon and French Guiana. Within three months the Atlantic colonies were to be back in French hands. Finally, under "additional" article 1, the British government officially sanctioned the reopening of the French slave trade for five years.[17] It was this article that shattered the harmony of Parliament. Where Castlereagh saw the end of destruction in Europe, and Wilberforce its renaissance in Africa, the slave interest saw the destruction of their capital. West Indians, abolitionists, and bankers all spoke of the "inevitable consequence" of exposing the planters to "an unequal and uncommercial competition."[18] Not a single voice, even among those defending the government, challenged this inference.

For Castlereagh and the government, Britain's chief priority was to insure the durability of peace and the equilibrium of Europe. Colonial cessions to France were part of a strategy "fully to open to France the means of peaceful occupation, and to transform her from a conquering and a military to a commercial and a pacific nation." Permanent peace required capitalism. French capitalism apparently required the slave trade for the time being. Perhaps the psychological key to why the restoration of the slave trade to France seemed so natural may be found in the negotiators' nostalgia for the eighteenth century. Hawkesbury, now Lord Liverpool, was convinced that Europe had never enjoyed so much happiness as from the time of the English Revolution in 1688, to the French Revolution in 1789. It was his object therefore to bring things back as much as possible to the state they were in at that period.[19] How could restored France be denied an attempt to retrieve some of her golden age, including slavery, even at the cost of discomfort to British abolitionists and West Indians? Talleyrand, speaking for the French government, had shrewdly pointed out that if the restored colonies were to play their allotted capitalist role in the reform of France, they must be permitted to stock their recovered colonies, as the British had proceeded to do after their initial resolutions on the slave trade. The British government had submitted to the force of this argument, although it was a step toward lessening British tropical hegemony.

Even more indicative of the government's position were the arguments presented to show the futility of any attempt to revoke the clause. The fundamental and traditional argument was that it was simply not within the power of Britain, short of war, to prohibit the international slave trade. The ministers pointed out that if they had withheld British sanction, France would have returned to the slave trade without a time clause. Britain could not forbid the restoration of the French slave trade to St. Domingue, which it did not control. Guiana, the other major French frontier, was occupied by the Portuguese, the largest slave-trading colonial power in the world. Areas such as Madagascar, long an object of French colonial ambition, could serve equally well as the new French base for slavery. The British had only the small and developed French islands as bargaining pawns. Finally, even without French dependencies, the Spanish and Portuguese colonies alone furnished an ample base for a thriving French slave trade. Thus the abolitionist demand for retaining Martinique and Guadeloupe, contingent upon French abolition, was beside the point. Only an internal political decision by France to abandon the slave trade altogether could resolve the international question in favor of abolition.[20]

Significantly, the abolitionists accepted the same economic point of departure. Tropical frontiers everywhere were targets of developmental opportunity. The reduction of Haiti was obviously a dominant motive behind the revival of the French slave trade: "St. Domingo would in itself be an immense vortex of human calamity." Wilberforce estimated, not unrealistically, that just to repopulate that colony alone with slaves would mean half a million human beings landed, many more sacrificed in Africa, and tens of thousands of ex-slaves butchered and exterminated. Abolitionist fears of a French expedition against the black state, and its implications for an indefinite extension of the slave trade, were not just propaganda weapons. Castlereagh never challenged the plausibility of their argument. If invasion rumours about Haiti panicked the abolitionists, the return of Guadeloupe to France mocked their conviction of inevitable progress. Prohibited by the earlier terms of British cession to Sweden, the slave trade was shamelessly restored with formal British approval.[21]

The abolitionists freely admitted that unilateral British abolition had only laid the groundwork for a larger African trade. Lord Holland foresaw an exportation of 20,000 African slaves from Senegal alone during the first year, if it were reopened to the trade. This would have been up sharply from the year just prior to abolition. The old west coast of Africa, now fully "stocked" by the British suppression, would be ready for a magnificent harvest by French slavers, with Madagascar and Bourbon thrown in for good measure.

France represented only the start of the nightmare. The colonies of Spain and Portugal would import at full capacity with their diplomatic bargaining positions now toughened by French power.[22] Brazil continued to be served by the traders with the regularity of the tides. Cuban growth would no longer be hampered by the war. A new and more vigorous Latin American bond gave a new collective economic strength to the slave trade. The Iberian systems were no longer weak satellites of the British maritime system, subject to powerful economic and political pressure.

If one had to choose a single word to describe the mood of both sides in this debate, at the very moment of victory, it would be helplessness. The government had announced that the treaty of Paris represented the limit of its ability to contain the slave trade. The opposition sounded an even more painful note. However strong they might appear to be within the confines of Britain, they, like the West Indians, realized that the power to control events might be fast ebbing away from them. May 1814 had marked the apogee of Britain's ability to affect world colonial policy through military power. With the departure of troops from France and her colonies, Britain would have voluntarily returned "those conquests, which, while they remained in our possession, afforded to us sure pledges for the attainment of our object."[23] Opportunity had knocked and might never return.

The future would be worse economically as well as politically. It might well turn out that the five-year clause was worse than nothing. By setting a term to the trade which might or might not be enforced, the article breathed a warning which would immediately unfurl every spare sail in Europe. It was an open invitation to stocking. In 1814 France possessed no slave trade, no interest which could present a sunken capital argument to the French government. In five years it would be "a revived and existing commerce." The five-year clause would be a wedge for continuing the trade "to all eternity."[24]

Samuel Romilly voiced the abolitionists' greatest fear, the fear of economic power. "Let Nantes and Bordeaux and other maritime towns become the Bristols and Liverpools of France; let large capitals be embarked in the Trade; let the support of many thousands of individuals be made to depend on its continuance; enlist the activity and zeal of commercial enterprise and adventure against you; multiply without number the enemies to the abolition and then wisely trust to reason to refute their arguments, and silence their clamours."[25] If the contest for St. Domingo were long and bloody, how could the slave trade fill that island within the five-year limit, or for a long time thereafter?[26]

The abolitionists, like the slaveowners, felt themselves at a peak with a gloomy prospect before them. The total victory of 1814 was an opportunity as fleeting as it was unpredictable. The moment had been lost and, as it seemed to the abolitionists, probably lost forever. New markets in Africa and America, new fleets plying the Atlantic, new industries for the slaving empires—this was the grim outline of a new era of European peace and African carnage.[27] The commercial outlook was clearly unfolding on the French, Portuguese, Brazilian, Dutch, and Spanish flags covering the slavers and in the parliamentary reports on the state of the slave trade. Economic interests could always be counted upon. But how could abolitionists know whether there would ever be another movement such as theirs? The prospects in Paris were not bright.

The consequences to the colonies of the unimpeded renewal of the slave trade seemed no less clear. Alexander Baring concluded that "whatever colony had the command of the slave trade would also command the sugar trade, and every other."[28] Joseph Barham, one of the first West Indians in Parliament to support abolition, agreed. He carefully collected data from both West Indian and abolitionist sources on the price of African slaves in both hemispheres. His conclusion was that the overall cost of fresh African labor was already one-fourth the price of slaves on

British plantations. Profits were thus far higher in slave-importing areas than in the British colonies.[29] This may go far to explain a Cuban slave import rate in 1816–1820 which was 200 percent greater than its previous peacetime levels of 1803–1804.

The most thoroughgoing analysis of the revival of the foreign slave trade was provided once again by the abolitionist, and now MP, James Stephen. In a long letter to Lord Liverpool in October 1814, the old pragmatic protagonist of abolition outlined the economic consequences of the French revival.[30] Stephen acknowledged that he was moving onto unholy ground, where most abolitionists feared to follow. "They have maintained that the breeding system is less expensive than the *buying;* but I have never countenanced that error." In his first published book on the colonies Stephen had already concluded that, contrary to Adam Smith's generalization, voluntary labor could not drive out slave labor in the West Indies on economic grounds.[31] Now he extended the same conclusion to breeding vs. buying. He acknowledged the truth of the planters' original claim. The slave trade offered the most inexpensive and effective form of labor in the West Indies.

Stephen had arrived at his conclusions and drawn in some other abolitionists "by admitted facts and dry calculations." In his letter, he maintained that his view was the common opinion of the planters, except when they wished to make Machiavellian use of abolitionist support for their own political purposes. For the most part, even mature plantations had maintained their numbers by supplementing natural increase with buying. Their "situation must now inevitably deteriorate." An enormous new input of capital had to be made so that "in sickly as well as in healthy situations, and where provision grounds are more scanty as well as where they more abound, and on laborious estates as well as those of easy cultivation, the superfecundity of nature may replace extraordinary as well as ordinary losses by mortality; because the inadequacy of the number of labourers, or want of strength, as it is called on a Plantation, will be an evil not to be repaired. It will be long at least before a resource can be found in the redundancy on other estates, except upon ruinous terms."[32] This was a remarkably frank recognition of the diversity of plantation conditions, which abolitionists had shrewdly refused to acknowledge in 1807.

Stephen had already presented this elaborate argument in a paper on the labor problem in Trinidad. He now extended it to the old colonies, estimating the postabolition net loss of labor on Jamaica in the course of one year at ten thousand slaves, or 3 percent of the slave population.[33] The implications for the British slave system were disastrous: an importing

power would "be able to raise sugar without the same costly improvements to guard against, but 'with the present benefit of the superior
economy of the *buying* as compared with the breeding system." Thus
British slave costs would be rising steadily while French or Spanish slave
costs were declining. The differential would extend to credit as well as
costs. Metropolitan credit had always been lent on the premise that increased production would, in three years, repay the original loan. If one
offered the potential creditor only an increase of production based on
internal demographic growth, wrote Stephen, you might "as well offer
to the stockbrokers a lottery to be drawn in the next generation. But the
French planters will be able to say, let me draw on you at three years for
the purchase of 100 new Negroes, and I will send you henceforth 100
Hhds. of sugar per annum." Whether the loan was paid in time or not,
the French planter would get the loan and the British planter would not.

Stephen went on to picture other aspects of French expansion, including the horrors of a war of extermination on Haiti. But he knew well
that he was addressing a man who had opposed abolition for twenty years
and whose convictions were molded by statistics of trade, not human
lives. He concluded with a prophecy of decline based solely on economic
and demographic extrapolation. The British colonies would be undersold
by competitors who could produce at lower costs. The only resource of
British planters would be the home market, whose demand they already
exceeded as a result of prior expansion and recent acquisition. But soon
the British would be confronted with the double irony of a superabundant
tropical frontier coinciding with insufficient and diminishing production.
The deficiency might have to be made up by East Indian growth. Stephen
overestimated the swiftness of the sugar decline by not allowing for labor
shifts. But he also failed to realize that his parting argument was precisely
the one which would make the French, lacking an India, regard total
abolition as a Machiavellian device to replace Latin American by East
Indian tropical agriculture.

The situation was critical for the British colonies. As long as the slave
trade continued to foreign colonies, some British capital could indirectly
finance it. While laws could be passed against any direct flow into the
slave trade, it was almost impossible to design legislation preventing
British capital from fueling the system at other points. British manufactures could be used to form the credit base of penetration as easily as
slaves, and the credit would be guaranteed by mortgages. British capital,
wrote a West Indian MP, would flow to the Spanish colonies as it had
flowed into Guiana after 1796. "Cuba and Puerto Rico will, like Surinam
and Demerara, become the property of British speculators (the sovereignty

remaining with those who may be your enemies)" and they would grow "on the ruins of your own colonies." The African expert, Macaulay, agreed. "If British capitalists are allowed to advance money on Brazilian or Cuba Estates, the money so advanced will inevitably find its way into the slave market."[34] Economically, British capital could always find a way of entering the larger slave system.

Given the premises of British abolition and French sanction, the future of the British slave system looked bleak. It appeared quite clear that other societies were not prepared to forego the economic benefits of the slave trade and were as suspicious of British motives after abolition as they had been before. In Parliament, Romilly fumed at foreign cynicism: "if to have relinquished this trade, when we almost singly, of all the nations of the earth, might have carried it on; and when we might have prosecuted it to a greater extent, and with a much greater profit, than we, or any other country had ever before derived from it; if to have persevered steadily for seven years in this self-denial, and never to have shown the least symptom of an inclination to yield to the strong temptation which this lucrative monopoly was holding out—if facts like this left France unconvinced, then indeed, is she not open to conviction."[35] Romilly, like all the abolitionists, exaggerated the British position in 1807. But Britain might easily have sustained her hegemony. Nor was it yet too late.

Was the situation one in which Britain, even if she ruled out the use of military force, was really helpless? If Europe was not open to conviction, was she open to competitive retaliation? By reversing itself until international abolition could be effectively guaranteed, the British government could have maximized the competitiveness of its slave system and maintained its position in tropical production. The whole rationale was already there. Wilberforce, in his opening motion against the slave-trade article with France, provided the premise, if not the conclusion. "As a matter of policy, some individuals, connected with the West India trade, might think that they should be seriously injured by the monopoly that France would acquire. They had consented formerly for the general benefit, to submit their opinions and to abolish the Slave Trade; but they did it under an implied contract that supposed benefits, of which they were deprived, should not be enjoyed by others."[36] This idea was important in the political economy of the abolitionist argument. Members of the government had asserted in 1807 that because Britain had a virtual monopoly of the slave trade, and of naval power, it could render abolition universal. The impact of abolition would be equally distributed. If the planters did not gain, they would not lose.[37] Now the implicit contract was broken. The abolitionists claimed that the government would not use its full power to secure total abolition. The government claimed that it could not, short of war. If Britain risked using its full power against France over Africa she would smash the fragile new European equilibrium. The pressure of economic competition provided an alternate lever.

The purely economic argument for reinstituting the slave trade seemed overwhelming. What interest in Britain opposed it, or what economic principle? European demand was obviously beckoning colonial supply. The market for all tropical goods was nothing less than superb. British capital, manufacturing, and shipping were obviously in the best position in Europe to take advantage of expanding tropical production. The British colonies were also endowed with the full range of managerial skills, access to British capital, undermanned plantations, and immense fertile frontiers. There were no huge social obstacles such as confronted the French in St. Domingue. The traditional political justification of "balancing" French gains with British ones was provided by the very terms of the treaty of Paris. A British government had sanctioned the French trade for five years. If the record of "abolitionist" legislation in the United States or Denmark was any indicator, postponed abolitions like that of the French, or pressured abolition like that of the Netherlands, clearly had to be discounted from face value at date of issue. No more was required to insure the British slave system against European non-compliance than to reestablish a British "interim" trade.

Some individuals were apparently prepared to think the unthinkable in 1814. British capital had made covert attempts to elude the ban on the foreign slave trade just after abolition. Earl Grey reported to a public meeting in June 1814 that some spokesmen for the slave interest intended to apply for a renewal of the African slave trade for the same period allowed to the French, and he allowed that the arguments would be difficult to answer.[38] A government of Castlereagh and Liverpool, which could recognize the legitimate claims of French capitalism to the trade, might have thought carefully before refusing it to British colonial capitalists. Privately, James Stephen warned the government that while the colonists "most reasonably complained against" the coupling of abolitionist articles in the treaty with the return of the French sugar colonies and the slave trade as a hardship on themselves, some had cynically muted their protests. "They will not all complain, because many of them, not without reason, regard the revival of the French slave trade as promising them a certain release from the restraints of our own abolition."[39] Britain would possess all of the advantages in rapidly making such a countermove. She was still the central manufacturing center of goods required for the African trade. The large orders which the French slave merchants were placing in England for the supply of iron collars, handcuffs, and other articles of their trade, could more easily and more quickly have been ordered from Liverpool than the French ports. Nearly a million excess guns were in stock "and Birmingham had to export again."[40]

Ships were fitting out in Havana by the summer of 1814, but here too the British merchant fleet would have had an enormous momentary advantage. It had a slave fleet in being which had merely been redeployed after abolition. Britain, which had subsidized the exhausted Continental powers against Napoleon, certainly possessed all the advantages of ready capital. The American fleet, the only potential competitor of scale, was prevented by war from operating. The British were thus in a position to reap windfall benefits, with a brief total monopoly of the Caribbean and Eastern slave trades. Never in time of peace had their monopolistic position as carriers been so favorable.[41] What Romilly said they had surrendered was still theirs for the taking.

We can summarize the picture in 1814–1815. With the collapse of Napoleon's Continental system, the British slave colonies, still capable of vigorous growth and expansion, were faced with vast new opportunities and threats: (1) high prices and a backlog from the Continent; (2) the return of some of the captured colonies to prewar possessors; (3) the restoration of the slave trade to Latin America and the East with their large undeveloped frontiers. Cuba and Brazil, as well as French and Dutch colonies, were capable of absorbing massive new numbers of fresh laborers from Africa. Finally, without the slave trade, British slavery was an increasingly costly luxury, not allowed even a free inter-island trade to produce at least an imperial slave market.[42]

The British government's theoretical alternatives were clear: (1) they could refuse to return any colonies except on condition of abolition of the trade (this was in fact easily done with small powers like Sweden); (2) they could employ a variety of diplomatic, economic, and military pressures to check or choke off the trade in Africa and the Americas while enforcing abolition in the British colonies; (3) they could conditionally restore the African trade to the British system, until an effective international agreement outlawed the traffic, as with piracy.

The first option, for reasons of general European policy was not attempted with France. The second option was employed over two full generations, despite considerable expense, endless diplomatic complications, and enormous opportunities for evasion by other powers. The third strategy relied only on effective reciprocity, while protecting British imperial and colonial positions. It was never tried and never seriously suggested, although it would have minimized diplomatic complications, maximized the competitive position of British slavery, and slowed or stopped the decline of Britain's world position in tropical production. It would also have lowered the policing costs of the British navy and would certainly have benefited the British consumer. The costs would have been borne chiefly by Africans who had neither capital nor votes. But British economic power was never unleashed on Africa or Europe. Forced to fight the battle of world sugar production in untenable terms, Britain did not even so much as threaten to employ its potent precautionary weapon, the reopening of the British slave trade. It was as though the most articulate element of world capitalism had lost even the power of speech. If revival remained an unspeakable alternative in 1814, it was because the aversion relied on something independent of capitalist arguments, old or new. The source of silence, inexplicable within contemporary economic parameters, probably lay in the thunderous popular petition against the slave-trade article which covered the tables of both Houses of Parliament in June and July of 1814.[43] When all the economic and demographic indicators pointed in one direction, the empire took the other.

10
Beyond Economic Interest

We have attempted to look systematically at two fundamental concepts which have become embedded in almost all historical works on British abolition since the appearance of Williams's seminal study. The first is that the decline of British slavery occurred before and was a prerequisite of abolitionist successes. The second assumes that abolition can be successfully explained in the framework of two variants of capitalist political economy, one of them tying abolition to the emergence of interests connected with laissez-faire capitalism hostile to the mercantilist nexus of slavery, and the other linking abolition to interests connected with mercantilist capitalism. A survey of these concepts in historical context is the prerequisite for studying abolition in a different framework.

The Age of Slavery

We begin with the central image of British slavery from Ragatz to the present. The British slave system supposedly died because, in some global sense, it was old. Old soil, old habits, old techniques, made for old colonists and old defenders. Do we not aways refer to the "old" empire of the eighteenth century and the "new" empire of the nineteenth? What is more inevitable than death for the aged? Luckier than most, the British slave system was buried without great bloodshed. Was this because the old man of the empire had so little blood in him? The metaphors of aging set our minds at rest and turn our attention to the new, the vigorous, and the dynamic—elsewhere.

We have said enough about the configuration of geographical growth to show how much of the "new" empire of 1792–1807 was a slave empire.

We have cited the statistics of trade, analyzed the impact of the frontier. What we must finally do is show not only that the British slave system was young, but that it seemed so to contemporaries. This cannot be done with economic statistics alone. Adjectives of age, appended to economies or geographic areas, may imply many things. Barbados, which was colonized for slavery in the seventeenth century, was located in the New World. Bourbon, which began its most rapid development in the late eighteenth century, was in the old. The important historical question here is whether the part of the empire where slavery predominated was considered to be outworn or decrepit at the beginning of the nineteenth century.

The tropics were always regarded as an area of rapid ascent and decline. But balancing this impression were the persistent demands of the planters for more slaves and of the British metropolis for more tropical production. The abolitionists, with their special concern for heightening the danger of the status quo, were unlikely to stress the themes of complete maturity and satiety. The planters likewise argued that maturity would be reached "soon," until which time, however, the system had to import slaves limited only by demand. Both sides had a vested interest in the statement that without abolition the slave trade would continue. But how did slavery look to those who had no burning interest in its growth potential or its labor needs? It would be interesting to peer into every survey of British trade at the beginning of the nineteenth century to get a sense of contemporary perceptions. Lacking this, one should try to get as close as possible to the simple working assumptions of the economic experts. We have chosen two general economic surveys of the empire which were published as close to 1806–1807 as possible. They were not written by men who were directly interested in the West Indian trade. Their writings did not reflect a decided abolitionist position. Both writers felt that the most important factor in the British system was the metropolitan economy, and both favored metropolitan industry. The West Indian trade was merely one trade among others, peripheral to the focus of their work.

A survey by J. Jepson Oddy, who published *European Commerce, showing new and secure channels of trade with the Continent of Europe* in 1805, contained no comments on either slavery or abolition.[1] Oddy did not favor foreign trade. He preferred industries that used domestic raw materials and labor. He did not separate trades into slave and nonslave, but into old and new. His main point of reference was the Revolution of 1688, by which time England's commercial manufacturing and colonial greatness had clearly emerged. His terminal year for data was 1802. For this man of 1800, what was new and what was old in trade? *"The places with which we deal and the articles in which we deal,* at the present time, to and from America, the West Indies and Russia, are all branches of commerce almost totally unknown two centuries ago, and even 60 years past, still in their infancy. Their aggregate amount is now immense, and far exceed the whole of our trade at the end of the American War. The new branches are on the increase, and they already exceed in amount, the old. The case is precisely similar with regard to the articles of commerce, amongst which cotton (till very lately unknown) now ranks first."[2] These associations seemed as natural to a writer at the beginning of the nineteenth century as our association of the West Indies with an old commercial zone appears at the end of the twentieth.

Oddy went a bit further in his analysis, breaking down the principal British industries by degree of development between 1797 and 1804. Of thirty-one exporting industries surveyed, Oddy found only five to be advancing. Of the rest, eleven were stationary and fifteen declining. Of the five rapidly developing industries, three were directly related to the slave system: cotton, sugar refining, and cotton yarn. Wrought and cast iron, which were among the top five, were also major producers for the slave area.[3] Whether the perspective was 120 years, 60, or less than a decade, Oddy was struck by the vigor of the West Indies.

A second survey of 1805 is equally interesting. It was a general inquiry into the problem of economic growth and decline, entitled *An Inquiry into the Permanent Causes of the Decline and Fall of Powerful and Wealthy Nations.* It was by William Playfair, the popularizer so adept at the graphic representation of economic change.[4] Playfair believed that the most solid foundation of British trade lay not in any overseas possession but in domestic production and invention. External causes of greatness were seldom "of much importance, unless favored by interior ones." What was his perception of the place of the West Indian trade in the scale of history? He found it to be so recent, far more so than the East Indian trade, that no nation had ever yet "owed its greatness or decline to that single source." What of its projected role? "The British superiority in the West India Trade is so far of a permanent nature, that France never will again be a formidable rival there. St. Domingo is not only lost, but probably lost forever, while it is expected that Britain may retain her islands." Except for the possibility of a slave revolution, which Playfair now thought remote after the lessons of St. Domingue, he considered that the trade "may be set down as permanent; that is to say there does not seem to be any immediate cause for its decline." Regarding the East and West Indian trades, Playfair referred to the last ten years as "the last and most prosperous times."[5] Like Oddy, he aligned the West Indies unselfconsciously alongside the continental vastness of America and Russia as areas with a future.

The perception from abroad was much the same. An informed and detailed analysis of British trade (published in Germany in 1804 and in Britain the following year) came to the conclusion that the British colonies were actually the pacesetters of the empire: "It is a fact of public notoriety, that within the last fifty years almost all the English colonies have been improved, and made to yield more plentiful returns, and that their population, and even that of the three united kingdoms in Europe, has been considerably augmented."[6] The West Indies were not limited, nor aged, nor declining as a trading partner. Those who took inventory of world trade in 1805 saw no reason to view the West Indies in any age but their prime.

Slavery between 1787 and 1807 was not a wasted machine which the British government could phase out like a bankrupt venture, accumulating moral capital in return. The abolitionists were facing a dynamic system. It is doubtful if they ever seriously feared that slavery would become the prevailing form of labor in the empire. The metropolitan-colonial economic gap was too wide for that. But they feared, realistically, that if British slavery was so difficult to contain when the Afro-Caribbean network, excluding the United States, accounted for only one-fifth of British trade, what would happen if the network should ever reach a plateau of one-third or one-half of that trade?[7] The "numbers" of progressing capitalism produced daggers at their hearts, year in and year out. In reality they had to introduce a fundamental change into the indicators of imperial economic progress. It was a long and painful program of innovation in British culture. They had to attempt to force the political system to measure the quantum of misery in premature death, forced separation from community and family, and the whole panoply of pain revealed in the handbooks of Caribbean slavery.

The abolitionists, then, were not out of touch with their contemporaries in viewing the British slave system as a novelty in their economic and social order. For them it was a "new" abomination from the New World. After a century and a half Jamaica was still not sated. Would it take another century and a half to fill the mainland tropics? The metaphor of aging usually is applied to economic entities which have ceased to grow from economic causes. Where was the data for this in 1805? Only in the tiny specks of the Caribbean which had long ceased to be the main centers of tropical production. Metropolitan politicians would naturally think in imperial not regional terms. Barbados had no special economic status as against Jamaica in 1788, and Jamaica had none vis-à-vis Trinidad in 1805 or Demerara in 1815:

> The extension of territory, and the acquisition by the mother country of more fertile, and therefore valuable possessions, cannot reasonably be admitted as giving to any part of the more Ancient Empire, a right to be compensated for the depreciation of its produce. In the general advantages of that acquisition, be they more or less considerable, the whole Empire, domestic and colonial participates; and it would be as reasonable for an English landholder to complain of the effect of the corn and cattle of Ireland, admitted on the principle of the Union, as for a planter in Jamaica to urge that his produce is become cheaper since Demerara has been added to the British Dominions.[8]

The dynamic of the colonial system was no more measured by the statistics of the seventeenth-century pioneers than were metropolitan trends by the statistics of Old Sarum. British slavery was still riding the wave of the future in 1805.

Abolition may well have helped one form of British capital development rather than another, by slowly severing British capital from a tempting new planetary network of slave labor. There was certainly no overpowering inconsistency between coercive colonial agriculture and European capitalism in the sixteenth, seventeenth, and eighteenth centuries. Indeed, forms of indenture in plantation agriculture continued for generations after both the abolition of the British slave trade and emancipation. It would seem accurate, given the evidence available thus far, to say that abolitionism blocked at least one vigorous channel for British capital, and redirected its flow. The really simple fact about the economics of abolition is that political power was turned against a system which could not be defeated in 1800 by the unaided operation of the invisible hand. There is no reason why capitalism should be perceived as the great unmoved mover in this process.

While the British West Indies were still viewed as a relatively recent component of the imperial trade network in 1806, their deleterious social characteristics had been clear for a century before the triumph of abolition. The moral devaluation of slavery at the end of the eighteenth century did not excoriate the slave system for being either a capitalist dead end or an imperial failure. On the contrary, the abolitionists bemoaned the fact that so much material opulence could maximize so much moral poverty. The formidable task was to make the latter impression outweigh the former, in order to call a final halt to the growth of slavery.

If the tendency of eighteenth-century British capitalism was to reduce labor as far as possible to the status of an unregulated commodity, subordinate to the laws of the market, capitalism ironically reached its most successful eighteenth-century embodiment at the periphery of the empire. As Karl Polanyi notes, the rigorous logic of reducing labor to a commodity also disposes of the psychological and moral entity of the human being "attached" to the required labor power.[9] Where were these conditions so well fulfilled as in the West Indies, and more especially at their frontiers? Colonial slavery and the slave trade drew from this principle all its consequences. In this sense Davis's penetrating emphasis on the role of capitalist ideology in the transition to industrialism may provide a crucial symbolic clue to the destruction of slavery.[10]

Beyond the symbolic matrix, however, the social matrix of abolition still remains to be charted. Only this context will provide the clue to why colonial slavery, the bare bones of the acquisitive ethos, was nurtured and tolerated for a full century after its lineaments were known. It will also provide insight into a problem hitherto incompletely recognized. Why was slavery, which in many respects outperformed its traditional role in the imperial economy, aborted in its prime? Rather than seeking evidence of the failure of West Indian slavery in capitalist terms, we must seriously consider reducing the importance of slavery's performance as an independent variable in the story of abolition, except, perhaps, as a goad to militant action. British abolition was not a phenomenon that flowed logically from the evolution of colonial slavery narrowly considered. In order to understand fully what turned Britain around on slavery we must be prepared to ask what turned it around on capitalist slavery.

Seeds of Destruction

There was only one plausible way in which abolition could be linked to a decline in the potential, if not actual, economic value of the slave system between 1791 and 1807. That was to accept the fact of growth but reverse the policy implications which seemed to flow from it. It was only necessary to convince the nation that some massive new phenomenon had emerged, radically reversing or neutralizing all previous assumptions that the growth of the slave system was economically beneficial to the empire. The strategic opening for such a theme may be seen in Playfair's reservation that all growth predictions depended on the unlikelihood of a British slave revolution. If the very success of the slave trade was seen as a threat to the totality of the British economy, dialectical ingenuity could imaginatively convert boom into doom. The abolitionist's argument was quite simple: the revolution in St. Domingue had broken the spell of the master class. It destroyed forever the myth of impregnability. Each imported slave was, henceforth, a new "seed of destruction," and the slave trade little more than a mad scheme for multiplying enemies. The abolitionists pushed this interpretation for all it was worth after 1791, if only in shrewd self-defense against accusations that they were themselves fomenters of slave revolt.

If one simply assumes, without evidence, that this linkage was accepted by the majority of metropolitan members of Parliament after 1791, their voting pattern can only be read as a study in irrational behavior. In 1792, following the stunning news from St. Domingue, the Commons rejected immediate abolition in favor of gradual abolition. A sense of urgency should have suggested an immediate suspension of imports rather than a resolution to end the trade in 1796. The Lords' decisive vote to postpone any action whatever in favor of the most procrastinating mode of evidentiary hearings over the next few years implies an emphatic dismissal of the correlation between African imports and revolutionary risk. From 1792 on the peers would seem to have located a clear and immediate revolutionary threat among the native sons and daughters of France and Britain (including some abolitionists) rather than among African slaves imported into the British colonies. Moreover, although the revolutionary threat to the British colonies reached its height in 1795–1796, the Commons failed to sustain even its original resolution to abolish the trade by January 1, 1796.

The behavior of the overseas slave societies themselves did not reflect any belief in the argument that the fresh African imports were a source of peril. Throughout the Americas, such restrictions on imports as resulted from the collapse of the French slave empire favored the admission of slaves coming directly from Africa and the barring of Caribbean slaves. The danger argument was suspect because of its political base of support. The advocates were metropolitan abolitionists who were simultaneously attempting to justify the slave violence on St. Domingue. The opposition, on the contrary, came from the slaveowners who might have to pay for their misjudgment with their plantations and their lives. In the period preceding the victory of abolition, the evidence clearly points to a weakening of the perception of a revolutionary threat to the British islands. Until 1804, the abolitionists continued to refer to black victories in St. Domingue as an added incentive for haste. In May of that year the threat of revolutionary infection from newly independent Haiti was pushed with special vigor by Wilberforce and Pitt. The force of their argument was apparently blunted by the opposition's rejoinder that Dessalines, the Haitian commander-in-chief, had himself just asked the British to sanction fresh importations of Africans to Haiti. After Pitt acknowledged Dessaline's overture to Parliament, the abolitionists dropped the theme.

Wilberforce's threatening speech of 1804 was actually the swansong of the abolitionists' "imminent revolution" motif. The debates of 1805 were devoid of proabolition references to the peril from Haiti or St. Domingue. In introducing the foreign slave importation bill in 1806, Attorney General Pigott included St. Domingue as one of the foreign markets which were being supplied by the British reexport trade. If slave importations had been regarded as a significant menace to colonial capital, it is hard to see, short of a conspiracy thesis, why Parliament was asked to vote first to abolish the British slave trade to enemy colonies on the grounds that such a trade was building up rivals.

Actually, by 1807, the old line of imminent peril had been completely reversed. The abolitionists now contemptuously brushed aside attempts to connect revolution with abolition. The very idea of internal revolution in the British West Indies was treated as ridiculous: "Look at the state of these islands for the last 20 years," declared Foreign Secretary Howick, "and say, is it not notorious, that there never were so few insurrections among the negroes, as at the very time they knew that such an abolition of this infamous traffic was under discussion?"[11] Howick's description of the behavior of the British West Indian slaves, at least during the nineties, must have raised some eyebrows. But the authority of the foreign secretary was now behind the proposition that no security threat existed. For the first time since 1791 Parliament was asked to act out of calm deliberation. Grenville might still forecast that African imports would bring ruin to the colonies in the long run, but abolition was no longer tendered as a measure of strategic urgency.

If slave property no longer seemed as secure after two decades of revolution and war, all other titles to absolute dominion, whether in Europe or the colonies, had been similarly shaken. The clearer risks to imperial authority entailed in racial slave empires after 1791 had to be placed alongside the equally obvious risks in European settler colonies after 1775. Yet, although imperialism must have seemed less secure in 1800, after a generation of revolutions, than in 1770, after a century of stability, Britain continued to increase her colonial roster in Asia, Africa, and the Americas. There is no reason to assume that the balance of insecurity resulting from these volatile threats to power and property everywhere were registered, consciously or unconsciously, in votes on the slave trade between 1792 and 1807.

On the contrary, during the decade before 1807 the British were turning increasingly to imported Africans to defend their tropical empire. R. N. Buckley has detailed the unpublicized process by which the Atlantic slave trade replenished the black units which helped to stem the revolutionary tide in the British islands and to restore the military initiative to Britain. Purchases for the West India regiments were probably never at higher levels than in 1806. The British were no less enterprising in the east, where the governor of Ceylon was authorized to purchase Africans from the Portuguese for a military campaign. By 1806 the British had not only learned how to employ "new Negroes" to divide and rule, but to join and conquer.[12]

An analysis which attempts to add the psychological risk factor into the balance of forces against the extension of colonial slavery in 1807 must at the same time answer more general questions about imperialist policies: Why did British ministers, who warned that they would tolerate no obstruction by antiabolitionists, insist that they must keep Demerara, seize the Cape Colony, hold Buenos Aires, and covet Cuba? Why did the British press hail the news of captured foreign colonies as glorious exploits, as additions to the resources, security, and potential of the empire? Why did the British government continue to depend on African slaves even beyond abolition, as the best source of troops for the maintenance of their Caribbean empire? To conclude that they were consciously or unconsciously driven to stoke the furnaces of colonial self-destruction presumes that European imperialism in 1807 was wedded, not to political economy, but to Thanatos.

Abolition and Evolving Economic Policy

THE SHORT TERM

The basic interpretation of the economic reality behind abolition has hitherto been that the protected empire of the early eighteenth century, with its old mercantilist-capitalist ideology, aged and was replaced, ca. 1750–1830, by an informal, free-trade empire. The old empire upheld slavery as well as mercantilism. Both were born at the same time and died at the same time. They must therefore have outlived their usefulness at the same rate. This pairing of rising laissez-faire and declining slavery is an application of the principle of concommitant variation. It is made more plausible by the fact that British slavery was an economy producing for a protected market in both 1760 and again in 1830, as it became decreasingly competitive with externally produced tropical products.

Even if we accept for the moment that British slavery, including its metropolitan network, was principally a component of the protected, or "forced" trade sector of the empire, the timing of abolition in 1807 becomes more rather than less mysterious. Abolition occurred at the precise peak of a movement away from free-trade principles. The shift became evident during the last year of the Pitt government and was completed by the subsequent ministry in its famous orders-in-council of 1807. The policy continued for the duration of the blockade. In 1805–1807 Britain swung toward protection of her colonial commerce, and the funneling of the entire North Atlantic trade through either her own ships or her own ports. If ever a date represented the triumphant reassertion of mercantilism it was 1807. The orders-in-council were supported by the gentry, the great merchants of London and Liverpool, by the European, colonial, and Latin American trades, by the shipping interest, by the West India interest, and by the carrying trade.[13] But if mercantilism was in the saddle, and the West Indians argued that only labor maintenance of the imperial colonies was at stake by 1807, why was the restricted slave trade crushed so dramatically by Parliament at that moment?

Let us probe the implications of regarding abolition as a result of a conflict between laissez-faire and mercantilism. A few months before the abolition of 1807, foreign abolition had been introduced to Parliament on explicitly protectionist grounds. The old colonies were to be guarded against foreign competition. Six months later, in the same Parliament, under the same ministry, the protected sector was unable to protect itself against its "protectors." It might be argued that six months can be a long time, that the connection between the circumstances surrounding the passage of the foreign slave trade bill of 1806, and the domestic slave bill were different. This line of argument is foreclosed by the other vote on the slave trade in 1806. Foreign abolition was last debated in the Lords on May 16, 1806. Within a few weeks, resolutions for total abolition were introduced and passed in both Houses by large majorities. They passed over the protests of the slave interest and despite the fact that foreign abolition supposedly had been designed to give the British colonies a competitive advantage.

In terms of political economy one might explain the foreign abolition vote of May 1806 as a consequence of resurgent mercantilism, or the votes of June 1806 and February 1807 (for British colonial abolition) as a consequence of emergent laissez-faire capitalism, but an historian can hardly ask to have the cake of mercantilist antiforeign abolition and eat that of antimercantilist domestic abolition at the same time. The more abolitionist events we include between 1804 and 1807 the more strained this type of interpretation becomes. If we include the abolition votes of 1804–1805 and the order-in-council of 1805 in the chronological sequence, the British political system becomes antimercantilist on Mondays, Wednesdays, and Fridays, and mercantilist on Tuesdays, Thursdays, and Saturdays. Finally, on "Sunday" (1807), the famous orders-in-council on trade were issued, and British policy rested for the duration.

The votes of 1806–1807 illustrate the danger of applying generalizations drawn from secular trends in political economy over a century to shifts in votes. The difficulty exists if, and only if, one attempts to account for the abolitions of 1806–1807 in terms of political economy. If, on the other hand, a noneconomic motive is accepted as the decision factor, one requires only one consistent parliamentary motive to explain the votes on abolition (see Appendix III).

One must analyze the sequence of targets as well as the timing of abolitionist action. Progressive constriction had affected Trinidad and St. Vincent in 1798, Guiana in 1805, all foreign colonies in 1806, and the "old" empire in 1807. The restriction would have followed a different order if the logic of either political economy or national strategy had been the dominant force in slave-trade policy. The foreign slave trade was not a liability to metropolitan Britain, insofar as she had trade with, and profitable capital investments in, foreign colonies. But certainly, insofar as these colonies aided enemy metropolitan states in wartime, growth in this sector was proportionately least advantageous to British capitalism. Guiana was lucrative and booming, with British capital rushing in, but was also less secure from reversion to foreign control than Trinidad. The old colonies, with important exceptions (especially Jamaica and St. Vincent), had small proportions of virgin land available for development. Trinidad was securely British, competitive, and almost uncleared.

Assuming that abolition of the British slave trade stemmed from mercantilist or market pressures, the most logical progression in 1796–1807 would have been the following: abolition of the British trade to foreign areas; abolition of imports to Guiana; abolition of imports to the older British islands; and finally, abolition of imports to underdeveloped Trinidad, St. Vincent, and Jamaica. In the context of volatile and hostile alternative producers from 1803 to 1807, a premium would also be placed on the time period *between* successive abolitions, to allow maximum benefit to the British colonial system and minimum loss to the metropolitan slave trade. Above all, the action would have been cautious, flexible, and experimental. In the manner of other trade legislation, it would have contained within itself an explicit economic rationale for implementation and an implicit rationale for conditions of reversal. Such legislation, more than any other, was always formulated within a clearcut means-ends network.

The obvious significance of abolition to the frontier areas is shown by the numbers of African slaves going to Cuba in the early nineteenth century. British restrictions on intracolonial as well as on African slave mobility resulted in a postwar decline to Trinidad and British Guiana of between 85 and 90 percent of their annual average imports prior to 1805. Cuba almost doubled her preabolition imports during the decade after 1809. The postwar shift in the balance of slave imports between the British and Spanish Caribbean frontiers is shown in table 31. In 1803–1804, Trinidad and Demerara had imported more slaves than Cuba. In 1815–1819 the Trinidad and Demerara imports (from other British colonies) were less than one-thirteenth of legal imports of Africans into Havana alone. Between 1809 and 1820 Demerara acquired net imports of slightly more than 6,000 slaves (well below replacement), mainly from neighboring Berbice. The Cuban figure for the same period

TABLE 31: SLAVE IMPORTS TO DEMERARA, TRINIDAD, AND CUBA, 1803–1804 AND 1815–1819

	Demerara and Trinidad			Cuba[a]		
	Slaves Imported	Percent Change	Percent of Average for Three Colonies	Slaves Imported	Percent Change	Percent of Average for Three Colonies
1803–04 (annual average)	11,747	—	50.3	11,621	—	49.7
1815–19 (average best 3 yrs.)	1,700[b]	–85.5	6.0	26,450	+ 127.6	94.0
1815–19 (average all 5 yrs.)	1,450[b]	–87.7	6.2	21,935	+ 88.7	93.8

Sources: Table 19; Aimes, *Slavery in Cuba,* Appendix, p. 269; Humboldt, *Narrative,* VII, 146–47. Humboldt estimated that Havana figures had to be raised by at least a fourth, for illegal imports and those to other Cuban ports to determine its total. On British intracolonial imports see PP 1823 (XVIII), *Slave Population Papers and Returns* (Demerara and Trinidad).
a. Includes allowance for unrecorded Cuban imports.
b. From intracolonial trade.

was a minimum of 134,000, more than twenty times the Demerara figure. If Humboldt's estimates of legal imports into other entrepots and the illegal trade were accurate, Cuba's advantage was even more staggering.

The whole web of supposedly logical and empirical short-term links between economic and social conditions and abolition disintegrates when analyzed in these terms. From 1788 until 1806 the abolitionists seemed to be men hammering away at a rising system, who struck hardest when its prospects were brightest and where it was vigorous. This was an appropriate strategy for embattled militants, not for capitalists and MPs acting according to the norms of political economy.

STRUCTURAL TRENDS

British slavery's long-range relation to the imperial vacillation over protectionism at the end of the eighteenth century must also be treated in appropriate temporal perspective. One of the most important misjudgments about the evolution of the British involvement in slavery stems from the almost universal identification of that interest with the mercantilist, and therefore noncompetitive, sector of the imperial economy. Once this image is altered, a different sense of the relation of slavery to metropolitan economic change may be possible. It is true that the bulk of the system in 1760 was protectionist. Sugar was carried in protected shipping and sold in a protected market. It should also be noted, however, that sugar was exchanged for British manufactures and that some British manufacturers, including the leaders of industrialization, vociferously demanded certain forms of protection before 1807. As far as the West Indians were concerned, the imperial system became even more protectionist *against* their interests after 1783, when they had to rely exclusively on British carriers for their provisions in peacetime.

We have already noted that in terms of production and trade the expansion of slave capitalism paralleled that of metropolitan capitalism. We must also recall some of the structural changes that were occurring in British slavery itself. There may well have been a contrast between mercantilist and classical political economy and a division of the economic interests that supported them. But did the British slave system between 1760 and 1820 fit so neatly onto either side of the ledger? After 1766 the free port system and British customs policy encouraged the opening of the imperial market to foreign cotton. This policy continued throughout the period of abolition. The extension of cotton culture in the West Indies was a sign of responsiveness to the new opportunities of industrialization. Coffee production in the British colonies also rose sharply after the St. Domingue uprising. In 1807 the British slave system was the premier coffee producer under European control. And coffee, unlike sugar, had no market in Britain. Almost the entire crop was reexported to the European continent, where it competed without protection and under war-related disadvantages between 1795 and 1807. The coffee grower had no recourse to neutral ships to carry his goods directly to the Continent, avoiding war insurance and reexport costs.

Even sugar, the premier and totally protected crop of 1787, had burst through its mercantilist dimensions before 1800. At the time of the Peace of Amiens in 1802, or of Paris in 1814, almost 40 percent of British-produced sugar was moving on to the Continent. The British consumer had been paying more for his sugar than were his Continental counterparts for more than two generations before the French Revolution. In the years before abolition, the price of British sugar fell well below that of Continental sugar and stayed there. In 1807 the British consumer had less cause to be displeased with mercantilist restraints on British sugar than at any time before or afterward. Before abolition it was the planters who cried aloud for free trade.[14]

More important than the implication of changes in the sugar trade was the function of the slave trade itself in the nonmercantilist branch of the slave system. Long before any other branch of British slavery, it had operated largely in a competitive, free-trade zone. To the African slave dealers all European traders were similar. In the West Indies, purely "British" demand was always far less than British supply. The British retained their dominant position in the trade to the end, although the law made their position increasingly difficult. After 1788 they were subject to a kind of reverse mercantilism in which imperial regulation created a handicap vis-à-vis foreign competitors. Unlike the usual mercantilist legislation this produced no net gain for any identifiable imperial interest group, although it may have stimulated the business of some capitalists who helped to fit out American slavers. In any event, the British slavers asked for nothing more in 1806–1807 than adherence to the golden rule of unrestricted free enterprise.

The slave trade was more than just a competitive enterprise. It was a capitalist bridge to penetration of foreign slave systems. Slave purchases usually meant debts. Debts meant mortgages and control by British capital which had no great interest in supporting mercantilism. The same capitalists often had holdings in both .protected and unprotected areas and products. But slave traders, by the very structure of their trade, would almost always tend to think in terms of an international rather than an imperial market.

Of all the historians influenced by the decline theory, only Davis seems to have serious reservations about the correlation between free trade and abolition. Although he declares that "the antislavery movement, like Smith's political economy, reflected the needs and values of the emerging capitalist order," he also notes that Smith's principles provided no grounds "for opposing a hypothetical slave trade resulting from free trade principles."[15] We have but one comment to add to that perceptive reservation concerning the identity of laissez-faire and antislavery. There is no need to talk about a hypothetically competitive slave trade. The actual British trade will do. Smith posited only that abolition would occur if it did not clash with interest. That is why he opened his lecture on the subject with the following statement: "We are apt to imagine that slavery is quite extirpated, because we know nothing of it in this part of the world; but even at present it is almost universal. A small part of the West of Europe is the only portion of the globe that is free from it, and is nothing in comparison with the vast continents where it still prevails. We shall endeavor to show how it was abolished in this quarter, and for what reasons it has continued in other parts, and probably will continue."[16]

The "informal empire" of the nineteenth century was already in formation toward the end of the eighteenth. If British capital and ships had continued to furnish the most valuable single item of foreign frontier development, we might today think of the great "free trade" empire of Britain as the product of the slave trade, as well as of Manchester manufactures. There was no conflict between the slave and manufacturing trades, as the interest petitions of 1794–1807 testified. All slave frontiers were potential areas of British profit. As Keith Aufhauser has shown, both slave and free labor systems were capable of generating above-average profits, even in Barbados, until emancipation. The advantages of slave capital in British Guiana or Trinidad were even greater. Sugar in 1830 "was still a lucrative occupation to any man willing to take up the cat-o'-nine-tails. And from a business point of view, a slave owner could match any employer of free labor on the score which they both respected—profits."[17] Even after full emancipation in 1838, the planters' intensive search for indentured labor from Asia indicated a labor-starved system.

Britain's new empires of the nineteenth century, both formal and informal, could have been bound to Britain by the slave trade. The slave trade seemed as normal and necessary to the planter in Demerara or the shipowner in Liverpool in 1805 as it had seemed to the merchant of Bristol or the planter of Barbados a century before. In economic terms this perspective was not confined to slave capitalists. In January 1807 the abolitionist *Edinburgh Review* noted that anyone who rented out a slave in Demerara could safely count on paying off his original purchase price within a few years, without any maintenance costs or further bother to himself. It would seem that British slavery, in its widest sense, was proving economically capable of crossing the bridge between the two variants of capitalist political economy.

The Elusive Enemies of Slavery

From the logic of political economy we must turn to the choices of the economically interested. The decline theory entails more than a presumed economic logic for the dismemberment of slavery. It also takes for granted some combination of short- and long-term economic interest which apparently welcomed and guided the process of liquidation. For Williams the carriers of abolition were the "new" manufacturing interests. Roger Anstey has already noted the lack of cohesion among these groups at the beginning of the nineteenth century. Davis's more supple interpretation moves the Williams thesis onto broader, if vaguer, grounds. He concludes that it makes no difference whether the manufacturing or the landed interest fulfilled the role of executioner.[18] We wonder, however, whether it can be presumed *a priori* that any economic interest *qua* interest can be assigned the structural role presupposed by the decline theory. There are analytic tasks which must precede such an interpretation. The dividing lines between antagonistic interests must be established for both the short and the long term. Then differences of interest must be plausibly shown to have made some difference in the outcome.

If British slavery between 1775 and 1815 was not declining and if interested capitalists were behaving as they ought to, they had no incentive to force slavery to contract. However, rather than assume such rationality, it would be well to survey briefly the evidence for interest-group pressures on the slave system in the two-decade controversy over abolition. We do not have the detailed information necessary for following members of Parliament through their successive votes on abolition. Our survey will be confined to a statement of the minimally plausible inferences that can be drawn from the available data. We think that this will suffice.

Probably the most important evidence against any conflict-of-interest theories of abolition between 1788 and 1807 is that no explicit linkages have yet been shown to exist. In a period in which large and powerful economic groups made their influence felt at the Board of Trade, in Parliament, or in committees, by means of representations, petitions, and publications, this is a strange case of self-abnegation. On matters of trade, with potential gains and losses hanging in the balance, when broad moral approval was guaranteed, where were the abolitionist petitions of the "interested"? A "cloak of humanity" approach might have been excellent strategy in 1788, or 1792, or 1814, when numbers of other petitions were supporting total abolition on noneconomic grounds. But in 1793, 1794, 1799, or 1806, partial abolitions were being proposed on grounds of expediency. On those occasions the principal question was "who were the persons to be injured and to what amount?"[19] When there were no massive abolitionist petition campaigns to rely on, it would have been appropriate to offset the gains of those who traded in human beings by those of nonslaving merchants. Yet for two decades, year in and year out, whether in behalf of bills for partial or for total abolition, whether the public was mobilized or not, whether the prospects were bright or gloomy, no petitions came in from antislavery interests. If there were such interests, and they thus failed to act, a startling new page could indeed be added to the history of British capitalism. Until such a blank page is filled, Ockham's razor retains its edge.

Winnowing the Parliamentary debates produces equally little evidence of proabolitionist commercial interests. Provincial manufacturers and London merchants neither argued as a group for the abolition of the slave trade nor asserted the negligibility of the British slave system. Perhaps the most ironic comment on the decline thesis is that certain metropolitan commercial interests fought harder and more coherently to preserve all parts of the slave trade than did the West Indian planters themselves. One of the strongest supporters of the West Indies, foreign slave trade and all, was Robert Peel, Sr. No member of Parliament more clearly represented the dynamic cotton industry. None argued more forcefully for the bond between the slave trade and his own industry. None was more categorical in declaring that the whole abolitionist scheme, even when supposedly couched in terms of expediency as in 1806, had no economic foundation. No representative of Liverpool had ever put the case more forcefully in fifteen years of debate: "If we were to philosophize, let us do so while our looms were full. Was it a reason, because our artful enemy had at present succeeded in putting our trade to a stand, by driving our manufactures from the continent of Europe, that we should aid him in accomplishing his end, and should ourselves banish them from the colonies?"[20]

At the very least, representatives of "new" economic forces, if manufacturers of cotton are such, were divided in their attitudes toward the economic value of the slave trade. One must agree with Anstey's point that the new forces were as yet not well organized; they did not form a self-conscious nor a politically overpowering group. We would further insist that, even as a minor interest group, they did not cast their influence on behalf of abolition. Even in Liverpool, merchants and bankers did not all have their capital equally distributed over each overseas trade. Those whose primary interests were in the temperate zones, especially in the Americas, might be expected to have economic interests which differed from those in the tropical zones. After 1807 the interests of some shippers were in fact often in direct conflict in response to governmental policies to protect British overseas producers. Yet this was largely a postabolition division which became acute after the orders-in-council against the neutral trade.[21]

Having failed to locate coherent domestic commercial groups hostile to the slave trade in the record of debates, we may turn to the "imperial" rivals. Because of its incredibly poor performance from 1788 to 1807, we have discounted the role of the rising East India interest in abolition. In general, the problem faced by the West Indians with regard to East Indian produce before 1807 was very similar to that of the British cotton manufacturer, although less acute. Goods produced in India could often be shipped as dead weight in Indiamen and sold without consideration for the cost of transportation.[22] To move, however, from potential conflict on this ground to political conflict over abolition is a long step. Before 1807, the slave trade actually formed the strongest link between the two tropical systems. A proportion of goods bound for Africa were usually East Indian products. Only days before the final debates in 1807, an East Indian wrote to Henry Dundas (now Lord Melville) that the only part of their goods in any degree profitable were piece goods, and a considerable proportion of these were for the threatened slave trade.[23] For the East Indians, the slave trade was that element of the West Indian system least likely to be opposed.

In the East Indian case we can finally move from the logic of potential conflict to an actual voting list. Anstey has analyzed the vote of 1796, the one roll-call vote against abolition that we possess for the period 1787–1807, and discovered that the East India interest voted disproportionately to defeat abolition. He presents a compelling argument, seconded by Davis, that they were voting out of a concern for the maintenance of the imperial factor, broadly conceived.[24] This would mean that neither their potential interests as shippers of sugar to England nor their immediate ones as shippers of piece goods to Africa were decisive. Their common position as peripheral members of an empire may have given them an outlook such that, except in a case of deep conflict, they would vote with the West Indies on issues concerning broad values by which the dependencies should be ruled. This suggests that commodity politics may have taken second place to value politics. Motives aside, the East Indians as a collectivity came down on the side of their West Indian counterparts. What evidence we have from postabolition votes further implies that this was a general position, not an isolated moment. After studying the postabolition East Indian votes on slavery, P. F. Dixon found a correlation strongly suggesting "a certain community of political interest between the West Indians and supporters of the [East India] Company," running from 1788 to 1830.[25] Two analysts of East Indian voting behavior thus independently reached parallel conclusions. Neither found any evidence of an East Indian "block" aligned against the West Indians.

There is one last metropolitan interest which has received only passing reference in accounts of abolition. This is the British landed interest. Most contemporaries, including the West Indians, pictured the landowning groups on both sides of the Atlantic as natural and conservative allies. In time of peace there was no apparent clash of interest whatsoever. There was however, one recurring source of conflict at the beginning of the nineteenth century arising from the fact that sugar was a potential alternative to domestic grains in the production of alcoholic beverages. The war disrupted the flow of European goods to the British Isles, causing grain shortages which sometimes coincided with poor reexport markets for sugar. Substituting sugar for corn in the distilleries was a way of canceling out this double imbalance. At three points of maximum disequilibrium (1800, 1808, 1811), British distilleries were opened to sugar, an obvious conflict of interest between West Indian planters and certain metropolitan growers.

This conflict did not produce an automatic surge of support for abolition. From June 1801 to January 1802 distillation from wheat was forbidden in England, Scotland, and even Ireland.[26] Yet abolition was absolutely dormant as an issue. Distillation from sugar was again requested as a means of relief following the Berlin decrees, but was not sanctioned by Parliament until late in 1808.[27] Since the question of distillation was not even broached in Parliament before December 1806, It could not account for the abolitionist breakthroughs in the spring and summer of 1806, including the overwhelming resolution for total abolition. The landed interest felt no threat to their market in the spring of 1806. The crop outlook was unpromising, and war with Prussia had cut off the Baltic corn supply. It is even more difficult to see how the large abolitionist majority in the Commons in 1804 is to be related to an interest whose economic position was being sharply bolstered by short supply situations for their own crops.[28] The large landed interest was as likely to be represented in the Lords as in the Commons. Yet the Lords' opposition to abolition was longer and stronger.

The sugar distillery vote of 1808 points in another direction. Not only were the West Indies not declining in economic value between 1800–1808, but they could muster real political muscle. The 1808 vote to allow sugar distillation, opposed by a portion, though not all, of the landed interest, passed the second reading in the Commons by a thumping majority of 90 to 39.[29] A year after the West Indians had been "crushed" over abolition, they fought a pitched battle with the "corn" counties, and "achieved a signal triumph."[30]

In general, until it can be shown which groups opposed the slave trade, in or out of Parliament, it makes no sense to say that any economically definable group was so aligned and so acted. In the meanwhile, there is less reason for saying that the owners of factories, or of land, or of the national debt,[31] destroyed the slave trade, than for saying that the MPs, as owners of houses and horses, did so. Perhaps the most significant "fact" about all the interests referred to thus far is the limited nature of their conflicts with British slavery or the slave trade. Aside from the abolitionists, the only parliamentary group clearly identifiable as a structural (proabolitionist) element in the debate, and clearly sympathetic to at least a portion of the abolitionist program, was a branch of the West India interest.

Most explanations of abolition emphasize the split between the developed and undeveloped colonies in 1804–1807, which supposedly weakened the force of the slave-trade interest. The special political impact of this dissidence toward 1807 is questionable. At all times after 1793 there existed a "moderate" planter group of undetermined magnitude and influence, willing to support partial moves toward abolition. The split was evident in 1793–1794. Opposing petitions regarding the bill to abolish the foreign slave trade were submitted from capitalists already heavily extended beyond the imperial confines. Some West Indians, however, spoke out in favor of the bill, and a motion made before the West India committee, to present a corporate petition against the bill, was defeated by 56 to 36. Thus at least a substantial sector of the slave interest refused to campaign actively against abolition of the foreign trade. The failure of this first campaign against the foreign trade is also noteworthy in that its potential effect was less serious than in 1806. The British, in the spring of 1794, were in the process of conquering every French Caribbean possession. Foreign abolition would have affected only the still minor trades to the Spanish and Dutch colonies. The sudden incorporation of the French slave colonies also pushed sugar prices to their lowest point between 1788 and the end of the century.[32] Yet the bill was summarily thrown out by the Lords.

A second moderate initiative occurred at the end of the century. Several planters sought to blunt the abolitionist attack by proposing to Pitt and Wilberforce a temporary suspension of the slave trade. A public meeting of the West India interest rejected the move and shook the resolution of the more timid converts. Even the open support of some of the West Indian moderates failed to assure passage of the slave trade limitation bill in 1799. Another suspension move by the moderates in 1804 was again overruled by the majority, who feared that the trade would never again be reopened. In 1806, as in 1794, the West Indians presented no corporate petition either for or against the foreign bill.[33] The slave interest split over the bill, as it had over every partial bill since 1793. Since we do not know the proportion of the defections between 1793 and 1807, nor if they made any real difference in Parliament, there is no reason to suppose that the mere existence of a division was decisive in the triumph of abolition. The moderates were shown to have no bargaining power in 1800, or in 1804, when they were repudiated by the West Indian majority, or in 1807, when their interest was brushed aside by the vast metropolitan majority. If the West Indian moderates played any role in the triumph of abolition, it was as foot soldiers on a battleground chosen by others.

By elimination we are left with only one parliamentary group which can be firmly and consistently identified with the abolition of the slave trade. The hard-core abolitionists have not yet been characterized economically. Even they could hardly have been decisive in the victory of abolition. Their intrinsic voting power was about the same as that of the hard-core of the slavery interest.[34] If one chooses to construct a model of "virtual" representation in the manner of Burke, this group can of course be made to stand for any or all capitalist interests. In the absence of evidence, the abolitionists, and they alone, become the identifiable group uniquely endowed with the ability to inform metropolitan and overseas capitalists of their own interests. Without the establishment of any linkages to the economic forces they are supposed to represent, the abolitionists are an economic spearhead merely because the decline theory says that some group must fulfill that role. In economic terms, abolition may have been voted in 1807 solely on the negative grounds that it would not be immediately fatal to a very important interest. This affords no economic incentive for destroying that trade, nor does it presume that there were any anticipated benefits, either to specific or general economic interests. But a prior question is in order. When an economic interest is undermined, why must it be by, or in behalf of, some other economic interest or combination of interests?

On the other hand, after Williams and Davis, we cannot simply take the abolitionists at their word. They declared from beginning to end that they represented the "disinterested" people of Britain. But they were, after all, active members of a society already deeply committed to the market and its values. As a whole they represented that portion of European society most completely mobilized for living with the sense of individual power, responsibility, and insecurity that flowed from the market. Britain's metropolitan development may on inspection prove more central and more crucial in explaining the abolitionist victory than all the emergent forces of interest conjured up by *Capitalism and Slavery.* These were not necessarily rising, falling, or stationary capitalists, until research proves them to be. Nor should members of the artisan classes necessarily be excluded *a priori.* What united them may be far more significant than what they had to gain, or lose from abolition.

Nor must we assume that this "consensual" conjecture represents an action sponsored and channeled by the "ruling class," however defined. We do know that people well beyond the confines of the economically well-connected demanded that a portion of their own security against the excesses of the unfettered market be applied to British capitalism in Africa. The analysis of economic development in this fascinating drama has been detoured for too long into the appraisal of interests and of their supposed ideology. It is time to return to the exciting paradox of abolition with a new sense of the broad significance of economic development. We may even rediscover the enduring economic enemies of slavery in the mass petitions of the British people between 1788 and 1814.

Beyond Elites

Economic interests cannot account for either the timing, the occurrence, or the maintenance of the abolition of the slave trade between 1787 and 1820. First, there was no political opposition to the introduction of slavery when it still played a relatively minor role in the English economic system compared with alternative economic activities. The information in tables 2–5 suggests that it would have been easier to eliminate British slavery in 1685 than in 1785, and in 1785 than in 1815, although easier in 1833 than in 1815 because of the abolition of the trade. As we noted briefly in chapter 3, market pressures for British abolition were more visible in 1740 than in 1790. It was at the end of the twenties that the French islands caught up with the British in sugar production and won the European market. It was at that point that the British foreign slave trade helped to alter the balance of Anglo-French production. These decades of crisis caused the West India interest to issue loud appeals for relief and protection. They also stimulated determined counterattacks. The British sugar islands were condemned on free-market principles as a burden. They were condemned on mercantilist principles as inadequate imperial trading partners for the North American provision colonies. Finally, during these decades, the first British colony specifically to exclude slave labor was founded. Despite the signals of distress in the British West Indies and the original exclusion of slaves from Georgia by its trustees, antislavery "from above" could not hold its ground in a single colony in the 1740s, much less inspire a trend.[35] The end of the free labor experiment in Georgia was explicitly sanctioned by Parliament in 1750. As long as metropolitan action remained the preserve of a small cluster of interests and philanthropists, the slave trade endured.

Neither British economic survival nor growth was ever dependent totally on slavery. But to the extent that both were aided by overseas trade, slavery was more important to Britain during the last decade of the eighteenth and the first decade of the nineteenth centuries, than ever before or after. Moreover, no European slave power had ever considered risking abolition solely on the grounds that any self-inflicted economic wounds would probably not be mortal. The risk was also undertaken when the British metropolis was threatened by severe losses in other major trading areas. Whether one chooses to treat abolition relative to the choices made by other contemporary governments or to Britain's own minimum overseas requirements, it is not possible to view abolition as an economic appendectomy.

Economic development did trigger successive steps in the dismantling of British colonial slavery, but it was more often than not on upward surges of the trade curve until well after the crucial cutoff of the African slave supply. If one does not move beyond a model of economically determined pressures for social change, the politics of abolition become not only inexplicable, but perverse. One cannot account for the curtailment and destruction of Britain's slave labor system by separating, a priori, "political" from "humanitarian" activity. Neither ideas nor intellectuals were the immediate source of the movement's power. That lay in its massiveness, its ability to mobilize an innovative political pressure group and to demand potential economic risks which its members, as participants in the economy, had to be willing to share.

It may be that the balance of political and economic forces at the elite level in 1787 was such that no action could be taken or maintained against slavery until and unless a broader public opinion entered into the political equation. The years 1787–1792 marked an important moment in the mobilization of opinion in British politics. Similarly, 1805–1807 marked a return in Britain to an acceptance of controlled social change, an out-look which had all but disappeared in the great fear produced by Jacobin France and Radical England during the mid-1790s. Whether this "public" was held together by a common economic network or outlook which distinguishes it from those who were opposed or apathetic, has not yet been investigated.[36]

In the political context of Hanoverian England it would appear that the slave system had to be besieged at its peripheral fortifications before it could be frontally attacked. Humanitarian historiography rightly treated the abolitionist movement not simply as an ideology, but as a national political movement with a humanitarian ideology. It emphasized both the significance of the abolitionists' sophisticated "new politics" style and the role of radical political threats in undermining the unity of the move-ment.[37] It recognized the economic interests arrayed against the aboli-tionists, if only as the formidable barrier to abolition that they were. While the West Indian interest group could from time to time mobilize their hundreds, the abolitionists could rouse their tens of thousands and, in moments of supreme effort, their hundreds of thousands.

The humanitarian tradition, however, also assumed that once con-science had been aroused, it, like economic activity, was a self-sustaining process. The sources of the abolitionists' durability and of their ability to maintain continuous if intermittent pressure on the political system for a generation until victory, and for sixty years beyond, deserve further study. We have spoken of a realm of political and economic activity which directly involved only a relative handful of individuals. Perhaps the true indicators of the forces which successfully challenged the slave system and forced it to turn the corner toward contraction and destruction should be sought not in the elites of trade and Parliament, but in the regional and local networks of social and religious life. Just as there is no model which can explain the demise of the British slave system without taking careful measure of its economic power in 1800, there is no royal road to the history of abolition which can bypass the movement, the unfolding of its initiatives and its methods. These questions may prove especially amenable to comparative national, regional, and social analysis.[38]

Capitalism and Slavery contained one powerful message which shat-tered the filiopietistic framework of previous chronicles of abolition for good. Williams told historians to look at economic change if they wished to understand even so antimaterialistic a movement as abolitionism proclaimed itself to be. However, he tied the study of economic develop-ment so narrowly to interest and so tightly to one ideology, that the West Indies simply *had* to shrink to fit the premises. Williams's story was both timely and excitingly told. Having freed abolition from humanitarians, he had deservedly earned the respect of a prophet and pioneer.

The decline of the decline thesis would sharpen the general discussion of abolition as a response to social change. If one simply describes abolition as the result of certain economic, political, and ideological forces, all moving in the same direction and at a uniform speed, there seems to be neither the need for, nor the possibility of, analytically disentangling them. Lumping together the causes of abolition begs too much and yields too little. It is only by separating the elements that we sense just how they worked for or against each other. Human history is not a uniform stream of actions all moving in the same direction at the same pace, either in the short or the long term. It is only by the patient and painstaking comparison of one variable after another that historical explanation can hope to break the ultimately metahistorical, if enchanting, spell of inevitability. It may then, and only then, be possible to describe abolition as the probable result of a peculiar economic, political, and ideological interaction.

Inheriting a controversy in which "material" and "ideal" protagonists were divided from one another by self-definition, the historiography of abolition has either perpetuated the traditional dichotomy or dissolved it completely. There is a methodological economy to such explanations because, granted these premises, certain questions about the conditions of social change need never be broached. In the history of abolition, however, as of any other movement, we are dealing neither with pure ideas held by saints, nor even with the same ideas abstractly held by large numbers, but with a collective force for change. And social forces, slave interest or abolitionist, cannot be retroactively placed into unweighed boxes with predetermined addresses.[39] If abolitionism by itself seems too hollow or airy a term to describe a social force to generations bred on depressions, wars, revolutions, and genocides, we must imaginatively allow for the possibility that a century which produced both domestic security and rapidly multiplying avenues to economic development might have also produced a new balance of social power sufficient, for the first time, to redefine a thriving trade as manstealing, and then to destroy that trade, regardless of either its economic value or its stage of development.

Abbreviations

Add MSS	Additional MSS, British Museum
AN	Archives Nationales, Paris
BT	Board of Trade
CO	Colonial Office
DUL	Duke University, Perkins Library
HLR	House of Lords Record Office
LRO	Liverpool Record Office
PD	*Parliamentary Debates,* published by William Cobbett until 1812, thereafter by Hansard
PP	Great Britain, *Parliamentary Papers*
PR	Debrett's *Parliamentary Register*
PRO	Public Record Office
SRO	Scottish Record Office
WO	War Office

All translations in the text and notes are by the author.

I

Chronology

1783 British Quakers organize committees to publicize and to petition against the slave trade. A petition is presented to Parliament and received without further action.

1787 Formation of a Society for Effecting the Abolition of the Slave Trade in London and some provincial cities. Clarkson travels to get evidence on the trade. Pitt and Wilberforce attempt to initiate an Anglo-French suspension of the slave trade. The West Indian free port system is renewed and expanded (through 1792). Government seeks to expand British colonial cotton growth.

1788 Manchester launches a mass abolition petition campaign. Privy Council Committee for Trade and Plantations reports on the slave trade. Abolition is raised in Parliament. First slave carrying (Dolben) act is passed. Mass propaganda campaigns begin. Sugar prices begin a general rise (to 1792).

1789 Wilberforce introduces resolutions on the slave trade in Parliament. Commons agrees to hear evidence. The Dolben act is now renewed annually.

1790 Select Committee of Commons hears testimony on the slave trade.

1791 Commons rejects Wilberforce's first abolition motion. Commons approves a charter for Sierra Leone, its company pledged to oppose the slave trade in Africa. Massive slave uprising on St. Domingue. Sugar prices rise steeply.

1792 Mass petition campaign for abolition. Commons resolves on gradual abolition by 1796. Lords delays action in favor of preliminary hearings. Boycott of sugar begins. French Revolution begins to affect mass agitation. Sierra Leone settlement renewed. Denmark decrees gradual abolition by 1803.

1793   Commons narrowly rejects motions to reintroduce general abolition and to abolish the British foreign slave trade. Decline of public agitation and abolition society activity. Lords continues desultory hearings on the slave trade. Britain begins campaign to capture the French slave islands. Tobago and Cape Nicolas-Mole on St. Domingue are occupied.

1794   Commons passes a foreign abolition bill. Lords tables the bill in favor of continued hearings on general abolition. Britain temporarily conquers Guadeloupe, St. Lucia, and large sections of St. Domingue. Martinique is permanently occupied. France turns to revolutionary war in the West Indies. Sugar reaches its low point before 1799. French ships raid the African coast, including Sierra Leone.

1795   Commons again defeats abolition. British slave islands are attacked by French revolutionary forces. Grenada, St. Vincent, and Dominica are threatened. The Cape of Good Hope is captured from the Dutch.

1796   Commons narrowly defeats abolition. The Dolben act is not renewed because of oversight. British troops retake Grenada and St. Vincent, and their planters are indemnified. Britain is stalemated in St. Domingue, but St. Lucia is recaptured, and Demerara and Berbice are taken.

1797   Commons rejects abolition. The Dolben act is renewed. A West Indian-sponsored parliamentary resolution for colonial amelioration of slavery is passed. Trinidad is captured. Tropical prices remain very high through mid-1799. Trinidad and St. Vincent crown land sales are suspended. The British are pushed from St. Domingue by Toussaint L'Ouverture.

1798   Commons rejects abolition. Other motions are introduced for stiffening restrictions on the slave carrying act and for abolishing the slave trade along much of the West African coast. Negroes are eliminated from the list of "goods" favored under the free port system.

1799   Commons rejects abolition. Commons passes an African slave coast restriction act. Lords narrowly rejects it. Commons passes a stricter slave carrying act, which narrowly clears the Lords. Sugar prices begin to decline. Britain conquers Surinam.

1800   No motion is made for abolition. Curaçao is captured.

1801   Pitt government resigns. A struggle begins over the sale of St. Vincent and Trinidad crown lands. St. Bartholomew is captured, as are all the Danish West Indies. Peace preliminaries are signed.

1802 Wilberforce postpones a general abolition motion. Plantation expansion is blocked in Trinidad and St. Vincent. The Peace of Amiens restores slave colonies to prewar status except for Trinidad, San Domingo, and Louisiana.

1803 War resumes. The British move quickly to recapture Demerara, Tobago, and St. Lucia. The French are driven from St. Domingue by Dessalines. The British foreign slave trade partly shifts to neutral flags. Sugar prices begin to rise again.

1804 Commons passes a general abolition bill for the first time since 1792. Lords tables the bill on grounds of late reception. Abolitionists resolve to revive activity, but without mass petitioning. Surinam is recaptured by the British. Sugar prices are good.

1805 Commons narrowly defeats abolition. An order-in-council ends the African trade to conquered slave areas by 1807 and immediately reduces annual imports to 3 percent of the existing slave population.

1806 Pitt dies. The new Grenville-Fox ministry aids the abolitionists. Parliament passes a foreign abolition bill in May and a general abolition resolution in June. Parliament also prohibits new ships from entering the slave trade. Sugar prices fall during the summer and late fall. First Prussia, then France impose German port closures, restricting British commercial access to central Europe. The Cape of Good Hope is recaptured; Rio de la Plata is captured and lost by a British expedition. British reenforcements are dispatched.

1807 Parliament passes a general abolition act prohibiting the importation of slaves from 1808. Sierra Leone becomes a crown colony. Sugar prices continue downward. British retaliate against Napoleon's trade decrees with their orders-in-council. Madeira, Curaçao, and the Danish West Indies are captured by the British.

1808 Sugar prices continue very low. Mariegalante and Desirade are captured by the British.

1809 Sugar prices rise. Senegal, Martinique, and Cayenne are captured by the British.

1810 The Portuguese agree, under British pressure, to abolish the slave trade gradually. The revolutionary government of Caracas proclaims abolition. Mexican revolutionaries proclaim emancipation. Guadeloupe, St. Martin, Bourbon, and the Ile de France are captured by the British. Sugar prices rise. The slave trade shows signs of new vigor.

1811   Parliament makes slave trading a felony. Spain's revolutionary Cortes debates abolition and receives Cuban objections. Java is captured by the British and the slave trade to that island ends. Sugar prices fall sharply through 1811.

1812   A registry of slaves is begun in Trinidad. War is declared between Britain and the U.S.A. Sugar prices begin to rise.

1813   The Continental blockade disintegrates. Tropical prices rise sharply. The Spanish Cortes again discusses abolition. Sweden agrees to abolition on obtaining Guadeloupe from the British.

1814   The treaty of Paris restores the French slave trade for five years. A mass petition ensues in Britain. Britain begins a strong diplomatic effort for total international abolition. The Dutch accept abolition before their colonies are restored. The French agree to a restriction of the slave-trade coast. Guadeloupe and Martinique are returned to France. Sugar prices reach record heights.

1815   Bonaparte decrees abolition in France during the Hundred Days. The restoration government accepts the decree. Britain secures a declaration against the slave trade at the Congress of Vienna. Sugar prices continue high. Slave trade to Cuba begins to rise sharply.

II

Estimating the Sugar, Coffee, and Slave Trades

Sugar Imports Into the North Atlantic Area

Our starting point is the sugar exported from tropical America to the North Atlantic area in *1770*. The figures are based on McCusker's exhaustive census of sugar production in the period 1768–1772 for each New World colony ("The Rum Trade," chaps. 4, 5, tables IV–21B, V–3A; Cuban and Brazilian figures are given on pp. 104, 108, while Peru, New Spain, and the French Mascarenes, which do not seem to have exported sugar commercially to the North Atlantic, are omitted). Important features of McCusker's method of calculation have been incorporated into our estimates of sugar exports at other periods.

All colonial sugars were not exported at the same level of refinement. With two exceptions, the British colonies shipped out primarily brown or raw muscovado sugar. Some other systems exported part or all of their produce in a more concentrated form called clayed sugar (described by McCusker on pp. 33–34, 93–95). It is therefore necessary to expand the proportion of clayed sugar to what McCusker calls a "muscovado equivalent." His formula is that 150 pounds of muscovado was required to produce 100 pounds of clayed, and that eight more pounds of inferior muscovado drawn from the drainings must be allowed for. Thus every 100 pounds of clayed in each colonial tabulation is increased to 150 pounds muscovado equivalent, while 8 pounds are deducted from the same colony's muscovado total to avoid double counting of clayed drainings. In allowing a net rate of 1.42 units of muscovado for 1.00 units of clayed sugar we may have allowed too much. According to Bryan Edwards, "the loss in weight by claying is about *one-third*; thus a pot of 60 lbs. is reduced to 40 lbs., but if the molasses which is drawn off in

193

this practice be reboiled, it will give near 40 percent of sugar; so that the real loss is little more than one-sixth" (*History of the British West Indies,* II, 275–76 and note). James Stephen, in an argument designed to maximize the increase in value caused by claying, estimated the loss at one-fifth (*War in Disguise,* p. 230). Not knowing the exact percentage of claying residue exported as rum or molasses, or reboiled and exported as muscovado, we have kept to McCusker's relatively high conversion rate. Since the British exported very little clayed sugar, this approach insures a slight underestimation of British slavery's share of colonial sugar exports at the end of the old regime. Our allowance also underestimates British production as perceived by contemporaries in 1807. The sugar committee of 1808 allowed 1.33 muscovado units for 1.00, compared with our ratio of 1.42 to 1.00 (PP 1808 [IV], 216, account no. 42). Since clayed sugar in 1807 was produced almost exclusively in the Spanish and Portuguese colonies, outside British control, our estimate of the British colonial share is slightly on the low side compared with contemporary measures.

Weight equivalents for the different colonies also follow McCusker (p. 783, table C–1). Three sorts of data might appear in contemporary documents: total production figures, colonial export figures, and metropolitan import figures. There was some loss at each stage. The difference between the first and second reflected on-the-spot consumption. The difference between the second and third reflected transoceanic wastage. Contemporaries made allowance for average losses per stage. Where only one set of figures is given, the loss at each stage is estimated at 10 percent. Our tabular tonnage figures indicate long tons.

Other difficulties arise in estimating exports from each colonial area for various periods. All percentages for *1770* are based on McCusker's export estimate.

THE EIGHTEENTH CENTURY
The British Colonies

For British colonial exports in *1745* we used the estimates of 1743–1747 which appear in the Liverpool Papers, forming part of a general census of European colonial production for the period (Add MSS 38331). Muscovado equivalent is allowed for Barbados clayed. For *1770* we use McCusker's figures. In the *1787* estimate, we use the Privy Council report on sugar imported from each colony into Britain. Allowance is made for the claying of two-thirds of the sugar from Barbados and half of that from Grenada (see McCusker, pp. 207, 222, 232, and 298, note 296; and the Privy Council Report on the Trade to Africa [1789], part III, Grenada and St. Christopher, answer no. 31). Our estimate therefore assumes that British clayed amounted to 8.7 percent of sugar exports in *1787*. In corroboration, just beyond this period, Hawkesbury estimated that 7.8 percent of British West Indian sugar (7,000 of 90,000 hhds.) was clayed (Add MSS 38310, fol. 74, Hawkesbury to Lord Penrhyn, May 14, 1792).

No allowance is made for smuggling or wastage, since the figures were drawn from the British end of the network.

The French West Indies

St. Domingue. The estimate of St. Domingue's exports in 1788 most widely used by contemporaries was taken from Bryan Edwards's *Historical Survey of the French Colony of St. Domingue* (London, 1797), pp. 199–208. For us, a problem presents itself.

All calculations for the French colonies begin from accounts of official imports into France. But an unknown proportion of French colonial production was smuggled elsewhere. This is of some importance in estimating the relative share of the largest producer in the sugar world. The proportion of illicit exports was estimated by contemporaries at somewhere between one-eighth and one-quarter of the metropolitan figure. Barbé de Marbois estimated the smuggling factor at 10 percent (see PRO 30 8/349, part II, extract from "Compte rendu par M. Barbé de Marbois, 'Etat des produits de la partie française de St. Domingue pendant la cours de l'année 1788' "). Duharnilly estimated the pre-revolution smuggling proportion at "a quarter, or a least a sixth" (letter of Nov. 4, 1794), but inflated *post facto* estimates as vague as this are suspect. Long accepted one-sixth as the minimum rate for all goods (Add MSS 18961, fol. 43, "Hispanola"). An estimate for Guadeloupe in 1790 written in 1795 set the clandestine rate for that island at one-eleventh or 9 percent (PRO 30 8/351 [1795], "Imports into France from Guadeloupe 1790"). Mahy de Coromé, who drew up an estimate of St. Domingue production for the British during the French wars, estimated the "État des denrées enlevées par les navires des Etats-Unis pour la destination du continent Américain en contravention à l'arrêt du 30 août [1784], et en fraude des droits d'octroi." His figures allow us to estimate the sugar shipped out illegally in American ships at 11.5 percent of the official figures (CO 245/10 [St. Domingo], "Mémoire," fol. 115 ff.).

McCusker employs a lower-end estimate of one-eighth (I, 309).We have adopted that rate for all the French colonies. If we assume a steady rate of smuggling from *1770* to *1787*, the rate does not affect the argument about the relative performance over time of the French and British colonies. A larger French smuggling rate of one-fifth or one-quarter would alter the inter-colonial proportions. But more sugar in *1787* would also mean an even greater North Atlantic shortfall of imports in the first decade of the nineteenth century.

The starting point for the St. Domingue export figure in *1745* is the official French estimate for 1742 given in the general British survey cited above. According to McCusker, the percentage of clayed sugar rose from 7 percent in the 1720s to 40 percent by the 1770s (I, 309 and note). If we assume a constant rate of increase, the percentage should have been approaching one-quarter in 1742. This gives us the muscovado equivalent for 1745, to match the British figure for 1743–1747. The final problem for *1745* was to estimate the ratio of the illegal to the legal metropolitan trade. Lacking evidence, we allowed the customary one-eighth allotted for *1770* and *1787*. It is possible, however, that in 1740, the extralegal trade had not yet reached the proportions of 1770–1790. Therefore the St. Domingue figure was estimated to allow for an illegal trade of one-tenth the legal trade as well as one-eighth. This accounts for the range of two percentage points in our account when comparing St. Domingue's sugar export with that of the British colonies in *1745*.

St. Domingue's export figure for *1770* is taken from McCusker (I, 356). For *1787*, we started with the average exports of St. Domingue muscovado and clayed sugars for 1786–1789, inclusive (*Report from the Committee of Warehouses*, p. 25; and CO 318/2 BT 277, "Abstract of the products entered for the exportation from the colony of St. Domingo 1783–1789 from Almanack for 1791, by M. Mozard at Port-au-Prince," which employs the same source). To these figures are added factors for weight (100 French livres = 108 English pounds), for claying (100 clayed = 142 muscovado), and for smuggling (100 official exports = 112.5 total exports). The result we call St. Domingue's sugar export for *1787*.

Martinique. We have sugar export figures to France for 1786–1789, but they are not broken down into clayed and muscovado figures (Guy Josa, *Les Industries du sucre et du rhum à la Martinique, 1639–1931* [Paris, 1931], p. 110). Following McCusker, with some allowance for progression from *1770* to *1787*, we have calculated the proportion of clayed sugar at 95 percent. The year 1789 is excluded from the Martinique average because the export figure was less than 50 percent of the average of the three previous years. Its inclusion would bias Matinique's export figure sharply downward. Given the percentage of clayed and muscovado, and the total data, it then only remains to assign the smuggling percentage for the foreign trade. We have assigned the same proportion (one-eighth) to Martinique as to St. Domingue, lacking any authoritative figures or other indicators.

Guadeloupe. Guadeloupe presents a further difficulty. We lack a series of figures for sugar exports between 1786 and 1789. Given the fact that Martinique and Guadeloupe developed along parallel lines and were almost equal in their slave labor forces at the outbreak of the French Revolution, I have taken the year 1790, for which we have figures for Guadeloupe, as the basis for calculating the *1787* estimate. In 1790 its sugar production was 90 percent of Martinique's. Guadeloupe's average for *1787*, by analogy, can be regarded as its 1790 ratio to Martinique. In calculating Guadeloupe's average export we used Martinique's two "middling" years between 1786 and 1789 as the base.

Guadeloupe's proportion of sugar in 1790 compared with Martinique's is discussed in *Memoir on the Sugar Trade of the British Colonies with Tables* (p. 3); and in Deerr's *History of Sugar*, I. Another estimate (PRO 30 8/351, "An Account of Imports into France from the Island of Guadeloupe in the year 1790"), contains three separate and conflicting figures on exports. Another was addressed to Dundas in 1794 from John Drummond (CO 166/1 [Martinique], letter of May 19, 1794).

St. Lucia. For St. Lucia we begin with Deerr's figure of 1223 tons of sugar produced in 1780, indicating approximately 1100 tons available for export. With a conversion of French to English pounds, and with an assumed Martinique clayed sugar percentage of 95 percent, there were an estimated 1662 tons of muscovado-equivalent sugar available for export in 1780. Allowing for another increase of 10 percent in production from 1780 to *1787*, St. Lucia's average yearly export is 1850 tons. St. Lucia would have exported about 1850 tons in *1787*. Tobago, as a British colony until 1783, is classified as a pure muscovado exporter in *1787*. The export figures are taken from the Colonial Office records (CO 285/2 [Tobago, 1789], "Etat des revenus").

An alternative account by Irving, ca. 1790–1791, shows the total amount of sugar imported into France from its West Indies as equal to 75,000 long tons exclusive of muscovado conversion. Adding one-eighth for smuggling the total would be 84,000 tons of sugar. Allowing for claying conversion, the North Atlantic, according to Irving, received 123,000 tons of muscovado-equivalent French West Indian sugar, compared with our own estimate of 125,000. (Add MSS 38350, fols. 213–14, "An Account of the Quantity and Value of the Principal Articles imported into France from the French West Indies, annually, upon a medium of eight years ending with 1790 . . . from Mr. Irving"). If an MP had simply followed Irving's account, at the nominal figures (without considering claying), British West Indian sugar exports would actually have appeared greater than those of the French West Indies, even if he allowed for a smuggling rate of one-sixth. Thus, the more one trusted the raw Anglo-French figures at the end of the old regime, the stronger the British system appeared.

The Dutch Colonies

Surinam. The Dutch colonies were, like the British, exporters of muscovado sugar. The figures available are for exports to Amsterdam only (A. van C. Sijpesteijn, *Beschrijing van Suriname, Historisch-Geographisch-en Statistisch Overzigt, uit Officiele Bronnen Bijeengebracht* [s' Gravenhage, 1854], p. 225). McCusker estimates that in 1771, 81 percent of Surinam's sugar went to Amsterdam and 19 percent to Rotterdam (I, 341). Our figure assumes that Amsterdam received 80 percent of Surinam's exports and converts Dutch weights into English pounds.

Demerara, Essequibo, and Berbice. The export figures for the years 1784–1785 were taken from Henry Bolingbroke's *A Voyage to Demerary, Containing a Statistical Account of the Settlements There* (London, 1807), p. 397. The result was checked for reliability against the export data for Demerara in 1789–1790 in the British Colonial Office records (CO 111/3 [Demerara and Essequibo], Exports of Demerara and Essequibo, 1789–1798). In these accounts, the export from Essequibo into nonmetropolitan areas is given. The Demerara figures give only shipments to Holland. We have assumed that the same percentage of sugar went to foreign parts from Demerara as from Essequibo. Once the Demerara-Essequibo export total is calculated, we deduct 10 percent for wastage in shipment to make the figures comparable to the data for Surinam, drawn from the European end of the process.

Dutch East Indies. The export of this colony is calculated from Deerr's *History of Sugar*, I, 224.

The Danish West Indies

Our base figure for *1787* is that given by Westergaard for the mid-1780s (Waldemar Westergaard, *The Danish West Indies, 1671–1917* [New York, 1917], p. 255) and checked against Deerr's figures for 1785, 1793, 1796 (*History of Sugar*, I, 245). All Danish sugar is calculated as muscovado. The *1770* percentile is from McCusker.

The Spanish Colonies

Cuba. Cuba is the only Spanish colony considered to be an exporter to the North Atlantic market. The *1770* percentage is from McCusker, I, 102–04. The base figure for *1787* is from Humboldt, *Narrative of Travels*, VII, chap. 28, p. 163. Following McCusker, all Cuban sugar is assumed to be clayed both in *1770* and in *1787*, before the great expansion of Cuban production. The import figures for 1790 from the *American State Papers, Commerce and Navigation*, would indicate that a substantial proportion of Cuban sugar was in muscovado form by 1790. However, we have caculated for 100 percent clayed for *1787*. This is in order to keep the *1787* figures consonant with those of *1770*.

Brazil. Brazil's figure for *1787* is taken from the figure for 1788 given in the report of the Privy Council (PP 1789 [XXVI], vol. 646a, part VI). The muscovado equivalent is reached by considering all its production to be clayed until *1787*.

THE NINETEENTH CENTURY

For eighteenth-century sugar exports we relied on a method of adding the estimates for individual exporting areas in order to arrive at a North Atlantic import total. For the early nineteenth century we adopt a different strategy. From 1797 through 1814, except for the brief truce of 1802–1803, Britain was at war with almost all the colonial powers of Europe. This resulted in "broken voyages" for sugar from hostile colonies, to conform with the principle of British wartime policy until 1807. Our information for the sugar censuses of 1800–1801 and 1805–1806 is therefore drawn from the records of the two maritime powers whose flags virtually monopolized the trade in those two clusters of years. Our calculations for colonial imports and reexports to Europe are taken from the combined figures in the British *Sessional Papers* and the *American State Papers*. British figures for 1798–1806 are from PP 1808 (IV), 304; subsequent years, PP 1812 (X), 53. See also PP 1813–1814 (XII), 199–200; PP 1847–1848 (LVIII), 528, sugar imported into the United Kingdom. For American import and reexport figures, see *American State Papers, Documents Legislative and Executive, of the Congress of the United States*, 38 vols. (Washington, D.C., 1832–1861), class IV, *Commerce and Navigation*, vols. 14, 15, 1789–1823.

The British West Indian figures for 1800–1801 and 1805–1806 were derived from British and American import figures for these areas with a very minor adjustment for the small percentage of clayed sugar. The British East Indian figure is derived from the same two sources, and is treated as muscovado sugar. All other figures are taken from American accounts. They include figures for Florida, Mexico, Honduras, Bourbon, Mauritius, Spanish Africa, the Philippines, the Dutch East Indies, China, and goods reexported from the Cape Colony.

West Indian totals are calculated from the American import figures, converting clayed figures to muscovado equivalents. The French, Danish,

Dutch, and Swedish figures should not be too rigorously separated, since so much sugar traveled between islands before crossing the ocean. The problem of clayed percentages is actually easier for 1800–1815, because the American import figures, and reexport figures after 1802, always divide sugar into clayed and muscovado. For the muscovado/clayed proportion of United States reexports before 1802, we assume the same ratio for reexports as for imports. Therefore, if the United States imported 33 percent clayed sugar in 1800, the reexport proportion is estimated at one-third clayed. It is also probable that much of the sugar carried under the Danish flag in 1800 and 1805–1806 entered American ports to comply with the British regulations forbidding direct trade by a neutral between hostile colonial and metropolitan ports.

To the United States import total was added the estimated production of Louisiana, which would not be recorded in its import figures for 1805–1806. John G. Clark estimates Louisiana production at between 3.5 and 6.2 million pounds in 1804 (*New Orleans 1718–1812: An Economic History* [Baton Rouge, 1970], p. 219). We chose an average of 6 million in 1805–1806. Following McCusker, standard deductions for local consumption and loss of weight in transit reduce the estimated amount of sugar imported from Louisiana to 2,170 tons in 1805–1806.

Brazil's exports are also calculated separately, since Brazil was largely outside the Anglo-American shipping network before 1807. In 1806 Brazil exported 36,018,000 kilograms of sugar to Portugal. In the early 1820s the ratio of brown to clayed sugar was apparently about one-quarter, (Humboldt, *Narrative of Travels,* VII, 174–75). Projecting this ratio backward to 1806 we find that Brazil exported 35,450 tons of sugar, at a clayed/muscovado ratio of 3:1, the equivalent of 46,600 tons of sugar. We have not deducted for wastage because it is unclear from Humboldt's wording whether the measure was made in Brazil or in Portugal. For the period 1800–1801, our starting point is the average Brazilian export for 1796 and for 1806 (the two years given by Humboldt for the period ca. 1800). Brazil was the only area outside the Anglo-American circuit between 1800 and 1807.

Our estimate of 46,000 muscovado-equivalent tons of sugar for Brazil in 1806 is also quite close to contemporary estimates. In 1808, George Hibbert estimated Brazilian production at between 50,000 and 60,000 hhds. (PP 1808 [IV], 168). He referred, in general, to hhds. of 13 cwt. each. If we use 14 cwt. per hhd. for Brazil, at Hibbert's maximum of 60,000 hhds. Brazil would have produced 42,000 tons of all types of sugar in 1808. If three-quarters of its production was clayed, its total muscovado-equivalent production (using the McCusker conversion and at 14 cwt. per hogshead) was 55,200 tons. Deducting 10 percent for local consumption, Brazil's *maximum* export would have been 49,700 muscovado tons. If we calculate its production at the average of Hibbert's range, or 55,000 hhds., Brazilian production was around 50,630 muscovado tons and its export 45,600 tons. If we use Hibbert's own multiplier of 13 cwt. instead of 14 cwt. per hhd., the estimated Brazil export would have been 46,160 tons at 60,000 hhds. and 42,300 tons on the average (55,000 hhds.) of Hibbert's two estimates. (McCusker, in "The Rum Trade," II, 860, note 122, rates the average Brazilian chest at 12¼ cwt. in 1780.) The significant point is that the range of these estimates remains quite close to our own figure of 46,600 exported tons of muscovado-equivalent sugar in 1805–1806. Given their access to both American export and Brazilian production estimates, the Sugar Distillation Committees of Parliament in 1807–1808 were in an excellent position to appraise the level of Continental consumption at the moment of abolition.

As a check on the reliability of the "Anglo-American" method of calculation, we repeated the eighteenth-century area-by-area approach. We calculated the average export of sugar to Europe for the years 1804–1806 by adding the following areas:

The British West Indies, including the conquered Dutch colonies, are estimated to account for 174,000 tons of the North Atlantic sugar import (PP 1808 [IV], 304).

For Martinique, an estimate of 20,400 was based on the total export from Sept. 1802 to Sept. 1803, allowing for 10 percent wastage between the island and the ports of landing (Add MSS 38356 [Liverpool Papers], fol. 264).

For Guadeloupe, we have both acreage and export figures for the year VIII, and acreage figures only for the year XI, parallel to the export year for Martinique. We estimate Guadeloupe's muscovado-equivalent export in this latter, peacetime year as proportionate to the acreage/export ratio of the year VIII, allowing for 10 percent wastage between the island and Europe. The total export estimate for the year XI is therefore 7,220 less 10 percent, or 6,500 tons of muscovado landed, slightly more than one-third its prerevolutionary figure. James Stephen (*Crisis of the Sugar Colonies*, p. 17) estimated Guadeloupe's production at a minimum of one-third its old regime level, almost exactly in conformity with our estimate based on French archival figures (AN C⁷ᴬ85 [Guadeloupe], dossier 3, pièces 25, 26 [ans 8, 9], and dossier 5, pièce 37 [an 11]). Again, if we allow Guadeloupe a level of exports equal to its 1808–1810 average, we have an export of 5,450 tons (Crouzet, *L'Economie britannique*, II, 579n.). Of this, less than 12 percent was now clayed

(*American State Papers, Commerce and Navigation*, imports for 1804–1806). Allowing for this proportion increases Guadeloupe's muscovado-equivalent export to 6,130 tons per year, or slightly more than one-third of its export in *1787*. Excluding independent Haiti, French West Indian exports reached about 27,000 tons in 1804–1806.

The export from the Danish West Indies for 1804–1806 is estimated as equal to the amount of 9,800 tons shipped to Britain in 1814, when foreign colonies no longer needed to reexport via the Danish colonies and when Britain was the sole carrier (PP 1814–1815). This figure may be an understatement. If we use the first postwar figures given by Deerr (a production figure of 11,300 for St. Croix in 1820, and 1140 for St. Thomas and St. John in 1821–1826), and reduce by 10 percent for internal consumption and 10 percent for wastage, imports from the Danish West Indies would have been close to 11,000 tons per year. These figures seemed too remote in time for use as proxies for 1804–1806 estimates.

The major Spanish exporter was Cuba. According to both Havana sources and U.S. import figures calculated at muscovado equivalents, the Spanish colonial ratio of clayed to muscovado sugar was 3 : 2 after 1800. (*American State Papers, Commerce and Navigation*, exports for 1805–1806; the *Liverpool Chronicle*, May 23, 1804, "Sketch of Havana," dated Havana, Dec. 30, 1803). Using Humboldt's figures and weight equivalents for 1804–1806, it would seem that in 1804–1806 Cuba exported 43,600 tons of muscovado-equivalent sugar (*Narrative of Travels*, VII, 163). This figure might be reduced by 10 percent to allow for wastage. Given the low United States import total for all listed Spanish American sugars (see table 17), we conclude that around 39,000 muscovado-equivalent tons of Cuban sugar reached the temperate ports of America and Europe.

For Mexico, data is available for the value and volume of exports for the years 1802–1804 (Humboldt, *Political Essay*, IV, 314 ff.). Allowing for a 3 : 2 "Cuban" ratio of clayed to muscovado, the result is an export of about 6,000 tons of muscovado sugar per year. The total Spanish colonial export is therefore just about 45,000 tons per year in 1804–1806.

East Asia figures add another 12,600 tons to the total.

For Louisiana, we use the figures in Clark, cited above.

Brazil, of course, is assigned the same value (46,600 tons) as calculated above. The results are as follows:

British-controlled West Indies	174,000
French West Indies	27,000
Danish West Indies	9,800
Spanish America	45,000

Asia	12,600
Louisiana	2,200
Brazil	46,600
Total	317,200

We have not attempted to allot any export figures for St. Domingue/Haiti in this period. However, since the United States import average for 1805–1806 gives a figure about 3,000 tons higher than our combined Martinique/Guadeloupe total for French colonies, the difference may roughly represent the Haitian export average for those years. Deerr's first postwar report on Haitian exports (1818) lists a figure of 2,630 tons of muscovado and no clayed.

By relying on the Anglo-American–Brazilian sum for 1805–1806, when the maritime conflict had thrown a greater percentage of the trade to America, the total is 317,000 tons compared with ca. 317,000–320,000 counting by area.

A final word should be said about combining the British and American annual trade reports. British trade years ran from January to January. American trade years ran from October to October. This means that British trade data for January 1805 through December 1806 are being compared, in our table, with American data for October 1804 through September 1806. However, since we are principally interested in measuring the availability of imports in the North Atlantic market, the distortion is less serious. One must recall that reexports from the United States required far more time to reach the European market than did reexports from Britain. In terms of Continental supply, we must allow for a time lag between American and British products of up to six weeks. Of course, in figuring imports for United States consumption alone, the time lag works in reverse with less time required for shipment. However, American consumption amounted to less than 10 percent of the North Atlantic total. Using the retained American import figures for 1806–1807 for the American import market instead of 1805–1806 would raise American consumption figures by one-eighth and the world market total by only 1 percent. But this would be a greater distortion than using 1805–1806, since more than one-third of the 1806–1807 American figures would be outside our critical period (ending with Dec. 31, 1806).

SUGAR AVAILABLE TO THE EUROPEAN CONTINENT

For *1787*, British Isles' retained sugar imports, plus American imports for 1789–1790, are deducted from the total sugar imports to the North Atlantic. The remainder is the figure for European consumption in *1787*.

For 1800–1801 and 1805–1806, the sugar available to Europe is estimated to be equal to American and British reexports, plus the estimate of Brazilian exports for each period. While our figures make no allowance for the unknown quantity of Danish-carried sugar, there is a corresponding overestimation of the total amount of refined sugar consumed by Europe in 1800–1806 as compared with 1785–1789. By 1800, West Indian planters, both in the British-controlled and Spanish systems, had turned to a new variety of cane, called Tahiti or Bourbon cane. This variety produced an increased yield of sugar per plant, which appears in the export and import figures of sugar by weight. However, at the refining stage, the sugar made from Tahiti cane produced far less than the old variety. In 1806, Europeans were offering only two-thirds as much for Tahiti sugar as for the older variety (see Pons, *Voyage*, I, 254). For a complete comparison with refined consumption in *1787*, European imports in 1800–1806 would have to be reduced by anywhere up to 30 percent of the listed figures. The quality of clayed sugar was also not everywhere the same. Pons spoke of the inferior technology of mainland Spanish claying and claimed that they also sold as sugar a mass "completely composed of molasses" (ibid.).

Our procedure of calculating the 1806–1807 Continental supply from British and American reexport totals is the one which was also used by the British in 1808 (see PP 1808 [IV], 216, account no. 42, citing the proceedings of the Jamaica House of Assembly, Nov. 13, 1807). Thus our mode of estimating sugar available to Europe was applied both in Jamaica and at Westminster.

Coffee Production

Our estimate of Anglo-French coffee production in 1787–1789 involves three basic documents. The Privy Council report furnishes the figures on British West Indian exports from 1783 to 1788. Information on St. Domingue's production is based on the *Report from the Committee of Warehouses*, and CO 318/2 BT 277, "Abstract of the Products entered for the exportation from the colony of St. Domingo 1783–1789 from Almanack for 1791, by M. Mozard at Port-au-Prince." In dealing with the remaining French West Indies, we have complete data only for the year 1788 (*Statistique générale*, table 11, "Denrées coloniales"). On the basis of this we assume that the proportion of coffee exported by Saint Domingue was the same in 1787 and 1789 as in 1788. The average St. Domingue production for 1787–1789 is then prorated upward to yield the total French Caribbean export for 1787–1789. For purposes of comparison with Britain, no smuggling factor is included, nor any estimate for old world slave production. The resulting figure therefore probably represents the minimal strength of French production vis-à-vis British-grown coffee in *1788*.

Volume and Proportions of the Slave Trade, *1761–1807*

In estimating the total North Atlantic traffic at the end of the eighteenth century and the volume of the British trade we have recourse to both previous estimates and fresh calculations. Our point of departure is provided by Curtin's *Atlantic Slave Trade: A Census*, and especially by Anstey's various essays: "Volume and Profitability"; "The Volume of the North American Slave-Carrying Trade from Africa, 1761–1810," *Revue française d'historie d'Outre-Mer* 62 (1975), 47–66; and "The Slave Trade of Continental Powers and the United States" (MS kindly provided by the author). Dr. J. E. Inikori has, however, argued for a drastic upward revision of both the Curtin and Anstey estimates ("Measuring the Atlantic Slave Trade: An Assessment of Curtin and Anstey," *Journal of African History* 17 [1976], 197–223). While it is impossible to offer a systematic discussion of Inikori's essay, we must assess his arguments and figures at relevant points in our calculations.

The International Dimension

With a few alterations indicated below, we employ Anstey's estimates for all the non-British slave trades after 1761. Inikori insists that there are gaps in Curtin's *Census*, and of necessity in Anstey's estimates, some of which derive from the *Census*. Regarding the Spanish colonial trade, Inikori insists on a large slave trade to Spanish America, ignored by Curtin. In evidence, he cites a colonial census figure of 1,219,470 "negroes in Mexico and Peru" in 1796 (p. 204), from a document collected in an 1804–1805 survey of the slave trade by British African merchants (see PRO T70/1585, Wm. Walton to George Case, Whitehaven, Jan. 19, 1805). The document, apparently drawn from Spanish contacts, does affirm the existence of large slave imports into Mexico and Peru toward the end of the old regime. However, it also notes that these continental imports were "purchased from the different European Nations in their various islands including what were brought to the Havana, etc. for sale" (ibid.). Since continental purchases were based on reexports, any addition of them to the African trade would entail double counting. Regarding the Portuguese trade, Inikori cites only one secondary work which gives the

Negro population of Brazil in a single year (1798). Since he does not deal with the scholarly studies on which the figures of Curtin and Anstey are based, including the archival studies of Herbert Klein, we must continue to rely on the Curtin-Anstey estimate. Inikori's treatment of the French slave trade involves similar difficulties. We thus follow Anstey's estimates for the Spanish, Portuguese, and French trades. We combine his Dutch and Danish figures in one category. Anstey's most recent information from the two principal researchers in each trade indicate that he underestimated the Dutch totals, and overestimated the Danish, for 1761–1810 by almost identical amounts. We have assumed that any distortions also balanced out in each decade. In view of the relative insignificance of both carriers, especially after 1780, the percentages shown in table 9 are not likely to be significantly altered by more definitive Danish and Dutch figures (see Anstey, *British Abolition,* 57n.).

On the American trade, we have used Anstey's estimate with some selective adjustments for 1801–1805 which do not alter any national shares by more than 1 percent. The American slave-carrying trade may be divided into three parts, domestic (destination United States), overseas (Spanish and French colonies), and Louisiana. On the overseas slave trade we employ Anstey's mode of calculating the U.S. share of the Cuban slave trade and his method of calculating the American slave trade to the rest of Spanish and French America. Regarding the Afro–United States trade, we have considerably lowered Anstey's estimate for the period 1801–1810, following a suggestion by Stanley Engerman, and in consultation with Anstey.

Our final estimate is 23,400 slaves carried to the overseas colonies, 32,200 to the United States, and 3,500 to Louisiana, in 1801–1805. American slavers were responsible for loading close to 12,000 Africans a year at the beginning of the nineteenth century, or about one-sixth of the transatlantic trade. If we have overestimated the American figure, the British percentile of the slave trade would be marginally higher than it appears in table 9. If, as is much less likely, we have underestimated the American volume, the British share would be marginally lower. In either event, the percentiles do not include British capital that moved slaves under the American flag—Britain's own war-trade in disguise.

THE BRITISH SLAVE TRADE

Here, Inikori's call for some upward revision of Curtin's census figure for Britain, even beyond Anstey's original revision of 10.3 percent, seems justified. Inikori employs a set of documents not previously used. These are the Customs 3 and 17 series at the PRO, which give accounts of ships and tonnage clearing for Africa. Anstey acknowledges the need for a higher estimate ("A Note on J. E. Inikori, 'Measuring the Atlantic Slave Trade: An Assessment of Curtin and Anstey,' " *Journal of African History* 17 [1976], 606–07).

Inikori further argues for a volume of the British slave trade for 1771–1807 which increases Curtin's figure by a minimum of 43 percent (see our table 8), and a maximum of 50 percent. Anstey's estimate is similarly raised by a minimum of 40 percent (ibid.) and a maximum of 47 percent. For the longer period 1751–1807, Inikori's minimum figure is 46 percent above Curtin's, and 33 percent above Anstey's (see Inikori, "Measuring," p. 214, table 4). Anstey, however, concedes only an increase on the order of 7 percent rather than the one-third to one-half espoused by Inikori (see Anstey, "A Note on Inikori"). The difference between Anstey and Inikori arises primarily from the fact that Inikori calculates on the basis of an increase in both the number of ships/tons clearing for the slave trade, and in the ratio of slaves boarded per ship or ton. Since the figures have some bearing on our study, we must briefly analyze the principal assumptions behind the estimates of both Anstey and Inikori. Since our thesis would be marginally enhanced by each relative inflation of the British slave trade, we will also attempt to guard against double counting or improbable inflations.

We have inspected and retabulated the PRO Customs 17 series, recording the ships and tonnage clearing for Africa from British ports from 1775 to 1808. There are some slight discrepancies between our tonnage totals and those of Dr. Inikori, which may be due to faulty copying or addition, e.g., our tonnage total for 1801–1807 is 263,964 tons compared with Inikori's 259,039 (see "Measuring," p. 217, and our table 8, col. 2). I have excluded from my account, as has Inikori, ships clearing for the Cape of Good Hope. Inikori treats all ships clearing for Africa as a homogeneous lump for purposes of calculation. We feel that a preliminary division must be made among four classes of shipping, each of which has a different bearing on the total volume of the slave trade as it may be calculated from Customs 17. First, Customs 17 makes no distinction between slavers and nonslavers. Allowance must therefore be made for nonslavers. Both Anstey and Inikori arrive at a similar standard deduction. Following their principle of an annual deduction we must presently discuss the reasons for accepting the standardized rate. Apart from the nonslavers, the remaining ships listed in Customs 17 should be considered in three categories, each of which could have carried substantially different numbers of slaves per ton at different times. First, there was the "imperial" trade, in which British carriers sailing from Britain landed slaves in British colonies. Second, there was the

"British foreign" trade, in which British carriers sailing from Britain landed slaves directly in foreign areas. These two classes of the trade are not distinguished in the Customs 17 list. Third, there was a "foreign" carrying trade, in which non-British vessels, sailing from British ports, landed slaves in foreign areas. These ships are listed as a separate (foreign) category in Customs 17. They are fused with the British trade in Inikori's calculations. Our table 8, cols. 1 and 2, distinguishes between the British and the total tonnage. This distinction is of some importance. Foreign tonnage constituted only 3.2 percent of the African trade tonnage between 1777 and 1807. Just before abolition, however, the foreign tonnage rose to nearly 9 percent. And, as will be shown below, foreigners could transport slaves at over twice the rate *per ton* as could British ships. There are very good reasons for including foreign tonnage, probably largely laden with British and India goods, within the "British" category. But there are also reasons for keeping them distinct for certain estimates. One is that, while Anstey uses lists of "British" shipping as his basis of calculation, Inikori's method includes as British ships those which are listed under non-British carriers. He therefore includes a "hidden" inflator of almost one-half (3.2 percent) of what Anstey acknowledges as the necessary upward revision (7.3 percent) of his own figures.

Finally, we must take note of a class of slavers financed partly or wholly by British capital but which cleared for Africa from foreign ports, under foreign flags, unloading slaves in foreign ports. These are not estimated in table 8. During the Peace of Amiens the size of this trade was probably indicated by the drop in British African tonnage from 43,530 in 1802 to only 30,350 in 1803. If we allow that 95 percent (see below) of the difference was sent abroad to take advantage of the unregulated Dutch, French, and Spanish trades, we might assume that British capital stood behind another 25,000 slaves in that year. To avoid double counting, this uncertain figure is omitted from tables 8 and 9.

Tonnage of Nonslavers

We will deal first with the area of greatest agreement, the proportion of African ships/tons to be deducted as nonslavers. Anstey and Inikori are both satisfied that 5 percent is ample allowance. Anstey relies primarily on a Liverpool shipping list indicating the number of slave and nonslave ships from 1783 to 1793 ("Volume and Profitability," p. 6; Gomer Williams, *History of the Liverpool Privateers and . . . the Liverpool Slave Trade* [1897; rpt. New York, 1966], p. 685, Appendix XIV). In fact, this Liverpool list probably exaggerates the nonslave trade because it counts ships, not tons. It gives a nonslave rate of 4.7 percent. A manuscript list by ship *and* tonnage for 1789 shows the degree of distortion this entails. While nonslavers represented 4.6 percent of the total number of Liverpool ships clearing for Africa, they represented only 2.4 percent of the tonnage (PRO T/64, 286, "An Account of All Vessels Which Have Cleared Outwards . . . for Africa"). Inikori's evidence for 5 percent nonslave allowance is even more persuasive. It is based on customs accounts of the weight of the principal African products imported into England in the two peak years of imports ("Measuring," p. 216). Our own estimates of the British slave trade, based on this allowance, is reflected in col. 6 of table 8.

We have one hesitation about the 5 percent allowance. The same document which shows the Liverpool African trade to be 98 percent slaving (by tonnage) in 1789, shows the Bristol African trade to be over 10 percent nonslaving. Although Liverpool was the African trading giant during the entire period 1777–1807, it might be that the small British ports would also have weighed more in the direction of Bristol; they lacked the sophisticated capital, credit, and commodity networks of London and Liverpool, which were necessary for the slave trade. Together the small ports might conceivably bring the nonslave trade tonnage slightly over 5 percent. It is also possible that at certain periods during the war years slavers were not able to load to capacity, although Anstey's Customs House lists do not indicate that this was a serious problem. Finally, deducting 5 percent from the Customs 17 figures still leaves 237,800 slaving tons in the trade in 1801–1807, compared with the 218,700 tons of Anstey's more specfic Customs House list. The gap between them might not be entirely due to inefficient compilation of individual ships in the trade. We have therefore prepared a calculation of slavers sailing under the British flag at a rate of 8 percent below the Customs 17 tonnage figure (table 8, col. 7). This comes quite close to maximizing the allowance for nonslavers. Above 8 percent, the estimate of slaves loaded from Customs 17 begins to fall below Anstey's annual estimates. For example, at a deduction of 8 percent there is only one such year. At 9.5 percent, five out of the eight years between 1797 and 1804 show estimates below Anstey's. Column 7 of table 8 thus represents the highest plausible deduction one can assume for the nonslave trade. It allows for a maximum of one ship out of twenty to have gone unrecorded on Anstey's lists between 1801 and 1807. It must be reemphasized that col. 7 is more precautionary than probable. In calculating the British national share of the slave trade in table 9 we use col. 6 in table 8.

Slaves per Ton of Slave Shipping

Beyond the question of finding out the proportion of slave shipping clearing from Britain, there remains the question of how many slaves were loaded into each of those vessels. Using Customs 17, Inikori calculated the ratios in terms of slaves per *ship* before 1788, and slaves per *ton* thereafter. I have used the tonnage figures throughout, to avoid the thorny question of allowances of slaves per undifferentiated ship (see Inikori, "Measuring," pp. 212–13, on Curtin; and pp. 217–18, on Anstey). One alteration of Customs 17 figures was required in order to use the tonnages before 1787. Customs 17/9 (1785–1786) lists 1786 clearances for Africa as 152 ships of 66,917 tons. This would make the average ship in 1786 more than three times as large as in previous years, and the total tonnage more than three times as great. We substituted a probable tonnage estimate, derived from multiplying the 1786 shipping figure (152) by the average annual tonnage for African shipping in 1784–1788 (excluding 1786). The resulting figure (22,768) was entered as our tonnage for 1786.

Christopher French's "Eighteenth Century Shipping Tonnage Measurements," *Journal of Economic History* 33 (June 1973), 434–43, suggests that for proper comparisons between tonnages for 1777–1807, all pre-1786 figures should be raised an average of 34 percent because of changes in recorded tonnage due to the general registry act of that year. However, adopting this procedure would force us to conclude that the average African trade ship decreased from about 192 tons in 1783–1785 to 159 tons in 1787–1789, a fall of over 17 percent. Without French's conversion factor the Customs 17 ledgers indicate an average rise of 11 percent (from 143 to 159 tons) over the same period. The unconverted trend is more congruent with the general African trend for the surrounding periods. From 1779–1781 to 1783–1785 the average weight of African ships rose 9.8 percent. Again, from 1787–1789 to 1791–1793, the rise was 9.3 percent. Thus, on either side of 1786 the data indicate a smooth upward rise of about ten percent every four years between 1779 and 1793. Rather than assuming that the African ships suddenly shrank by over a sixth after 1786, it seems more reasonable to assume that either the post-1786 Customs 17 figures were recorded so as to be directly comparable to those before that date, or that the conversion required by the act of 1786 produced measured tonnage figures which were only a small fraction of the 34 percent differential in French's sample (drawn from the West India trade). Except for the 1786 figure we therefore use the Customs 17 figures as the basis of calculation for all loading ratios. The anomaly of the 1786 figure may itself be the result of momentary confusion caused by the registry act.

The completed tonnage list is then multiplied by Anstey's annual ratios of slaves loaded per ton of British slave shipping from 1777–1807 (see Anstey, "Volume and Profitability," pp. 6–10). These work out as: 2.10 slaves per ton for 1777–1780; 2.18 for 1781–1788; 1.58 to 1.62 slaves per ton from 1789 to 1796; and thereafter a fluctuating decrease to an average of 1.03 slaves per ton for 1802–1807.

Inikori, by contrast, rejects Anstey's ratios. He uses a slaves per *ship* ratio (derived from a small sample) until 1788, and thereafter the 1.6 slaves per ton which the Dolben act roughly required. We prefer Anstey's pre-1788 ratio because of the large sample size and its tonnage base. Inikori's rejection of Anstey's annual variations after 1789 is unconvincing. He insists on using 1.6 slaves per ton, despite the fact that the amended regulation act of 1799 drove the ratio down to 1.03 per ton. His decision is based on a premise of widespread evasion of the 1799 act. Yet his own evidence for such evasion is not only scattered, but some of it goes to prove that evasion under the British flag was almost impossible ("Measuring," p. 220, case of the Vanguard). Even more decisively, Inikori accepts without demur the ratio of 1.6 slaves per ton imposed by the act of 1788 ("Measuring," p. 220; Anstey "Volume and Profitability," p. 10n.). Why the law of 1788 should have been totally effective, and that of 1799 effective only to the exact demands of the act of 1788 is unexplained. If easy evasion were characteristic of the trade, Inikori should more consistently have used pre-Dolben ratios of over 2 slaves per ton for the whole period. (This would increase Curtin's estimate of the slave trade for 1789–1807 by over 98 percent instead of 45.5 percent.)

Given that the awards to informers for violations were lucrative, even for minimal evasion, and that Anstey's ratios are verified by near complete information on slaves *landed* in the British West Indies, we use Anstey's ratios as holding for all British ships. In fact, Anstey's annual ratios may reflect the loading figures even more precisely than he himself was aware. His slaves per ton ratios fall from just under 1.6 between 1789 and 1796 to between 1.47 and 1.33 in 1797–1799. This would accord with the fact that the first increase in stringency over the Dolben act was an amended regulation act of 1797 (see *Statutes at Large*, vol. 41, 37 Geo 3, July 19, 1797). The Anstey ratios are used in our table 8.

However, if Anstey's ratios apply for British vessels landing slaves in the British West Indies, do they apply equally to British vessels landing in foreign areas? Anstey conceded that they do not, on the assumption that the regulating acts could not be enforced there. But his estimate makes no allowance for what would have affected up to a quarter of the British slavers clearing for Africa ("Volume and Profitability," p. 9n.). On these grounds Inikori argues that a ratio of 1.6 for the whole British trade is a closer approximation of the real ratios to be computed per ton than Anstey's samples, based on British West Indies landings alone ("Measuring," p. 220 and note).

In this case we disagree with Anstey's premise, and therefore with Inikori's inference. The regulatory act applied to all registered British vessels and therefore to those in the British direct trade to foreign colonies. The British "foreign" trade ships had the number of slaves allowed registered and painted on each ship before clearance. Any member of the crew who could count, and who reported a violation on return to England was entitled to a moiety of a heavy fine levied for each excess slave. Even a small overload amounted to a sailor's, if not to a slave's, ransom. British landings were often advertised by ship, captain, and number of slaves in foreign port newspapers. Massive violations meant massive risks to the merchant and massive rewards to the informer. Moreover, continuous violations over the course of two decades must sooner or later have come to the attention of a well-informed abolitionist network, primed to crying up every extraordinary incident in the slave trade or on the slave islands. They would have pounced on convictions or even indictments as prime evidence that, contrary to the claims of the slave merchants, there could be no regulation short of total prohibition. The abolitionists did claim that such "evasion" took place under foreign flags, which was quite legal for British capitalists. The abolitionists did not extend that accusation to British carriers. Lacking even accusations of evasion under the British flag, Inikori's claim for a 1.6 ratio for any category of ships categorized as British on the Customs 17 list after 1799 seems unwarranted.

If Inikori's post-Dolben ratio of 1.6 probably inflates the British trade after 1799, the same ratio certainly deflates the volume of the foreign flag trade from 1789 to 1806. None of the regulatory acts applied to foreign ships. They could continue to carry over two slaves per ton from Africa beyond 1788. For example, an "account of Negroes advertised for sale in the Charleston, [S.C.] newspapers, 28th February 1806" showed that the American vessels averaged 311 slaves per ship. The British ships averaged 158 slaves per ship. No British vessel carried as many as any of its American counterparts (see PRO T70/1585).

To estimate the numbers carried under this category of the Customs 17 ledgers after 1788, we multiply the number of tons by Anstey's pre-Dolben ratio of 2.18 slaves per ton (1780–1788), rather than Inikori's post-Dolben 1.6 per ton. The total British and foreign slave-carrying figures from 1777 to 1807 are represented in table 8, col. 8. As indicated above, this total excludes all British ships or merchandise that sailed for the slave trade directly from foreign ports. It may even underestimate the number of foreign ships sailing for the slave trade from British ports. The highest number of listed foreign clearances occurred in 1805, the last full year of the unrestricted foreign slave trade (Customs 17/27). This, however, was just about half the number (a minimum of 30 to 35 American ships alone) that the African merchants claimed had been fitted out for the slave trade in different ports of the United Kingdom (PRO T70/1585, "Remarks on the Impolicy of Preventing Foreigners carrying British manufactures to Africa" [1806]). The Customs 17 accounts could not record clearances of American vessels going first to Europe before clearing finally for Africa. This may account for the discrepancy. However, even the listed "foreign" ships, after deducting 5 percent for nonslavers, were capable of transporting over 10,000 slaves from Africa to the Americas in 1805. If the British flag trade that year was 36,000, the listed foreign trade out of Britain added more than 25 percent to the unofficial British total. This is already within hailing distance of James Stephen's claim that 40 percent could be added to the official British slave trade. And, if the British slave merchants' *minimum* estimate of 30 slavers fitted in British ports was more accurate than the Customs 17 African trade figure of 19, the total number of Africans transported in foreign slavers clearing from Britain was around 16,000, or 44 percent of the British carrier total. Stephen's claim of a 40 percent invisible slave trade does not appear unreasonable, at least for the three years preceding the passage of the foreign abolition act in 1806. To avoid double counting, however, all officially foreign carriers are excluded from the "British" share of the slave trade in our table 9.

III

The Relative Strength of Suggested Motives in the Votes of 1806–1807

Roger Anstey argues that the foreign slave trade bill of 1806 was really a humanitarian sheep in the fox's clothing of British material interest. He emphasizes that it was cleverly introduced by the ministerial abolitionists as a measure of economic expediency which simply reinforced the capital restriction principle of the order-in-council of 1805 (*British Abolition*, pp. 363–75; also PD 6 [1806], 597–99, Mar. 31, 1806). In the salty expression of the representative of Liverpool, the abolitionists "were now coming by a side wind on the planters" (PD 6 [1806], 919, speech of Tarleton, April 25). In support of his position Anstey cites the small attendance at the only recorded vote in the Commons.

Davis, in turn, uses Anstey's account to affirm the strength of economic motives in the passage of the bill. He emphasizes that what counted was not the ulterior motives of the humanitarian sponsors but the fact that the members of Parliament thought they were voting for economic interests. His significant point is that, if Anstey is right, Parliament shifted ground against the foreign slave trade in 1806 only when aroused to its economic danger to the old colonies (*Slavery In Revolution*, p. 348).

I would agree with Davis that what counted for success was not the intentions of the sponsors but the motives and understandings of the voters. However, both Davis and Anstey may not take sufficient account of the "foreign" bill as it moved from stage to stage and House to House. My contention is that ultimately most members of Parliament voted openly and self-consciously for the bill of 1806 as an integral step toward total abolition.

What has been overlooked in both the above accounts is a crucial and dynamic element in the debate. The Commons bill, as Anstey indicates, started on the lowest of notes. It was introduced on the same day as the debate on the budget. The attorney general, in bringing it in on March 31, 1806, deliberately muted its potential impact and actually seemed to be confused over the proper form in which to enter it. The bill was ostensibly designed to prevent British capital from going to enemy colonies and from contributing to the development of those areas. It was also meant to help "carry into effect" the order-in-council of August 1805 (PD 6 [1806], 598). Even the representative of Liverpool, Tarleton, was uncertain of its meaning. He simply noted that it would have to be studied by the merchants (ibid., pp. 557–59). No opposition was expressed in principle. On the second reading, three weeks later, only four speakers participated. The House was not even counted. However, General Gascoyne, Liverpool's other representative, now objected in principle. For the first time in the debate he opposed the bill as a scheme for indirect abolition.

Only at the last possible moment in the Commons, on the occasion of the third reading, were ramifications and motivations seriously discussed. This debate was unusual in having twice as many speakers and in being eight times as long as the previous one. It was also the only discussion that resulted in a recorded vote. One member of the opposition now openly accused the bill of "false humanity." An alarmed Sir Robert Peel admitted that he had been lulled into not attending previous sessions. Three of the five who spoke against the bill addressed themselves principally to its humanitarian motives. More significant, however, is the fact that the abolitionists came out from behind their disguise. Foreign Secretary Fox explicitly declared that he would support a total abolition bill whether brought forward in the session of 1806 or 1807, whichever Wilberforce preferred (ibid., pp. 1024–25). On both sides, every new speaker took the view that the basis of the bill was humanity (true or false, of course, depending on their point of view). The fact that the bill won by a vote of 35 to 13 was therefore not testimony to the "significance" of economic interest in deciding the issue (see table 32).

The heart of our argument, however, does not lie in these speeches. The fate of the bill now rested with the Lords, who had not clearly pronounced on abolition since the narrowly defeated slave trade restriction bill of 1799. If the interests had been awakened belatedly to the Commons' debate, they appeared in force at the upper House. Petitions against the bill came in from a dozen interests representing manufacturing, shipping, and West Indian capital. And from Manchester, for the first time since 1792, came a "noninterest" abolitionist petition, but containing more signatures than all the others combined. There was vigorous canvassing by the opponents of the bill just before the third reading. James Stephen had his *Facts and Observations* written up and printed virtually overnight for distribution among the peers in anticipation of the possible impact of opposing evidence.

The humanitarians must have sensed their strength because they dropped all pretense of pure expediency. In the debate of May 16, 1806, the opposition treated the bill as the preamble to total abolition. Six of eight spoke against it as a broadly conceived abolition bill. Only two opposition speakers treated it in the narrow terms of its original presentation. The proponents of the bill showed the same perceptual ratio as its

TABLE 32: RECORDED VOTES ON ABOLITION, MAY 1806–FEBRUARY 1807

	Foreign Trade Bill		Resolution for Total Abolition		Bill for Total Abolition	
	Pro	Con	Pro	Con	Pro	Con
	May 1, 1806 3rd Reading		June 10, 1806		Feb. 23, 1807 2nd Reading	
Commons						
Total vote	35	13	114	15	283	16
Percentage	73	27	88	12	95	5
	May 16, 1806 2nd Reading		June 24, 1806		Feb. 5, 1807 2nd Reading[a]	
Lords						
Total vote	43	18	41	20	100	36
Percentage	70	30	67	33	74	26

Source: Cobbett's *Parliamentary Debates*.

a. Excluding proxies, the vote totals are 72 and 28.

antagonists. Like the opposition, six of the eight supporters of the bill insisted that their decision was inspired by its humanity and by the fact that it would contribute to total abolition. If this three to one ratio of humanity to interest on each side represented a rough proportion of the sixty-one voters concerned with broader humanitarian rather than with narrow economic implications, there is no doubt in what terms the decision was being viewed.

Perhaps the keynote on both sides was sounded by the men who had, from the outset, clearly represented the fundamental clash of values involved. Grenville's vigorous speech scorned the idea that abolition required subterfuge. If the opposition chose to score the bill as being "abolition in disguise," Grenville replied, he was glad to accept the valuation, while rejecting the moral implication. Were this abolition in disguise, he said, "he should be glad indeed, not of disguise but of the abolition. . . . But he could see no reason for disguise, on such a subject. He had heard of fraud in disguise, of injustice and oppression in disguise; but justice and humanity required no disguise. Those who felt those virtues, would also be proud to acknowledge them" (PD 7 [1806], 232). Thus far Grenville seemed to be preparing the ground to argue that he was *not* taking Parliament down the broad road but that the bill was what it was purported to be, an abolition of a trade which would exclude any discussion of general abolition. But his very next words threw the argument not onto interest but onto moral grounds. He asked not for the restriction of capital but the removal of guilt. "It had been argued, that if we laid down the trade, others were ready to take it up. This, however, was a mode of reasoning that could not stand the test of examination. Were we to act unjustly in order to prevent others from doing so? Let us clear ourselves of the guilt, and if they thought proper to take it up, let the guilt be upon their heads. To the cause of humanity let them be answerable for the consequences" (ibid., p. 233).

What did the question of removing guilt and laying down the trade have to do with the British West Indies, which could continue to purchase slaves from Africa, or with British capitalists who could continue to purchase them and transport them in British ships? Who could possibly hear those words and believe he was merely listening to a carefully bounded argument about controlling the flow of British capital and African labor to the enemy? Fortunately, we have the explanation of Grenville's strategy. He abandoned the narrow economic ground because it was no longer necessary. "I saw our strength," wrote Grenville to Wilberforce the next day, "and thought the occasion was favorable for launching out a little beyond what the measure itself actually required. I really think a foundation is laid for doing more and sooner than I have for a long time allowed myself to hope" (*Life of Wilberforce,* III, 261, letter of May 17, 1806). Since the "launching out" was toward total abolition on openly humanitarian grounds, the "strength" Grenville perceived was obviously in that direction.

What had happened was that the initial abolitionist strategy had actually underestimated parliamentary willingness to move toward total abolition. James Stephen, outlining possible parliamentary strategies only three days after the Lords' vote, noted that the speech had provided both the crucial link and the proving ground for a general bill on humanitarian grounds: "The late speeches of Mr. Fox and Lord Grenville on the foreign abolition bill, would have made this disposition [toward immediate total prohibition] undeniable, if it could have been doubted before . . . and this, not on cold views of national policy alone, but on those high and sacred principles, which, as Lord Grenville observed in the late debate, constitute the true strength of our cause (DUL Hamilton [Grenville MSS], reel 17, "Observations in answer to the Question 'Whether a general Abolition Bill should be brought into Parliament' " [in James Stephen's hand], May 19, 1806, p. 1). Another reason for immediate action was the prospect that "an early dissolution of Parliament will strongly influence in our favour many Members of the House of Commons who have been instructed by large bodies of their Constituents to vote for an abolition of the Slave Trade" (ibid., p. 2). The abolitionists, who were convinced that they could not carry total abolition relying on their hard core alone (ibid., p. 7) believed that a significant number of "neutrals" were already under constituent pressure to vote for total abolition in May 1806.

Equally revealing were the reasons given for postponing the general bill to the beginning of the next session. First, the abolitionists felt the embarrassment that their "colonial protection" argument for the foreign act might engender if they were to instantly turn around and introduce a new bill which totally ignored the protection of the colonies. More decisive, however, was the lateness of the session, which made it impossible for a bill "of so much importance to be deliberately and fully considered by the two Houses." The abolitionists keenly recalled that the Lords had overwhelmingly voted to table their bill of 1804 on just such due process grounds (ibid., pp. 6–10). The rank and file of the movement were informed that this was the reason for the postponement (Friends House, London, Antislavery Tracts, Box H, printed circular dated July 30, 1806.) What characterizes both these considerations for delay is the fact that they were the outcome of abolitionist strategy, not opposition maneuvers. Made overcautious by their narrow defeat in 1805, the abolitionists attempted to outdo their opponents in tactical manipulation. As a result they may have just been too clever by half a year, and delayed total abolition for another session.

The opposition also acknowledged the power of the noneconomic factor in May 1806. The speaker who replied to Grenville was Lord Hawkesbury, for twenty years the spokesman of imperial economic values. He pointed out that humanity had been fraudulently brought into the debate and tried to force the bill back into a discussion of interest. From over two decades on the Board of Trade, Hawkesbury knew the "rules" of economic legislation. Each interest presented its case and a decision or a compromise was reached. The only question proper to a bill of economic expediency was who was injured by the bill and who was benefited. But, despite himself, he felt he had to follow Grenville onto the grounds of humanity even while he wished only to emphasize the bill's threat to British capital already invested in the conquered colonies and Cuba (PD 7 [1806], 234).

Now we must turn to an analysis of the votes themselves (see table 32). The immediate result in the Lords, on May 16, 1806, was a victory of more than two to one for the foreign bill. Of the 43 Lords who voted for the bill and of the 18 who voted against, how many voted on the narrow, and how many on the broad basis? We will never know exactly. We do know, however, that just one month later, the same House voted for a resolution for total abolition by almost exactly the same vote, 41 to 20 (ibid., p. 809). Six months later, the bill for total abolition carried in the Lords by 100 to 36 (or 72 to 28 of those present).

We know of no member in either House who voted both against the partial bill of 1806, on grounds of insufficiency, and for the total abolition resolution of 1806. In other words, there were no "radical" abolitionists in either house who announced that they would vote against the foreign bill because it did not go far enough. It is reasonable to suppose that any erosion which took place in the voting on the total abolition resolution would have had to come from those who had explicitly voted for the foreign bill on economic grounds. At least they might have moved to amend the "all practical expedition" clause in the "total" resolution of June 1806, so as to give the *de jure* islands some time to benefit by the foreign trade act. Total abolition, of course, nullified any differential economic benefit from the foreign bill to the British colonies.

It is also theoretically possible that one or more voters crossed over from opposition to support between votes. Possible but not probable. One must first be able to explain why anyone who voted against the foreign bill should wish to vote *for* total abolition. Would anger at their having lost half their business cause some foreign slave-trade sympathizer to now punish the two West Indians who had gone along with the foreign bill? No member of Parliament is mentioned in the literature as pursuing such a *politique de pire*. The figures on both votes give an indication of the insignificance of the mercantilist motive. Even without a voting list we can measure the net increase of total votes against abolition from the foreign bill of May to the "total" resolution of June. It amounted to only two votes in each House or a loss of 4 percent of the affirmative vote on the partial bill. To strengthen our case in this regard, we recall that only two (of the six) lords who spoke for the foreign trade bill did so on the narrow grounds of protecting the British colonies or restricting British capital. For them, and for them only, the bill of 1806 was what its preamble said it was, a bill of expediency.

Among the lords who spoke on both foreign and total abolition, Sidmouth was the only one who shifted from pro to con, insisting he was a gradualist. Lord Darnley, who also supported the foreign bill strictly on policy grounds, does not appear thereafter in the debates or on the list of lords who voted for total abolition on its second reading in 1807. We may assume that he was the only other defector. (For the 1807 list, see Lambeth Library, Porteus MSS 2104, fol. 86v.) A shift of two votes between May and June 1806 is not very impressive evidence for the significance of the economic factor.

No full roll-call analysis is available for any of the votes of 1806–1807. It is theoretically possible that many of the lords who attended one session were absent from the other. But our working assumption is that we should extrapolate from the known to the unknown and assume that any replacements fit roughly into the ratios of pro and con and of "broad-" and "narrow-minded" voters. In this connection, we note that the very full Lords' ballot for abolition in 1807 produced a slightly higher percentage for abolition than the moderately full Houses of 1806. It would seem that the larger the vote in Lords, the greater was the abolitionist margin.

We have given more weight to the debate in the Lords because they were aroused, and all their debates were fairly well attended. But the votes in the Commons are also of interest. Considering the volatility of the pro-slave-trade vote in the Commons from one division to the next from May 1804 to May 1806, its stability between May 1806 and February 1807 is significant. In February 1805, before the invocation of imperial economic motives, the slave-trade interest polled more than half the vote, 77 to 70. In May 1806, after that strategy was invoked, its share dropped to one-third, 13 to 35. Can this drop be attributed to the supposed derogation from morality? Why then, with the scrapping of the expediency strategy, did the slave-trade interest's share fall even more dramatically to one-eighth of those polled (15 to 114)? In February 1807, again without an appeal to expediency, the interest was reduced to one-sixteenth of the poll (16 to 263). Its greatest proportionate loss occurred, not when the standard of expediency was raised, but between May and June 1806, when it was lowered.

The absolute figures for the slave-trade vote are revealing in another way. In the Commons, the resolution for total abolition on June 10, 1806, produced 114 votes for and only 15 against. This represented a net increase of only two negatives over the Commons' ballot against the foreign slave bill on May 1, 1806. The yea vote, however, showed a net increase of 79. We know that two West Indian members of Parliament spoke for the May bill and then against the June resolution. Both did so on economic grounds. We are tempted to say that these two members represented the total group for whom the foreign bill had been primarily a means of defining imperial economic policy. This would mean that in the vote to abolish the foreign trade, not a single *metropolitan* vote in the Commons was gained by the "expediency" rationale.

In addition to the two West Indian members who voted for the foreign bill and against the general abolition, we know of three antiabolitionist speakers who voted against both measures (Rose, Tarleton, Gascoyne). This means that of the fifteen votes against the resolution of June 10 in the Commons, a maximum of ten (excluding the two West Indians) could have switched between May and June. Presuming, against all plausibility, that every last one of the unknown negatives of June 10 had swung from "foreign" yeas to "total" nays, and that all these nays were swayed primarily by economic arguments to vote for the foreign slave bill in May and against the total abolition resolution in June, a total of twelve voters in Parliament could possibly have taken the expediency argument seriously enough to stick with their economic convictions for even one month. That more than a fraction of the unknown ten were either so convinced in May, or so converted in June, seems unlikely. Not a single metropolitan speaker against the June resolution announced that he had just moved over to the antiabolitionist side *for any reason whatsoever.*

In any event, the total gain for the opposition from both Houses between May and June 1806 amounted to four members, or just over 4 percent of the total votes in both Houses for the foreign bill. Lest it be thought that the resolution won because it was merely a resolution, the vote on the total abolition bill in the Commons (Feb. 23, 1807) was 283 to 16. In considering the votes of January–February 1807 there is also the possibility that some members of Parliament were psychologically intimidated by the overwhelming sense of the June 1806 votes into not voting their "economic" conscience. This would only emphasize how potent the humanitarian sentiment appeared to the opposition by 1807. Nothing better demonstrates abolitionist strength than its ability to exercise a tyranny of the majority to effect the outcome. (On the silence and desertions of the leading metropolitan antiabolitionists, such as Castlereagh, Rose, and the Addingtonites, see Add MSS 52204 [Allen Papers], Political Journal, Jan. 21, 1806–Mar. 23, 1807, p. 48, entry of Feb. 26, 1807.)

We have not discussed the issue of the political significance which should be assigned to the fact that the foreign bill was a government measure. It is quite possible that the difference between the abolitionist defeat of 1805 and the victory of 1806 reflects the fact that the full weight of the Cabinet, with dissident members silenced by collegial ethics, was behind it. Yet it must be recalled that the votes of June 1806 and of February 1807 were not ministerial measures. They fared as well or better than the foreign bill. This may be a testimony less to what pressures a government could exert than to what a single-minded prime minister could do against an opposition worn down by twenty years of public dissociation (see Anstey, *British Abolition*, pp. 393–98; Smith, *Whig Principles and Party Politics* [Manchester, 1975], pp. 286–87). The resolution of June 1806, moreover, was freer from ministerial pressure than the substantive votes of May 1806 and February 1807. Anstey is therefore right in dating a significant shift of opinion by the *middle* of 1806 (*British Abolition*, p. 400). Our principal contention is that it must have occurred by May 1806.

In retrospect, the recorded vote on the foreign bill in May 1806 must have seemed to the slave traders like a "golden age" of equilibrium compared with 1807. Even more clearly than in the Lords, the fuller the House the greater was the margin, for abolition. Thus, while Davis is right in suggesting that Anstey's analysis of abolitionist motives begs the question of parliamentary motives, we not only agree with Anstey's conclusion that the votes of 1806–1807 reflect the abolitionist motives behind all the actions of 1806, but contend that they are the testing ground for a point at which the logic of imperial interest conflicted with the logic of humanity.

However, the argument just outlined does less than full justice to the significance of the passage of foreign abolition as interpreted by Anstey and Davis. Abolition progressed by incremental steps in volume reductions from 1799 onward. Strategy likewise shifted by degrees from the strict expediency preamble of the order-in-council of 1805, to the openly transparent expediency rationale of the foreign bill of May 1806, to the pure but symbolic humanitarianism of the resolution of June 1806, to the hotly contested humanitarian preamble of the bill of 1807.

The accounts of both Anstey and Davis show the enormous significance of piecemeal steps at the psychological level. The process reveals the gentlest of gradients between economic and moral rationalization. Anstey's focus on the abolitionist leadership's tactics is thus of capital importance as a clue to general parliamentary attitudes. Foreign abolition in 1806 was presented as both expedient in itself and as the natural complement to the "expedient" order of 1805. The enemies of this abolition exposed the maneuver and were routed all the same. One must therefore make as much allowance for both the psychological complexity and the intelligence of the rank and file as for the dexterity of the opposing spokesmen. In acting against a trade, those broadly responsible for its political consequences needed assurance that they were not violently departing from standards of trade regulation. The foreign bill provided such an opportunity. Its economic argument was vaguely plausible, if not compelling under close scrutiny. It provided a bridge for moving imperceptibly from political economy to humanity. The Lords consciously marched across that bridge in May 1806. And the bill's sponsor, taking his cue from the House, was as much a follower as a leader. This may also explain why not one parliamentary opponent of abolition thereafter raised the issue of political deception as a motive for voting against the quick successive moves toward total abolition.

Davis suggestively describes abolitionism as a mediating ideology between two stages of a society increasingly dominated by the market. It might be fruitful to conceive of the special role of the foreign bill, described by Anstey, as constituting the political mechanism mediating between two societal concepts of what was susceptible to the market.

Notes

A list of abbreviations will be found on page 188.

Chapter 1: The Decline Theory of Abolition

1. Eric Williams, *British Historians and the West Indies* (New York, 1966), p. 233. See also Elsa V. Goveia, *A Study on the Historiography of the British West Indies to the End of the Nineteenth Century* (Mexico: Inst. Panamericano de Geografía e Historia, 1956). Typical of the "moral progress" history is Frank J. Klingberg, *The Anti-Slavery Movement in England: A Study in English Humanitarianism* (1926; rpt. Hamden, Conn., 1968), echoing the views of abolition's first historian, Thomas Clarkson, *The History of the Rise, Progress and Accomplishment of the Abolition of the African Slave-trade by the British Parliament*, 2 vols. (London, 1808; rpt. London, 1968), II, chap. 10. Reginald Coupland, *Wilberforce: A Narrative* (1923; rpt. New York, 1968), is the representative of the humanitarian tradition most clearly singled out by Williams as a foil for his own interpretation.

2. Cf., for example, F. J. de Pons, *Perspectives des rapports politiques et commerciaux de la France dans les deux Indes*(Paris, 1807), pp. 184–86; Thomas Jollivet, *Des Missions en France de la société abolitioniste et étrangère* (Paris, 1841), and *De la Philanthropie anglaise* (Paris, 1842); Betty Fladeland, *Men and Brothers: Anglo-American Antislavery Cooperation* (Urbana, Ill., 1972), pp. 123–34, 151; Franz Hochstetter, *Die wirtschaftlichen und politischen Motive für die Abschaffung des britischen Sklavenhandels im Jahre 1806/1807* (Leipzig, 1905).

3. See Adam Smith, *An Inquiry into the Nature and Causes of the Wealth of Nations* (1776; rpt. New York, 1937), pp. 80–81; A. von Humboldt, *Political Essay on the Kingdom of New Spain*, 4 vols. (London, 1811), III, 9–18. For an early verification of the decline theory see A. H. L. Heeren, *Manual of the Political System of Europe and its Colonies* (London, 1846), p. 356.

4. See especially J. P. Greene's review article, "Society and Economy in the British Caribbean during the Seventeenth and Eighteenth Centuries," *American Historical Review* 79 (1974), 1499–1517.

5. Lowell J. Ragatz, *The Fall of the Planter Class in the British West Indies, 1763–1833* (1928; rpt. New York, 1963); Eric Williams, *Capitalism and Slavery* (1944; rpt. New York, 1966). Williams reiterates his thesis without qualification in *From Columbus to Castro: The History of the Caribbean, 1492–1969* (New York, 1970), pp. 280–81.

6. For a discussion of the development of slavery based on economic models, see E. D. Domar, "The Causes of Slavery or Serfdom: A Hypothesis," *Journal of Economic History* 30 (1970), 18–32; Douglass C. North and Robert P. Thomas, "An Economic Theory of the Growth of the Western World," *Economic History Review* 22 (1970), 1–17; and above all, Stanley L. Engerman, "Some Considerations Relating to Property Rights in Man," *Journal of Economic History* 33 (1973), 43–65.

7. On Williams's view of the role of the abolitionists and of Pitt, see *Capitalism and Slavery*, pp. 146–50, repeated in his *From Columbus to Castro*, pp. 243–45. On the critiques of this view see esp. G. R. Mellor, *British Imperial Trusteeship, 1783–1850* (London, 1951), pp. 50–60, 75, 118–20; Roger T. Anstey, "Capitalism and Slavery: A Critique," *Economic History Review*, 2nd ser. 21 (1968), 307–20; and Patrick C. Lipscomb, "William Pitt and the Abolition of the Slave Trade," Ph.D. dissertation, University of Texas, 1960.

8. Mellor, *British Imperial Trusteeship*, p. 424.

9. David Brion Davis, *The Problem of Slavery in Western Culture* (Ithaca, N.Y., 1966), p. 153 and note. Davis repeats the affirmation for British, although explicitly not American, abolition, in *The Slave Power Conspiracy and the Paranoid Style* (Baton Rouge, La., 1969), p. 33. See also Patrick Richardson, *Empire and Slavery* (New York, 1972), p. 87. Elsa V. Goveia, in *Slave Society in the British Leeward Islands at the End of the Eighteenth Century* (New Haven, 1965), pp. 335–36, agrees fully with Williams on the significance of West Indian economic decline for abolition, as does Jack Gratus, *The Great White Lie* (New York, 1973), p. 14. Howard Temperley, criticizing Williams on virtually every other point, does not dissent from the theory of West Indian decline. See his *British Anti-Slavery, 1833–1870* (London, 1972), appendix on Williams, p. 276. For the fullest statements of the decline thesis see Williams, *From Columbus to Castro*, pp. 226 ff; *Capitalism and Slavery*, pp. 120–27. Ragatz, in *The Fall of the Planter Class*, chap. 4, sets the turning point as early as 1763. Ragatz himself separated the question of the secular decline of the slave system from that of the slave trade. Others refer to the American Revolution or more vaguely to the end of the eighteenth century. See Eugene D. Genovese, *The World the Slaveholders Made* (New York, 1969), p. 128. Also accepting the Ragatz-Williams decline thesis are Alan Adamson, *Sugar Without Slaves: The Political Economy of British Guiana, 1838–1904* (New Haven, 1972), pp. 8–9; John Hatch, *The History of Britain in Africa* (New York, 1969), pp. 85–86; Stiv Jakobson, *Am I Not a Man and a Brother? British Missions and the Abolition of the Slave Trade and Slavery in West Africa and the West Indies, 1786–1838* (Uppsala, 1972), p. 592; Sidney Mintz, *Caribbean Transformations* (Chicago, 1974), pp. 85–86; Richard Pares, *Merchants and Planters* (Cambridge, 1960), pp. 40–41; and Richard B. Sheridan, *Sugar and Slavery: An Economic History of the British West Indies, 1623–1775* (Baltimore, 1974), pp. 447, 485–86.

10. Davis acknowledges that Ragatz and Williams exaggerated the economic decline of the British West Indies, but he maintains that "regardless of short-term fluctuations, there can be no doubt that by 1822, the West Indies were of far less value to Britain than they had been a half-century earlier. Nor can there be any doubt that even in the eighteenth century Barbados and the Leeward Islands had become economically stagnant; or that the entire British Caribbean suffered a continuing exodus of white settlers" (*The Problem of Slavery in an Age of Revolution, 1770–1823* [Ithaca, N.Y., 1975], p. 55n). We wish to take issue with this statement insofar as the term applies to economic measurements and their impact. Davis implies that increases in West Indian value were short term and that the trend over the fifty years from 1770 was downward. We select his statement because it represents a judicious distillation of the prevailing interpretation, gained from broad and scrupulous reading of the available scholarship. It is sufficient to note that Davis's

leitmotif in the text is also the standard statement of the decline thesis: a "golden age" before the American Revolution, the fragility of the West Indian economy, speculative concentration on sugar, the spectacular rise of St. Domingue, and British planters on the verge of final ruin in the 1780s, due to fundamental economic causes of decline—markets, credit, competition, etc. The British slave system remains a model of decline, part of the mercantilist system, and defended by "backward-looking" arguments, while a "second British empire was taking shape in the minds of British merchants and statesmen even before the American Revolution" (pp. 61–63, 162, 351). The two most recent works, apart from Davis, which support the decline thesis are Michael Craton's *Sinews of Empire: A Short History of British Slavery* (New York, 1974), pp. xiii, 243–47, 258–59; and Robin Furneaux's *William Wilberforce* (London, 1974), pp. 256–58. The former work leans strongly toward the perspective of Williams; the latter is in the Coupland tradition. An unqualified supporter of the Williams general thesis is Johnson U. J. Asiegbu, *Slavery and the Politics of Liberation, 1787–1861* (New York, 1969), pp. xiii–xvi, 157–59. There are important parallels to the decline thesis in the historiography of other slave economies. On the centrality of the concepts of "decay" and "capitalist" abolition in Brazilian historiography, see Richard Graham, "Brazilian Slavery Re-examined," *Journal of Social History* 3 (Summer 1970), 431–53, esp. pp. 441 ff.

11. Roger T. Anstey, "A Re-interpretation of the Abolition of the British Slave Trade, 1806–1807," *English Historical Review* 87 (1972), 304–22. Anstey ingeniously stood the Williams thesis on its head in accounting for the passage of abolition, clarifying the peculiar combination of ideological and political circumstances that allowed abolition to pass into law in 1806–1807. In his full-length study, *The Atlantic Slave Trade and British Abolition, 1760–1810* (London, 1975), p. 42, the author has, with his usual grace, acknowledged the force of the argument which we present below.

12. C. Duncan Rice, " 'Humanity sold for sugar.' The British Abolitionist Response to Free Trade in Slave-Grown Sugar," *The Historical Journal* 13 (1970), 403; *The Rise and Fall of Black Slavery* (London, 1975), chap. 5.

13. Since Ragatz and Williams are in accord on this point we will henceforth use the term "Ragatz-Williams" decline theory when referring to that aspect of Williams's account which relies on the "fall" of the British plantation system. Where he adds his own powerful dynamics to Ragatz's account, mapping the twin trajectories of rising metropolitan capitalism and falling slavery, the decline theory is credited only to Williams. Reference to the decline theory without reference to Ragatz is to be understood as denoting the total Williams version, i.e., the "decline *and* rise" theory. Our attribution of the theory to other scholars applies insofar as the deline theory is used by them as a significant element of their argument. In general, while historians have by no means adopted Williams's entire model of short- and long-run economic mechanisms, they have often absorbed his general premises about economic development. Thus the decline of British slavery is linked to the rise of laissez-faire in many histories, even when the author is at pains to emphasize other logical or empirical weaknesses in the details of Williams's account.

14. On C. L. R. James's hypothesis, see *The Black Jacobins: Toussaint L'Ouverture and the San Domingo Revolution* (1938; rpt. New York, 1963), pp. 51–53; on the shifting political economy of the empire and the new imperialism, see R. Coupland, *The American Revolution and the British Empire* (1930; rpt. New York, 1965), esp. pp. 160–219. For arguments connecting the rise of laissez-faire to the triumph of abolition, see Williams, *Capitalism and Slavery*, chap. 7; Williams, *From Columbus to Castro*, pp. 280–85; Richardson, *Empire and Slavery*, pp. 76, 30–31; Craton, *Sinews of Empire*, pp. xiii, 239–40, 256–58; Rice, *Rise and Fall*, p. 222; and Davis, *Slavery in Revolution*, pp. 352–53. Rice, and especially Davis,

harbors doubts about the degree of significance to be assigned to the shift in the early abolitionist period but assumes that the shift was under way during the period 1775–1815 and had a positive effect on the abolitionist cause. Davis also suggests that there was an ambivalence between antislavery and laissez-faire doctrines (*Slavery in Revolution*, p. 358). For an even more skeptical appraisal of the link, see Anstey, "Capitalism and Slavery: A Critique." The terms "mercantilism" and "laissez-faire" are used in the same sense that they were in the studies above. There was, of course, a very large area of agreement between protectionism and free trade. By 1780, both systems presupposed an economy operating through investments of privately owned capital acting in a free internal market without monopolistic interference. The real difference between them derived from the extent to which the world was considered either a single unified market or a zero-sum battlefield requiring political mechanisms to protect national capital and labor.

15. William Playfair, *The Commercial and Political Atlas: Representing By Means of Stained Copper Plate Charts, The Exports, Imports, and General Trade of England* (London, 1786), p. v. A second edition appeared in 1787, a third, in French, in 1788, and another in 1801.

16. See PP 1790–1791 (XXXIV), vol. 745, *Minutes of the Evidence taken before a Committee . . . of . . . Commons . . . respecting the African Slave Trade* (1791), p. 265.

17. PD 2 (1803–1804), 942–43, cotton manufacturers' bill.

18. See Clarkson, *History*, I, chaps. 15, 17.

19. PP 1789 (XXVI), vol. 646a, *Report of the Lords of the Committee of Council for Trade and Plantations*, part V. The Privy Council relied heavily on M. R. d'Auberteuil, *Considérations sur l'état présent de la colonie française de Saint-Domingue*, 2 vols. (Paris, 1776–1777).

20. See *Morning Chronicle*, Feb. 7, 1788; *Bristol Journal*, Mar. 22, 1789; *Bath Chronicle*, Jan. 31, 1788; *Whitehall Evening Post*, Feb. 5–7, 1788. It is quite clear that only after the beginning of the abolitionist agitation were the higher economic organs of the government stimulated to obtain accurate information. See BT 6/12 (1788), copy of a letter from the Duke of Dorset to the Marquis of Carmathen, Mar. 20, 1788. Major works were used as sources even if their data were a full generation out of date. Long's *History of Jamaica*, although published in the 1770s and often using data of the late 1760s, still formed the basis of many numerical statements about the island in 1787.

21. Tables 9 and 10, "Denrées coloniales," and "Commerce des Colonies," in the *Statistique générale et particulière de la France, et de ses colonies, par une société de gens de lettres et de savans* (Paris, 1804), referred only to pre-Revolutionary figures.

22. BT 318/2, pp. 292 ff., a note to J. Stephen from J. Dobson on Cuban exports, Feb. 7, 1807. Dobson was unable to give figures for Cuban exports, and the total trade estimate by value was for 1801! The *Liverpool Chronicle and Commercial Advertiser*, May 23, 1804, in a "Sketch of . . . Havana," dated Dec. 30, 1803, gave figures for the year 1803.

23. The estimate, in 1788, by Robert Norris, a Liverpool merchant, was 74,200 slaves exported from Africa by all European powers. See also *London Chronicle*, Feb. 5, 1788; *Whitehall Evening Post*, Feb. 2–5, 1788. See Add MSS 34427 (Auckland Papers, XVI) Nov. 1787–Feb. 1788, Wilberforce to Eden, Nov. 23, 1787. He estimated the total export of slaves at over 100,000 per year. The *General Evening Post*, Nov. 13–15, 1787, put the figure at over 90,000 annually, plus those lost in transit. The Bishop of Rochester, Dr. Porteus, used the figure of 80,000 per year in 1794 (speech of Mar. 10, 1794, in *Woodfall's Parliamentary Reports*, II [1794], 218). Long's estimate for his *History of Jamaica* was 60,000 slaves per year (Add MSS 18961 [Long Papers, "Collection for the History of Jamaica"], fol. 37). *Aris' Birmingham Gazette*, Jan. 28, 1788, cited the round number 100,000, as did the *Bristol*

Gazette, Feb. 14, 1788. Estimates for the total export of Africans over three centuries ranged from 9 million (*Leeds Mercury,* Jan. 29, 1788, and *Stamford Mercury,* Jan. 13, 1792), to 50 million (letter in *The Diary,* April 16, 1790), to 375 million (*Leeds Intelligencer,* May 12, 1806). As for ratios of increase, the *Glocester Journal,* Feb. 13, 1792, estimated that the British trade had risen from between 4,000 and 5,000 per year in 1660 to 40,000 in 1791.

24. See the excellent analysis by Davis, *Slavery in Revolution,* chap. 10. See also F. O. Shyllon, *Black Slaves in Britain* (London, 1974); and James Walvin, *Black and White: The Negro in English Society, 1555–1945* (London, 1973), pp. 105–43. For the general chronology of the abolitionist movement see Appendix I, and the books by Davis and Anstey cited above. On the early parliamentary tactics of abolition, see also Lipscomb, "William Pitt and the Abolition of Slavery," especially for the period 1787–1804.

25. See the response of members of the political elite on reception of copies of *The Case of Our Fellow Africans,* distributed by the Quakers in 1784. Friends House Library, London, Box F, Minutes of Meeting for Sufferings, Committee on the Slave Trade, 1783–1792, minutes of May 5, 1784.

Chapter 2: The 1770s as the Pivot of British Slavery

1. Williams, *Capitalism and Slavery,* pp. 52 ff.; Sheridan, *Sugar and Slavery,* pp. 470 ff. Stanley L. Engerman, "The Slave Trade and British Capital Formation in the Eighteenth Century: A Comment on the Williams Thesis," *Business History Review* 46 (Winter 1972), 430–43; and Roger T. Anstey, "The Volume and Profitability of the British Slave Trade, 1761–1807," in *Race and Slavery in the Western Hemisphere: Quantitative Studies,* ed. Stanley L. Engerman and Eugene Genovese (Princeton, 1975), pp. 22–24, and in his *British Abolition,* chap. 2, take issue with William's assertions on the significance of the slave trade for British economic growth. See also R. P. Thomas, "The Sugar Colonies of the Old Empire: Profit or Loss for Great Britain?" *Economic History Review* 21 (1968), 30–45; Richard B. Sheridan, "The Wealth of Jamaica in the Eighteenth Century," *Economic History Review* 18 (1965), 292–311, and his "Rejoinder" to Thomas, *Economic History Review* 21 (1968), 46–61; Parry, *Trade and Dominion,* p. 284; Davis, *Slavery in Revolution,* pp. 61–63; Craton, *Sinews of Empire,* pp. 147–56.

2. See chap. 1, notes 9 and 10.

3. Ragatz, *The Fall of the Planter Class,* pp. 111–13; Williams, *Capitalism and Slavery,* pp. 120–25; Davis, *Slavery in Revolution,* p. 52; Richardson, *Empire and Slavery,* pp. 60–70; Craton, *Sinews of Empire,* p. 243.

4. Our principal source here is B. R. Mitchell and P. Deane, *Abstract of British Historical Statistics* (Cambridge, 1962).

5. Williams, *Capitalism and Slavery,* pp. 52–55, and for statistical tables, 225–26.

6. PP 1808 (X), 262, evidence on petitions related to the orders-in-council of 1807.

7. In 1791 an abolitionist valued the colonies at the mean between Privy Council and colonial estimates, i. e., at a little over £50 million (PR 29 [1791], 272). See Williams, *From Columbus to Castro,* p. 125; Bryan Edwards, *The History, Civil and Commercial, of the British West Indies,* 5 vols. (1819; rpt. New York, 1966), II, 473; Thomas Southey, *Chronological History of the West Indies,* 3 vols. (1827; rpt. [London], 1968), II, 14, for estimates. Williams used the figure of £50 million for 1775 as given in Frank Pitman's *The Settlement and Financing of British West India Plantations in the Eighteenth Century* (New Haven, 1917), p. 271. This would make the gain from 1775 to 1788 even greater. Since the method of valuation was based on the number and value of slaves for each colony, times a constant

multiplier, we have a way of checking the uniformity of British assessments of foreign colonies as well. In 1795, newly conquered Martinique was valued at about £6.8 million. Its slave population was estimated at about 90,000. The slave population of the British West Indies, at about 480,000, was 5.3 times as large as Martinique's. Its proportionate valuation should thus have been £36 million—exactly the figure given in the Privy Council report.

8. See Patrick Colquhoun, *A Treatise on the Wealth, Power and Resources of the British Empire* (London, 1815), p. 59. In 1798 Pitt acknowledged the West Indies as *the* major nondomestic source of British income in the empire. The West Indian share was estimated by Pitt at four-fifths of the "whole produce of income arising beyond the seas, and enjoyed by persons in this country." See Cobbett's *Parl. History,* 34 (1798–1800), 13–14.

9. For slave prices, see Anstey, "Volume and Profitability," p. 20, table 6. For British general price indices, see Mitchell and Deane, *Abstract*, pp. 469–70. The Schumpeter-Gilboy, and Gayer, Rostow and Schwartz indices were not available to contemporaries. They did not apply any criteria of fluctuating prices to assessments.

10. T. S. Ashton, "Introduction," in Elizabeth Schumpeter, *British Overseas Trade Statistics, 1697–1808* (Oxford, 1960), p. 11.

11. Based on Anstey, "Volume and Profitability," p. 20, table 6.

12. Philip Curtin, *The Atlantic Slave Trade: A Census* (Madison, Wis., 1969), p. 136, table 38 and p. 154. Curtin's decennial pattern creates difficulties for measuring the impact of events. See R. N. Bean, "The British Transatlantic Slave Trade, 1650–1776," Ph.D. dissertation, University of Washington, 1971, p. 2. The British thought they were carrying about 38,000 slaves annually across the Atlantic around 1789. See PP 1789 (XXVI), vol. 645a, part 1, *Minutes of Evidence on the Slave Trade,* evidence of Mr. Norris. For Anstey's figures see "Volume and Profitability," pp. 8–10, tables 1 and 2.

13. See CO 137/91 (Jamaica), extract of a letter dated Feb. 20, 1793; *Glasgow Advertiser,* Mar. 23–26, 1792, extract of a letter from Liverpool; Bodleian Library, Clarendon Deposit (Barham Papers), c. 357, Jamaica Correspondence, Jamaica agents to J. F. Barham, June 12, July 30, Sept. 13, 1792. See also Peter J. Marshall, *The Anti-Slave Trade Movement in Bristol* (Bristol, 1968), p. 22.

14. James Stephen, *The Dangers of the Country* (London, 1807), pp. 187, 210.

15. This subject is discussed at greater length in chap. 5.

16. The estimates on the Liverpool trade of 1805 are in Barry F. Drake, "Continuity and Flexibility in Liverpool's Trade with Africa and the Caribbean," *Business History* (in press). On British slave-trade profits, see Anstey, "Volume and Profitability," pp. 20–22. E. Phillip Le Veen, in another estimate of the profitability of the slave trade, arrives at a figure of 9.5 percent per year at the turn of the century ("British Slave Trade Suppression Policies 1821–1865: Impact and Implications" Ph.D. dissertation, University of Chicago, 1971, p. 28, table 3). See also chap. 5, note 21, below.

17. [James Wallace], *A General and Descriptive History of . . . the Town of Liverpool . . . together with . . . its extensive African Trade* (Liverpool, 1794), p. 232n. Wallace's was probably the best documented account of the Liverpool African trade available to contemporaries between 1787 and 1807.

18. On the French trade, see Perry Viles, "The Slaving Interest in the Atlantic Ports, 1763–1792," *French Historical Studies* 7 (1972), 529–43.

19. On the comparatively modest rate of profit in the Levantine trade, see Ralph Davis, *Aleppo and Devonshire Square: English Traders in the Levant in the Eighteenth Century* (London, 1967), pp. 223, 234. Professor Davis, who is undoubtedly well qualified to

judge the subject, expressed the opinion to me that expectations of profit were extraordinarily low in the eighteenth century. Expectations for returns from international trade were only slightly higher than from domestic investment. See also chap. 10, note 14, below.

20. Regarding the pre-Revolutionary value of the various British colonies for British exports, Arthur Young, in 1772, described the West Indies as Britain's most valuable cluster of colonies. He concluded that "every soul in the West Indies is worth better than 68 in the northern colonies, eighteen in the tobacco, and rather better than one and a half in the southern [continental] ones" (*Political Essays Concerning the Present State of the British Empire* [London, 1772], pp. 338). Trade was of course the criterion of imperial value.

21. During the revolutionary war, the trade was legally prohibited to Massachusetts, Rhode Island, Virginia, North Carolina, Georgia, and Pennsylvania. On American anti-slavery, see Winthrop D. Jordan, *White Over Black: American Attitudes Toward the Negro* (Chapel Hill, N.C., 1968), pp. 294-304, 316-31, 342-74; Arthur Zilversmit, *The First Emancipation: The Abolition of Slavery in the North* (Chicago, 1967), chaps. 4-8; Davis, *Slavery in Revolution*, pp. 119-31.

22. On total slave imports see Robert W. Fogel and Stanley L. Engerman, *Time on the Cross: The Economics of American Negro Slavery*, 2 vols. (Boston, 1974), I, 24-25, and figure 6, "U.S. Imports of Slaves per Decade, 1620-1860." On the recovery of staple agriculture even before the introduction of Witney's machine, see Lewis C. Gray, *History of Agriculture in the Southern United States to 1860*, 2 vols. (Washington, D.C., 1933), II, 610-11, 674-86, 1023-24.

23. Elizabeth Donnan, *Documents Illustrative of the Slave Trade to America,* 4 vols. (Washington, D. C., 1933), IV, 525. On the major role of British capital in the American slave trade and the reopening of South Carolina, see DUL, Hamilton microfilms of the Grenville papers originally at Boconnoc, Cornwall (hereafter cited as DUL Hamilton [Grenville Mss]), reel 17, Papers in support of the Foreign Abolition Bill, "B", "American Slave Trade," May, 1806 (probably by James Stephen). Stephen also claimed that only *one* American slave ship serving Charleston was not British-financed (ibid., "Observations on the claim of a more extended term than a month for the fitting out Foreign Slave Ships from British Ports").

24. Fogel and Engerman, *Time on the Cross*, I, 29. One could easily give this the fully/only twist, and note that importations contributed *fully* one-third of the increase of slave labor before 1808.

25. The American figures are calculated from table 2 of John Cummings, *Negro Population in the United States, 1790-1915,* (New York, 1968), a reprint of the Department of Commerce publication, *Negro Population, 1790-1915* (Washington, 1918). To show the possible significance of even American abolition, it should be noted that the peak decade of the slave trade, 1800-1810, ending three years after abolition, was the *only* decade after 1750 in which the Negro percentage of the total population actually increased.

Chapter 3: The Protected Economy Before the French Slave Revolution

1. See Sheridan, *Sugar and Slavery*, p. 472; Herman Merivale, *Lectures on Colonization and on Colonies, Delivered before the University of Oxford in 1839, 1840, and 1841* (1861; rpt. New York, 1967), p. 62. In terms of public revenue, the slave islands were regarded as the only imperial net asset to the metropolitan budget (John Sinclair, *The History of the*

Public Revenue of the British Empire, 3 vols. [1803; rpt. New York, 1966], II, 91–103). Henry Brougham believed that the civil establishments of the West Indian islands yielded the British treasury over £50,000 net annually (exclusive of crown land sales) and could easily be made to yield £70,000 (*An Inquiry into the Colonial Policy of the European Powers*, 2 vols. [Edinburgh, 1803; rpt. New York, 1970], I, 559.

2. See Ragatz, *The Fall of the Planter Class*, esp. chaps 6, 7; Williams, *Capitalism and Slavery*, pp. 113–14, 121–23, 145–50.

3. Sheridan, *Sugar and Slavery*, p. 385. The planters were also accused of technological inertia for failing to use the plough instead of the hoe, thereby raising the labor needs for any given sugar plantation, However, it was the number of hands required for the cane harvest, with its critical time factor between cutting and boiling, which determined what the minimum slave requirement should be (HLR MSS, May, 31, 1792, evidence on the slave trade, p. 3).

4. See, for example, Robert Wallace, *Characteristics of the Present Political State of Great Britain* (1761; rpt. New York, 1969).

5. Thomas Tryon, *Letters, Domestick and Foreign* (1700), pp. 192–93, quoted in K. G. Davies, *The North Atlantic World in the Seventeenth Century* (Minneapolis, 1974), p. 189. For Jamaica on the eve of the American Revolution, see PR 1 (1774–1775), 342, "Testimony of John Ellis esq. of Jamaica, in Parliament."

6. See Douglas Hall, "Absentee-Proprietorship in the British West Indies, to about 1850," *Jamaican Historical Review* 4 (1964), 15–35. R. B. Sheridan, "The Sugar Trade of the British West Indies from 1660 to 1756, with Special Reference to Antigua," Ph.D. dissertation, University of London, 1951, p. 100, notes complaints of soil exhaustion as early as the 1660s and increasingly from the 1680s. See also his *Sugar and Slavery*, pp. 106, 111–12. On contemporary statements about Barbados, see *Representation of the Board of Trade relating to the State of the British Islands in America* (London, 1734), p. 14, a copy of which is in Add MSS 35807 (Hardwicke Papers), fol. 60–66. On exhaustion in the Leeward Islands, see Josiah Tucker, of Bristol, *An Essay on the Advantages and Disadvantages which respectively attend France and Great Britain with regard to Trade* (Glasgow, 1756), p. 22. From the agronomic perspective British tropical agriculture was simply part of the imperial continuum. West Indian, like British soils, could go through cycles of relative exhaustion and rejuvenation. See Archibald Cochrane, Earl of Dundonald, *A Treatise shewing the intimate connection . . . between agriculture and chemistry . . . in Great Britain and Ireland and . . . [the] West India estates* (London, 1793, 1803), pp. 197–252.

7. On absenteeism as characteristic of St. Domingue, see Add MSS 38351 (Liverpool Papers), fol. 214, memoir dated "after 91." Sheridan, *Sugar and Slavery*, p. 386, points out that each generation saw the rise of new men alongside the indebted and absentee planters. On the indebtedness of Dutch Surinam at the outbreak of the American Revolution, see Brougham, *An Inquiry*, II, 356.

8. LRO Picton Library (Tarleton Papers), 920 TAR, John to Clayton Tarleton, April 29, 1790. The French planters also considered heavy indebtedness endemic to the system. See M. De Buc de Marentille, *De l'Esclavage des Nègres dans les colonies de l'Amérique* (Pointe-à-Pitre, 1790), p. 13. A copy is in CO 71/20 (Dominica, 1791).

9. Gabriel Debien, *Les Esclaves aux Antilles Françaises, XVII–XVIII siècles* (Basse Terre et Fort-de-France, 1974), pp. 164, 167. An argument for the relative efficiency of the British colonial planters is found in W. A. Green, "The Planter Class and British West India Sugar Production, Before and After Emancipation," *Economic History Review* 26 (1973), 448–63. In 1807, F. J. de Pons, who favored the reconquest of St. Domingue, admitted that many plantations, especially in the north, had already ceased to be profitable before the

revolution because of soil exhaustion. There were also many estates in the hills which were on the point of being abandoned (*Perspective des rapports*, p. 275). Despite their expanding culture, the Cuban *hacendados* were also bemoaning their "imminent ruin" around 1790. See Manuel Moreno Fraginals, *The Sugarmill: The Socioeconomic Complex of Sugar in Cuba, 1760–1860* (New York, 1976), p. 17; also p. 156, note 16.

10. Fogel and Engerman, *Time on the Cross*, I, 21, figure 4, based in turn upon the careful estimates of John James McCusker, "The Rum Trade and the Balance of Payments of the Thirteen Continental Colonies, 1650–1775," 2 vols., Ph.D. dissertation, University of Pittsburgh, 1970, I, 712.

11. Ragatz, *The Fall of the Planter Class*, pp. 142–91; Williams, *Capitalism and Slavery*, pp. 121–23; Davis, *Slavery in Revolution*, pp. 52–53. The inspiration for the "rising East" theory probably owes much to Alexander von Humboldt, who, as early as 1809, drew attention to "the future direction of [sugar] commerce" in the East Indies and the "astonishing rapidity" of sugar expansion in Bengal (*Political Essay*, III, 15–18). The original essay was published in Germany, 1809–1813. The general theme of a *Drang nach Osten* at the end of the eighteenth century is reiterated by Vincent T. Harlow, *The Founding of the Second British Empire, 1763–1793*, 2 vols. (London, 1952, 1964), I, p. 48, and rightly challenged by Parry, *Trade and Dominion*, p. 277.

12. Add MSS 12407 (Long Papers), fol. 27. Lisbon was simultaneously deprived of Brazilian sugars due to a conflict with Spain (ibid., 12404, fol. 445).

13. The Jamaican House of Assembly reported that the hurricane of 1785 hit the French and Spanish possessions harder than those of the British. See *Two Reports from the Committee of the Honorable House of Assembly of Jamaica on the Subject of the Slave Trade* (London, 1789), second report, p. 13, a copy of which is in CO 137/88 (Jamaica, 1789–1791). On July 10, 1787, the *Manchester Mercury and Harrop's General Advertiser* reported heavy losses from a hurricane in Mauritius, and on Oct. 9, 1787 that "a dreadful gale has visited the French West India Islands; its Ravages continued for the greatest part of the 9th and 10th of August last; happily our own Possessions escaped, and did not feel the Effect of the Hurricane in the least degree." Britain itself was not weatherproof from 1790 to 1807. The abolition petitions peaked in the especially cold winter of 1791–1792, which carried off many of the most ill-housed. And what can one make of the storms, lightning, thunder, floods, and hailstones five inches in diameter, which visited abolitionist Yorkshire, Wilberforce's own constituency, at the very moment abolition took effect? (*The Iris, or the Sheffield Advertiser*, May 5, 1807).

14. Ragatz, *The Fall of the Planter Class*, p. 206.

15. Ragatz, *The Fall of the Planter Class*, pp. 186–87; Williams, *Capitalism and Slavery*, pp. 121–22; Richardson, *Empire and Slavery*, pp. 65–66.

16. See Ragatz, *The Fall of the Planter Class*, p. 192; Williams, *Capitalism and Slavery*, p. 123. The document was from the *Proceedings of the Hon. House of Assembly of Jamaica, on the Sugar and Slave Trade* (Oct., 1792), also published in London in 1793. A copy is in CO 137/91 (Jamaica, 1792–1793), Appendix 13.

17. Michael M. Edwards, *The Growth of the British Cotton Trade, 1780–1815* (Manchester, 1967), p. 22; *Proceedings on the Sugar and Slave Trade*.

18. Ragatz, *The Fall of the Planter Class*, pp. 184–85; Williams, *From Columbus to Castro*, pp. 226–27; PP 1789 (LXXXIV), vol. 646, part II.

19. Williams, *Capitalism and Slavery*, pp. 122–23.

20. *Proceedings on the Sugar and Slave Trade*, pp. 4–6.

21. Ibid, p. 9.

22. Ibid, p. 7.

23. *A Jamaican Plantation: The History of Worthy Park, 1670–1970* (Toronto, 1970), pp. 116–18.

24. Add MSS 38346 (Liverpool Papers, 1785–1786), fol. 85, "A Comparative view of the produce and the supplies of the British West Indies with shipping employed both in Carrying to and from North America, before and since the war."

25. PP 1778–1782 (XLIV), vol. 35, *Report From the Committee to Whom the Petition of the Sugar-Refiners of London was Referred,* 1781, p. 35; PP 1790–1791 (XXXIV), vol. 745, "Minutes of Evidence," p. 265, Mr. Irving; SRO (Melville Papers), GD 51/1/361/14, declaration of the London Sugar Brokers, Mar. 23, 1792.

26. Williams, *Capitalism and Slavery,* p. 146.

27. Ibid., p. 122; also *From Columbus to Castro,* p. 237. Ragatz, *The Fall of the Planter Class,* p. 125, also qualifies St. Domingue's output for 1783 as "amazing."

28. As in the previous discussion, *1787* refers to an average of four or five years with 1787 at its center. In this case we use 1785–1789 because these were the years used for comparison down through 1792. If the percentage of smuggled goods was constant we can use the official figures as reliable estimates of ratios over time. If it fell, by using a constant for French smuggling we are inflating French colonial exports, and biasing the British share downward. The British colonies might also have engaged in the practice, but we assume zero smuggling so as not to inflate the British total. See also McCusker, "The Rum Trade," I, 310–15.

29. See Appendix II. According to accounts in the *Report from the Committee of Warehouses of the United East India Company Relative to the Culture of Sugar* (London, 1792), which did not allow for clayed conversion, St. Domingue production in 1742 amounted to 51.7 percent of the total combined sugar production of the French colony and the entire British system. Measured against the peacetime British average (Britain was at war with Spain), St. Domingue's share was 45.9 percent.

30. Ragatz, *The Fall of the Planter Class,* pp. 125–26.

31. See Appendix II.

32. See the Privy Council Report in PP 1789 (XXVI), vol. 646a, Supplement to Accounts, no. 10. See CO 318/2 for the Jamaican figures; and *A Report from the Committee of Warehouses,* p. 25, for the St. Domingue figures. As of 1792, the "latest accounts made up" for that island ran only through 1789. Michael Craton asserts that Jamaica's "general rate of expansion had slowed almost to a stop" by 1788 ("Jamaican Slavery," in *Race and Slavery in the Western Hemisphere: Quantitative Studies,* ed. Stanley L. Engerman and Eugene D. Genovese [Princeton, 1975], p. 268).

33. Using Richard Dunn's rough estimate of colonial sugar output in 1700, we calculated the relative standing of British colonial production for a full century before abolition. Dunn's figures are 25,000 tons for the British colonies, 20,000 for Brazil, 10,000 for the French colonies, and 4,000 for Dutch Surinam. If Brazilian production is calculated at its nominal weight, with no allowance at all for conversion of clayed sugar, British colonial output was 42 percent of total European colonial production in 1700. If Brazilian production is converted to muscovado equivalence at our 1806 proportion of 75 percent clayed sugar, British output was 38 percent of the total. If we assume, with McCusker, that *all* Brazilian sugar was clayed, the British share was 37 percent. Under any of these assumptions Britain's share in *1787* was almost identical to that of 1700. See Richard S. Dunn, *Sugar and Slaves: The Rise of the Planter Class in the English West Indies, 1624–1713* (Chapel Hill, N.C., 1972) p. 234.

34. Williams, *Capitalism and Slavery,* pp. 145–46.

35. Noel Deerr, *The History of Sugar,* 2 vols. (London, 1949–1950), II, 529–30,

accounts for the lower price of French raw sugar in terms of differences in refining techniques which do not imply lower costs of production. A large proportion of French production was clayed; the "equivalent" of English muscovado in the French market was really a compound of English-grade raw sugars plus the drainings of the claying process. For testimony on the noncompetitive status of British sugar see that of Mr. Irving, PP 1790–1791 (XXXIV), vol. 745, "Minutes of Evidence," p. 266.

36. The tables may be found in the *Report of the Committee of Warehouses*, pp. 21–23; Sheridan, *Sugar and Slavery*, pp. 493–95. My conversion of refined to raw sugar equivalents in the tables is at the official rate of 34:20, or 1.7:1. For some of the earlier literature on the subject see *The Present State of the British Sugar Colonies Consider'd* (London, 1731), pp. 6–16; *Remarks upon a Book Entitled, the Present State of the Sugar Colonies Consider'd* (London, 1731), p. 5; *The Importance of the Sugar Colonies to Britain Stated* (London, 1731), p. 9; Mr. Bennett, *Two Letters and Several Calculations on the State of the Sugar Colonies and Trade* (London, 1738); William Perrin, *The Present State of the British and French Sugar Colonies, and our own Northern Colonies Considered: Together with some Remarks on the Decay of our Trade, and the Improvements made of late years by the French in Theirs* (London, 1740), p. 43. Perrin dates the decay from the late twenties.

37. PP 1790–1791 (XXXIV), vol. 745, "Minutes of Evidence," p. 265.

38. Williams, *Capitalism and Slavery*, p. 122.

39. Ralph Davis, *The Rise of the Atlantic Economies* (London, 1973), p. 251; see also Sheridan, *Sugar and Slavery*, pp. 30–35.

40. See *York Chronicle*, Jan. 13, 1792; *Sheffield Advertiser*, Jan. 6, 1792; E. G. Thomas, "The Treatment of Poverty in Berkshire, Essex, and Oxfordshire, 1723–1834," Ph.D. dissertation, University of London, 1970, Appendix D, "Family Budgets in Oxfordshire, 1795," pp. 307–09; also pp. 18, 52, 149, 155, 319. Thomas also cites the "typical" budget of David Davies, in *The Case of the Labourers in Husbandry stated and considered* (1795). See also the broadside in the Manchester Central Library, Political Tracts Collection, 2770, "The Committee . . . for the . . . Relief of the Poor [introducing] Rice . . . amongst the lower class . . . ," Feb. 19 and Mar. 17, 1800; and Thomas Troughton, *The History of Liverpool* (Liverpool, 1810), pp. 293–94.

41. Contrast with Williams, *Capitalism and Slavery*, pp. 145–50; *From Columbus to Castro*, pp. 235–40, 280–92.

42. *A Report from the Committee of Warehouses*, pp. 19–20.

43. Williams, *Capitalism and Slavery*, p. 123. See the response to this East Indian thesis in Mellor, *British Imperial Trusteeship*, pp. 50–57.

44. Williams, *Capitalism and Slavery*, p. 123. Ironically, Williams's "swing-to-the-East" theme is vintage Coupland. See Coupland, *The American Revolution and the British Empire*, pp. 201–09. Coupland cites Pitt's India bill speech of 1784 to the effect that India's value, "had of course, increased in proportion to the losses sustained by the dismemberment of other great possessions, by which losses . . . the remaining territories became more valuable" (p. 208). But, according to Pitt, all remaining possessions had thereby increased in relative value. Moreover, British interest in India in the late 1780s was falling, not rising (P. J. Marshall, *The Impeachment of Warren Hastings* [London, 1965], p. 189). The pace of British expansion in India also slowed down in the 1780s and 1790s, after Pitt's India Act of 1784 forbade the Company from undertaking further aggressive wars (P. J. Marshall, *Problems of Empire: Britain and India, 1757–1813* [London, 1968], pp. 74–75).

Chapter 4: The Unprotected Economy Before the French Slave Revolution

1. Williams, *Capitalism and Slavery*, pp. 135–68; Ragatz, *The Fall of the Planter Class*, pp. vii–ix.

2. See, for example, Coupland, *The American Revolution*, pp. 83–84, 196–201; and a number of books cited in chap. 1, notes 9 and 10.

3. Eric Hobsbawm, *Industry and Empire* (London, 1968), p. 41.

4. Williams, *Capitalism and Slavery*, p. 128. Note the familiar data gap between 1790 and the mid-1820s.

5. See Edwards, *The Growth of the British Cotton Trade*.

6. J. H. Clapham, "The Industrial Revolution and the Colonies, 1783–1822," in *The Cambridge History of the British Empire* (Cambridge, 1940), II, 225.

7. Frances Armytage, *The Free Port System in the British West Indies* (London, 1953), pp. 42–44, 61–63.

8. Irving's note is in PRO Customs 17/14 (1792), fol. 80; the West Indian cotton and slave accounts are in Customs 17/13 (1791), fol. 107. Of the cotton so imported, 40 percent came from the French settlements, 32 percent from the Spanish, 26 percent from the Dutch, and 2 percent from the Danish and Swedish colonies. Under the free port act of 1766 French colonial cotton could be purchased for up to 30 percent below its price in metropolitan France (Witt Bowden, *Industrial Society in England Towards the End of the Eighteenth Century* [New York, 1925], p. 202).

9. The *Diary* of Aug. 12, 1790, assigned the British West Indies 31 percent of British imports in 1789. See also *Diary*, Aug. 13, 1789, letter of "Leo Africanus," assigning 25 percent.

10. Cobbett's *Parl. History*, 26 (1786–1787), 532, speech of Feb. 23, 1787. Britain's approaching self-sufficiency in cotton was reiterated by Buckingham on Mar. 1, 1787 (ibid., p. 538). See also BT 6/140 (1788–1792), "Cotton," fols. 15, 56, 57; and BT 6/103, Circular, May 3, 1786; Add MSS 38392 (Liverpool Papers), Minutes of the Committee of Trade, Jan. to Dec. 1790, fol. 96, April 20, on varieties of cotton ordered distributed to the West Indian governors; and Edwards, *The Growth of the British Cotton Trade*, pp. 75–88. Colonial agents were also looking for new strains of cotton on their own account (DUL, Stephen Fuller Letterbook, May 2, 1787). Even when seeming to look east, the British government had its eye on the west. In 1787 the first British emissary to Saurashtra, India, was dispatched to assess the prospects of cotton purchases. Significantly, however, his "real, but secret, mission was to determine whether Indian varieties of cotton could be grown in the West Indies" (Howard Spodek, "Rulers, Merchants, and Other Groups in the City-States of Saurashtra, India, around 1800," *Comparative Studies in Society and History* 16 [1974], 450n.).

11. Armytage, *Free Port System*, p. 153, table J; Mitchell and Deane, *Abstract*, pp. 177–78; PRO 30 8/351, an account of cotton imports, 1789–1794; PP 1808 (IV), 319, Reports from Committees, Appendix C, cotton imported from the West Indies, 1761–1806.

12. CO 101/28 (Grenada, 1788), E. Matthews to Lord Sydney, Feb. 12, 1788, on the impact of the free port act of 1787; Add MSS 38416 (Liverpool Papers), fol. 29, William Walton to Hawkesbury, Liverpool, Feb. 24, 1788.

13. Add MSS 38350, "Brief Statement."

14. Add MSS 38416 (Liverpool Papers), Henry Wilkens to Hawkesbury, Mar. 15, 1788. See also BT 6/140, "Cotton," fol. 34, on African cotton, 1787–1788; and fol. 260, Remarks on

the Cotton Manufacturers, Mar. 19, 1789.

15. See *Shrewsbury Chronicle*, Feb. 3, 1792; *Manchester Mercury*, Mar. 11, 1788.

16. BT 6/40, fols. 36–39.

17. See PP 1785–1786 (VII), vol. 39.

18. BT 6/40, fols. 56, 102, 121–27; *An Important Crisis in the Calico and Muslin Manufactory Explained* (April 9, 1788). See *Morning Chronicle*, Jan. 3, 1792; Add MSS 38392 (Liverpool Papers), fol. 19, Minutes of the Committee of Trade, 1790, noting receipt of a memorial of the merchants of Lancaster, asking for a duty on cotton-wool imported in foreign ships, April 17, 1790.

19. See above all, John Ehrman, *The Younger Pitt: The Years of Acclaim* (New York, 1969), pp. 330–36, and the same author's *The British Government and Commercial Negotiations with Europe, 1783–1793* (Cambridge, 1962), chap. 8; and Parry, *Trade and Dominion*, pp. 277–80. If acceptance of the Anglo-French treaty were made the litmus test of inclinations toward commercial liberalization, the slave interest would have passed it. In February 1787, the West India committee voted not to petition against the treaty, despite the added advantage it might give to French brandy over Caribbean rum (DUL, Stephen Fuller Letterbook, letter to Jamaica, Feb. 28, 1787). In the spring of 1787 Pitt was also still "a great favorite with our West India gentlemen" (ibid., Jan. 20 and Feb. 28).

20. Ehrman, *The Younger Pitt*, pp. 335–36. See also Ralph Davis, "The Rise of Protection in England, 1689–1786," *Economic History Review* 19 (1966), 306–17; and Harlow, *The Founding of the Second British Empire*, II, chap. 5.

21. Williams, *Capitalism and Slavery*, p. 136.

22. See Anstey, "Volume and Profitability," p. 2, and table 6. The growth from 1775 was acknowledged by the abolitionists. See Thomas Clarkson, *An Essay on the Comparative Efficiency of Regulation or Abolition Applied to the Slave Trade* (London, 1789), p. 19. For contemporary estimates of profitability and the general state of the trade, see Add MSS 38416 (Liverpool Papers), fol. 103, Tarleton to Hawkesbury, June 3, 1788, which accurately rated the profit at 10 percent. For other ratings see ibid., fols. 37–42, 204. On prior profitability see PP 1777 (LIX), vol. 9, *Return from the Commissioners for Trade and Plantations . . . In Consequence of the Address to His Majesty . . . 29th day of January 1777*, p. 11. On the public's early awareness of its profitability, see *Diary*, April 17, 1789, letter from Liamuiga to Charles Spooner, esq.; *Northampton Mercury*, Feb. 2, 1788; *Lincoln Rutland and Stamford Mercury*, Jan. 25, 1788; *Leeds Mercury*, Feb. 26, 1788. See esp. Engerman, "The Slave Trade and British Capital Formation," pp. 430–43. Even those who consider the administrative and monopoly costs of the sugar colonies as a burden on the empire in the eighteenth century do not apply this characterization to the slave trade. Thomas, in "The Sugar Colonies of the Old Empire," pp. 39–40, shows a profit-sales ratio of 0.20 for the slave trade in the latter 1780s (table 3A), compared with a profit-sales ratio of 0.09 in fine broadcloth, 1781–1796, and 0.19 in cotton textiles in the 1760s and 1830s (table 2A).

23. See Add MSS 38416 (Liverpool Papers), fols. 79–80, extract of the petition of the planters of Berbice, March 1788. The Dutch opened St. Eustasius to slaves in foreign ships in 1789 (CO 71/15 [Dominica, 1788–1789], Governor Orde to Lord Sydney, May 31, 1789). On Dutch subsidies to their slave trade, see PP 1789 (XXVI), vol. 646a, Privy Council report, part VI. On the Danish factories, see Sv. E. Green-Pederson, "The Scope and Structure of the Danish Slave Trade," *Scandinavian Economic History Review* 19 (1971), 175. On French and Spanish lures to British traders, see Add MSS 38416, fols. 60, 81, 120; DUL, Stephen Fuller Letterbook, Feb. 17, 1788. On French subsidies and a prospectus for a joint venture from Bordeaux, see LRO (Tarleton Papers),

920 TAR/5, John to Clayton Tarleton, April 29, 1790; PP 1789 (XXVI), vol. 646a, Privy Council report, part V, C. no. 6 and 7; and CO 137/88 (Jamaica, 1790–1791), a copy of a St. Domingue ordinance of May 9, 1789, opening a free trade in slaves to the south of the island. See also *Diary,* Sept. 7, 1789. On the opening up of the Spanish colonies, see Add MSS 38416, fol. 24, from the African Office, Feb. 19, 1788; fol. 29, William Walton to Hawkesbury, Feb. 25, 1788; fol. 83, Th. Sandoff to Hawkesbury, April 17, 1788; fol. 103, Tarleton to Hawkesbury, June 9, 1788; CO 71/15 (Dominica, 1788–1789), Orde to Sydney, May 31, 1789. On the volume of the British slave trade to Spanish America before 1788, see Add MSS 38416, fol. 114.

24. Pp. 146–47; *From Columbus to Castro,* pp. 244–45.

25. Add MSS 38416 (Liverpool Papers), fol. 221, Mr. Pownal's account of the slave trade, n.d. (published in Donnan, *Documents of the Slave Trade,* II, 507). The data year referred to was 1753. See also fols. 114, 24; CO 101/28 (Grenada, 1788); PRO 30 8/349, part 1 (Chatham Papers), Whitehall, Nov. 3, 1797, letter from the Jamaica Committee of Correspondence, May 15, 1797; Frank Pitman, *The Development of the British West Indies, 1700–1763* (1917; rpt. Hamden, Conn., 1967), p. 138.

26. Add MSS 38416, fol. 221. In 1753 the French colonies were already purchasing more slaves from British vessels alone than were the British colonists themselves. On public knowledge of the antiquity of the trade, see *Morning Chronicle,* July 1, 1788.

27. For the 1787–1789 data see the sources cited in chap. 3, note 32. For the 1767 production figure we use Add MSS 18961 (Long Papers), vol. 43, "Hispanola," citing official figures. For British imports from the French West Indies see the figure in our table 12, column 3.

Lacking the figures for the French Windward Islands, we used as our base their percentage of total French colonial exports in 1788, as it appears in the *Statistique Générale,* table 9, assuming that exports in 1786–1787 were roughly proportionate to those of 1788. If one is wary of using 1788 to calculate proportions for 1786–1787, the Anglo-French comparison for 1788 alone gives almost identical results. On the impact of the trade treaty with France, see Add MSS 38350 (Liverpool Papers), fols. 6–18, "Brief Statement Relative to the Growth of Cotton (after January 1790)." It was noted before the American Revolution that one-sixth of St. Domingue's cotton went as barter for slaves (PRO 30 8/349, part II).

28. *Diary,* May 9, 1792.

29. BT 6/75, Correspondence 1785–1790, fols. 377–79; PP 1789 (XXVI), vol. 646a, part VI (France); and PP 1794–1795 (XL), vol. 810, *Papers . . . relative to Sir Charles Grey,* nos. 4, 6.

30. Add MSS 38416, fols. 103–10, Tarleton to Hawkesbury, June 3 and 9, 1788; see also fol. 168, Henry Ellis to Hawkesbury, Marseilles, April 12, 1788. One of the major reasons given for extending the West Indian free port system in 1787 was the need to undercut French attempts to take the slave trade from the British. See H. T. Manning, *British Colonial Government After the American Revolution, 1782–1820* (New Haven, 1933), pp. 276–77. From our table 9 this appears to have been a well-grounded concern.

31. On the foreign trades in 1788 see PP 1789 (XXV), vol. 644, pp. 243–54; Add MSS 38416, fol. 81, John Reiden to Hawkesbury, Mar. 7, 1788, and fol. 155, James Jones to Hawkesbury, July 26, 1788. See also *Diary,* June 12, 1789, July 23 and Sept. 17, 1791; *Northampton Mercury,* April 7, 1792.

32. Add MSS 38350 (Liverpool Papers), fol. 217; ibid., 38387, fol. 12, "Thoughts," 1778–1779; PRO 30 8/348, Privy Council examination of Charles Spooner (Mar. 1, 1788), p. 181.

33. Add MSS 18961 (Long Papers), fol. 60; *Diary,* Feb. 16, 1790. See also *Morning Chronicle,* July 1, 1788, letter of "Humanitas"; *Diary,* April 9, 1790, letter of "Leo Africanus."

34. Add MSS 38416 (Liverpool Papers), fol. 153, letter of James Jones, July 26, 1788; *Morning Chronicle*, April 3, 1788, letter of "Pyrrho"; *Diary*, April 10, 1789, West India Merchants and Planters advertisement; *Public Advertiser*, Mar. 25, 1788, third letter of "Niger" to Wilberforce; CO 71/21 (Dominica, 1791), Governor Orde's Report, May 19, 1792. On labor shortages, even for established planters who did not want to buy Africans, see the Bodleian Library, Clarendon Deposit (Barham Papers), c. 357, Jamaica Correspondence, C. Rowe to Barham, Jan. 17, 1785, Feb. 4, 1786, Feb. 13, 1787, June 23, 1788, Oct. 13, 1788, Dec. 31, 1788, July 30, 1792.

35. See Dundas's and Pitt's speeches in the Commons, April 23, 1792, account in *Diary*, April 24, 1792, and April 26, 1792. On the need for the slave trade for new plantations and as an aid to maintaining the managerial class, see HLR MSS, May 31, 1792, Evidence on the Slave Trade, pp. 4–7.

Chapter 5: The Growth of Slavery in the Era of British Supremacy

1. For an example, see Add MSS 38356 (Liverpool Papers), "Histoire de la Martinique," fols. 263–64, "Commerce en 1806."

2. *The West India Common-Place Book, Compiled from Parliamentary and Official Documents* (London, 1807). See also Stephen, *The Dangers of the Country.*

3. See J. W. Fortescue, *A History of the British Army,* 14 vols. (London, 1910–1930), IV and V, passim.

4. In 1793–1794 the British appeared to be on the verge of capturing the entire French West Indian system. In 1797–1802, the British had come into possession of Dutch Guiana, Trinidad, all the Dutch, Danish, and Swedish West Indies, the French African dependency of Gorée, and the Dutch Cape Colony. In 1807, the British had regained Tobago, St. Lucia, Guiana, the Danish West Indies, the Cape Colony, and (temporarily) Buenos Aires.

5. See Henry Hamilton, *An Economic History of Scotland in the Eighteenth Century* (Oxford, 1963), pp. 411–12, Appendix 7; G. Stewart, *Progress of Glasgow* (Glasgow, 1883), pp. 165–69, Appendix.

6. See Williams, *Capitalism and Slavery,* pp. 154–61, for the assertions about the cotton and iron industries; PP 1812 (X), 79 ff, "Account of the . . . Value of all the imports . . . and exports [1805–1810]"; PP 1813–1814 (XII), 225.

7. See Edwards, *The Growth of British Cotton,* p. 97; Michel Crouzet, *L'Economie britannique et le blocus continental, 1806–1813,* 2 vols. (Paris, 1958), I, 211–15.

8. PD 9 (1807), 137.

9. Mitchell and Deane, *Abstract,* p. 311.

10. See Add MSS 38416 (Liverpool Papers), printed sheet, July 28, 1802, pencil-marked "with Mr. Crawford's compliments," a summary of Dutch encouragements and British legal sanction (opinion in Doctor's Commons, July 2, 1803). There was "no limitation to the number of Negroes in their [Dutch] ships," as well as a "triangular" trade profit in freight to Holland.

11. DUL Hamilton (Grenville MSS), reel 17, "Observations on . . . Foreign Slave Ships" [June or July 1806], pp. 12–14. See also Appendix II.

12. CO 111/6 (Demerara, 1805–1806), "Observations respecting the Order . . . in Council of the 15th August 1805 . . ." See also Sheffield City Libraries (Fitzwilliams Papers), F/65/72, "Observation."

13. Because of the rising costs of British-regulated trade, the Spanish began to turn

elsewhere for their supply immediately after Amiens. See PD 8 (1806–1807), 989, speech of Hibbert, Feb. 23, 1807. On the drop in the slave trade in 1803, see Anstey, "Volume and Profitability," p. 12, table 3, and Appendix II.

14. [James Stephen], *Foreign Slave Bill: Facts and Observations,* from a copy annotated by Stephen [May, 1806], p. 2 and note. See also Anstey, *British Abolition,* p. 11, note 31.

15. PRO, HCA 10/19, Admiralty Prize Lists, Danish Prizes (1807–1808).

16. *Dangers of the Country,* p. 210. See also Appendix II.

17. *Foreign Slave Bill,* pp. 3–4; DUL Hamilton (Grenville MSS), reel 17, "Remarks on the claims of compensation by the proprietors of Bance Island."

18. See D. M. Williams, "Abolition and the Re-Deployment of the Slave Fleet, 1807–1811," *Journal of Transport History,* 2 (1973), 103–15, esp. table 1 and 2. See also G. Rees, "Copper Sheathing: An Example of Technological Diffusion in the English Merchant Fleet," *Journal of Transport History* 1 (1971), 87–89. At the moment of abolition, 101 of 104 traceable slave ships were copper sheathed.

19. See Michael W. B. Sanderson, "English Naval Strategy and Maritime Trade in the Caribbean, 1793–1802," Ph.D. dissertation, University of London, 1969, p. 174. Along the same lines we took large samples of ships clearing for Africa in 1786, 1796, 1804, and 1806 from Lloyd's *Register of Shipping.* The proportion of ships for each year which were either new, or had had large capital investments in major overhauls, in the three years immediately preceding, was 40 percent in 1786, 29 percent in 1796, 40 percent in 1804 and 41 percent in 1806.

20. Crouzet, *L'Economie britannique,* I, 284–321.

21. See Sheffield City Libraries (Fitzwilliams Papers), F/65/72, "Observations" etc.; and the protests of London and Liverpool merchants in HLR MSS, May 6, 1806, petitions on the slave trade. See also Drake's "Continuity and Flexibility." Reviewing Anstey's *British Abolition* (*Times Literary Supplement,* Oct. 24, 1975, p. 1263), David Brion Davis refers to Anstey's figures, indicating a sharp fall in slave-trade profits from 1801 to 1807, as a statistic in favor of the decline thesis. It is questionable whether Anstey's estimates can fulfill the empirical role which Davis assigns to them. They refer only to a drop in profits between 1791–1800 and 1801–1807 on slaves carried in British ships. They do not allow for higher rates of return to British capital moving under neutral flags, unrestricted by the load and crew limits of the act of 1799, and unthreatened by loss to privateers. Moreover, Anstey's calculation explicitly excludes all returns on staples carried homeward from the Americas. Since this trade was far less significant in the 1790s than in the following decade, Anstey's percentage point fall between the two periods is exaggerated. The merchants of Liverpool, in an 1806 statement on their capital investment in the slave trade, claimed that two-thirds of their African ships returned laden with West India produce, which accounted for "nearly half of the West India trade of the port" (PRO T70/1585, bundle marked "Abolition 1806–1807"). Therefore, although British traders indicated a wide profit differential between British and American slavers after 1800, only more comprehensive estimates could determine whether a substantial decline in the rate of return to British slaving capital occurred after 1791–1800.

22. *Leeds Mercury,* Mar. 17, 1792; *Sheffield Advertiser,* Nov. 4, 1791; *Edinburgh Advertiser,* Nov. 1, 1791; *Shrewsbury Chronicle,* Nov. 4, 1791; *Diary,* Oct. 27, 1791, Jan. 30, Mar. 26, May 28, and June 15, 1792; *General Evening Post,* Jan. 14–17, 1792.

23. See PRO 30 8/349, part 2, an estimate made by General Forbes at Port-au-Prince, April 2, 1796. See also ibid., "An account of produce exported to British and Foreign ports" from ports under British control, Sept. 1793–Mar. 1794. For Dundas's estimate of the exports of British-controlled St. Domingue in 1797, see PR 2 (1797), 503. According

to official French records, sugar production in 1801 was down about 90 percent to just under 9,000 tons. See J. N. Leger, *Haiti: Son Histoire et ses detracteurs* (New York, 1907) pp. 294–95. Humboldt estimated a drop of just over 75 percent (without allowing for conversion of clayed to muscovado) in his *Political Essay*, III, 14. Richardson, in *Empire and Slavery*, p. 72, cites figures for 1802 which would make the drop only two-thirds (excluding conversion of 1791 clayed sugar).

24. The British colonial share of sugar exports calculated at *nominal* figures would have been a maximum of 65 percent for 1802–1806. See my essay "Le 'Déclin' du système esclavagiste britannique et l'abolition de la traite," *Annales: ECS* 31 (1976), 414–35. The data in the essay are derived mainly from Deerr's *History,* and are in nominal figures.

25. In 1800–1802 more sugar was coming to Europe via Britain, both absolutely and relatively, than in 1805–1806.

26. Spanish colonial sugar exports in 1800–1801 and in 1805–1806 have been calculated by region and checked against United States imports for those years. See Appendix II.

27. See Edwards, *History of the British West Indies,* II, 597–98, table 2; and *Report . . . of the . . . East India Company relative to . . . Sugar,* 21–23.

28. For such calculations see PP 1808 (IV), "Fourth Report," June 22, 1808, 4, imports and reexports of sugar to foreign parts, 1781–1785 to 1807–1808.

29. Ibid., report of July 24, 1807, introductory statement.

30. Ibid., 265–74, 300–01, evidence of Wedderburn and of Henry Shirley, a Jamaica resident from 1773 to 1801, in Appendix C to the report of July 1807. An incidental remark by Shirley is of interest in this connection. He noted that when he became a planter, *before* the American Revolution, the price of sugar was also very low.

31. PP 1805 (X), Papers Respecting the Slave Trade, 639–92, Report from a Committee of the House of Assembly of Jamaica . . . Relative to the Slave Trade (London, 1805), p. 26 of the original printed report.

32. See Young, *West India Common-Place Book,* pp. 37–38, 51–52.

33. PP 1808 (IV), report of July 24, 1807, p. 78, Appendix, cotton imported from the British West Indies, selected periods 1761–1806; Mitchell and Deane, *Abstract,* pp. 177–78.

34. HLR MSS dated May 12, 1806, "An Account of the quantity and value of cotton wool imported into Great Britain from all parts of the world in . . . the last ten years. . . ." The Lords' data went back to 1796 rather than 1792 or 1793, and we use the time-scale presented by William Irving, and that of the decision makers in 1806.

35. See chapter 4 for figures on 1771–1775.

36. The data given to the Lords also indicated whether or not the cotton imported was shipped in British or foreign vessels. Even at a glance it was obvious that, with a single exception, almost all cotton entering Britain between 1796 and 1805 came in British ships. The exception was for cotton from the United States, which came almost exclusively in American ships.

37. See *Diary,* Aug. 11, 1790.

38. See Add MSS 18961 (Long Papers), fol. 44, for the St. Domingue figure for 1767. The Jamaican figure for 1768 is in Young, *West India Common-Place Book,* p. 74. Alternative figures for Jamaica may be used. Jamaica's export in 1768 was 4,203 cwt., according to Young. In 1771–1774 its average rose to 6,370 cwt. See Jamaica House of Assembly Report of 1792, Appendix II. The figure for British West Indian exports to Britain in the 1760s is taken from PP 1808 (IV), 307, Appendix C, account of coffee imported 1761–1806. See Add MSS 18961 (Long Papers), fol. 44, for our source of the 1767 production figures. The estimate for St. Domingue's coffee increase from 1767 to 1789 is based on Long's figure of 12,197,977 pounds as the official estimate. Long may be translating directly from

the French tables, in which case the recorded weight would have to be multiplied by 1.08 to get the equivalent between the French *livre* and the English pound. One could also add anything from one-twelfth to one-sixth to the St. Domingue figure for illicit exports. Finally, Long's figure may be an undervaluation. Ramsay, relying on Hilliard d'Auberteuil's *Considérations,* estimated the coffee export figure for 1767 at 15,600,000 pounds. See Add MSS 27621 (J. Ramsay Papers), fol. 206. The Privy Council report relied heavily on the same author. But our point is equally well made with *any* combination of the Jamaica and St. Domingue figures cited.

39. Ragatz, *The Fall of the Planter Class,* pp. 42, 199.

40. CO 137/91 (Jamaica, 1792–1793), "Observations to Show the immense cultivation of Coffee that will immediately take place in Jamaica . . . ," Dec. 3, 1792.

41. The doubling of St. Domingue's slave trade began after the peace, in 1783. Its coffee exports leapt from an official average of 49 million pounds in 1784–1785 to 72 millions in 1788–1789. See CO 318/2, 276 ff., "Abstract of Products . . . from the Colony of St. Domingue 1783–1789, from the Almanac at Port-au-Prince, 1791," by M. Mozard; and *A Report from the Committee of Warehouses,* p. 25. For the estimate of total French colonial production on the eve of the Revolution, see Appendix II.

42. PP, 1812 (X), 319, petition of the Jamaica House of Assembly, Dec. 10, 1811.

43. CO 137/91 (Jamaica, 1792–1793), "Observations."

44. PRO 30 8/349, part 2, and PRO 30 8/351, "An Account of Cotton Wool and Coffee imported into Britain 1789–1794." By the same account Guadeloupe (also in 1790) exported almost twice the coffee of the British system. By 1799 Jamaican exports to Britain were six times as large as those of Martinique.

45. See Leger, *Haiti,* pp. 294–95, citing official documents for 1800–1801; and Charles Mackenzie, *Notes on Haiti,* 2 vols. (1830; rpt. London, 1971), II, Note (FF), p. 297. In 1801 the United States was the only remaining neutral carrier of French West Indian produce from St. Domingue and Guadeloupe. In that year they exported into the United States 38 million pounds of coffee. This would imply a 55 percent drop in coffee exports from the same islands as of 1788. By 1804–1805, following the Haitian war of independence, American imports, which now included Martinique as well as Guadeloupe and Haiti, dropped to 23.5 million, which was over 70 percent below the 1788 figures. After 1802 Jamaican coffee exports to Britain also began to exceed those of the French West Indies to the United States. See *American State Papers, Class IV, Commerce and Navigation,* 2 vols. (Washington, 1832), I, pp. 391–718, tables of imports, 1797–1807. In 1804–1805, Jamaican coffee exports were over 23 million pounds. On the estimate of Cuba in 1804, see Alexander von Humboldt, *Personal Narrative of Travels to the Equinoctial Regions of the New Continent During the Years 1799–1804,* 7 vols. (1829; rpt. New York, 1966), VII, 209–10. We employ Humboldt's high allowance of 75 percent above official figures for smuggling. On the estimate for Caracas in 1804, see Humboldt, *Political Essay,* IV, 22.

46. The official rates of value were fixed at the end of the seventeenth century, so that both coffee and cotton were overvalued by the end of the eighteenth century. See [John Marshall], *A Digest of all the Accounts Relating to the Population, Productions, Revenues . . . of the United Kingdom of Great Britain and Ireland* (1833; rpt. Westmead, England, 1969), p. 57. Because of the value added in processing the raw material, cotton was actually the more valuable import. See Add MSS 38350 (Liverpool Papers), fol. 10, "Brief Statement . . . of Cotton." The official values did give a clear idea of trends in the short or medium run.

47. Estimates are derived from table 10, and from decennial figures in Mitchell and Deane, *Abstract,* pp. 5–6.

Chapter 6: The New Frontier and Abolition

1. On the long run, see Ragatz, *The Fall of the Planter Class,* p. 113; Williams, *Capitalism and Slavery,* p. 115. On the rivalry after 1797, see Williams, *Capitalism and Slavery,* pp. 149–50, and *From Columbus to Castro,* pp. 273–74. For a similar perspective see Craton, *Sinews of Empire,* pp. 263–76.

2. See *Morning Chronicle,* April 3, 1788, letter of "Pyrrho"; ibid., June 30, 1788, letter of "Humanitas to Civis"; *Public Advertiser,* Mar. 25, 1788, letter of "Niger" to Wilberforce; *Diary,* April 10, 1789, account of the West India Planters and Merchants meeting; ibid., April 9, 24, 26, 1792, speeches of Vaughan, Dundas, and Fox.

3. *St. James's Chronicle,* April 3–5, 1798; PP 1805 (X), 639, papers respecting the slave trade; CO 137/119 (Jamaica, 1807), No. 115, "Secret and Confidential," June 14, 1807.

4. *Diary,* April 26, 1792, speech of Lord Mornington; *Morning Chronicle,* Mar. 16, 1796; ibid., April 7, 1797; *St. James's Chronicle,* April 3–5, 1798.

5. CO 142/21 (Jamaica), Sept. 1802–1804; see also HLR MSS, May 14, 1806, reexport trade to the Spanish dominions.

6. CO 295/6 (Trinidad), fols. 131–33, letters of Feb. 7 and 15, 1803.

7. CO 111/1 (British Guiana, 1781–1783); CO 111/3 (Demerary and Essequibo, 1795–1799). Berbice, with one hundred plantations in 1789, added sixty more before the British conquest in 1797.

8. CO 111/3, (Demerary and Essequibo, 1795–1799), memorial of the proprietors of Demerara and Berbice to H. Dundas, 1795, with observations by Hawkesbury to Dundas, Sept. 24, 1795.

9. Ibid.; and SRO (Melville Papers), GD 51/1/542, Dawson to Dundas, Mar. 19, 1799; CO 111/4 (Demerara and Essequibo), draft letter dated "Downing Street, April 3, 1802" to Governor Beaujon; CO 111/5, George Baillie to John Sullivan, June 6, 1803.

10. On the demand for reconquest see CO 111/5, Baillie to Sullivan, May 21, 1803. On technological improvement, see H. G. Dalton, *The History of British Guiana,* 2 vols. (London, 1855), I, 275–76.

11. Colquhoun, *A Treatise on the British Empire,* p. 384.

12. CO 111/5 (Demerara and Essequibo, 1803–1804), "Observations on the Colony of Essequibo and Demerary," by A. Dalzell, Commissary (Barbados, 1804).

13. For James Stephen it was a recurrent nightmare. See his *Crisis of the Sugar Colonies* (London, 1802; rpt. New York, 1969), p. 157; *The Opportunity, or Reasons for an immediate alliance with St. Domingo* (London, 1804); pp. 141–43; *Dangers of the Country,* p. 207; and Add MSS 31237, fol. 185, memoranda on Brazil, 1808.

14. See Bodleian Library, Clarendon Deposit (Barham Papers), c. 362, correspondence of J. Plummer (sugar wholesaler) to J. F. Barham, Nov. 23, 1801, Jan. 11, and Aug. 25, 1802; *Edinburgh Review,* XVIII (Jan. 1807), 314.

15. See Cobbett's *Parl. History,* 36 (1801–1803), 143, 863.

16. *The Opportunity,* p. 137. As to how long the unimpeded slave trade would continue, Wilberforce's estimate was as "long as there remained cultivable land in the Western hemisphere" (*A Letter on the Abolition of the Slave Trade* [London, 1807], p. 290).

17. Williams, *Capitalism and Slavery,* pp. 149–50; *From Columbus to Castro,* pp. 273–74.

18. On Guiana, see PP 1806 (XIII), 775, account printed July 3, 1806. On Cuba, see Humboldt, *Personal Narrative,* VII, 146. Moreover, even if Cuban imports during 1805, allowing for imports outside Havana, were double the figure of 5,000, Guiana was still the larger importer. The peak year for Guiana imports under British rule was 1801, when 14,774 slaves were imported into Demerara and Surinam (see HLR, "An Account of . . .

Negroes Imported into the Conquered Colonies," May 12, 1806). Wilberforce also reckoned the Guiana purchases at 12,000 to 15,000 per year (R. I. Wilberforce and S. Wilberforce, *The Life of William Wilberforce*. 5 vols. [London, 1838], III, 234). On Brazilian imports for 1800–1810, see Philip Curtin, *The Atlantic Slave Trade: A Census* (Madison, Wis., 1969), p. 207, table 62. On United States imports, see Fogel and Engerman, *Time on the Cross*, I, 25.

19. *Life of Wilberforce*, II, 368, III, 183–84, 216–17, 231–34; R. I. Wilberforce and S. Wilberforce, eds., *The Correspondence of William Wilberforce*, 2 vols. (London, 1840), II, 14–15, 33–34.

20. Stephen, *Crisis*, pp. 158–59; *Life of Wilberforce*, III, 166. The West Indian moderates may have played a role in pushing for the order (ibid., p. 217).

21. CO 111/5 (Demerara, 1803–1804), Dalzell, "Observations."

22. See CO 111/6 (Demerara, 1805–1806), "Observations respecting the Order . . . in Council of the 15th August 1805. . . ." See also Sheffield City Libraries (Fitzwilliams Papers), F/65/72, "Observations"; for the protests of London and Liverpool merchants, see HLR MSS, petitions, May 6, 1806.

23. PP 1808 (X), 187. In 1806, using averages from Thomas Tooke's *History of Prices*, 2 vols. (London, 1838), II, 401, 414, for cotton wool (Mar.–July 1806), and for sugar (Nov. 1806–Jan. 1807, a low point in sugar prices), the real value of Demerara cotton exports still exceeded that of sugar.

24. See note 22.

25. See Anstey, *British Abolition*, p. 314.

26. See PD 8 (1806–1807), 146–49, 178, 194.

27. University of Durham (Earl Grey Papers), letter from Grey to Holland, Sept. 28, 1806. This was also the recommendation of the Demerara interest.

28. Ibid., letter from Grey to Lauderdale, one of the British negotiators, Oct. 1, 1806. The Dutch had already hinted at their willingness to abolish the slave trade to Guiana in exchange for its return. This feeler to the Pitt administration in 1804 was not pursued at the negotiations in 1806. See *Life of Wilberforce*, III, 195–96.

29. For Cuban sugar exports in 1805–1806, see Appendix II. Total Demerara sugar exports in 1806 are estimated at 11,000 tons, using CO 111/7 (Demerara, 1807), trade account for 1806; the figures in hhds. are converted to pounds as reported in CO 111/5 (1803–1804), Dalzell, "Observations." (See note 12.)

30. The *Sun*, April 6, 1806.

31. Fortescue, *History of the Army*, V, 310–19, 368–436. The La Plata campaign ran from the spring of 1806 through the summer of 1807.

32. The *Morning Chronicle*, Jan. 31, 1807, declared that seventeen slave ships, capable of carrying over 5,000 slaves, were under orders for La Plata, and a larger number would have changed direction had the government not intervened. Elena F. Scheuss De Studer, *La Trata de Negros en el Rio de la Plata durante el siglo XVIII* (Buenos Aires, 1958), pp. 319–20, shows that the British, Portuguese, and American trades to La Plata were all increasing between 1802 and 1805.

33. See J. Millette, *The Genesis of Crown Colony Government: Trinidad, 1783–1810* (Curepe, Trinidad, 1970), pp. 15–19; L. M. Fraser, *History of Trinidad*, 2 vols. (1891; rpt. [London], 1971), I, 149; Add MSS 38356 (Liverpool Papers, 1800–1808), fol. 95, "Notes sur l'Isle de la Trinité," pencil-dated Nov. 29, 1801; and PP 1801–1802 (IV), 425–26, information relating to Trinidad, May 19, 1801. See also SRO (Melville Papers), GD 51/1/529/9, Huskisson to Dundas, "Private," Jan. 20, 1800; GD 51/1/526, Dundas's memorandum on Trinidad as a possible British possession; CO 295/2, extract of Governor Picton's

letter, Trinidad, Feb. 18, 1802; and HLR MSS, Feb. 13, 1807, papers on the slave trade, extract of a letter from Picton to Dundas, Trinidad, May 14, 1799, beginning "Trinidad should be regarded as a sugar colony. . . ."

34. See CO 295/2, letter of Picton, Feb. 18, 1802; Millette, *The Genesis*, pp. 19-20; Add MSS 38356 (Liverpool Papers, 1800-1808), fol. 95, "Notes sur l'Isle de la Trinité." Port of Spain was made a free port from the outset, on a par with those of the older British colonies (BT 5/11, minutes of the Board of Trade, 1797-1808, fol. 68).

35. Coupland, *Wilberforce*, p. 285; *Life of Wilberforce*, III, 35-36, Wilberforce to Addington, Jan. 28, 1802. Williams asserts (*From Columbus to Castro*, pp. 262-63) that no steps against the slave trade were attempted by Pitt because of the conquest of Trinidad and Guiana. As we have already seen, the assertion is erroneous. Equally so is Williams's assertion that Pitt opposed the bill to restrict the slave trade from part of the African coast. See *Life of Wilberforce*, III, 331, 337-40.

36. HLR MSS, Feb. 13, 1807, papers on the slave trade, extracts of letters from Thomas Picton to Dundas, May 14, 1799, and to Lord Hobart, Sept. 8, 1801. In the abolition debates of 1806-1807 the Trinidad crown lands policy was clearly dated back to Pitt's action in 1797 (PD 8 [1806-1807], 618).

37. Pp. 148-49; on his estimate of the contribution of Trinidad and Demerara in pulling Britain away from abolition after the St. Domingue uprising, see also *From Columbus to Castro*, pp. 262-63.

38. Eric E. Williams, *History of the People of Trinidad and Tobago* (Port of Spain, Trinidad, 1962), pp. 66-67. On the indiscriminate enslavement of Creole prisoners of war, see Granville Sharp's letter to Wilberforce of June 4, 1795, in DUL (Wilberforce MSS). Williams considered that Trinidad had come into the empire too late because Parliament had already voted for abolition in principle in 1792. This is to assign, rightly or wrongly, the ultimate force to a causal network not mentioned in *Capitalism and Slavery*, and to date the essential victory from 1792.

39. See Cobbett's *Parl. History*, 36 (1801-1803), 26 ff. On the importance of Trinidad to the empire, James Stephen wrote in *The Crisis*, p. 153, "That you have the means of immediately opening a new slave colony of great agricultural capacity, is indeed true. . . . Open the floodgates of the Guinea market upon this new soil, and it will soon be saturated with many millions of British capital spent in improvements. . . ." Against such a policy Stephen cited not economic but a purely strategic consideration. Trinidad would grow so fast as to tempt the cupidity of France (p. 157).

40. Ragatz, in *The Fall of the Planter Class*, pp. 322-23, devotes more space to Trinidad's potential than does Williams, but deals with the island only in a post-Napoleonic context.

41. See Patrick C. Lipscomb, "Party Politics, 1801-1802: George Canning and the Trinidad Question," *Historical Journal* 12 (1969), 449. On Wilberforce, see Cobbett's *Parl. History*, 36 (1801-1803), 143, Nov. 3, 1801. No speaker challenged the government's assessment of Trinidad as a balance to St. Domingue.

42. CO 295/2 (Trinidad), fols. 40-53, letter to Governor Picton, "Private," Feb. 18, 1802, and Picton's reply, April 12, 1802. Government apologists evisioned Trinidad as capable of rapid returns to Britain, not to mention the prospects of the slave trade itself: "The slave trade (I speak of it only in a commercial point of view) promises to open new sources of commercial profit. The demand for negroes must, for some years to come, be very great; St. Lucia, Martinico, and Trinidad may still be supplied" (F. M. Eden, *Eight Letters on the Peace* [London, 1802], pp. 70, 95).

43. PR 16 (1801-1802), 444-45, Feb. 2, 1802. On the Trinidad question in 1801-1802, see esp. Lipscomb, "Party Politics," pp. 442-46; and *Life of Wilberforce*, III, 28 ff.

44. In addition to Picton's letters (note 42 above), see CO 295/2 (Trinidad), letter from a merchant, Jan. 30, 1802, and from A. Layman, July 16, 1802.

45. CO 295/2, fols. 205 ff.; CO 295/5, fols. 130, 198–99; CO 295/6, fols. 38–39, 148, 152, 156–63, 188. See also WO 1/20 (Guadeloupe, 1810), Abercromby to the Earl of Liverpool, Basseterre, Sept. 20, 1810; PRO 30 8/350, part 2, letter from a proprietor in Trinidad, Feb. 8, 1802; BT 6/70, Chinese settlers, various plans in 1806.

46. HLR MSS, Feb. 13, 1807, extract of a letter of J. Hislop to Lord Hobart, Nov. 24, 1803.

47. CO 28/71 (Barbados, 1804–1805), copy of the *Barbadoes Mercury*, Oct. 29, 1805.

48. This was pointedly noted by Sir William Young, referring to Demerara on Mar. 1, 1799 (PR 8 [1799], 146–47), and by Doctor Lawrence on April 7, 1803 (PR 1 [1803], 608).

49. Cobbett's *Parl. History*, 33 (1797–1798), 124–25, "Papers respecting the Negotiation for Peace with France," no. 14, dated July 8, 1797, Lille. These papers were presented to Parliament on Nov. 3, 1797. See also Pitt's rationale for retaining Trinidad in his defense of the negotiations (ibid., pp. 1008–09, Nov. 10, 1797). In 1800 the cabinet still thought that Trinidad and Tobago, or Martinique and St. Lucia, would be the compensatory colonies. See SRO (Melville Papers), GD 51/1/556/1, "Sketch of a Plan of Peace . . . [settled at the cabinet, 1800], communicated to Mr. Addington," April 1801.

50. See esp. Edwards, *The History of the British West Indies*, III, 241–84, "A tour through . . . Barbadoes, St. Vincent . . . in the years 1791 and 1792 by Sir William Young." See also Ragatz, *The Fall of the Planter Class*, pp. 116, 220–21; Sheridan, *Sugar and Slavery*, pp. 455–58; Fortescue, *History of the British Army*, III, 41–43, IV, 441–48, 493.

51. PR 41 (1795), 571–73, 614, 629–30 (June 11 and 18, 1795); and CO 261/9, "Report of the Committee, appointed by both Houses in November 1796, on losses suffered in Rebellion and Invasion." Crown holdings in Jamaica were also enlarged by the Maroon revolt and subsequent deportations. They were too far into the interior to be considered ready for immediate development. See also Lipscomb, "Party Politics," p. 447 and note.

52. CO 261/9, letter from D. Ottley to S. Boddington, esq.; Edwards, *History of the British West Indies*, III, 282, Young's diary, St. Vincent, April 19, 1792. See also, in CO 261/9, pp. 109, 121–23, letter of Drewry Ottley, chairman of the Committee of Correspondence to Sir William Young and William Manning, Feb. 24, 1797; a private letter from the Committee to Young, Mar. 24, 1797; memorial from Young and Manning to the government, May 5, 1797.

53. CO 261/9, p. 177, Committee of Proprietors' response to Pitt, Mar. 13, 1799.

54. Ibid., letter from Young to Ottley, April 4, 1798; Cobbett's *Parl. History*, 33 (1797–1798), 1376–1415.

55. CO 261/9, letter of Dec. 10, 1800; see also PR 8 (1799), 146–47, for Sir William Young's speech of Mar. 1, 1799; and CO 261/9, letters of Ottley, Mar. 3, 1797, and Young, April 4, 1798; memorials of Mar. 12, 1799, and Dec. 10, 1800.

56. Lipscomb, "Party Politics," p. 457. See also *Life of Wilberforce*, III, 331, Diary, April 18, 1799; CO 261/9, Young's letters of April 4 and May 4, 1798; memorial of Mar. 13, 1799. On the critical role of Stephen, see his undated letter to Wilberforce [1798], DUL (Wilberforce MSS).

57. Lipscomb, "Party politics," pp. 454, 457; CO 261/9, p. 16, Young's note on a conversation with Lord Hobart, Nov. 5, 1801.

58. CO 261/9, pp. 217–18, note on a meeting with Addington, Oct. 5, 1802; and a memorial by Young to Addington, Oct. 15, 1802.

59. Ibid., Addington to Young, Oct. 19, 1802. See also, in *Life of Wilberforce*, III, 35–37, 41, Wilberforce to Addington, Jan. 27, 1802, and Diary, Feb. 4, 1802; Pitt to Wilberforce,

Feb. 4, 1802. According to Lipscomb, "Party Politics," pp. 459–63, Pitt's attitude was decisive in forcing the prime minister to give way.

Chapter 7: Economic Conjuncture and Abolition Bills, 1791–1806

1. See Ragatz, *The Fall of the Planter Class,* p. 113; Williams, *Capitalism and Slavery,* pp. 112–15. On overproduction generally, see chap. 8, note 1, and Ragatz, pp. 287 ff.

2. *Capitalism and Slavery,* p. 152; *From Columbus to Castro,* pp. 288–89.

3. For the votes and debates, see Cobbett's *Parl. History,* 29 (1791–1792), 359, 1158, 1292, 1293.

4. See PP 1792 (XXXV), vol. 770, "Committee of the Bill for Regulating the Exportation of Sugar," pp. 4–7.

5. Add MSS 38351 (Liverpool Papers), fols. 116 ff., 137, "History of the Policy hitherto pursued by this country with respect to the Trade of Sugar."

6. PR 29 (1791), 575–83, debate of May 30. Also Add MSS 41262A (Clarkson Papers), letter of Henry Thornton to John Clarkson, Dec. 30, 1791, marked *"Duplicate, Private."* See also Philip D. Curtin, *The Image of Africa: British Ideas and Action, 1780–1850* (Madison, Wis., 1964), pp. 106–14.

7. Curtin, *Image of Africa,* p. 583.

8. Add MSS 41262A (Clarkson Papers), Thomas Clarkson to John Clarkson, Jan. 1792; and the *General Evening Post,* Mar. 27–29, 1792.

9. See, inter alia, *Diary,* June 13, Oct. 27, Nov. 1, 5, 8, 22, Dec. 1 and 28, 1791; *Edinburgh Advertiser,* Nov. 1, 8, 25, 1791.

10. On the implications of St. Domingue events, both confidential and public, see Add MSS 38351, fol. 137; and *Diary,* Jan. 1, 6, 15, 16, 18, and 24, 1792.

11. *Diary,* Jan. 27, 30, 31, and Feb. 7, 1792.

12. See *General Evening Post,* Jan. 6, 1792; *Newcastle Courant,* Jan. 7, 1792; *Public Advertiser,* Jan. 22, 1791.

13. *Northampton Mercury,* Jan. 21, 1792. Licorice roots as well as honey had been considered as early as 1788 (*Sheffield Register,* Feb. 23, 1788).

14. See *Sheffield Advertiser,* Dec. 23, 1791; *Edinburgh Evening Courant,* Mar. 19, 1792; *Glocester Journal,* Jan. 2, 1792; *Leeds Mercury,* Jan. 21, 1792; *Diary,* Dec. 8, 17, 27, 30, 1791, and Jan. 9, 25, 26, 28, 31, Mar. 17, 1792; *Newcastle Courant,* Feb. 4, 1792.

15. See also the *Shrewsbury Chronicle,* Nov. 4, 1791. We will not deal here with the boycott movement against sugar that was developing at the end of 1791. It had little effect against the countervailing opening of the Continental market to British sugar.

16. For volume see Mitchell and Deane, *Abstract,* p. 178. On prices see *Diary,* Nov. 26, 1791, Jan. 24, 1792; Mitchell and Deane, *Abstract,* p. 178; LRO Picton Library (Tarleton Papers), 920 TAR, Clayton to John Tarleton, Feb. 29, Mar. 16, 1792. For the connection with the slave trade, see Add MSS 38416 (Liverpool Papers), fol. 260 (1791 or 1792), "Answers to Mr. Pitt."

17. LRO, Picton Library (Tarleton Papers), 920 TAR, Clayton to Thomas Tarleton, May 2 and Sept 24, 1792; ibid., Liverpool Letterbook of Robert Bostock, letters of Bostock to captains Flint and Payne, April 9 and May 2, 1792; the *Glasgow Advertiser,* Mar. 23–26, letter from Liverpool.

18. See *Diary,* Feb. 3, 1792, quoting the *Bahama Gazette;* and Mar. 14, 1792, containing an offer of £40,000 sterling for a West India estate. See also *General Evening Post,* Feb. 2–4,

1792; *Northampton Mercury,* Jan. 21, 1792; *Sheffield Advertiser,* Jan. 6, 1792, *Diary,* Feb. 10, April 17, May 4, June 22, 1792; *General Evening Post,* Mar. 24–27, 1792.

19. *Sinews of Empire,* p. 262. The point is not further elaborated. It is based on Williams, *Capitalism and Slavery,* pp. 146–47, 219n.

20. PD 29 (1791–1792), 1153.

21. *Sinews of Empire,* p. 262.

22. On the voting lists for abolition, see Anstey, *British Abolition,* pp. 282–83, 307–10.

23. PD 29 (1791–1792), 1055–58.

24. Ibid., 1142–45.

25. Ibid., 1206–13, Dundas's resolutions of April 23, 1792. The House of Commons voted not to give the British colonies the "grace period" of six years for colonial abolition requested by Dundas, but only two, voting for total abolition in 1796.

26. See Tooke, *History of Prices,* I, 190–91, II, 399, 401, 414; and Ragatz, *The Fall of the Planter Class,* pp. 340 and 350, charts 19 and 20.

27. Mitchell and Deane, *Abstract,* p. 311.

28. The contemporary political significance assigned to this bill, and to the narrowly defeated slave trade limitation bill has been too rarely recognized. The first bill passed the Lords by the slimmest margin of any abolition vote between 1788 and 1807. Grenville's major speech in its behalf was described as "very rarely, if ever surpassed by any speech ever delivered within the wall of the Upper House." Given the final edge, his eloquence was well timed. The slave trade limitation bill was even more bitterly fought, and the margin of defeat was almost as narrow. The *Times* claimed that the question was canvassed "with greater interest and zeal than any that has occurred since the Regency." Grenville learned a sharp lesson in proxy hunting which was to serve abolition well eight years later. On the slave carrying bill, see the debates in the *Senator or Parliamentary Chronicle* 23 (1799), 1545–47, 1556, 1734; and the *True Briton,* June 20–22, 1799. On the slave trade limitation bill, see Anstey, *British Abolition,* p. 331; and PR 6 (1798), pp. 100, 257; PR 7 (1799), pp. 146–60, 172–75; 312; PR 9 (1799), pp. 501–88. The bill, first moved in 1798, would have prohibited the trade along 1200 miles of the African slave coast.

29. See Tooke, *History of Prices,* II, 414.

30. Anstey, *British Abolition,* chap. 15.

31. *War in Disguise; or the Frauds of the Neutral Flags* (London, 1805). Other contemporary surveys corroborated Stephen's findings. The transportation rates on sugar between Jamaica and London doubled between 1803 and 1806. See Arthur D. Gayer et al., *The Growth and Fluctuation of the British Economy, 1790–1850* (Oxford, 1953), p. 65.

32. PP 1808 (X), 392. The figures presented by J. Marryat, of the Trinidad interest, were for the period before the American embargo took effect. They may be broken down as follows:

	Prices in $		Ratio of Trinidad to Martinique
Product	Trinidad	Martinique	
Flour (per barrel)	14	7	2.0 : 1
Beef (per barrel)	30	12	2.5 : 1
Salt Fish (per quintal)	16	7	2.3 : 1
Salt Pork (per barrel)	36	16	2.3 : 1
Rice (per cwt.)	10	7	1.4 : 1
Board (per 1,000 ft.)	64–70	30–40	1.75 : 1–2.13 : 1
Sugar (per cwt., outward bound)	2.25	4.43	0.5 : 1

Marryat noted that sugar bound outward from Trinidad was often forced to sell to particular British correspondents.

33. In 1807 a West Indian spokesman cited the accounts of an estate in Danish St. Croix, an "old" foreign island, to show that differential prices went far back into the war and were not related to differences in quality or soil. The Danish estate, owned by a British planter, had been returning profits to him at twice the rate of his British estate. When the island had been temporarily seized by the British just prior to the Peace of Amiens, eighty hogsheads of the St. Croix estate had been sold in London and forty sent on to Copenhagen. The proprietor had received more for the third sold in Denmark than for the two-thirds sold in England. See Charles Bosanquet, *A Letter to W. Manning, esq., M.P., on the Causes of the Rapid and Progressive Depreciation of West India Property*, 2nd ed. (London, 1807) pp. 52–53.

34. *War in Disguise*, pp. 70, 107 (my emphasis).

35. See Stephen's confidential report to the prime minister, Add MSS 49183 (Spencer Perceval Papers), IX, James Stephen correspondence, "Coup d'Oeil on an American War" (probably Jan. or Feb. 1808).

36. *War in Disguise*, p. 204.

37. PD 5 (1805), 847, act no. 34, April 10, 1805, to permit trade with American colonies; PD 7 (1806), 33, 228, 234 speeches of Clarence and Hawkesbury, May 7 and 16; *Cowdroy's Manchester Gazette*, May 10, 1806, speech of R. Peel, May 1; Armytage, *Free Port System*, pp. 104–05; Judith Blow Williams, *British Commercial Policy and Trade Expansion, 1750–1850* (Oxford, 1972), p. 381. The impact of the free port system on Spanish slave-trade imports was increasing at the beginning of the nineteenth century. In 1804, 3,583 slaves were sent from the British to the Spanish colonies, compared with an average of 2,544 in 1789–1792. See PRO T70/1584, *Speech of... Westmorland... 16th May 1806*, p. 10 for the 1804 figures; and T70/1585, bundle marked "Abolition 1806–1807" for the 1789–1792 figures.

38. See DUL (Wilberforce Papers), Grenville to Wilberforce, May 20, 1806; DUL Hamilton (Grenville MSS), reel 17, "Lord Ellenborough's opinion respecting the importation of slaves, Trinidad," Sept. 20, 1806.

Chapter 8: The Market Mechanism and Abolition

1. See Williams, *Capitalism and Slavery*, p. 152; and Davis, *Slavery in Revolution*, p. 439. See also Peter F. Dixon, "The Politics of Emancipation: The Movement for the Abolition of Slavery in the British West Indies, 1807–1833," D. Phil. Oxford, 1971, pp. 74–76. While Anstey concludes that "overall Caribbean production was in excess of demand," he explicitly dissociates overproduction from abolition, noting that contemporaries made no connection between them. See Anstey, "A Re-interpretation," pp. 316–19. Ragatz's original account of the tropical market after 1799 is also a cautious and nuanced account with no broad statements about overproduction. See *The Fall of the Planter Class*, chap. 9.

2. *The McGraw-Hill Dictionary of Modern Economics*, 2nd ed. (New York, 1973), deals with overproduction as follows: "*underconsumption (overproduction)*, the manufacture of goods in excess of consumer demand." The theoretical debate involves argument about *general* overproduction or glut, but the decline school particularizes it to apply to sugar. See Maurice Dobb, *Theories of Value and Distribution Since Adam Smith* (Cambridge, 1973), pp. 92–94, 215–16; Joseph A. Schumpeter, *History of Economic Analysis* (New York, 1954), pp. 538–39, 621–25, 740–43; Henry W. Spiegel, *The Growth of Economic Thought* (New York, 1971), pp. 260–64, 295–96.

3. We assume, though the historians of decline do not define the term, that by overproduction they mean that supply grew more rapidly than demand, causing a fall in price and profit margins.

4. We must again note that a very short-term response to conditions is implied by this market-cum-abolition argument from overproduction. The way in which information on West Indian development was presented to Parliament in 1805–1808 implies that their time perspective was a much longer one.

5. For a similar contemporary estimate of the balance of supply and demand in 1800, see Humboldt, *Political Essay,* III, 14–15.

6. Tooke, *History of Prices,* II, 414; also PP 1806 (XII), 314, *An Account of the General Average prices of Brown . . . Sugar, exclusive of all Duties,* Feb. 1793–Jan. 1806, printed April 3, 1806.

7. See Ragatz, *The Fall of the Planter Class,* p. 380, chart 23.

8. On differential sugar consumption by class, see T. R. Gourvich, "The Cost of Living in Glasgow in the Early Nineteenth Century," *Economic History Review* 25 (1972), 65–80.

9. Mitchell and Deane, *Abstract,* p. 356.

10. Ibid., p. 355.

11. See table 24, and PP 1808 (IV), report of April 13, 1808. Ragatz, whose account follows the sugar market year by year, although in scattered form, notes this sharp revival of demand (*The Fall of the Planter Class,* p. 293.)

12. See Marcel Reinhard, "Bilan demographique de l'Europe, 1789–1815," *Comité Internationale des Sciences Historiques, XII Congrès International* (Vienna, 1965), Rapports, I, Grands Thèmes, pp. 457–71, on the populations of continental Europe. On France, see also C. H. Pouthas, *La Population française, pendant la première moitié du XIXe siècle* (Paris, 1956); and J. Bourgeois-Pichat, "The General Development of the Population of France Since the Eighteenth Century," in *Population and History,* ed. D. V. Glass and D. E. C. Eversley (London, 1965), pp. 474–506, Appendix 2, table 1. Both estimate the French increase at 9 percent or more between 1786 and 1806. On Britain's population growth, see Mitchell and Deane, *Abstract,* pp. 5–8. On Italy, see C. M. Cipolla, "Four Centuries of Italian Demographic Development," in *Population and History,* pp. 578–87.

13. Our calculation is from Humboldt's *Narrative of Travels,* VII, note A of Book the Tenth, esp. pp. 356–63. Playfair, in his edition of Smith's *Wealth of Nations,* first published in 1805, noted that because of St. Domingue, tropical production was only then "fast approaching an equilibrium of supply and demand." See Smith, *An Inquiry . . . ,* from the 11th London edition, 2 vols. (Hartford, 1818), I, chap. 11, part 1, p. 113, note r. See also note 5 above.

14. AN C⁸ᴬ110 (Martinique), fol. 24, report of Villaret to Napoleon, May 12, 1805; C⁸ᴬ111, fol. 111, report of Prefect Laussat, June 10, 1805. For the 1788 figures, see *Statistique générale,* table 9; for 1806, AN AFᴵⱽ1060, dossier 1, p. 68, "Relève des quantités des Denrées Coloniales importées en France pendant 3 mois de l'an 14 et l'année entière de 1806, formant en tout une série de 15 mois." Our figure for the year 1806 is four-fifths of the fifteen-month archival figure.

15. See Deerr, *History of Sugar,* I, 471–79; Eli F. Heckscher, *The Continental System: An Economic Interpretation,* 2nd ed. (Gloucester, Mass., 1964), pp. 291–94. Retail sugar and sugar products showed the same trend in London and Amsterdam. Compare W. W. Posthumous, *Inquiry into the History of Prices in Holland,* 2 vols. (London, 1964), II, 378–79, with William Beveridge et al., *Prices and Wages in England,* 2nd ed. (New York, 1966), I, 431. The Continent was not experiencing even a short-run "glut" when either the abolition bills of 1806 or 1807 were introduced. The weekly average prices of all grades of Paris sugars were

rising both in the spring of 1806 and at the beginning of 1807. See AN AF^{IV} 1060, dossier 1, pp. 70 ff.

16. Deerr, *History of Sugar*, I, 530–31. In attempting to outline the context of the tropical market in 1800–1807, we have confined ourselves largely to sugar, the product which usually monopolizes the attention of historians of abolition. Yet, as we have indicated before, coffee was a more dynamic British crop than sugar. It was still an expanding industry in Jamaica, Cuba, and Brazil on the eve of British abolition. British foreign abolition was hardly a gem of economic belligerency against the French imperium. The act would and did have least effect on Brazil, the slave-importing colony which was most important to the French cotton industry. In 1806, 52,000 bales of Brazilian cotton wool went to France, compared with 41,000 to Britain. See AN AF^{IV} 1060, dossier 1, p. 80.

17. PP 1806–1807 (II), 84, report from the Sugar Distillery Committee of the Commons, testimony of William Cole, sugar broker. See also PP 1808 (IV), 179 ff., accounts of imports from British plantations, 1803–1805, of American exports of sugar, 1806, and of sugar in the warehouses and at the West India docks at year's end 1804, 1805, 1806. See also Bodleian Library, Clarendon Deposit (Barham Papers), c. 362, Plummer to Barham, Sept. 25, Dec. 11, 1804, Feb. 5, Sept. 25, Oct. 2, 1805, June 5, June 19, 1806. Barham's low-grade Jamaica brown sugar, which sold at 83 shillings per cwt. in December 1804, was still selling at 80 in September of the following year. By June 1806 it had dropped 25 percent to 60 shillings. All subsequent testimony dated the downturn in colonial trade somewhere between May 1806, when Prussia closed the ports of northern Germany to Britain, and November 1806 when Napoleon attempted to close down the whole continent (PP 1808 [X]), *Minutes of Evidence Respecting the Orders-in-Council*, Mar. 18, 1808, pp. 214, 239, 294, 295, 299, 302, 346; PP 1806–1807 (II), 85, report from the Sugar Distillery Committee.

18. Charles Reinhard, *Remarks on the Trade with Germany* (London, 1806), pp. 18–52, 108–16.

19. PP 1806–1807 (II), report from the Sugar Distillery Committee, Feb. 7, 1807, pp. 73, 83–85. Anstey notes that three separate committees in two years "failed to make a single reference to abolition as relevant to overproduction" ("A Re-interpretation," p. 318).

20. Heckscher, *The Continental System*, pp. 164–65; Crouzet, *L'Economie Britannique*, I, 240 and note; PP 1808 (X), evidence respecting the orders-in-council, pp. 299–301.

21. PD 8 (1806–1807), 619–55.

22. See Appendix II.

23. AN AF^{IV} 1060, dossier 1, esp. p. 34, petition from Lyon, December 1806.

24. AN C^{8A}115 (1807), fols. 1, 92, reports of Mar. 10 and April 17, 1807; AN C^{8A}112 (1806), fol. 266, Dec. 10, 1806.

25. Anstey, *British Abolition*, pp. 347, 386–87. If underselling by foreign colonies is considered tantamount to overproduction by the British colonies, Anstey's claim is understandable. He notes (p. 371) that Grenville linked the two concepts in his speech of May 7, 1806. At the same time, however, Grenville did not even go so far as to assert that the British were actually being undersold. He only hypothesized that foreigners might be able to compete on equal terms or "perhaps . . . undersell us." Nor did he imply that underselling was equivalent to driving the British produce from the market rather than only reducing the level of profits. His brief statement was entirely hypothetical in presentation.

26. *Cowdroy's Manchester Gazette*, May 10, 1806, reporting on the debate of May 1 in the Commons. *Cowdroy's* account is more extensive than Cobbett's.

27. DUL Hamilton (Grenville MSS), reel 17, [James Stephen], "Observations on Mr. Roses Objections . . . as to the Free Port Trade," [April 1806]; ibid., "Observations on . . . Foreign Slave Ships" [June or July 1806], p. 18; and Stephen, *Foreign Slave Bill*, p. 7.

28. *Foreign Slave Bill,* p. 4. Anstey's analysis is justifiable in one significant respect. Grenville, in vaguely referring to a possible sequence of growing foreign production and competition may have wished to associate the two points psychologically without pressing the issue to the point where it might be challenged and require real demonstration. This would then explain why he briefly made the point only in his introductory remarks on May 7 and did not mention it at all during the major debate of May 16. A subtle psychological association, however, is something different from a powerful argument.

29. The only use of the glut argument in 1806–1807 was Grenville's assertion that abolition would save the slave colonies from ruin due to accumulated produce (PD 8 [1806–1807], 659, Feb. 5, 1807). In the next sentence, however, he reverted to the long-run theme of expansion, noting that the Jamaica and Trinidad frontier would keep the slave trade operative "for two or three centuries," and two million Africans more. Not a single speaker on either side took note of Grenville's offer to save the colonists from themselves. Anstey points out the unimportance of this argument in Grenville's strategy ("A Re-interpretation," p. 319n.) and notes that the one minor speaker who mentioned the point at the very end of the debate in the Commons only aroused impatience and loud calls for the question. On "seasoning," see Orlando Patterson, *The Sociology of Slavery* (London, 1967), pp. 98–101; Ragatz, *The Fall of the Planter Class,* p. 87; Craton and Walvin, *A Jamaican Plantation,* p.131. On the early discussion of "seasoning" in Parliament, see Cobbett's *Parl. History,* 29 (1791–1792), 1141, debate of 1791.

30. See, for example, the emphasis of Davis's *Slavery in Revolution,* p. 440–52, compared with the passing reference to oversupply on p. 439.

31. Anstey, *British Abolition,* pp. 52–53.

32. "The planters proved the stronger and achieved a signal triumph" (Ragatz, *The Fall of the Planter Class,* p. 319).

33. On alternative traders see PD 8 (1806–1807), 659, 664–66, 670, 671, 954–55, 960, 988–90. On the unbridled Portuguese trade, see DUL (William Smith Papers), Grenville to Smith, Feb. 11, 1807. On the estimate of Bonaparte's hostility, see DUL Hamilton (Grenville MSS), reel 17, "Observations in Answer to the Question whether a general Abolition Bill should now be brought (May 19, 1806)," p. 4. It is significant that the assertion of near monopoly was made only once by the ministerial movers in each house. When it was repeatedly challenged, no reply was forthcoming. Even more than with the demographic aspect of the debate, the abolitionists sidestepped the issue of rivals and relied on the sheer power of their plea to extricate at least all British subjects from the slave trade.

34. HLR MSS, May 6, 1806, petition of merchants, ship owners and manufacturers of Liverpool in the slave trade, and "Trade Bill," dated July 17, 1806, authorizing an export trade to all Latin America.

35. HLR MSS, May 13, 1806, petition of "the town and neighborhood of Manchester."

36. See PP 1806–1807 (II), 64–68, Sierra Leone Company report; BT 6/70, "Sierra Leone Charter, Report of the Court of Directors, March 29, 1804"; report of Gov. Ludlam, Nov. 19, 1805, and correspondence received through Jan. 7, 1807. In Parliament, see PR 2 (1803), 609, 612; PD 9 (1807), 1001–03.

37. Cobbetts' *Parl. History,* 29 (1791–1792), 1290–91, speech of W. Grant, April 27, 1792. Pitt's classic demographic calculation of 1791 asserted that the excess of deaths over births in Jamaica for 1768–1788 was merely 1 percent. Noting that the secular trend was toward a further narrowing of the demographic gap Pitt concluded that Jamaica must have already reached a rough natural equilibrium. His figures were challenged (ibid., pp. 303, 307, 1290, 1231, 1263–64). But a more fundamental methodological challenge was aimed at his use of aggregate population figures to estimate plantation labor needs.

The figures used by Pitt included the slave population in the towns and grazing pens. Stephen Fuller, the agent for Jamaica, gathered population data for a few of the largest plantations in each parish of Jamaica. His total of seventeen accounts shows excesses of deaths over births ranging from 1.68 percent to 5.88 percent per year with a mean of 3.11 percent and a median of 2.7 percent (DUL, Stephen Fuller Letterbook, May 4, 1791). Edward Long also estimated annual plantation deficits at up to 6 percent (PRO 30 8/153, 40, Long to Pitt, March 7, 1788; also cited in Michael Craton, "Jamaican Slavery," in Engerman and Genovese, eds., *Race and Slavery*, p. 267 and note). By 1805, a deficit of 3 percent per year was the officially accepted replacement requirement for the conquered colonies, indicating that the planters' claim of a 2.5 percent yearly deficit was considered more accurate than Pitt's estimate of under 1 percent. After abolition, James Stephen openly acknowledged the accuracy of the higher figure.

38. Bodleian Library, Clarendon Deposit (Barham Papers), c. 366, Barham to Wilberforce, Sept. 2, 1806; and c. 381, miscellaneous political papers, sketch of a speech. It has been questioned whether the Caribbean *Creole* birthrate under slavery was any lower than it would have been under another legal status (see Jack Ericson Elben, "On the Natural Increase of Slave Populations: The Example of the Cuban Black Population, 1775–1900," in Engerman and Genovese, eds., *Race and Slavery*, pp. 211–47). The economic issue, however, was not the native birthrate but the short- and medium-run negative growth-rate of plantation labor in the absence of African imports. Slave deaths continued to outrun births in Jamaica after Waterloo. See George W. Roberts, *The Population of Jamaica* (Cambridge, 1957), p. 39, table 6.

39. Cobbetts' *Parl. History*, 29, (1791–1792), 348; Stephen, *Dangers of the Country*, pp. 210–11.

40. PD 11 (1808), 818–19, speech of Bragge Bathurst, June 3, 1808.

Chapter 9: Abolition and the Decline of British Slavery, 1808–1814

1. Williams, *Capitalism and Slavery*, p. 136; *From Columbus to Castro*, p. 281.

2. PP 1812 (X), 7, 25, accounts of official and real values of British exports through 1811.

3. John Marshall, *A Digest of all the Accounts relating to . . . Great Britain and Ireland*, 2 vols. in 1 (London, 1833), II, 82; PP 1808 (IV), Report of April 13, 1808, p. 307, Appendix C. If we compare 1805–1807 with 1808–1810 the result is even more unfavorable to the latter period. In 1805–1807 retained imports accounted for only 2 percent of coffee brought to Britain, compared with the 38.8 percent in 1808–1810. Although the lowering of duties in October 1808 caused domestic consumption to rise briefly to thirty-three times the previous rate, the situation was still unsatisfactory. In 1808–1810 Britain was importing almost 70 percent more coffee than in 1805–1807.

4. See Crouzet, *L'Economie Britannique*, II, 579n.

5. See PD 11 (1808), 506, 538, speeches of Barham and Whitbread.

6. PP 1813–1814 (XII), 199–200.

7. See table 10.

8. This percentile was estimated following the method in Appendix II, using averaged British and American import figures and Brazilian exports.

9. Tooke, *History of Prices*, II, 398–401, 414; and Beveridge et al., *Prices and Wages*, pp. 429–31.

10. The *Times*, June 22, 1814.

11. PD 27 (1813–1814), 645, speech of J. Marryatt, May 2, 1814.

12. Humboldt, *Narrative of Travels,* VII, 146. His table shows sharp drops from 1804 to 1805, 1806 to 1807, 1812 to 1813, and sharp rises between 1809 and 1810, and 1814 and 1815.

13. See Leslie Bethell, *The Abolition of the Brazilian Slave Trade* (Cambridge,1970), pp. 8–9; Arthur F. Corwin, *Spain and the Abolition of Slavery in Cuba, 1817–1886* (Austin, Texas, 1967), pp. 22–25. According to Wilberforce the 1814 motion was to have been introduced by Don Augustin Arguelles. He was arrested in the antiliberal reaction of 1814 (PD 28 [1814], 440, Wilberforce on the peace treaty with France, June 29, 1814).

14. PD 27 (1813–1814), 243–44; PD 28 (1814), 470. See also Martha Putney, "The Slave Trade in French Diplomacy from 1814 to 1815," *Journal of Negro History* 60 (1975), 411–27.

15. PD 28 (1814), 637–47. Some abolitionists themselves woefully admitted that they had completely underestimated the possibility that France would request the reopening of the slave trade (PD 27 [1813–1814], 320–21, speech of Grenville, June 27, 1814; see also 387, speech of Horner, June 28, 1814).

16. PD 27 (1813–1814), 1078–79.

17. PD 28 (1814), 173–99.

18. Ibid., pp. 274, 332, 352, 443.

19. Ibid., p. 462, speech of Castlereagh; and p. 371, speech of Liverpool.

20. Ibid., pp. 278–83, 338–40, speeches of Castlereagh and Liverpool in the Commons and the Lords, June 27, 1814.

21. Ibid., pp. 272–327, speeches of Wilberforce and Grenville, in the Commons and the Lords, June 27, 1814. It was estimated that peopling St. Domingue, Brazil, and the Guianas could require the transfer of a million to a million and a half slaves, exclusive of deaths in Africa (*Morning Chronicle,* June 18, 1814, speech of James Mackintosh). This is the actual number transported to Cuba and Brazil between 1821 and 1865. The French apparently calculated their labor requirements with curious precision. One Paris newspaper article stated that St. Domingue's annual requirements would be 10,971 slaves (quoted in the *Courier,* Aug. 18, 1814). The French had prepared and presented estimates of the number of slaves wanted for each island (*Carlisle Journal,* July 30, 1814). On Castlereach's response, see DUL (Wilberforce Papers), Stephen's comments on a conversation with Castlereagh, Aug. 24, 1814.

22. PD 28 (1814), 328, 351, 404.

23. Ibid., pp. 329, 352, 388.

24. Ibid., p. 349.

25. Ibid., p. 398. See also p. 446.

26. Ibid., pp. 354, 400.

27. Ibid., pp. 355, 408, 656.

28. Ibid., pp. 443–44.

29. Bodleian Library, Clarendon Deposit, (Barham Papers), c. 337, bundle labeled "Foreign Slave Trade (1806)." This bundle contains papers running through 1814–1815. Barham's sources for African and American slave prices were the abolitionist Zachary Macaulay and the antiabolitionist George Rose, a West Indian proprietor.

30. Add MSS 38416 (Liverpool Papers), Stephen to Liverpool, Chelsea, Oct. 17, 1814. From Paris, Alexander von Humboldt had reported that the French talked without qualms about shipping another hundred thousand Africans to a reconquered St. Domingue (Bodleian Library [Wilberforce MSS], 13, Humboldt to Wilberforce, Paris, Aug. 30, 1814. On the subsequent French slave-trade revival, see Serge Daget, "Long cours et

négriers nantais du traffic illégal, 1814–1833," *Revue française d'histoire d'outre-mer* 62 (1975), 90–134.

31. "I have a clear conviction, that such cheapness of labor is by no means to be expected from the voluntary industry, however great, of negroes in a state of freedom, as now excites the enterprize, and splendidly rewards the success of the planter, in places where slavery is established" (*Crisis,* p. 191).

32. Add MSS 38416, Oct. 17, 1814.

33. Stephen's Jamaica figures were from a volume, *Notices Respecting Jamaica in 1808–1809–1810* (London, 1811), by Gilbert Mathison.

34. Bodleian Library, Clarendon Deposit (Barham Papers), c. 377, "Foreign Slave Trade."

35. PD 28 (1814), 396.

36. Ibid., pp. 275–76.

37. PD 8 (1806–1807), 663, 995, speeches of Grenville and Howick, Feb. 5 and 23, 1807.

38. *Morning Chronicle,* June 18, 1814.

39. Add MSS 38416, Stephen to Liverpool, Oct. 17, 1814.

40. Gavin White, "Firearms in Africa: An Introduction," *Journal of African History* 12 (1971), 182; *Morning Chronicle,* June 30, 1814; *York Herald,* July 4, 1814; and *General Advertiser,* July 9, 1814.

41. But in July 1814, a newspaper noted that the restored king of Spain had allowed Spanish permission to export British cotton goods to South America to expire. There was fear that Ferdinand wished to give preference to French cotton goods. The days of the British nonslave monopoly to Spanish America might be lost in addition to the slave trade. See the *Northampton Mercury,* July 9, 1814.

42. Williams argues that the inter-colonial trade permitted significant transfers of slave labor from low to high profit areas. However, this has been perceptively disputed by D. Eltis, in "The Traffic in Slaves Between the British West Indian Colonies, 1807–1833," *Economic History Review* 25 (1972), 55–64.

43. See Betty Fladeland, "Abolitionist Pressures on the Concert of Europe, 1814–1822," *Journal of Modern History* 38 (1966), 355–73.

Chapter 10: Beyond Economic Interest

1. Oddy was a member of the Russian and Turkey or Levant companies. His book was well received by the *Edinburgh Review* 8 (1806), 128–37, "Oddy's *European Commerce.*"

2. *European Commerce,* p. 472.

3. P. 474.

4. (London, 1805).

5. P. 184.

6. Charles Reinhard, *A Concise History of the Present State of the Commerce of Great Britain* (London, 1805), p. 43, translated from the German edition of 1804. See also Monbrion, *De la Préponderance maritime et commerciale de la Grande Bretagne* (Paris, 1805), pp. 100, 218.

7. Slave-grown products around 1800 accounted for a disproportionate share of Britain's increasing control of world trade. See W. W. Rostow, "The Beginnings of Modern Growth in Europe: An Essay in Synthesis," *Journal of Economic History* 33 (1973), 547–80.

8. PP 1831–1832 (XX), *Report from a Select Committee of the House of Commons on the Commercial state of the West India Colonies,* p. 671.

9. Karl Polanyi, *The Great Transformation* (London, 1944), chap. 6.

10. Davis at one point acknowledges the difficulty in linking the fortunes of abolition to declining mercantilism but later reinforces Williams's connection between rising capitalism and declining slavery (*Slavery in Revolution,* pp. 63 and 350–51). He reworks the Williams thesis so that declining British slavery and rising British capitalism take on additional ideological significance, but the central juxtaposition and dynamic ethos remain the same. The same economic situation, the same men, and the same ideological nexus, account for the laissez-faire assault on the remnants of paternalism in Britain and the abolitionist attack on overseas slavery. Davis also maintains that the fact of fundamental importance is that the early antislavery decades also witnessed the climax of an attack on traditional paternalism toward British labor (pp. 357–58). This interesting extension of the Williams thesis lies beyond the limits of our discussion. On the relationship see also Engerman, "The Slave Trade and British Capital Formation," and Anstey, "Capitalism and Slavery: A Critique."

11. PD 8 (1806–1807), 952. While there is no explicit evidence of a parliamentary concern in 1807 with danger arising from the African slave trade, is abolitionist silence suggestive of a "repressed" obsession with slave violence? It seems quite unlikely. The French, after all, had far more cause than the British to be traumatized by both colonial and domestic revolution after 1790. Yet successive French governments were patently unimpressed by the relative risks entailed in expanding their slave empires. Psychologically, Calais was still somewhere east of Suez. The Spanish, Portuguese, and Dutch also failed to follow Britain's lead. And even the Danes, who had officially abolished the slave trade to their islands as of 1802, used their colonies as an entrepot for the trade until the British occupied them in 1807. Thus, one would not only have to postulate an unconscious obsession on the part of the British, but account for its lack of impact everywhere else but in the United States.

12. R. N. Buckley, "The Early History of the West India Regiments, 1795–1815: A Study in British Colonial Military History," Ph.D. dissertation, McGill University, 1975, esp. pp. 158–67, 253–63, 341–43.

13. Heckscher, *The Continental System,* pp. 120–212, and Crouzet, *L'Economie britannique,* II, 827.

14. The prevailing image of the slave economy has been built around the premise that slave production, and especially the slave trade, were systems which returned noncompetitive economic profits. However, "the staple crop industries in colonial America [and the transatlantic slave trade] very closely approximated the competitive ideal." See R. P. Thomas and R. N. Bean, "The Fishers of Men: The Profits of the Slave Trade," *Journal of Economic History* 34 (1974), 888–93. The West Indian planters demanded either a "fair price" for sugar in Britain or a "free market" in the islands. See "Resolutions of a General Meeting of the West Indies Planters," Feb. 26, 1807, cited in Joseph Lowe, *An Inquiry into the State of the West India Colonies* (London, 1807), pp. 88, 134; and *A Letter to W. Manning on The Causes of the Rapid and Progressive Depreciation of West Indian Property* (London, Jan. 1807), p. 28. For a similar free-trade proposal representing British-American interests, see Medford Macall, *Oil without Vinegar, and Dignity without Pride, or, British, American, and West India Interests considered* (London, 1807), p. 35.

15. Davis, *Slavery in Revolution,* pp. 350, 353.

16. Adam Smith, *Lectures on Justice, Police, Revenue and Arms, delivered at the University of Glasgow,* ed, Edwin Cannan (Oxford, 1896), p. 96. Smith did not always make a clear distinction between human beings and domestic animals. In the *Wealth of Nations,* pp. 263, 344, he referred without qualms to "the labourers and labouring cattle" employed in agriculture. It was thus still possible in 1776 for political economists to define cattle as

"productive labor" and their maintenance as "a circulating capital in the same manner as that of the labouring servants."

17. R. Keith Aufhauser, "Profitability of Slavery in the British Caribbean," *Journal of Interdisciplinary History* 5 (Summer 1974), 45–67.

18. Williams, *Capitalism and Slavery,* pp. 135–36, 154–68; Davis, *Slavery in Revolution,* p. 348.

19. PD 7 (1806), 234, speech of Hawkesbury, May 16, 1806.

20. PD 6 (1806), 1022, speech of May 1. The slave merchants linked their cause with the cotton industry to the very end. See PRO T70/1585, bundle marked "Abolition 1806–1807," S. Cock to Lord Howick, Feb. 13, 1807, enclosing accompanying documents. In this they were cognizant of Peel's position. "By all means," wrote one of them when they were mobilizing their evidence, "insert in your pamphlet what is said of the joint houses of the Peels, because it will particularly please Sir Robert Peel, who is a member of Parliament, and has Interest with several other members" (ibid., Walton to Case, Whitehaven, Jan. 1, 1805, "Inclosed the Cotton Manufacturers' Statement").

21. See *Liverpool Chronicle and Commercial Advertiser,* Feb. 27, 1805; Crouzet, *L'Economie britannique,* II, 813–14. Ralph A. Austen and Woodruff D. Smith, in "The Images of Africa and the British Slave-Trade Abolition: The Transition to an Imperialist Ideology, 1787–1807," *African Historical Studies* 2 (1969), 73, present a variant of the decline thesis. They assume that West Indian influence was declining and that "other groups, merchants and industrialists as well as landowners, possessed an increasingly greater share of the money represented in Parliament, while the West Indian economy began experiencing difficulties." *Capitalism and Slavery,* which is their authority for that structural shift, does not discuss proportions of representation or wealth either before or after 1807. Anstey finds no swing in the direction assumed by Williams (*British Abolition,* p. 323), nor does G. P. Judd (*Members of Parliament, 1734–1832* [New Haven, 1955], p. 94). The evidence seems to point slightly in the opposite direction down to 1832. If either house changed at all during Pitt's hegemony it was the Lords. Pitt's tenure coincided with an enormous expansion of the upper house. Yet socially, Pitt's peers were virtually business-proof, as they had to be under George III. Of over one hundred appointments "in the whole of his career, Pitt recommended but one [businessman], Robert Smith, the banker" (A. S. Tuberville, *The House of Lords in the Age of Reform, 1784–1837* [London, 1958], p. 50).

22. Dixon, "Politics of Emancipation," p. 58.

23. Add MSS 38416, fol. 23; SRO (Melville Papers), GD 51/1/441 (I), T. Browne to Melville, Jan. 30, 1807.

24. Anstey, *British Abolition,* pp. 307–08; and Davis, *Slavery in Revolution,* p. 430.

25. Dixon, "Politics of Emancipation," p. 61.

26. Ragatz,*The Fall of the Planter Class,* p. 290. On the major distillery debate of Dec. 14, 1801, see PR 16 (1802), 387–415. Sympathy for capitalist co-proprietors was not a negligible factor. In 1792 Earl Fitzwilliam and his supporters were reluctant to follow Fox on abolition because of its interference with rights of property (E. A. Smith, *Whig Principles and Party Politics* [Manchester, 1975], p. 135). The Irish members, who at first voted as a bloc for abolition, largely deserted the cause in 1805 out of fear that abolition endangered property. See Clarkson, *History,* II, 499–500; *Life of Wilberforce,* III, 212–13.

27. Ragatz, *The Fall of the Planter Class,* pp. 318 ff.

28. Tooke, *History of Prices,* I, 266. From Jan. 1804 through Dec. 1806 the price of flour and malt purchased by Greenwich hospital was higher at *every* quarter than it had been at any quarter from Dec. 1800 through June 1803 (Beveridge et al., *Prices and Wages,* p. 291). The same was true for annual averages of oats and malt at Winchester College

(ibid., p. 795), for bread at the Charterhouse grammar school in London (ibid., p. 210), and for flour and malt for the Naval Stores in London and Portsmouth.

29. PD 11 (1808), 824.

30. Ragatz, *The Fall of the Planter Class,* p. 319. William Wilberforce, in the name of the "inseparable interests" of the planters and the farmers, and in the name of the manufacturers of Yorkshire as well, cast his vote for the West India interest (PD 11 [1808], 819–20, speech of June 3, 1808). He also voted with the sugar interest in the debates of 1801.

31. The decision to pay for the war with higher duties on sugar and to repay the enormous postwar national debt without a domestic income tax after 1814, while retaining the wartime duty on colonial produce, was a fiscal choice made at the expense of the tropical trade complex. However, this interest was not antagonistic either to the slave system or to the slave trade. On the contrary, the greater the volume of tropical imports, the easier would be their own fiscal position.

32. DUL, Stephen Fuller Letterbook, letters of Mar. 4, and Dec. 1, 1794.

33. On the bills of 1798, see PR 6 (1798), 100, speech of B. Edwards. On the suspension of the slave trade, see Barham's letter to proprietors of the West Indies, Bodleian Library, Clarendon Deposit (Barham Papers) c. 377, bundle entitled "Slave trade papers"; and *Life of Wilberforce,* II, 367–68. On the minority status of the moderates in 1804, see DUL (Wilberforce Papers), Pitt to Wilberforce, May 30, 1804. On the West Indian split in 1806 see ibid., Brougham to Wilberforce, n.d. [1806].

34. Anstey, *British Abolition,* p. 298. Anstey aptly concludes: "It is striking that the West Indian interest enjoyed the parliamentary support of two loose but significant groupings of MPs over and beyond those representing the slave-trading ports. The abolitionists, on the other hand, had no such allies. There may, of course be more profound senses in which abolition expressed the emergence of an ideology of Free Trade: but of parliamentary support from any new interest group representing the rising forces in the economy—indeed of the existence of any such groups—there is at this time not a trace" (p. 285). Our sole reservation to this well-documented estimate is to its own reservation on ideology as it relates to the international market. Free trade was a submerging, not an emerging ideology during the French Wars.

35. Pitman, *The Development of the British West Indies,* pp. 168–74, 242–66; Cobbett's *Parl. History,* 8 (1722–1733), 1197–98; Trevor Richard Reese, *Colonial Georgia: A Study in British Imperial Policy in the Eighteenth Century* (Athens, Ga., 1963), pp. 32, 40, 47–50; C. C. Jones, *The History of Georgia,* 2 vols. (Boston, 1883), I, 110–12, 423–26.

36. David Brion Davis, in his discussion of the legal status of slavery in eighteenth-century England, has superbly demonstrated the struggle to "balance the needs of domestic ideology against commercial and imperial interests" (*Slavery in Revolution,* chap. 10). He notes that after the abolition of the slave trade, "English courts were more inclined than before to endorse antislavery principles" (p. 501n.).

37. See Coupland, *Wilberforce,* pp. 154–61.

38. James Walvin, in his manuscript essays "How Popular was Abolition? Popular Dissent and the Negro Question, 1787–1833," and "The Impact of Slavery on British Radical Politics, 1787–1838" (publication forthcoming), has made an especially interesting foray into the question of popular participation; see also E. M. Hunt, "The North of England Agitation for the Abolition of the Slave Trade, 1780–1800," M.A. thesis, University of Manchester, 1959. On the comparative study of abolition see Davis's *Slavery in Revolution,* esp. chaps. 2, 3, and 5. Duncan Rice's "The British Provinces and their Anti-Slavery Loyalties" (MS kindly sent by the author), touches on both the regional and religious

aspects of abolitionism. A very interesting hypothesis on abolition as a venture in metropolitan cultural imperialism is provided by Howard Temperley's essays, "The Anglo-American Antislavery Connection," presented at the American Studies Association in April 1976, and "Capitalism, Slavery and Ideology," *Past and Present* (in press). My own tentative perspective on this problem, has been presented in "Capitalism and Abolition: Values and Forces in Britain, 1783–1814," *Liverpool, The African Slave Trade and Abolition,* ed. Roger T. Anstey and P. E. H. Hair (Liverpool, 1976), pp. 167–95.

39. Philip Curtin warned against the danger of reading twentieth-century West Indian problems back into the mid-nineteenth century. See "Sugar Duties and West Indian Prosperity," *Journal of Economic History* 14 (Spring 1954), 157–64.

Bibliography

Manuscript Sources

Archives Nationales, Paris
  AF^{IV}1060
  C^{7A}85 (Guadeloupe)
  C^{8A}112, 115 (Martinique)

Bodleian Library, Oxford
  Clarendon Deposit, Barham Papers.
  Wilberforce Papers.

British Museum, Add. MSS.
  12404–07, Long Papers.
  18961, Long Papers.
  21254–56, London Abolition Committee Minute Books, 1787–1819.
  27621, J. Ramsay Papers.
  31237, Vansittart Papers.
  34427, Auckland Papers.
  38310–416, Liverpool Papers.
  41262A, Clarkson Papers.
  49183, Perceval Papers.
  52204, Allen Papers.

Friends House Library, London
  Minutes of Meeting for Sufferings, Committee on the Slave Trade, Box F.

House of Lords Record Office MSS (HLR)
  May 31, 1792. Evidence on the slave trade.
  May 6, 1806. Petitions on the slave trade.
  May 12, 1806. Cotton imports, 1796–1805.

261

May 12, 1806. Slaves imported into conquered colonies.
May 13, 1806. Petitions on the slave trade.
May 14, 1806. Trade with Spanish America.
July 17, 1806. Trade with Spanish America.
Feb. 13, 1807. Papers on the slave trade.

Perkins Library, Duke University (DUL)
Stephen Fuller MSS.
Grenville MSS (on microfilm reels).
William Smith MSS.
James Stephen MSS (on microfilm reels of Grenville Papers).
Wilberforce MSS.

Picton Library, Liverpool
TAR 920, Tarleton Papers.

Public Record Office, London (PRO)
30 8/349, 351, Chatham Papers.
HCA 10/19. Admiralty prize lists for Danish vessels, 1807–1808.
Board of Trade (BT)
5/11, 6/12, 6/40, 6/70, 6/75, 6/103, 6/140, 318/2
Colonial Office (CO)
28/71 (Barbados); 71/15, 20, 21 (Dominica); 101/28 (Grenada); 111/1, 3, 5, 7 (British Guiana); 137/88, 91, 119 (Jamaica); 142/21 (Jamaica); 245/10 (St. Domingo); 261/9 (St. Vincent); 285/2 (Tobago); 295/2, 6 (Trinidad); Customs 17/4–30; Treasury (T) 1583–86.
War Office (WO)
1/20 (Guadeloupe)

Scottish Record Office, Edinburgh (SRO)
Melville Papers.

Sheffield City Libraries
Fitzwilliam Papers.

University of Durham
Grey Papers.

Official and Semiofficial Documents

Great Britain
Parliamentary Papers: Reports (R), Accounts and Papers (AP), Sessional Papers (SP)
R 1785–86, VII (66). Report on trade with Ireland.
AP 1777, LIX (9).
AP 1778–82, XXXV (44). Report on sugar.
AP 1789, XXVI (646a). Privy Council report on the slave trade.
AP 1790–91, XXXIV (745). Evidence on the slave trade.
AP 1792, XXXV (770). Sugar bill report.
AP 1794–95, XL (810). Charles Grey affair.
SP 1801–02, IV.
SP 1805, X. Slave trade papers.

SP 1806, XII. Sugar prices, 1793–1806.

SP 1806, XIII. Slave trade accounts.

SP 1806–07, II. Report of the sugar distillation committee.

SP 1808, IV. Sugar distillation reports.

SP 1808, X. Hearings on orders-in-council, 1807.

SP 1812, X. Accounts of trade.

SP 1813–14, XII. Accounts of trade.

SP 1823, XVIII. Slavery papers.

SP 1847–48, LVIII.

Parliamentary Debates

Cobbett, William, ed. *The Parliamentary History of England from the Earliest Times to the Year 1803.*

Cobbett, William [subsequently Hansard, T. C.], ed. *The Parliamentary Debates from the Year 1803.*

Debrett's *Parliamentary Register,* 1774–1802.

Proceedings of the Honorable House of Assembly of Jamaica on the Sugar and Slave Trade (London, 1793).

The Senator, or Parliamentary Chronicle.

Woodfall, William. *An Impartial Report of the Debates that Occur in the Two Houses of Parliament,* 1794–1796.

United States

American State Papers. *Documents Legislative and Executive, of the Congress of the United States,* 38 vols. (Washington, D.C., 1832–1861), class IV, *Commerce and Navigation,* vols. 14, 15, 1789–1823.

Newspapers

Aris' Birmingham Gazette. 1788.

Bahama Gazette. 1792.

Barbadoes Mercury. 1805.

Bath Chronicle. 1788.

Bristol Gazette. 1788.

Bristol Journal. 1789.

Carlisle Journal. 1814.

Cowdroy's Manchester Gazette. 1806.

Diary. 1789–1792.

Edinburgh Advertiser. 1791.

Edinburgh Evening Courant. 1792.

Edinburgh Review. 1806–1807.

General Advertiser. 1814.

General Evening Post. 1787, 1792.

Glasgow Advertiser. 1792.

Glocester Journal. 1792.

The Iris, or the Sheffield Advertiser. 1807.

Leeds Intelligencer. 1806.

Leeds Mercury. 1788, 1792.

Lincoln, Rutland, and Stamford Mercury. 1788.

Liverpool Chronicle and Commercial Advertiser. 1788, 1805.

London Chronicle. 1788.
Manchester Mercury and Harrop's General Advertiser. 1787, 1788.
Morning Chronicle. 1788, 1792, 1796, 1807, 1814.
Newcastle Courant. 1792.
Northampton Mercury. 1788, 1791, 1792, 1814.
Public Advertiser. 1788, 1791.
Sheffield Advertiser. 1791, 1792.
Sheffield Register. 1788.
Shrewsbury Chronicle. 1791–1792.
St. James's Chronicle. 1798.
Stamford Mercury. 1792.
Sun. 1806.
Times. 1799, 1814.
Whitehall Evening Post. 1788.
York Chronicle. 1792.
York Herald. 1814.

Individual Studies

Adamson, Alan. *Sugar Without Slaves: The Political Economy of British Guiana, 1838–1904.* New Haven, 1972.

Aimes, Hubert. *A History of Slavery in Cuba, 1511 to 1868.* New York, 1967.

An Important Crisis in the Calico and Muslin Manufactory Explained. 1788.

Anstey, Roger T. *The Atlantic Slave Trade and British Abolition, 1760–1810.* London, 1975.

_____. "Capitalism and Slavery: A Critique." *Economic History Review,* 2nd ser. 21 (1968), 307–20.

_____. "A Note on J. E. Inikori, 'Measuring the Atlantic Slave Trade: An Assessment of Curtin and Anstey.'" *Journal of African History* 17 (1976), 606–07.

_____. "A Re-interpretation of the Abolition of the British Slave Trade, 1806–1807." *English Historical Review* 87 (1972), 304–22.

_____. "The Volume and Profitability of the British Slave Trade, 1761–1807." In *Race and Slavery in the Western Hemisphere: Quantitative Studies,* ed. Stanley L. Engerman and Eugene Genovese. Princeton, 1975.

_____. "The Volume of the North American Slave-Carrying Trade from Africa, 1761–1810." *Revue Française d'histoire d'Outre-Mer* 62 (1975), 47–66.

Armytage, Frances. *The Free Port System in the British West Indies.* London, 1953.

Asiegbu, Johnson U. J. *Slavery and the Politics of Liberation, 1787–1861.* New York, 1969.

Aufhauser, R. Keith. "Profitability of Slavery in the British Caribbean." *Journal of Interdisciplinary History* 5 (Summer 1974), 45–67.

Austen, R. A., and Smith, W. D. "The Images of Africa and British Slave Trade Abolition: The Transition to an Imperialist Ideology, 1787–1807." *African Historical Studies* 2 (1969), 69–83.

Baines, E. *History of Cotton Manufacture.* London, 1835.

Bean, R. N. "The British Transatlantic Slave Trade 1650–1776." Ph.D. dissertation, University of Washington, 1971.

Bennett, *Two Letters and Several Calculations on the State of the Sugar Colonies and Trade.* London, 1738.

Bethell, Leslie. *The Abolition of the Brazilian Slave Trade.* Cambridge, 1970.

Beveridge, William, et al. *Prices and Wages in England.* 2nd ed. New York, 1966.

Bolingbroke, Henry. *A Voyage to Demerary, Containing a Statistical Account of the Settlements There.* London, 1807.

Bosanquet, Charles. *A Letter to W. Manning, esq., M.P., on the Causes of the Rapid and Progressive Depreciation of West India Property.* 2nd ed. London, 1807.

Bourgeois-Pichat, J. "The General Development of the Population of France Since the Eighteenth Century." In *Population and History,* ed. D. V. Glass and D. E. C. Eversley, pp. 474–506. London, 1965.

Bowden, Witt. *Industrial Society in England Towards the End of the Eighteenth Century.* New York, 1925.

Brougham, Henry. *An Inquiry into the Colonial Policy of the European Powers.* 2 vols. Edinburgh, 1803; rpt. New York, 1968.

Buc de Marentille. *De l'Esclavage des Nègres dans les colonies de l'Amérique.* Pointe-à-Pitre, 1790.

Clark, John G. *New Orleans 1718–1812: An Economic History.* Baton Rouge, 1970.

Clarkson, Thomas. *An Essay on the Comparative Efficiency of Regulation or Abolition Applied to the Slave Trade.* London, 1789.

———. *The History of the Rise, Progress and Accomplishment of the Abolition of the African Slave-Trade by the British Parliament.* 2 vols. London, 1808; rpt. London, 1968.

Cochrane, Archibald, Earl of Dundonald. *A Treatise shewing the intimate connection . . . between agriculture and chemistry . . . in Great Britain and Ireland and . . .* [the] *West India estates.* London, 1793, 1803.

Colquhoun, Patrick. *A Treatise on the Wealth, Power and Resources of the British Empire.* London, 1815.

"The Committee . . . for the . . . Relief of the Poor . . . Amongst the lower class. . . ." Feb. 19 and Mar. 17, 1800. Manchester, n.d. Political Tracts Collection, no. 2770. Manchester Central Library.

Corwin, Arthur F. *Spain and the Abolition of Slavery in Cuba, 1817–1886.* Austin, Texas, 1967.

Coupland, Reginald. *The American Revolution and the British Empire.* 1930; rpt. New York, 1965.

———. *Wilberforce: A Narrative.* 1923; rpt. New York, 1968.

Craton, Michael. "Jamaican Slavery." In *Race and Slavery in the Western Hemisphere: Quantitative Studies,* ed. Stanley L. Engerman and Eugene Genovese. Princeton, 1975.

———. *Sinews of Empire: A Short History of British Slavery.* New York, 1974.

Craton, Michael, and Walvin, James. *A Jamaican Plantation: The History of Worthy Park 1670–1970.* Toronto, 1970.

Crouzet, François. *L'Economie britannique et le blocus continental, 1806–1813.* 2 vols. Paris, 1958.

Cummings, John. *Negro Population in the United States, 1790–1915.* 1918; rpt. New York, 1968.

Curtin, Philip D. *The Atlantic Slave Trade: A Census.* Madison, Wis., 1969.

———. *The Image of Africa: British Ideas and Action, 1780–1850.* Madison, Wis., 1964.

———. "Sugar Duties and West Indian Prosperity." *Journal of Economic History* 14 (Spring 1954), 157–64.

Daget, Serge. "Long cours et négriers nantais du traffic illégal, 1814–1833." *Revue française d'histoire d'Outre-Mer* 62 (1975), 90–134.

Dalton, H. G. *The History of British Guiana.* 2 vols. London, 1885.

Davies, K. G. *The North Atlantic World in the Seventeenth Century.* Minneapolis, 1974.

Davis, David Brion. *The Problem of Slavery in the Age of Revolution, 1770–1823.* Ithaca, N.Y., 1975.

_____. *The Problem of Slavery in Western Culture.* Ithaca, N.Y., 1966.

_____. *The Slave Power Conspiracy and the Paranoid Style.* Baton Rouge, La., 1969.

_____. Review of *The Atlantic Slave Trade and British Abolition, 1760–1810,* by Roger T. Anstey. *Times Literary Supplement,* Oct. 24, 1975.

Davis, Ralph. *Aleppo and Devonshire Square: English Traders in the Levant in the Eighteenth Century.* London, 1967.

_____. "The Rise of Protection in England, 1689–1786." *Economic History Review* 19 (1966), 306–17.

_____. *The Rise of the Atlantic Economies.* London, 1973.

Debien, Gabriel. *Les Esclaves aux Antilles Françaises, XVII–XVIII siècles.* Basse Terre et Fort-de-France, 1974.

Deerr, Noel. *The History of Sugar.* 2 vols. London, 1949–1950.

Dixon, Peter F. "The Politics of Emancipation: The Movement for the Abolition of Slavery in the British West Indies, 1807–1833." D. Phil., Oxford, 1971.

Domar, E. D. "The Causes of Slavery or Serfdom: A Hypothesis." *Journal of Economic History* 30 (1970), 18–32.

Dobb, Maurice. *Theories of Value and Distribution Since Adam Smith.* Cambridge, 1973.

Donnan, Elizabeth. *Documents Illustrative of The Slave Trade to America.* 4 vols. Washington, D.C., 1933.

Drake, Barry F. "Continuity and Flexibility in Liverpool's Trade with Africa and the Caribbean." *Business History,* in press.

Drescher, Seymour. "Le 'Déclin' du système esclavagiste britannique et l'abolition de la traite." *Annales: ESC* 31 (1976), 414–35.

Dunn, Richard S. *Sugar and Slaves: The Rise of the Planter Class in the English West Indies, 1624–1713.* Chapel Hill, 1972.

Eden, F. M. *Eight Letters on the Peace.* London, 1802.

Edwards, Bryan. *The History, Civil and Commercial, of the British West Indies.* 5 vols. London, 1819; rpt. New York, 1966.

_____. *Historical Survey of the French Colony of St. Domingo.* London, 1797.

Edwards, Michael M. *The Growth of the British Cotton Trade, 1780–1815.* Manchester, 1967.

Ehrman, John. *The British Government and Commercial Negotiations with Europe, 1783–1793.* Cambridge, 1962.

_____. *The Younger Pitt: The Years of Acclaim.* New York, 1969.

Elben, Jack Ericson. "On the Natural Increase of Slave Populations: The Example of the Cuban Black Population, 1775–1900." In *Race and Slavery in the Western Hemisphere: Quantitative Studies,* ed. Stanley L. Engerman and Eugene Genovese. Princeton, 1975.

Eltis, D. "The Traffic in Slaves Between the British West Indian Colonies, 1807–1833." *Economic History Review* 25 (1972), 55–64.

Engerman, Stanley L. "The Slave Trade and British Capital Formation in the Eighteenth Century: A Comment on the Williams Thesis." *Business History Review* 46 (Winter 1972), 430–43.

_____. "Some Considerations Relating to Property Rights in Man." *Journal of Economic History* 33 (1973), 43–65.

Engerman, Stanley L., and Genovese, Eugene D., eds. *Race and Slavery in the Western Hemisphere: Quantitative Studies.* Princeton, 1975.

Fladeland, Betty. "Abolitionist Pressures on the Concert of Europe, 1814–1822." *Journal of Modern History* 38 (1966), 355–73.

_____. *Men and Brothers: Anglo-American Antislavery Cooperation.* Urbana, Ill., 1972.
Fogel, Robert W., and Engerman, Stanley L. *Time on the Cross: The Economics of American Negro Slavery.* 2 vols. Boston, 1974.
Fortescue, J. W. *A History of the British Army.* 14 vols. London, 1910–1930.
Fraser, L. M. *History of Trinidad.* 2 vols. London, 1891; rpt. [London], 1971.
Furneaux, Robert. *William Wilberforce.* London, 1974.
Gayer, Arthur D., *et al. The Growth and Fluctuation of the British Economy, 1790–1850.* Oxford, 1953.
Genovese, Eugene D. *The World the Slaveholders Made.* New York, 1969.
Gourvich, T. R. "The Cost of Living in Glasgow in the Early Nineteenth Century." *Economic History Review* 25 (1972), 65–80.
Goveia, Elsa V. *Slave Society in the British Leeward Islands at the End of the Eighteenth Century.* New Haven, 1965.
_____. *A Study on the Historiography of the British West Indies to the End of the Nineteenth Century.* Mexico, Inst. Panamericano de Geografía e Historia, 1956.
Graham, Richard. "Brazilian Slavery Re-examined." *Journal of Social History* 3 (Summer 1974), 431–53.
Gratus, Jack. *The Great White Lie.* New York, 1973.
Gray, Lewis C. *History of Agriculture in the Southern United States to 1860.* 2 vols. Washington, D.C., 1933.
Green, W. A. "The Planter Class and British West India Sugar Production, Before and After Emancipation." *Economic History Review* 26 (1973), 448–63.
Green-Pederson, S. E. "The Scope and Structure of the Danish Slave Trade." *Scandinavian Economic History Review* 19 (1971), 149–97.
Greene, J. P. "Society and Economy in the British Caribbean during the Seventeenth and Eighteenth Centuries." *American Historical Review* 79 (1974), 1499–1517.
Hall, Douglas. "Absentee-Proprietorship in the British West Indies to about 1850." *Jamaican Historical Review* 4 (1964), 15–35.
Hamilton, Henry. *An Economic History of Scotland in the Eighteenth Century.* Oxford, 1963.
Harlow, Vincent T. *The Founding of the Second British Empire, 1763–1793.* 2 vols. London, 1952, 1964.
Hatch, John. *The History of Britain in Africa.* New York, 1969.
Heckscher, Eli F. *The Continental System: An Economic Interpretation.* 2nd ed. Gloucester, Mass., 1964.
Heeren, A. H. L. *Manual of the Political System of Europe and its Colonies.* London, 1846.
Hilliard d'Auberteuil, M. R. *Considérations sur l'état présent de la colonie française de Saint-Domingue.* 2 vols. Paris, 1776–1777.
Historical Statistics of the United States, Colonial Times to 1957. Washington D.C., 1960.
Hobsbawn, Eric. *Industry and Empire.* London, 1968.
Hochstetter, Franz. *Die wirtschaftlichen und politischen Motive für die Abschaffung des britischen Sklavenhandels im Jahre 1806–1807.* Leipzig, 1905.
Humboldt, Alexander von. *Personal Narrative of Travels to the Equinoctial Regions of the New Continent During the Years 1799–1804.* 7 vols. London, 1829; rpt. New York, 1966.
_____. *Political Essay on the Kingdom of New Spain.* 4 vols. London, 1811.
Hunt, E. M. "The North of England Agitation for the Abolition of the Slave Trade, 1780–1800." M.A. thesis, University of Manchester, 1959.
The Importance of the Sugar Colonies to Britain Stated. London, 1731.
Inikori, J. E. "Measuring the Atlantic Slave Trade: An Assessment of Curtin and Anstey."

Journal of African History 17 (1976), 197–223.

Jacobson, Stiv. *Am I Not a Man and a Brother? British Missions and the Abolition of the Slave Trade and Slavery, 1786–1838.* Uppsala, 1972.

James, C. L. R. *The Black Jacobins: Toussaint L'Ouverture and the San Domingo Revolution.* 1938; rpt. New York, 1963.

Jollivet, Thomas. *De la Philanthropie anglaise.* Paris, 1842.

_____. *Des Missions en France de la société abolitioniste et étrangère.* Paris, 1841.

Jones, C. C. *The History of Georgia.* 2 vols. Boston, 1883.

Jordan, Winthrop D. *White Over Black: American Attitudes Toward the Negro.* Chapel Hill, N.C., 1968.

Josa, Guy. *Les Industries du sucre et du rhum à la Martinique 1639–1931.* Paris, 1931.

Judd, G. P. *Members of Parliament, 1734–1832.* New Haven, 1955.

Klingberg, Frank J. *The Anti-Slavery Movement in England: A Study in English Humanitarianism.* 1926; rpt. Hamden, Conn., 1968.

Leger, J. N. *Haiti: son histoire et ses detracteurs.* New York, 1907.

Le Veen, E. Phillip. "British Slave Trade Suppression Policies 1821–1865: Impact and Implications." Ph.D. dissertation, University of Chicago, 1971.

Lipscomb, Patrick C. "Party Politics, 1801–1802: George Canning and the Trinidad Question." *Historical Journal* 12 (1969), 442–66.

_____. "William Pitt and the Abolition of the Slave Trade." Ph.D. dissertation, University of Texas, 1960.

Lowe, Joseph. *An Inquiry into the State of the West India Colonies.* London, 1807.

McCusker, John James. "The Rum Trade and the Balance of Payments of the Thirteen Continental Colonies, 1660–1775." Ph.D. dissertation, 2 vols., University of Pittsburgh, 1970.

Macall, Medford. *Oil Without Vinegar and Dignity without Pride, or British, American, and West India interests considered.* London, 1807.

Mackenzie, Charles. *Notes on Haiti.* 2 vols. 1830; rpt. London, 1971.

Manning, H. T. *British Colonial Government After the American Revolution, 1782–1820.* New Haven, 1933.

[Marshall, John]. *A Digest of all the Accounts Relating to the Population, Productions, Revenues . . . of the United Kingdom of Great Britain and Ireland.* London, 1833; rpt. Westmead, England, 1969.

Marshall, Peter J. *The Anti-Slave Trade Movement in Bristol.* Bristol, 1968.

_____. *The Impeachment of Warren Hastings.* London, 1965.

_____. *Problems of Empire: Britain and India, 1757–1813.* London, 1968.

Mathison, Albert. *Notices Respecting Jamaica in 1808–1809–1810.* London, 1811.

Mellor, G. R. *British Imperial Trusteeship, 1783–1850.* London, 1951.

Millette, J. *The Genesis of Crown Colony Government: Trinidad, 1783–1810.* Curepe, Trinidad, 1970.

Memoir on the Sugar Trade of the British Colonies, with Tables. London, 1793.

Merivale, Herman. *Lectures on Colonization and on Colonies, Delivered before the University of Oxford in 1839, 1840, and 1841.* London, 1861; rpt. New York, 1967.

Mintz, Sidney. *Caribbean Transformations.* Chicago, 1974.

Mitchell, B. R., and Deane, P. *Abstract of British Historical Statistics.* Cambridge, 1962.

Monbrion. *De la Préponderance maritime et commerciale de la Grande Bretagne.* Paris, 1805.

Moreau de Jonnes, A. *Recherches statistiques sur l'esclavage colonial et sur les moyens de le supprimer.* Paris, 1842.

Moreno Fraginals, Manuel. *The Sugarmill: The Socioeconomic Complex of Sugar in Cuba, 1760–1860.* Trans. C. Belfrage. New York, 1976.

North, Douglass C., and Thomas, Robert P. "An Economic Theory of the Growth of the Western World." *Economic History Review* 22 (1970), 1–17.

Oddy, J. Jepson. *European Commerce, Showing new and secure channels of trade with the Continent of Europe.* London, 1805.

Pares, Richard. *Merchants and Planters.* Cambridge, 1960.

Parry, J. H. *Trade and Dominion: The European Overseas Empires in the Eighteenth Century.* London, 1971.

Patterson, Orlando. *The Sociology of Slavery.* London, 1967.

Perrin, William. *The Present State of the British and French Sugar Colonies, and our own Northern Colonies Considered: Together with some remarks on the Decay of our Trade, and the Improvements made of late years by the French in Theirs.* London, 1740.

Pitman, Frank. *The Development of the British West Indies, 1700–1763.* New Haven, 1917; rpt. Hamden, Conn., 1967.

———. *The Settlement and Financing of British West India Plantations in the Eighteenth Century.* New Haven, 1917.

Playfair, William. *An Inquiry into the Permanent Causes of the Decline and Fall of Powerful and Wealthy Nations.* London, 1805.

———. *The Commercial and Political Atlas: Representing By Means of Stained Copper Plate Charts, The Exports, Imports, and General Trade of England.* London, 1786.

Polanyi, Karl. *The Great Transformation.* London, 1944.

Pons, F. J. de. *Perspective des rapports politiques et commerciaux de la France dans les deux Indes.* Paris, 1807.

Posthumous, W. W. *Inquiry into the History of Prices in Holland.* 2 vols. London, 1964.

Pouthas, C. H. *La Population française pendant la première moitié du XIXe siècle.* Paris, 1956.

The Present State of the British Sugar Colonies Consider'd. London, 1731.

Putney, Martha. "The Slave Trade in French Diplomacy from 1814 to 1815." *Journal of Negro History* 60 (1975), 411–27.

Ragatz, Lowell J. *The Fall of the Planter Class in the British West Indies, 1763–1833.* 1928; rpt. New York, 1963.

Remarks upon a Book Entitled, the Present State of the Sugar Colonies Consider'd. London, 1731.

Rees, G. "Copper Sheathing: An Example of Technological Diffusion in the English Merchant Fleet." *Journal of Transport History* 1 (1971), 87–89.

Reese, Trevor Richard. *Colonial Georgia: A Study in British Imperial Policy in the Eighteenth Century.* Athens, Ga., 1963.

Reinhard, Charles. *A Concise History of the Present State of the Commerce of Great Britain.* London, 1805.

———. *Remarks on the Trade with Germany.* London, 1806.

Reinhard, Marcel. "Bilan demographique de l'Europe. 1789–1815." *Comité Internationale des Sciences Historiques, XII Congrès International.* Vienna, 1965.

A Report from the Committee of Warehouses of the United East India Company Relative to the Culture of Sugar. London, 1792.

Representation of the Board of Trade relating to the State of the British Islands in America. London, 1734.

Rice, C. Duncan. " 'Humanity sold for sugar!' The British Abolitionist Response to Free Trade in Slave-Grown Sugar." *Historical Journal* 13 (1970), 402–13.

———. *The Rise and Fall of Black Slavery.* London, 1975.

Richardson, Patrick. *Empire and Slavery.* New York, 1972.

Roberts, George W. *The Population of Jamaica.* Cambridge, 1957.

Rostow, W. W. "The Beginnings of Modern Growth in Europe: An Essay in Synthesis."

Journal of Economic History 33 (1973), 547–80.

Sanderson, Michael W. B. "English Naval Strategy and Maritime Trade in the Caribbean, 1793–1802." Ph.D. dissertation, University of London, 1969.

Scheuss de Studer, Elena F. *La Trata de Negros en el Rio de la Plata durante el siglo XVIII,* Buenos Aires, 1958.

Schumpeter, Elizabeth B. *British Overseas Trade Statistics 1697–1808.* Oxford, 1960.

Schumpeter, Joseph A. *History of Economic Analysis.* New York, 1954.

Sheridan, Richard B. *Sugar and Slavery: An Economic History of the British West Indies, 1623–1775.* Baltimore, 1974.

_____. "The Wealth of Jamaica in the Eighteenth Century." *Economic History Review* 18 (1965), 292–311.

Shyllon, F. O. *Black Slaves in Britain.* London, 1974.

Sijpesteijn, A. van C. *Beschrijing van Suriname, Historisch-Geographisch-en Statistisch Overzigt, uit Officiele Bronnen Bijeengebracht.* s' Gravenhage, 1854.

Sinclair, John. *The History of the Public Revenue of the British Empire.* 3 vols. London, 1803; rpt. New York, 1966.

Smith, Adam. *An Inquiry into the Nature and Causes of the Wealth of Nations.* 1776; rpt. New York, 1937.

_____. *Lectures on Justice, Police, Revenue and Arms, delivered at the University of Glasgow.* Ed. Edwin Cannan. Oxford, 1896.

Smith, E. A. *Whig Principles and Party Politics: Earl Fitzwilliam and the Whig Party, 1748–1833.* Manchester, 1975.

Southey, Thomas. *Chronological History of the West Indies.* 3 vols. London, 1827; rpt. [London], 1968.

Spiegel, Henry W. *The Growth of Economic Thought.* New York, 1971.

Spodek, Howard. "Rulers, Merchants and Other Groups in the City-States of Saurashtra, India, around 1800." *Comparative Studies in Society and History.* 16 (1974), 448–70.

Statistique générale et particulière de la France, et de ses colonies, par une société de gens de lettres et de savans. Paris, 1804.

Stephen, James. *Crisis of the Sugar Colonies.* London, 1802; rpt. New York, 1969.

_____. *The Dangers of the Country.* London, 1807.

_____. *Foreign Slave Bill: Facts and Observations.* N.d.

_____. *The Opportunity, or Reasons for an immediate alliance with St. Domingo.* London, 1804.

_____. *War in Disguise; or the Frauds of the Neutral Flags.* London, 1805.

Stewart, G. *Progress of Glasgow.* Glasgow, 1883.

Temperley, Howard. *British Anti-Slavery, 1833–1870.* London, 1972.

Thomas, E. G. "The Treatment of Poverty in Berkshire, Essex, and Oxfordshire, 1723–1824." Ph.D. dissertation, University of London, 1970.

Thomas, R. P. "The Sugar Colonies of the Old Empire: Profit or Loss for Great Britain?" *Economic History Review* 21 (1968), 30–45.

Thomas, R. P., and Bean, R. N. "The Fishers of Men: The Profits of the Slave Trade." *Journal of Economic History* 34 (1974), 885–914.

Tooke, Thomas. *History of Prices.* 2 vols. London, 1838.

Troughton, Thomas. *The History of Liverpool.* Liverpool, 1810.

Tuberville, A. S. *The House of Lords in the Age of Reform, 1784–1837.* London, 1958.

Tucker, Josiah. *An Essay on the Advantages and Disadvantages which respectively attend France and Great Britain with regard to Trade.* Glasgow, 1756.

Two Reports from the Committee of the Honorable House of Assembly of Jamaica on the Subject of the Slave Trade. London, 1789.

Viles, Perry. "The Slaving Interest in the Atlantic Ports, 1763–1792." *French Historical Studies* 7 (1972), 529–43.

Wallace, James. *A General and Descriptive History of . . . the Town of Liverpool . . . together with . . .its extensive African Trade.* Liverpool, 1794.

Wallace, Robert. *Characteristics of the Present Political State of Great Britain.* London, 1761; rpt. New York, 1969.

Walvin, James. *Black and White: The Negro in English Society, 1555–1945.* London, 1973.

———. "How Popular was Abolition? Popular Dissent and the Negro Question, 1787–1833." Unpublished manuscript.

———. "The Impact of Slavery on British Radical Politics 1787–1838." In press.

Westergaard, Waldemar. *The Danish West Indies, 1671–1917.* New York, 1917.

White, Gavin. "Firearms in Africa: An Introduction." *Journal of African History* 12 (1971), 173–84.

Wilberforce, R. I., and Wilberforce, S., eds. *The Correspondence of William Wilberforce.* 2 vols. London, 1840.

———. *The Life of William Wilberforce.* 5 vols. London, 1838.

Wilberforce, William. *A Letter on the Abolition of the Slave Trade.* London, 1807.

Williams, D. M. "Abolition and the Re-Deployment of the Slave Fleet, 1807–1811." *Journal of Transport History* 2 (1973), 103–15.

Williams, Eric. *British Historians and the West Indies.* New York, 1966.

———. *Capitalism and Slavery.* 1944; rpt. New York, 1966.

———. *From Columbus to Castro: The History of the Caribbean, 1492–1969.* New York, 1970.

———. *History of the People of Trinidad and Tobago.* Port of Spain, Trinidad, 1962.

Williams, Glyndon. *The Expansion of Europe in the Eighteenth Century: Overseas Rivalry, Discovery and Exploration.* London, 1966.

Williams, Gomer. *History of the Liverpool Privateers and Letters of Marque with an Account of the Liverpool Slave Trade.* London, 1897; rpt. New York, 1966.

Williams, Judith Blow. *British Commercial Policy and Trade Expansion, 1750–1850.* Oxford, 1972.

Young, Arthur. *Political Essays Concerning the Present State of the British Empire.* London, 1772.

Young, William. *The West India Common-Place Book, Compiled from Parliamentary and Official Documents.* London, 1807.

Zilversmit, Arthur. *The First Emancipation: The Abolition of Slavery in the North.* Chicago, 1967.

Index

Abolition: arguments and motives, 3–4, 64, 136, 178–79, 214–23; economic significance of, 4–5, 6, 149; and humanitarianism, 5, 185–86; effect on slave population, 36; and mercantilism, 60–63; colonial attitudes toward, 63; interest group pressures, 68, 139, 177–81, 258n34; effect on shipping, 74–75; and overproduction, 113, 130–37; and Sierra Leone experiment, 115; French reaction to British, 133; and trade policy, 123–24; and the market, 125–41; effect on trade, 142–61; and capitalism, 166–67; sequence of targets, 172; petitions about, 177–78; chronology, 189–92; economic models, 226n6; in America, 231n21; and laissez-faire, 256n10; and fear of revolution, 256n11; and proprietary rights, 257n26. See also Acts, Bills, Resolutions; Parliament, abolition moves

Abolitionism: mass agitation, 12, 38; Quakers, 12; and slave trade, 25; in North America, 33–34, 35; sources, 38, 171–72, 182–83; and Anglo-French sugar trade, 52; and cotton protectionism, 59, 60; Pitt and, 61; activity in 1798–1799, 121

Absentee owners, 39, 40, 232n7

Acts, Bills, Resolutions: abolition bills, 12–14, 27, 113–24, 168, 182, 214–23, 248n28; slave transportation acts, 13, 29, 45, 60, 71–73, 134–35, 175, 248n28; free port act of 1787, 63; foreign abolition bill of 1806, 74, 101, 123–

24, 134; orders-in-council, 99–100, 101, 171; Sierra Leone bill, 115; sugar distillery vote, 181; Anglo-French treaty, 237n19

Addington, Henry, 106, 108, 110–11

Administrative costs: of slave and non-slave colonies, 39

Africa: trade with, 11, 25, 70, 137; as cotton source, 59; safety for shipping, 75. See also Sierra Leone; Slave trade; Triangularity

African Institution, 132

America: independence and the decline theory, 41; trade relations, 68, 70; slave trade, 73–74, 99, 136–37; cotton production, 83–86; coffee imports, 242n45

American Revolution, 15–16, 33, 164

Amiens, Peace of, 1802, 65, 66, 71–73, 105, 107–08, 128

Anglo-French treaty of 1787, 60, 62, 237n19

Anstey, Roger: opposition to Williams's interpretation, 6–7; analysis of slave trade, 28–32, 71, 73, 205–13, 240n21; on votes of 1806–1807, 121, 134, 141, 214, 222–23, 251n25, 252n28, 258n34; on manufacturing interests, 177; on "new" economic forces, 178–79; on vote of 1796, 179

Antislavery. See Abolition; Abolitionism

Asia: trade with Great Britain, 67, 70; cotton production, 83–84; as labor source, 176. See also India

Asiento. See Spain, colonies

Aufhauser, Keith, 176

273